ASCENT®
CENTER FOR TECHNICAL KNOWLEDGE

Creo Parametric 7.0 Behavioral Modeling

Learning Guide
1ˢᵗ Edition

ASCENT - Center for Technical Knowledge®
Creo Parametric 7.0
Behavioral Modeling
1st Edition

Prepared and produced by:

ASCENT Center for Technical Knowledge
630 Peter Jefferson Parkway, Suite 175
Charlottesville, VA 22911

866-527-2368
www.ASCENTed.com

ASCENT - Center for Technical Knowledge (a division of Rand Worldwide Inc.) is a leading developer of professional learning materials and knowledge products for engineering software applications. ASCENT specializes in designing targeted content that facilitates application-based learning with hands-on software experience. For over 25 years, ASCENT has helped users become more productive through tailored custom learning solutions.

We welcome any comments you may have regarding this guide, or any of our products. To contact us please email: feedback@ASCENTed.com.

General Disclaimer:

Notwithstanding any language to the contrary, nothing contained herein constitutes nor is intended to constitute an offer, inducement, promise, or contract of any kind. The data contained herein is for informational purposes only and is not represented to be error free. ASCENT, its agents and employees, expressly disclaim any liability for any damages, losses or other expenses arising in connection with the use of its materials or in connection with any failure of performance, error, omission even if ASCENT, or its representatives, are advised of the possibility of such damages, losses or other expenses. No consequential damages can be sought against ASCENT or Rand Worldwide, Inc. for the use of these materials by any third parties or for any direct or indirect result of that use.

The information contained herein is intended to be of general interest to you and is provided "as is", and it does not address the circumstances of any particular individual or entity. Nothing herein constitutes professional advice, nor does it constitute a comprehensive or complete statement of the issues discussed thereto. ASCENT does not warrant that the document or information will be error free or will meet any particular criteria of performance or quality. In particular (but without limitation) information may be rendered inaccurate by changes made to the subject of the materials (i.e. applicable software). Rand Worldwide, Inc. specifically disclaims any warranty, either expressed or implied, including the warranty of fitness for a particular purpose.

AS-CRP7-BMX1-SG   //   RS-CRP7-BMX1-SG

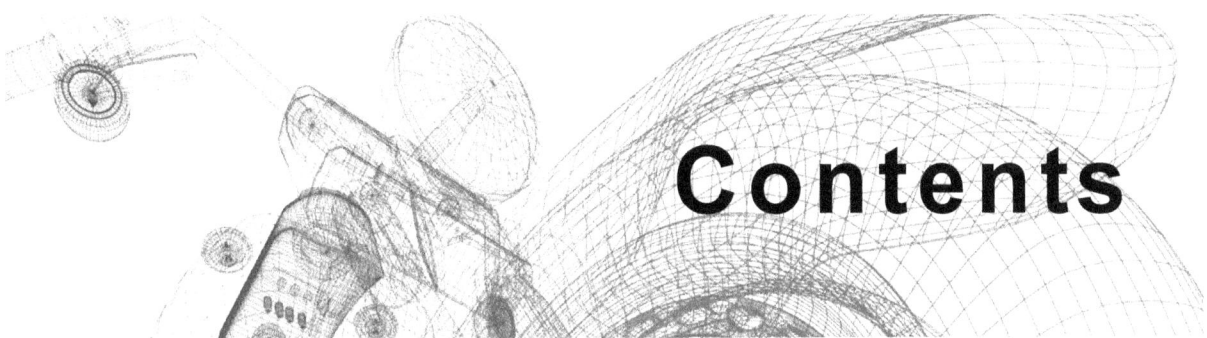

Contents

Preface

The *Creo Parametric 7.0: Behavioral Modeling* learning guide introduces the analysis tools available in the Behavioral Modeling Extension (BMX) for establishing and analyzing design goals. You will learn how to create analysis features and sensitivity and feasibility studies. Behavioral Modeling provides the ability to automatically change dimensions and parameters to meet specific design goals.

Topics Covered:

- Capabilities of BMX

- Analysis Features

- Sensitivity Analysis

- Feasibility and Optimization Analysis

- Multi-Objective Design Studies

- Graph Matching

- Excel Analysis

- Motion Analysis

Prerequisites

- Access to the Creo Parametric 7.0 software. The practices and files included with this guide might not be compatible with prior versions. Practice files included with this guide are compatible with the commercial version of the software, but not the student edition.

- It is highly recommended that you have completed the *Creo Parametric 7.0: Introduction to Solid Modeling*. Experience with MS Excel and Creo Mechanism Design is useful, but not required.

Note on Software Setup

This guide assumes a standard installation of the software using the default preferences during installation. Lectures and practices use the standard software templates and default options for the Content Libraries.

This content was developed using Creo Parametric 7.0, Build 7.0.2.0.

In This Guide

The following highlights the key features of this guide.

Feature	Description
Practice Files	The Practice Files page includes a link to the practice files and instructions on how to download and install them. The practice files are required to complete the practices in this guide.
Chapters	A chapter consists of the following - Learning Objectives, Instructional Content, Practices, Chapter Review Questions, and Command Summary.
	• **Learning Objectives** define the skills you can acquire by learning the content provided in the chapter.
	• **Instructional Content**, which begins right after Learning Objectives, refers to the descriptive and procedural information related to various topics. Each main topic introduces a product feature, discusses various aspects of that feature, and provides step-by-step procedures on how to use that feature. Where relevant, examples, figures, helpful hints, and notes are provided.
	• **Practice** for a topic follows the instructional content. Practices enable you to use the software to perform a hands-on review of a topic. It is required that you download the practice files (using the link found on the Practice Files page) prior to starting the first practice.

Practice Files

To download the practice files for this guide, use the following steps:

1. Type the URL *exactly as shown below* into the address bar of your Internet browser, to access the Course File Download page.

   Note: If you are using the ebook, you do not have to type the URL. Instead, you can access the page simply by clicking the URL below.

   ## https://www.ascented.com/getfile/id/coeloglossumPF

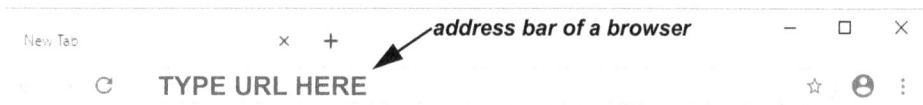

   address bar of a browser

   New Tab   ✕   +   — ☐ ✕

   ⟳   **TYPE URL HERE**   ☆   ☻   ⋮

2. On the Course File Download page, click the **DOWNLOAD NOW** button, as shown below, to download the .ZIP file that contains the practice files.

   DOWNLOAD NOW ▶

3. Once the download is complete, unzip the file and extract its contents.

   The recommended practice files folder location is:
   C:\Creo Parametric Behavioral Modeling Practice Files

   Note: It is recommended that you do not change the location of the practice files folder. Doing so may cause errors when completing the practices.

Stay Informed!

To receive information about upcoming events, promotional offers, and complimentary webcasts, visit:

www.ASCENTed.com/updates

Introduction to Behavioral Modeling

The Behavioral Modeling Extension (BMX) is an analysis tool for Creo Parametric models. BMX enables you to subject the model to a series of real world situations and problems. With BMX, you can test the behavior of your model before a physical model is created to generate and test the prototypes, saving time and money. This course provides examples and explanation of how behavioral modeling can be used to build a robust design.

Learning Objectives in This Chapter

- Review the capabilities of BMX.
- Understand where to use BMX.
- Learn the building blocks of BMX.

1.1 Capabilities of the Behavioral Modeling Extension

Unlike other analysis tools, the Behavioral Modeling Extension (BMX) works in a flexible environment. It enables you to capture the design intent that lies outside of that captured using standard dimension schemes. The results can then be used to drive the dimensions and features of your model.

BMX can be used to solve some of the following situations:

- Trial and error iteration of one or more design variables.

- Repetitive construction of a feature.

- Repetitive measurement of a feature.

- Feasibility or optimized solutions to a problem.

- Analyzing your model when standard functionality does not exist.

A BMX analysis is accomplished using Analysis features. The Analysis feature is not confined to a specific analysis type, but can be applied to extract virtually any type of data required from the Creo Parametric model. This enables you to apply BMX to many different analysis scenarios.

BMX enables you to do the following:

- Create feature parameters that result from measurement, model, surface, or curve analyses. For example, you can create a parameter that measures the length of a bolt. This parameter could then be placed in a family table.

- Create datum features based on analysis results from your model. For example, you can create datum points or a coordinate system on the model's center of mass.

- Create an Excel Analysis that integrates an Excel spreadsheet directly into a Creo Parametric model. Creo Parametric dimensions, parameters, and other analysis parameters are matched with corresponding cells in the spreadsheet.

- Create a User-Defined Analysis (UDA) feature specific to your design requirements.

- Create a Sensitivity Analysis to show how a design parameter reacts when a design variable is changed within a specific range.

- Create a Feasibility Study that adjusts design variables to meet specific design constraints. It determines if a feasible solution exists given the range of values for the design variables.

- Create an Optimization Study to adjust the design variables to meet specific design constraints. It optimizes the model with respect to a specific goal while maintaining design constraints.

- Create a Multi-Objective Design Study to report all of the values of the design parameters across a variation of design variables. The Multi-Objective Design Study provides access to all permutations and variations of a model within the bounds of the design variables.

- Compare two graphs to determine the difference in the distribution of one parameter along another parameter.

- Create a Motion Analysis that graphs design parameters with respect to time. This can only be created in the Assembly mode.

- Create a Simulation analysis that uses the results from a Creo Simulate analysis.

BMX Example

Creo Parametric has no standard solution for determining the holding capacity of a container (e.g., a bottle). You can solve this problem by using BMX analysis tools to create two volume calculations: one to measure the solid volume of the bottle and another to measure the volume of the bottle after it is shelled, as shown in Figure 1–1. You can then create a Relation analysis feature to measure the difference between solid and shelled volumes to determine the holding capacity of the bottle. The Relation analysis feature updates if changes are made to the model.

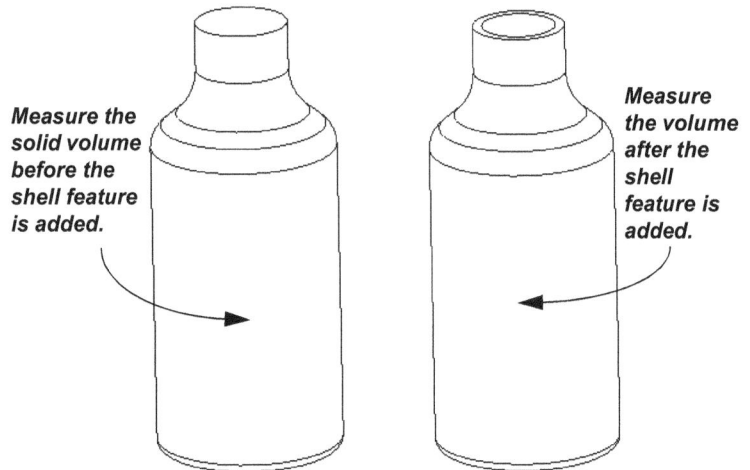

Measure the solid volume before the shell feature is added.

Measure the volume after the shell feature is added.

INTERNAL_VOL = SOLID_VOL - SHELLED_VOL

Figure 1–1

1.2 Building Blocks of BMX

In the past, standard CAD tools were limited to capturing design intent in the form of an electronic model. Some of the important design information could be transferred to the model using relations or dimension schemes, while other design requirements could not be incorporated. For example, CAD was used for design documentation. In many situations, the Engineering design of the model has been independent from the CAD system. BMX provides tools in Creo Parametric that enable you to further integrate your design goals with CAD modeling (e.g., minimize model weight).

The following describes some of the building blocks used in BMX:

- Analysis Features
- Field Points
- Construction Groups
- User-defined Analyses
- Design Studies

Analysis Features

Analysis features are discussed in more detail in later chapters.

An Analysis feature takes the Analysis setup and results and stores this information in a feature, as shown in Figure 1–2. The results can be stored as parameters. These parameters are updated each time the model is modified.

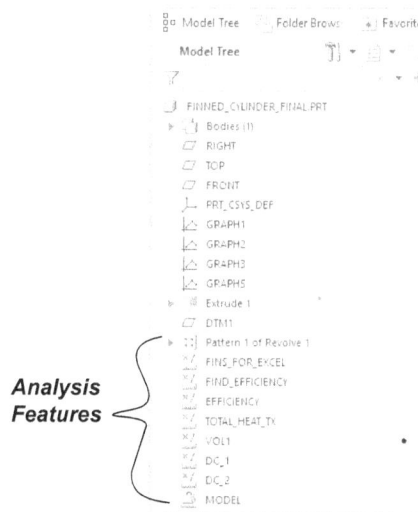

Figure 1–2

Field Points

Field points are special datum point features used in user-defined analyses (UDA). A field point is placed on a reference (i.e., curve, surface, quilt), but is not rigidly constrained. Therefore, it can capture data from anywhere on the geometry. Figure 1–3 shows a field point that was placed on a surface feature, which can be used to measure the shortest distance between the surface and the pipe.

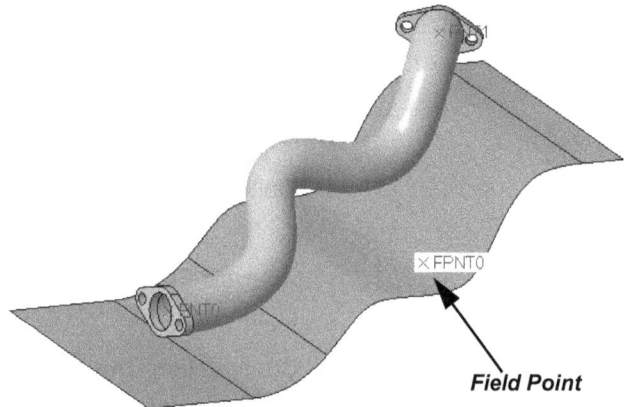

Field Point

Figure 1–3

Construction Groups

Construction Groups are discussed in more detail in later chapters.

A construction group (shown in Figure 1–4) is a group of features used to measure a design variable.

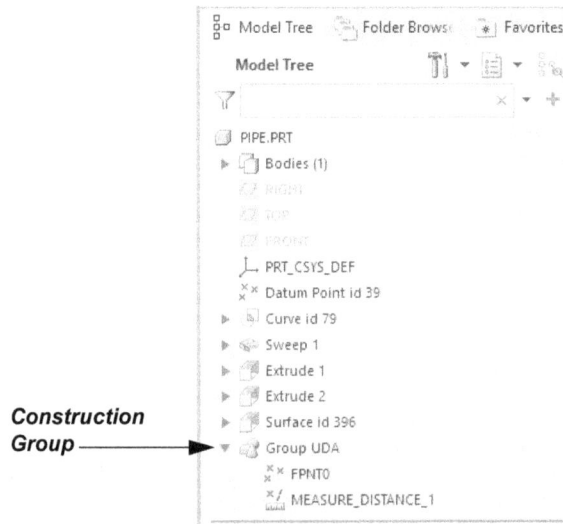

Construction Group

Figure 1–4

User-Defined Analyses

A User-defined analyses (UDA) provides modeling solutions that meet your user-defined constraints. To create a UDA, you have to define a construction group.

- UDAs are discussed in more detail in later chapters.

Design Studies

Design studies are discussed in more detail in later chapters.

Once Analysis features are added to the model to represent the design possibilities, you can run design studies that enable you to perform the following additional studies:

- "What if " analysis (Sensitivity Analysis)

- Goal-seeking analysis (Feasibility/Optimization)

- Simultaneous goal analysis (Multi-Objective Design Study)

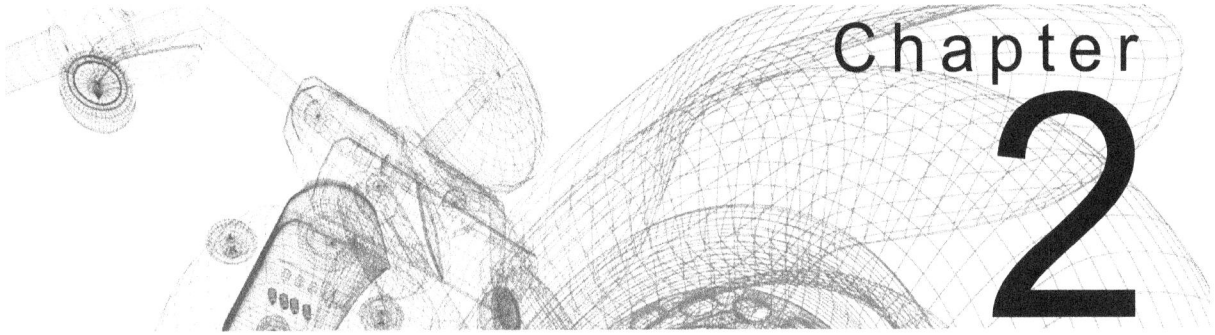

Analysis Features

Analysis features are used to generate parameters and datum features based on an analysis calculation on the model geometry.

Learning Objectives in This Chapter

- Learn how to create analysis features.
- Recognize the various analysis feature types and techniques.

2.1 Analysis Features

An analysis feature can be used to generate parameters and datum features based on an analysis calculation on the model geometry. An analysis feature, plus any dependent features and relations, update automatically when changes are made to the design.

An analysis feature has the following properties of a standard Creo Parametric feature:

- It is stored with the model.

- It is added as a feature to the Model Tree ($\times\!\!\!/$).

- It can be suppressed, reordered, deleted, etc.

- It reacts to feature order.

Figure 2–1 shows the Model Tree with multiple analysis features.

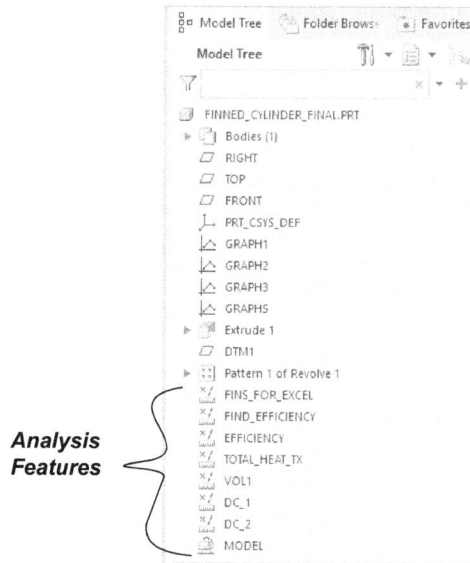

Figure 2–1

Once the analysis feature has been defined, the resulting parameters can be used in a relation. The relation can be written in the following way:

result_parameter_name: fid_analysis_feature_name

Where:

> **result_parameter_name =** The name of the results parameter created as a result of the analysis.

> **analysis_feature_name =** The name of the analysis feature.

In the example shown in Figure 2–2 and Figure 2–3, sweeping a section along a datum curve creates the solid geometry and the dimension d14 drives the height of the section of the geometry. The design intent of the part is to have the height of the protrusion equal to 50% of the distance around the trajectory. To accomplish this, a datum analysis feature is created to measure the distance around the trajectory. The analysis feature is then used in a relation to capture the design intent.

Before Analysis:

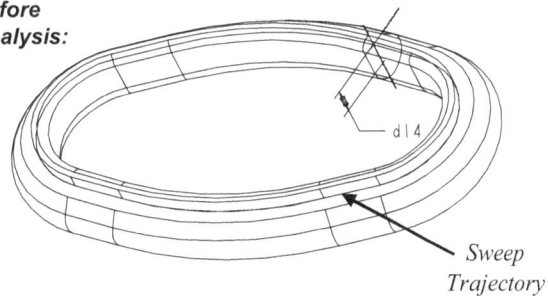

d14

Sweep Trajectory

Figure 2–2

After Analysis:

Analysis Information:
analysis_feature_name = ANALYSIS_LENGTH_1
results_parameter_name = LENGTH

Analysis created using the Length dialog box.
A measurement of the sweep trajectory length is generated.

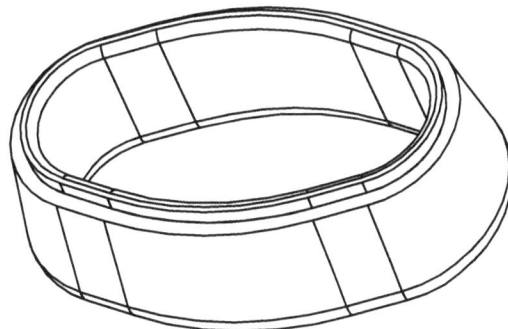

Relation:
d14 = 0.5 * LENGTH:fid_ANALYSIS_LENGTH_1

Figure 2–3

If parameters are defined in a part or assembly, they can be inserted directly into a relation. To insert a parameter into a relation, expand the *Local Parameters* area in the Relations dialog box and select the parameter name. Right-click and select **Insert to Relations**, as shown in Figure 2–4.

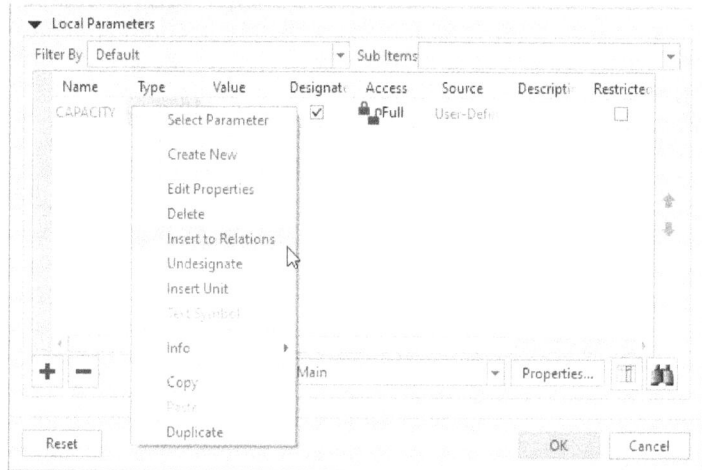

Figure 2–4

Creo Parametric enables you to create the following analysis types:

Analysis Type	Description
Measure	Measures distance, length, angle, area, volume or diameter of selected references. To create this type of analysis, select the *Analysis* tab, click (Measure), and select the appropriate option from the Measure dialog box, as shown below.
Model Report	Calculates model mass properties, finds short edges, or measures thickness of selected entities. To create this type of analysis, select the *Analysis* tab, and select the appropriate option, as shown below.

Inspect Geometry	Measures radius, curvature, dihedral angle, deviation, and slope of selected references. To create this type of analysis, select the *Analysis* tab, and select the appropriate option, as shown below. 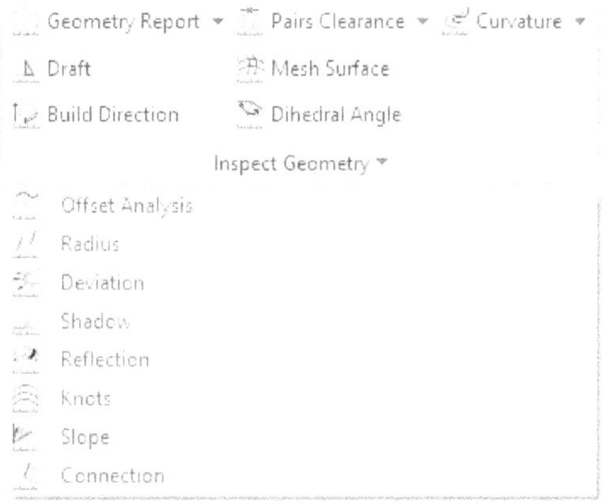 Geometry Report ▼ Pairs Clearance ▼ Curvature ▼ Draft Mesh Surface Build Direction Dihedral Angle Inspect Geometry ▼ Offset Analysis Radius Deviation Shadow Reflection Knots Slope Connection
Custom	This group contains **User-Defined**, **Excel**, **External**, **Mathcad**, and **Prime**, as shown below. The analysis available depends on the license available. Some of the more commonly used analysis in this group are **Excel** and **User-Defined**. 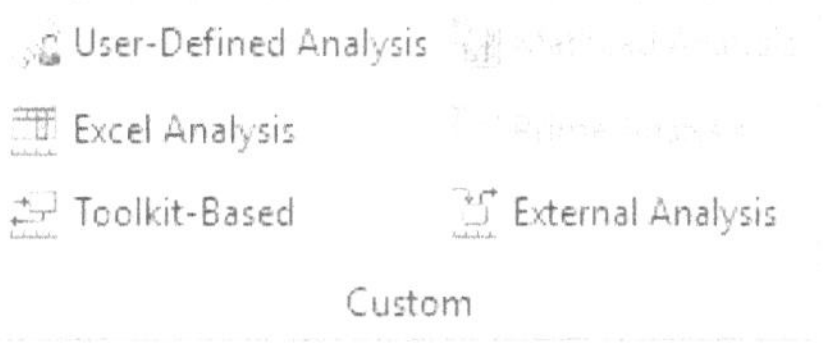 User-Defined Analysis Excel Analysis Toolkit-Based External Analysis Custom
Relation	This type of the analysis feature is defined by means of a relation(s). Relations enable you to define analysis feature parameters. To create this type of analysis, select the *Tools* tab and click $d=$ (Relations).

2.2 Analysis Feature Types

All the analysis features are created in the *Analysis* tab. The following types of analyses that can be created in an analysis feature:

*   Measure

*   Model Analysis

*   UDA (User-Defined Analysis)

*   Relation

*   Excel Analysis

*   Motion Analysis (Assembly mode only)

*   Simulate

Measure

The Measure analysis feature enables you to conduct a measurement on the model, including:

*   Length

*   Distance

*   Angle

*   Diameter

*   Area

*   Volume

*   Transform

How To: Create a Measure Analysis Feature

1. Select the *Analysis* tab. It activates as shown in Figure 2–5.

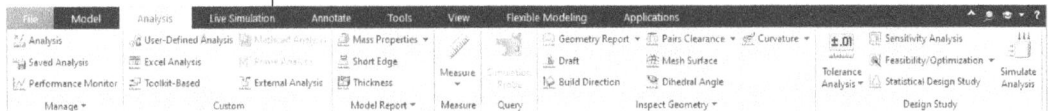

Figure 2–5

2. Select the type of analysis from the groups that you want to add to your model. A dialog box opens corresponding to the analysis type.

   For example, if you click ✎ (Measure), the Measure dialog box as shown in Figure 2–6.

Figure 2–6

3. When the Measure dialog box opens, you can select the type of measurement that you want to create and then click

   ⊕ (Expand The Dialog) to expand the dialog box, as shown in Figure 2–7.

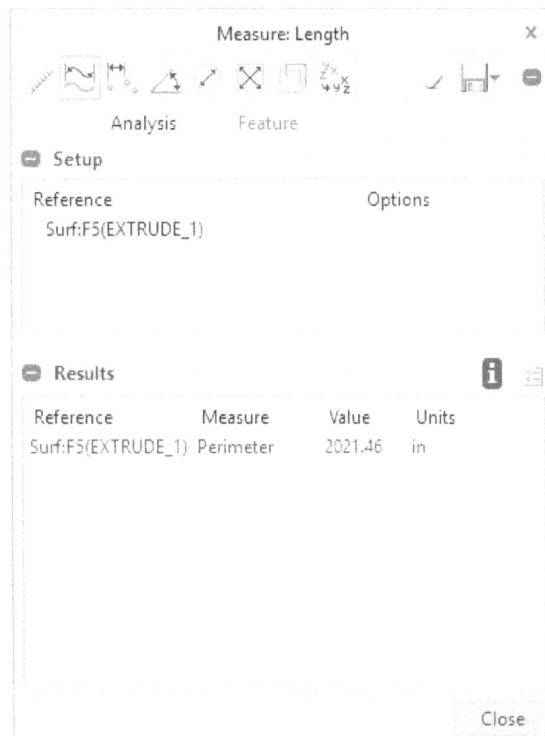

Figure 2–7

- The item to measure can be preselected or selected when the *Analysis* tab is active and displays in the Measure dialog box. The results also display in the View window.

4. Click ▤ (Open Options) in the Measure dialog box to set various options. For example, you can toggle the **Show Feature Tab** option, as shown in Figure 2–8. This will show or remove the *Feature* tab in the dialog box.

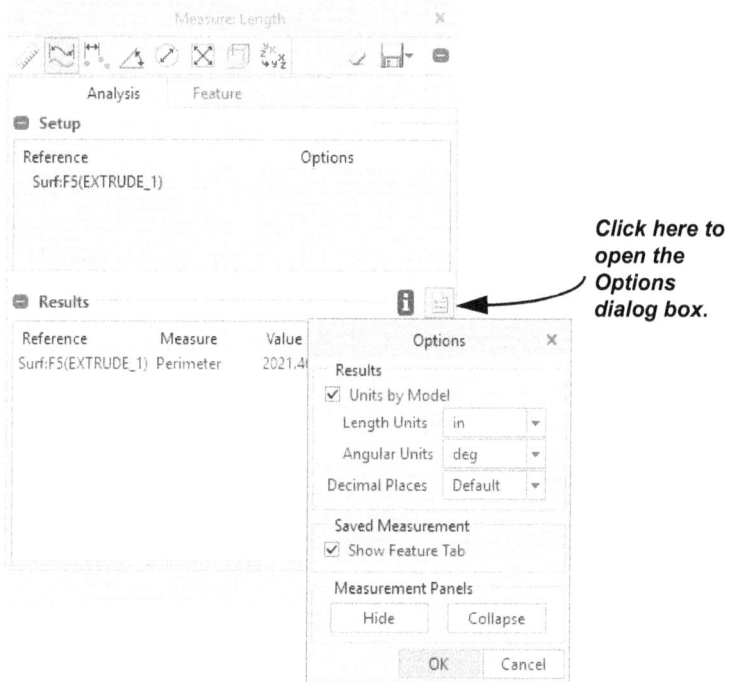

Figure 2–8

5. Select the *Feature* tab shown in Figure 2–9 to display the parameter.

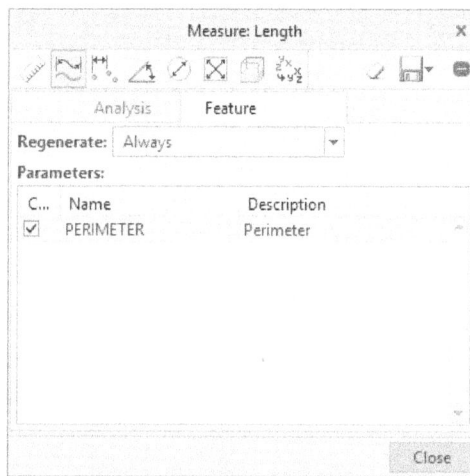

Figure 2–9

The Regenerate drop-down list enables you to assign when the analysis feature regenerates. The options include the following:

- **Always:** Regenerates the analysis feature during model regeneration.
- **Read Only:** Excludes the analysis feature from the model regeneration.
- **Design Study:** Only regenerates the analysis feature when it is used by a design study.

In the *Parameters* area, you can specify whether you want to create the displayed parameters. You can edit the names of these parameters as required.

6. By default, the **Make Feature** option is preselected in the Measure dialog box. The **Feature** option creates an analysis feature. Enter an appropriate name for the analysis feature. By default, the default name identifies the analysis type (e.g., **MEASURE_LENGTH_#** for length analysis feature). The updated dialog box is shown in Figure 2–10.

*Note that when you click **Save Analysis** or **Make Feature**, any parameter names you changed will be saved correctly with the analysis, but will revert to the original names in the dialog box. This way, you can use the dialog box to save multiple analyses without closing it.*

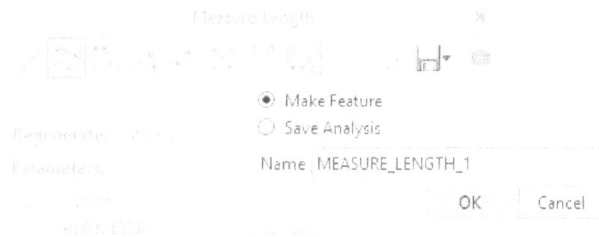

Figure 2–10

7. Click **OK** and then **Close** in the Measure dialog box to complete the feature.

Model Analysis

A model analysis feature calculates any of the following properties:

- Model Mass Properties

- X-section Mass Properties

- Clearance and Interference

Figure 2–11 shows the Mass Properties dialog box used to calculate and define the required information.

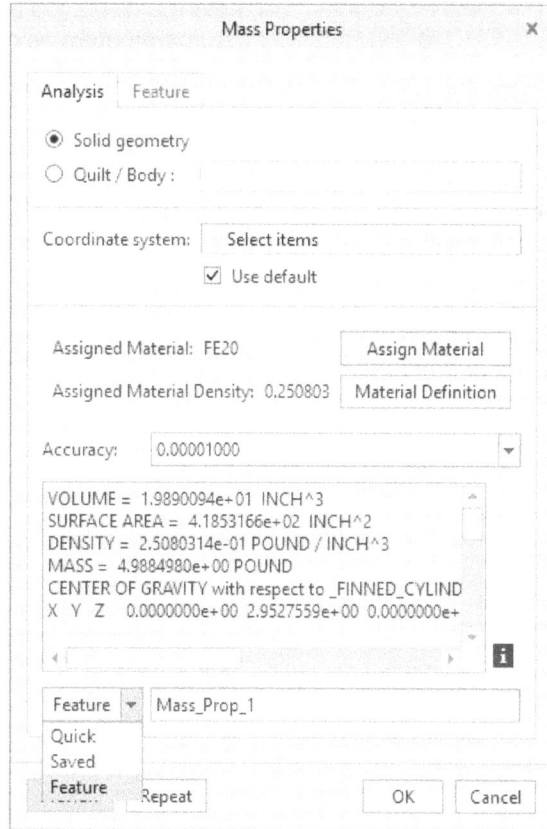

Figure 2–11

Model Analysis Example

The designer needs to ensure the center of gravity is correctly located on the model (shown in Figure 2–12) so that it does not tip over once used. You can create a Model Analysis analysis feature that measures the location of the center of gravity and creates a coordinate system at this location. The location updates as changes are made to the model, ensuring that design changes reflect in an updated center of gravity.

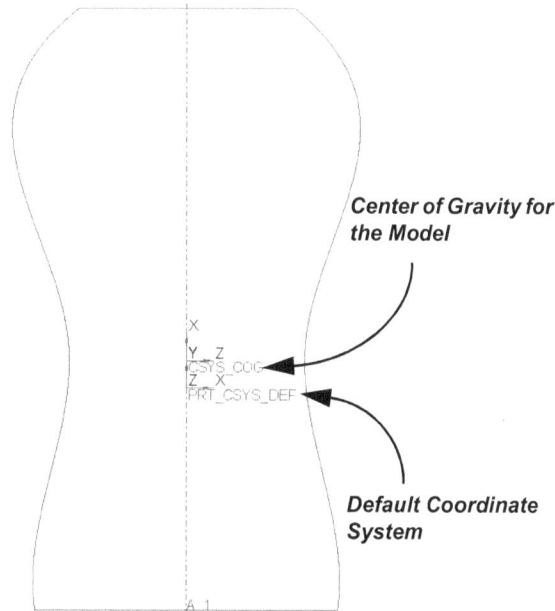

Center of Gravity for the Model

Default Coordinate System

Figure 2–12

UDA

The UDA analysis feature enables you to define, perform, and store non-standard geometric analyses.

A group must be defined consisting of all the datum features. The last feature in the group must be an Analysis feature. If the group contains a field point as the first feature, the measurement is used throughout the entire domain of the field point. The resulting parameters are the maximum and minimum values of the Analysis feature in the created group.

The analysis is performed during regeneration, so the location of the feature can impact results. These values can be used in other Analysis features later in the regeneration cycle.

UDA Example:

You must determine the distance between the two cylinders. A measurement between the two surfaces only reports the closest distance. You will require the distance at all locations.

How To: Perform a UDA Analysis

1. In the *Model* tab, in the Datum group, expand ⋰ (Point) and select ⬚ (Field). Select anywhere on the surface of one of the cylinders to place the point, as shown in Figure 2–13. The location does not matter because when it is used in the Analysis feature, it is permitted to move over the entire surface.

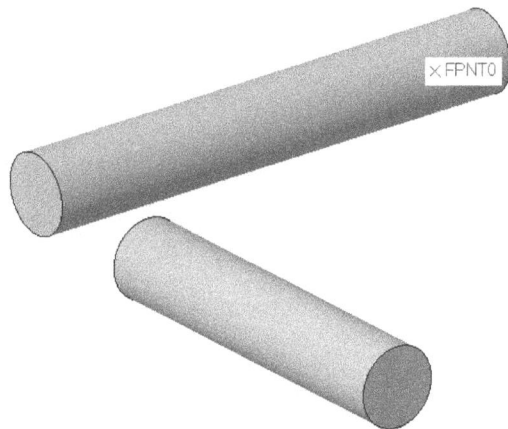

Figure 2–13

2. Create a distance measurement analysis feature with its associated parameter. This feature determines the distance between the field point and the other cylinder.
3. To run a user-defined analysis, a local group must be created that groups the analysis and field datum point feature. In the Model Tree, select the field point and analysis feature, and click ⬚ (Group) in the mini toolbar. Edit the group name in the Model Tree, to make it meaningful.

4. In the *Analysis* tab, in the Custom group, click

    (User-Defined Analysis). The dialog box displays as shown in Figure 2–14.

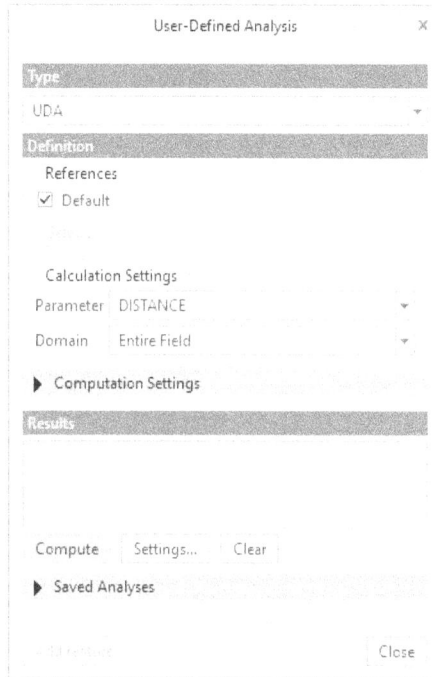

Figure 2–14

The elements in the dialog box required to create a User-Defined Analysis feature are described as follows:

Element	Description
Type	Select the UDA local group to analyze.
References	Enable the **Default** option to use default UDA references. In the example, the distance between the two protrusions was reported for the top surface. If the same information was required for the bottom surface, the references must be switched by clearing the Default checkbox and using **Select** to select the new references.
Calculation Settings Parameter	Lists all parameters belonging to the analysis in the UDA local group. Only one parameter can be analyzed at a time by the UDA.
Calculation Settings Domain	**Entire field -** Calculates the parameter for all the geometry associated with the field point. Reports a fringe plot. **Selected Point -** Prompts you to select a point on the geometry. Reports a single value in the results field.

The results of the analysis for the entire field are shown in Figure 2–15.

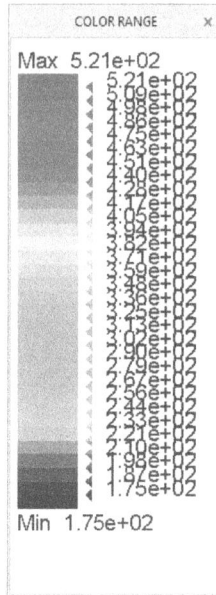

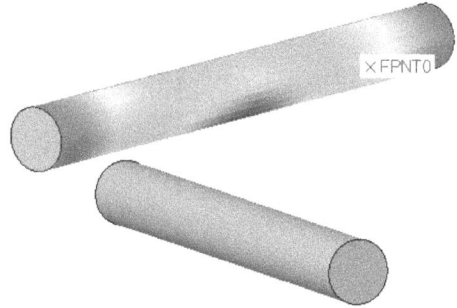

COLOR RANGE   x

Max 5.21e+02
5.21e+02
5.09e+02
4.98e+02
4.86e+02
4.75e+02
4.63e+02
4.51e+02
4.40e+02
4.28e+02
4.17e+02
4.05e+02
3.94e+02
3.82e+02
3.71e+02
3.59e+02
3.48e+02
3.36e+02
3.25e+02
3.13e+02
3.02e+02
2.90e+02
2.79e+02
2.67e+02
2.56e+02
2.44e+02
2.33e+02
2.21e+02
2.10e+02
1.99e+02
1.87e+02
1.75e+02
Min 1.75e+02

X FPNT0

Figure 2–15

Relation

The Relation analysis feature enables you to write a relation that calculates model information that cannot be directly derived from another type of analysis. A relation is written using the standard Creo Parametric editor.

Relation Analysis Example

For example, the vase shown in Figure 2–16 has been created by shelling a solid protrusion. If the internal volume of the vase is required, a Relation Analysis feature can be created that subtracts the volume of the vase before and after the shell feature. The parameter **INTERNAL_VOL** can then be optimized or included in other design studies.

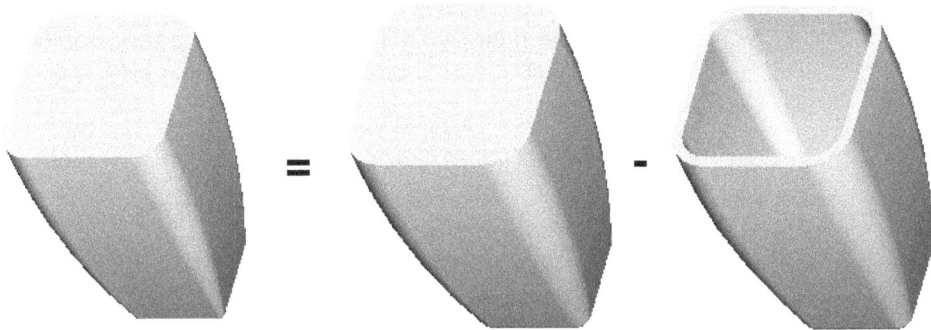

INTERNAL_VOL = SOLID_VOL - CUT_VOL

Figure 2–16

Motion Analysis

The Motion Analysis analysis feature enables you to evaluate parameters based upon the entire range of motion for an assembly. As the assembly is put in motion, results of the design parameters can be graphed with respect to time. This type of analysis feature is only available in the Assembly mode.

Motion Analysis is discussed further in a later chapter.

Motion Analysis Example

Figure 2–17 shows a model where a shaft rotates on its pin connection with a block. Two datum points have been created on each part. A Measure analysis feature was created to track the distance between the two points as the shaft rotates.

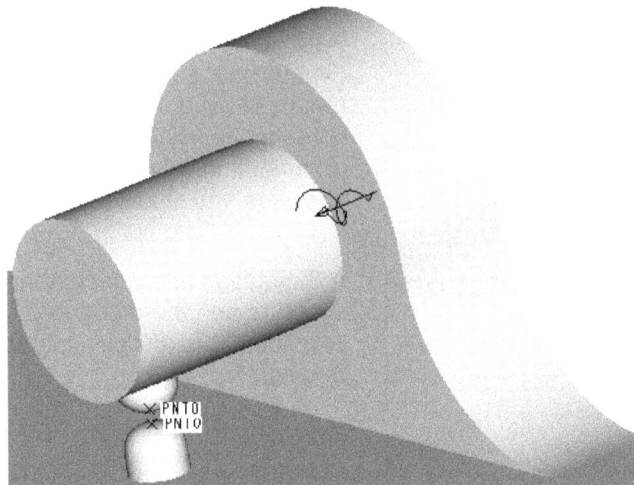

Figure 2–17

The graph shown in Figure 2–18 tracks the displacement between the two points throughout the range of the motion analysis.

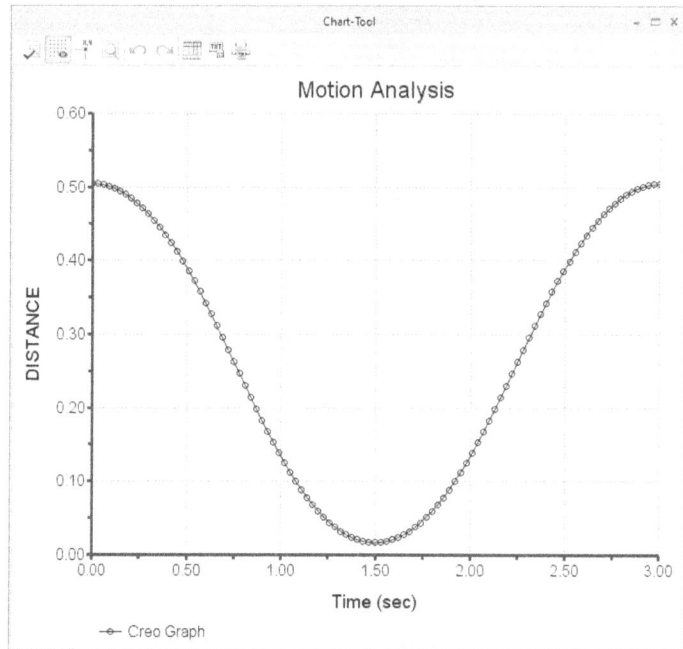

Figure 2–18

Excel Analysis

An Excel analysis feature enables you to use an Excel spreadsheet to define the analysis that is run on the Creo Parametric model. The spreadsheet links with Creo Parametric dimensions, parameters, and other analysis parameters. The results of the analysis can then be output and stored in the Excel spreadsheet. The data that is output can be stored as a feature parameter in the Excel Analysis feature and used in downstream analyses and studies.

Simulation Analysis

A Simulation analysis feature enables you to run both the structure and thermal analyses that have been defined in Creo Simulate. This analysis feature requires a license of Creo Simulate.

User-Defined, Relation, Excel, Motion and Simulate analyses can also be created using the $\overset{\times f}{\underset{\text{....}}{}}$ (Analysis) option in the *Manage* group in the *Analysis* tab.

How To: Create an Analysis Feature in the Manage Group, in the *Analysis* tab

1. To create an analysis feature, in the *Analysis* tab in the Manage group, click (Analysis). The ANALYSIS dialog box opens as shown in Figure 2–19. Enter a new name for the Analysis feature and press <Enter>. The default name is **Analysis#**.

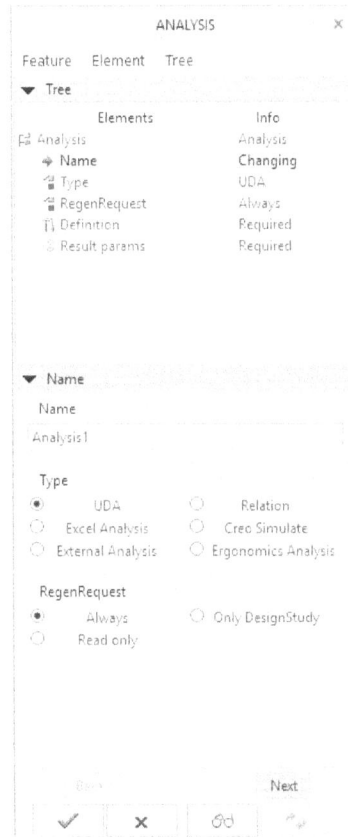

Figure 2–19

The *Tree* area in the Analysis dialog box lists the elements required for the selected Analysis feature. The elements required for the creation of an Analysis feature are described as follows:

Element	Description
Name	Defines the name of the Analysis feature. You must press <Enter> for the name to be assigned. Name Analysis1

Type	Defines the type of Analysis feature. The image below shows the available options. The Motion Analysis option is only available in Assembly mode. 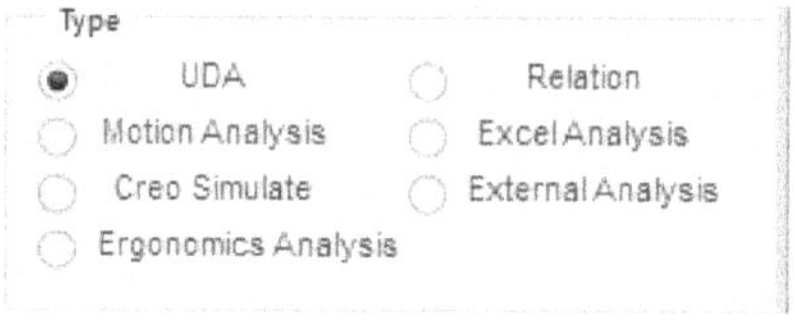

Regen Request	Defines how regeneration affects the Analysis feature. The *RegenRequest* options are shown below. 

	Always	The Analysis feature is regenerated each time the model is regenerated.
	Only DesignStudy	The Analysis feature is only regenerated when running a design study
	Read only	The Analysis feature is never regenerated.

Definition	Defines the calculations for the Analysis feature. This varies depending on the type of Analysis feature. This is accessed by selecting **Next** in the ANALYSIS dialog box.

Result Params	Defines the parameters that are added to the Analysis feature. This is only available for certain Analysis features. To add a parameter, select it in the *Result params* area, select **YES**, and enter a name, as shown below. 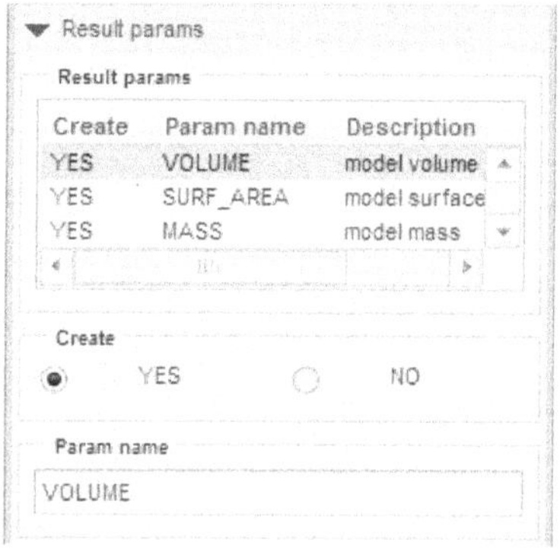

Result Datums	Defines the datum features that are added to the Analysis feature. This is only available for certain Analysis features. To create a datum feature, select it from the *Result datums* area, select **YES**, and enter a name, as shown below.

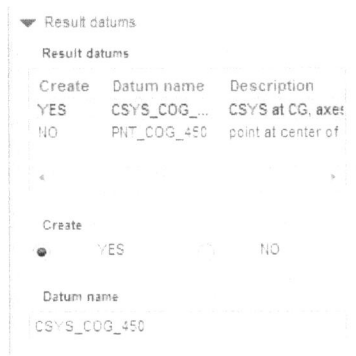

Persistent Display

For Curve, Surface and User-Defined Analysis (UDAs) features, their calculations generate graphs or a color fringe plot. In these situations, you have the ability to control the display of these features. The display properties can be accessed either through the Analysis feature or by clicking (Saved Analysis) in the Manage group of the *Analysis* tab. The Saved Analysis dialog box is shown in Figure 2–20.

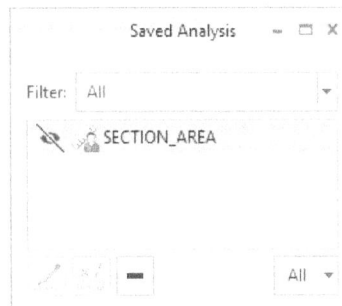

Figure 2–20

You can select the Analysis feature, expand **All** and click **Hide All** or **Unhide All** to toggle the display.

2.3 Customizing Graphs

Many analyses allow you to create graphs of the results. The Chart-Tool window can be customized to change titles, fonts colors, and so on.

In the image shown in Figure 2–21, the chart on the left is the default graph and the image on the right is a customized graph.

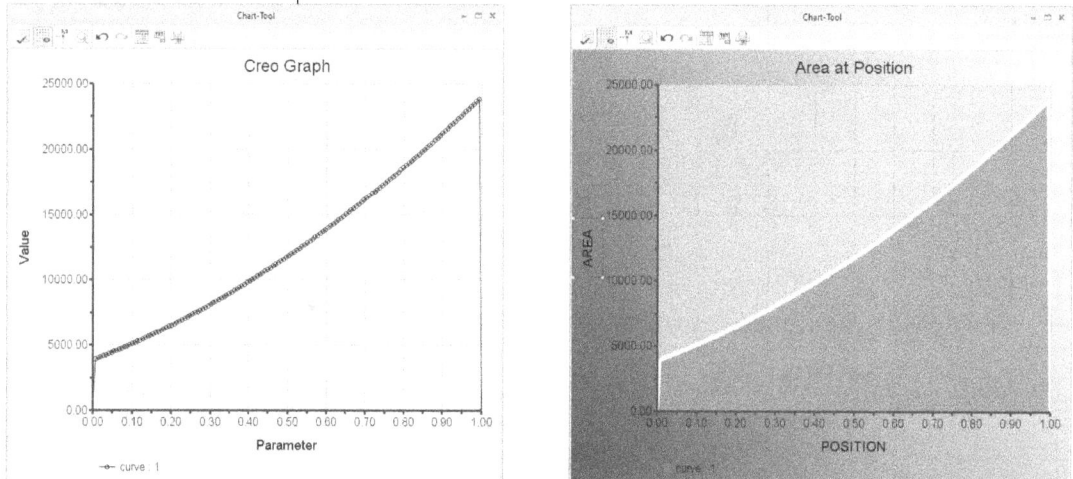

Figure 2–21

To customize a graph, click ✎ (Customize Graph) in the toolbar at the top of the Chart-Tool window. The window expands to show the customization options shown in Figure 2–22.

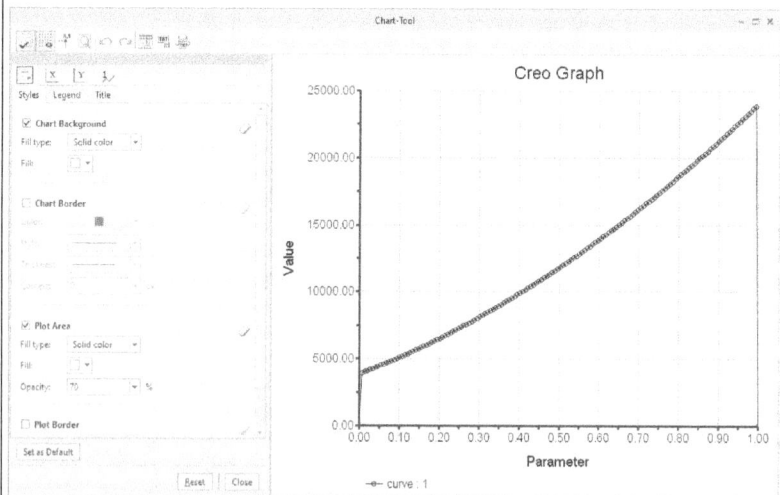

Figure 2–22

There are four areas you can customize:

- ‾。 (Format Chart) - Format the overall chart style and legend and title areas.

- ⊠ (Format X-Axis) - Format the x-axis style, gridlines, title and setup. The setup customizations include setting a user defined range, linear or logarithmic scale, and so on.

- ⊡ (Format Y-Axis) - Format the y-axis with the same options as the x-axis.

- ⋰⁄ (Format Trace) - Format the curve and data point styles as well as the setup which include the ability to switch from a line chart to a column chart.

Select the appropriate option from the customization area, and the available options display. In Figure 2–23, the ‾。 (Format Chart) option is selected.

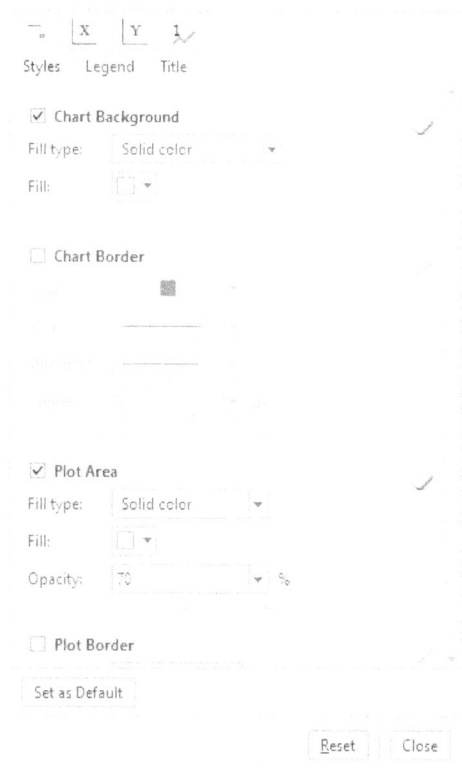

Figure 2–23

The background color can be changed by selecting a color from the color swatch. It can also be changed from a solid color to gradient. When the **Gradient** option is selected, two color swatches are available as well as an angle values, so you can select two colors and an angle, and the background will blend between them, as shown in Figure 2–24.

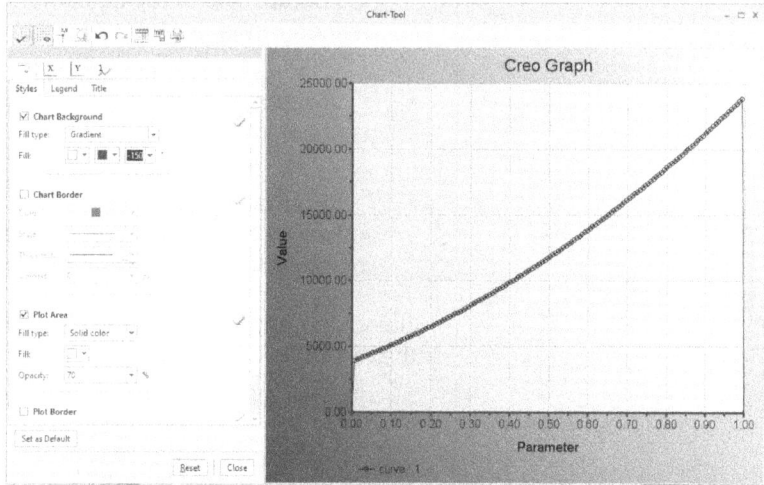

Figure 2–24

The *Legend* tab, shown in Figure 2–25, controls the display of the legend. The *Title* tab, also shown in Figure 2–25, controls the display of the chart title.

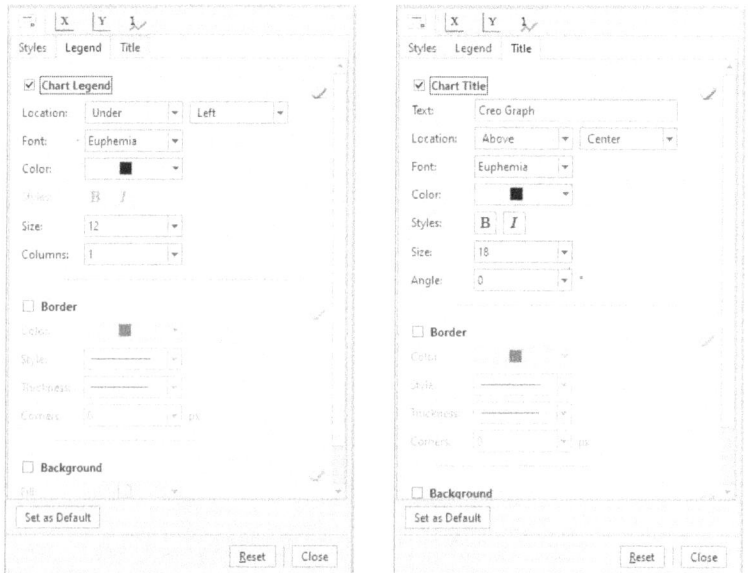

Figure 2–25

Similarly, you can make changes to the X and Y axis areas and the data curve.

Changes can be reset to default in multiple ways:

- Any individual changes can be reset to the original by clicking ✎ (Clear Formatting).

- All settings can be set to defaults by clicking **Reset**.

You can define the default style for new charts by making the edits you want and clicking **Set as Default**.

Graphs and underlying data are exported to an Excel spreadsheet by clicking ⊞ (Export To Excel). Note that customizations to the graph such as background color will not be carried forward into the Excel graph, although changes to the X and Y axis Titles will, as shown in Figure 2–26.

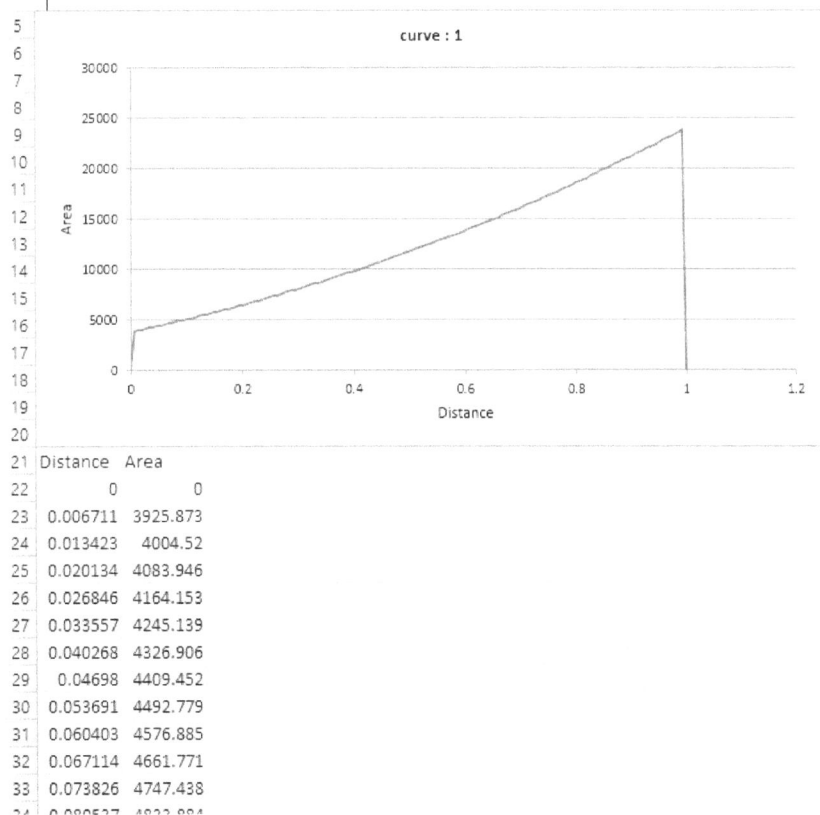

	Distance	Area
21	Distance	Area
22	0	0
23	0.006711	3925.873
24	0.013423	4004.52
25	0.020134	4083.946
26	0.026846	4164.153
27	0.033557	4245.139
28	0.040268	4326.906
29	0.04698	4409.452
30	0.053691	4492.779
31	0.060403	4576.885
32	0.067114	4661.771
33	0.073826	4747.438

Figure 2–26

Practice 2a | Analysis Features I

Practice Objectives

- Create a Measure Analysis feature.
- Create a Relation Analysis feature.
- Add Analysis feature parameters to the Model Tree.

In this practice, you will create three Analysis features to determine the internal volume of a canister. A shell feature is used to remove the material in the canister. The first two Analysis features measure the liquid volume that the model holds below a specified fill line. One of these Analysis features calculates the entire volume of the model, without the shell, and the second measures the volume with the shell. A final Analysis feature is added to the model as a relation to subtract the values for the solid and shell parameters.

Task 1 - Open the canister.prt model.

1. Set the working directory to *Analysis_Features_I*.

2. Open **canister.prt**.

3. Set the model display as follows:

   - *(Datum Display Filters)*: Only (Plane Display)
   - *View* tab: (Plane Tag Display)
   - *(Spin Center)*: Off
   - *(Display Style)*: (Shading With Edges)

   The model displays as shown in Figure 2–27.

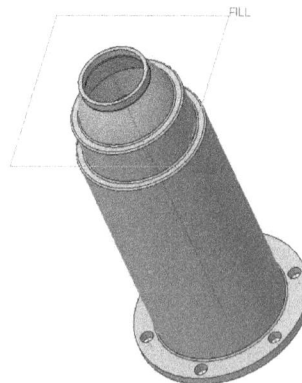

Figure 2–27

Task 2 - Use the Model Player to investigate the model.

1. Select the *Tools* tab.

2. In the Investigate Group, click ⟋ (Model Player).

3. Click ◁ (Go To Beginning) to rewind to the beginning of the feature list.

Note that the first four features are hidden datums, so they will not display while using the Model Player.

4. Click ▶ (Step Forward) repeatedly to review each feature in the feature list. The shell feature was added to the canister to create an internal cavity. The **FILL** datum plane was added to the model to mark the location of the water line for the canister.

Task 3 - Create the first Analysis feature.

1. Select the *Analysis* tab.

2. In the Measure group, expand ⟋ (Measure) and select ⬚ (Volume). The Measure: Volume dialog box displays as shown in Figure 2–28.

Your dialog box may already display as expanded.

Figure 2–28

3. In the Measure: Volume dialog box, click ⊕ (Expand The Dialog), if not already expanded.

4. Click in the *Plane* field and select the **FILL** datum plane from the model.

5. Note that if you are unable to click in the *Plane* field, right-click on **CANISTER.PRT** in the *Reference* area and select **Remove**. Then, select **CANISTER.PRT** in the Model Tree and the *Plane* field activates.

6. If required, click ⚲ (Measure Other Side) to flip the direction of the arrow so that it points down into the part, as shown in Figure 2–29.

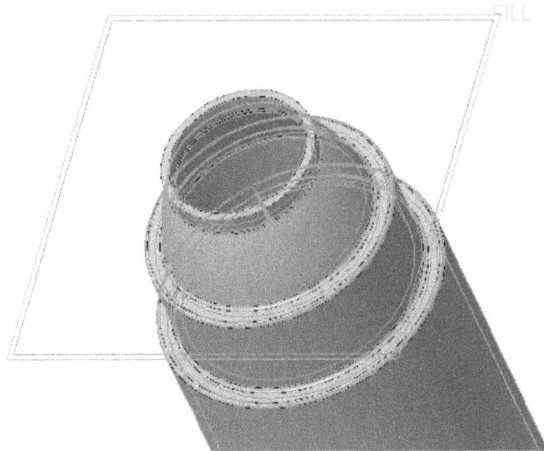

Figure 2–29

7. The part volume beneath the **FILL** datum plane is 926352 mm^3 (or approximately 1.0 L), as shown in Figure 2–30.

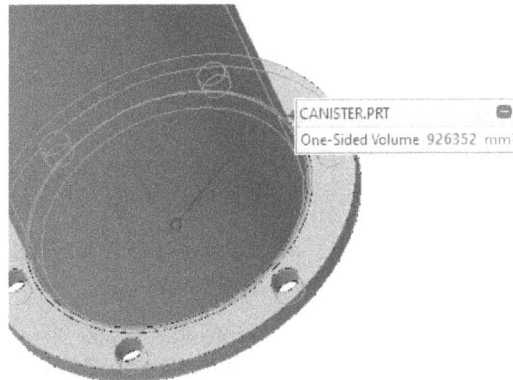

Figure 2–30

8. In the Measure: Volume dialog box, select the *Feature* tab.

9. Ensure that **Always** is selected as the default *Regenerate* option.

10. Select **ONE_SIDED_VOLUME** in the *Name* column, edit the parameter name to **CUT_VOL** and press <Enter>.

*After saving, the parameter name may change back to **ONE_SIDED_VOLUME** but this does not impact the analysis you just saved.*

11. In the Measure: Volume dialog box, click ⊟⁻ (Save).

12. Ensure that **Make Feature** is selected, set the name to **CUT**, and press <Enter>.

13. Click **Close** in the Measure: Volume dialog box.

Task 4 - Create a second Model Analysis feature.

Like all Creo Parametric features, Analysis features obey the regeneration order.

1. In the Measure group, expand ⟋ (Measure) and select ▢ (Volume).

2. Click in the *Plane* field and select the **FILL** datum plane from the model.

3. If required, click ⟋ (Measure Other Side) to flip the direction of the arrow so that it points down into the part.

4. Select the *Feature* tab.

5. Ensure that **Always** is selected as the default *Regenerate* option.

6. Select **ONE_SIDED_VOLUME** in the *Name* column, edit the parameter name to **SOLID_VOL**, and press <Enter>.

7. In the Measure: Volume dialog box, click ⊟⁻ (Save).

8. Ensure that **Make Feature** is selected, set the name to **SOLID**, and press <Enter>.

9. Click **Close** in the Measure: Volume dialog box.

Task 5 - Show the feature parameters in the Model Tree.

---

1. In the Model Tree, click ⫟ ⁻ (Settings)>**Tree Columns** from the drop-down list.

2. In the Type drop-down list, select **Feat Params**.

3. Enter **CUT_VOL** in the Name field and select ≫ (Add Column).

---

4. Enter **SOLID_VOL** in the Name field and click ➤ (Add
   Column) to add it to the *Displayed* column. The Model Tree
   Columns dialog box displays as shown in Figure 2–31.

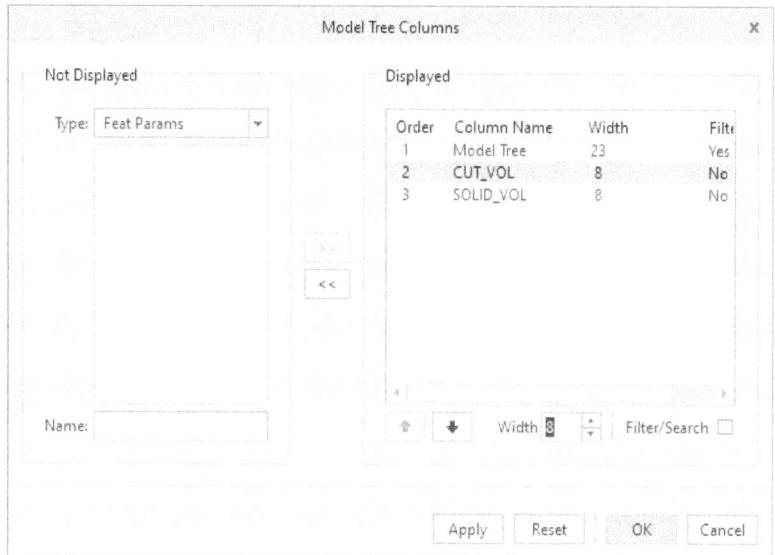

Figure 2–31

5. Click **OK**.

6. The new parameters display in the Model Tree, as shown in
   Figure 2–32. Note that both parameters have the same
   volume. This is because they were both created at the same
   point in the feature list.

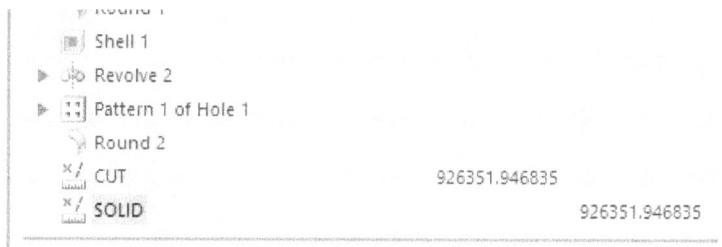

Figure 2–32

Task 6 - Reorder the SOLID and CUT Analysis features.

Design Considerations

You want to determine the difference between the solid volume and the shelled volume, which is the carrying capacity of the container. So the SOLID measurement has to be made prior to shelling the container, and the CUT analysis feature after the shell feature.

1. In the Model Tree, drag the SOLID analysis feature and drop it so that it comes before the **Shell 1** feature, then drag the CUT analysis feature so that it comes after **Shell 1**. The Model Tree displays as shown in Figure 2–33.

Analysis features behave like other features; their feature order can affect the resulting parameter values.

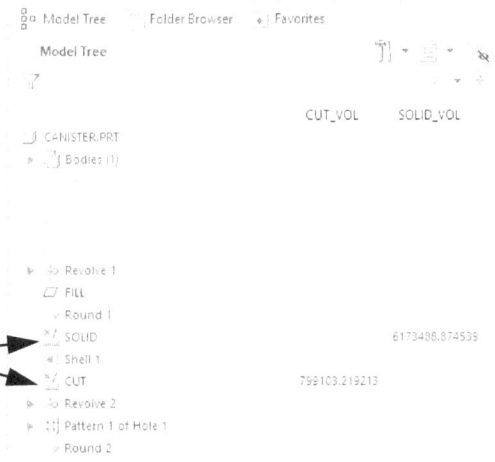

Reorder the SOLID Analysis feature before the Shell and CUT after the Shell

Figure 2–33

The **solid_vol** (6173488.87 mm^3) and **cut_vol** (799103.22 mm^3) will be used in a Relation Analysis feature to calculate the internal volume.

Task 7 - Create a Relation Analysis feature.

Design Considerations

In this task, you will add a relation to calculate the capacity. The relation will be of the form:

CAPACITY = SOLID_VOL:FID_SOLID - CUT_VOL:FID_CUT

The relation can be typed in as written or you can use the tools in the Relations dialog box to select the parameters.

In this relation, the two parameters **solid_vol** and **cut_vol** are subtracted. These parameters exist at the feature level and not at the part level. To indicate this, the feature name must be specified, as shown in Figure 2–34.

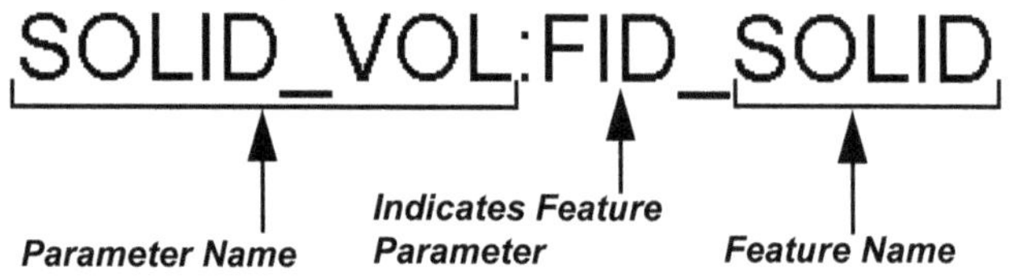

Figure 2–34

1. In the Manage group in the ribbon, click (Analysis).

2. In the Name field of the ANALYSIS dialog box, type **internal** and press <Enter>.

3. In the *Type* area, select **Relation**.

4. Ensure that **Always** is selected as the default *RegenRequest* option.

5. Click **Next**. The Relations dialog box displays, where you can enter the relation.

6. Type **CAPACITY =**.

7. In the Relations dialog box, click [ ] (Insert Parameter Name) and the Select Parameter dialog box opens, as shown in Figure 2–35.

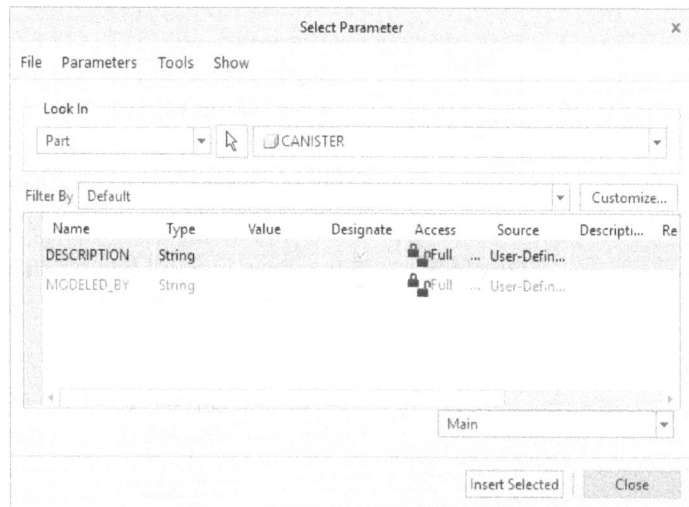

Figure 2–35

8. In the Look In drop-down list, select **Feature**.

9. In the Model Tree, select **SOLID** and click **Insert Selected**.

10. Type **-**.

11. Click [ ] (Insert Parameter Name).

12. In the Look In drop-down list, select **Feature**.

13. In the Model Tree, select **Cut** and click **Insert Selected**. The Relations editor displays as shown in Figure 2–36.

Figure 2–36

14. In the Relations dialog box, click ✓ (Verify) to verify the relation and click **OK**.

15. Click **OK** in the Relations dialog box.

16. Click ✓ (OK) to complete the Analysis feature.

Task 8 - Add the volume parameter to the Model Tree.

---

1. Add the **CAPACITY** feature parameter to the Model Tree. If required, refer to Task 5 for instructions on how to add this parameter. The calculated capacity of the canister is approximately 5.4 L.

Task 9 - Modify the location of the FILL datum.

---

1. Select the **FILL** datum plane and click 'd1' (Edit Dimensions) in the mini toolbar.

2. Change the offset dimension from *25* to **200**.

3. Regenerate the model. Note how the parameter values change in the Model Tree.

---

4. Restore the location of the **FILL** datum by modifying its offset value back to **25**. Regenerate the model.

5. In the Model Tree, click 📋 ▾ (Settings)>**Reset Tree Settings**>**Reset Tree Settings**.

6. Save the model and erase it from memory.

Practice 2b

Analysis Features II

Practice Objectives

- Create a Measure Analysis feature.
- Create a Relation Analysis feature.
- Create a Model Analysis feature.

In this practice, you will create Analysis features in a flower vase model. These features are required by the designer to design and manufacture a stable model. The following information is required:

- The height of the flower vase. This will be calculated using a Measure Analysis feature.

- The amount of paint required to paint the outside surface area of the flower vase. This will be calculated using both a Measure and Relation Analysis feature.

- The location of the center of mass to help ensure the stability of the flower vase when it is used. This will be calculated using both a Model Analysis and Measure Analysis feature.

Using Analysis features in this way enables you to quickly and easily review the parameter values without having to recalculate them each time a design change is made.

Task 1 - Open the flower_vase.prt model.

1. Set the working directory to *Analysis_Features_II*.

2. Open **flower_vase.prt**.

3. Set the model display as follows:

- *(Datum Display Filters)*: Only ˣˣ (Point Display)

- *View* tab: (Point Tag Display)

- *(Spin Center)*: Off

- *(Display Style)*: (Shading With Edges)

The model displays as shown in Figure 2–37.

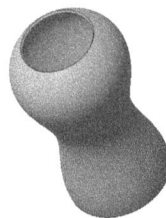

Figure 2–37

4. Select the *Tools* tab and use ⬛ (Model Player) to investigate the model.

Task 2 - Create an Analysis feature that measures the height of the model.

---

1. Create and place two datum points, the first at the bottom center of the vase and the second at the top center, as shown in Figure 2–38. To create these datum points, select the *Model* tab. In the Datum group, click ˣˣ (Point), then select the following:

   • Select the reference edge.
   • Expand **On** in the *References* area of the dialog box.
   • Select **Center** from the drop-down list.
   • Click **New Point** and select the top edge.
   • Click **OK**.

Both datum points can be created within the same feature, or they can be created separately.

Shading turned off for clarity.

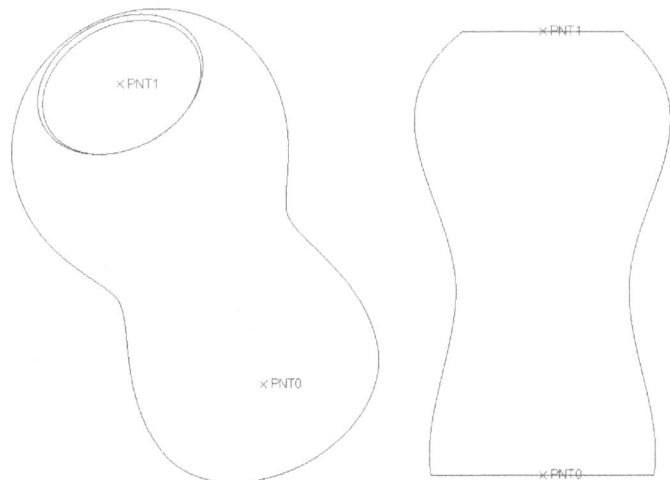

Figure 2–38

2. In the ribbon, select the *Analysis* tab.

3. In the Measure group, expand ⬛ (Measure) and select ⬛ (Distance).

4. The Measure dialog displays as shown in Figure 2–39.

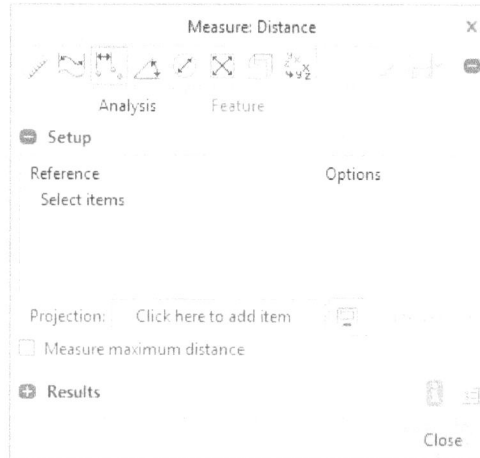

Figure 2–39

5. Select **PNT0**.

6. Press and hold <Ctrl> and select **PNT1**. Note that the vase part height is 270mm, as shown in Figure 2–40.

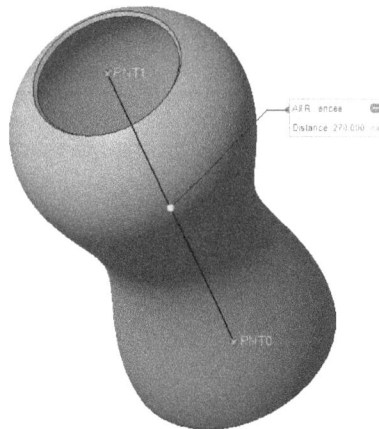

Figure 2–40

7. In the Measure: Distance dialog box, select the *Feature* tab.

8. Ensure that the **DISTANCE** parameter is selected.

9. Click ▭▾ (Save).

10. Ensure that **Make Feature** is selected, set the name to **HEIGHT**, and press <Enter>.

11. Click **Close** in the Measure: Volume dialog box.

Task 3 - Show feature parameters in the Model Tree.

1. In the Model Tree, click 🛠 ▾ (Settings)>**Tree Columns** from the drop-down list.

2. Select **Feat Params** from the Type drop-down list.

3. Set the parameter name to **DISTANCE** and select ≫ (Add Column).

4. Click **OK**.

5. The Model Tree shows the new parameter, as shown in Figure 2–41.

▸ 🔷 Surface id 39
　　▢ Protrusion id 78
　　🔩 Round id 155
　　ˣˣ Datum Point id 190
　　ˣ⁄ HEIGHT　　　　　　　　　　　　270.000000

Figure 2–41

**Task 4 - Create an Analysis feature that measures the
surface area that is required to be painted.**

1. In the Measure group in the ribbon, expand 📏 (Measure) and select ✕ (Area).

2. Select one of the outside surfaces of the part. Note that the area is 119001mm2.

3. In the Measure: Distance dialog box, select the *Feature* tab.

   • Note that the **AREA** parameter will be created.

4. Click 💾▾ (Save).

5. Ensure that **Make Feature** is selected, set the name to **PAINT_AREA**, and press <Enter>.

6. Click **Close** in the Measure: Volume dialog box. The feature is added to the Model Tree.

7. Show the **AREA** parameter in the Model Tree.

Task 5 - Create an Analysis feature that uses the Model Analysis to find the center of mass for the model.

1. Click **File>Prepare>Model Properties**.

2. In the Model Properties dialog box, click **Change** in the Mass Properties line.

3. In the Define Properties by field select Geometry and Parameters from the dropdown. Ensure that the value for the density is **1.00 e-9** and click **OK**, as shown in Figure 2–42.

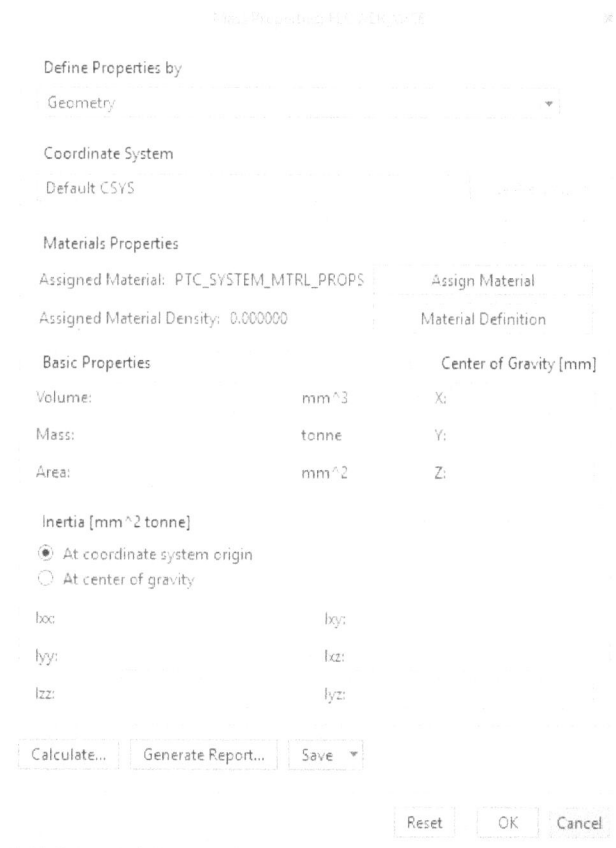

Define Properties by

Geometry

Coordinate System

Default CSYS

Materials Properties

| Assigned Material: PTC_SYSTEM_MTRL_PROPS | Assign Material |
| Assigned Material Density: 0.000000 | Material Definition |

Basic Properties   Center of Gravity [mm]

Volume: mm^3   X:

Mass: tonne   Y:

Area: mm^2   Z:

Inertia [mm^2 tonne]

◉ At coordinate system origin
○ At center of gravity

Ixx: Ixy:

Iyy: Ixz:

Izz: Iyz:

Calculate...   Generate Report...   Save ▾

Reset   OK   Cancel

Figure 2–42

4. Close the Mass Properties dialog box.

5. In the ribbon, in the Model Report group, click ⬚ (Mass Properties).

6. In the Mass Properties dialog box, click **Preview**.

7. The model mass properties display in the Results window, as shown in Figure 2–43.

Figure 2–43

Note that the mass of the part is 0.5Kg and that its center of mass is located approximately 12 mm from default coordinate system in the Y-direction, as shown in Figure 2–44.

Shading turned off for clarity.

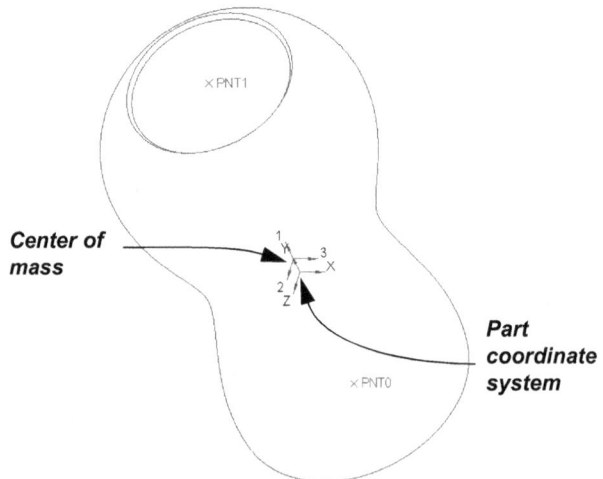

Figure 2–44

8. In the Quick drop-down list, select **Feature** and edit the name to **CENTER_MASS** and press <Enter>.

9. Select the *Feature* tab.

10. Remove the checkmark in the *Create* column next to the **VOLUME** parameter, so it is not created.

11. Add a checkmark in the *Create* column next to the **PNT_COG** parameter, as shown in Figure 2–45, to create it.

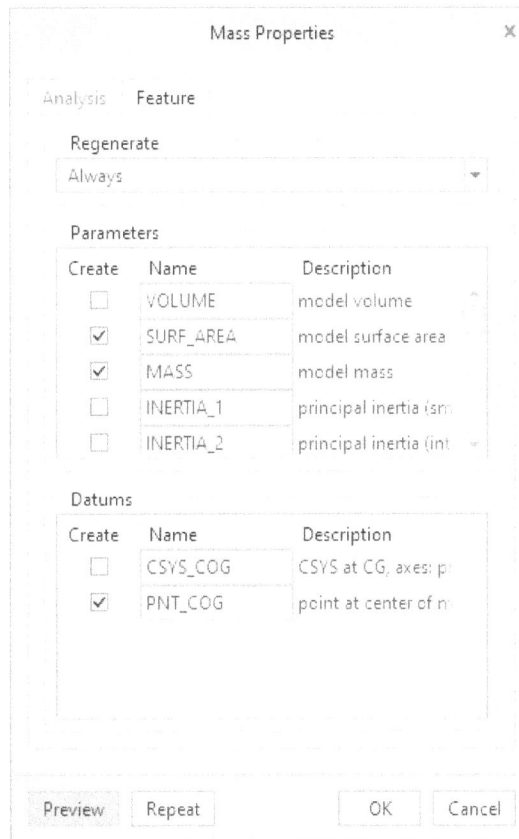

Figure 2–45

12. Select **OK** to complete the feature. The feature is added to the Model Tree and a point displays at the part's center of mass, as shown in Figure 2–46.

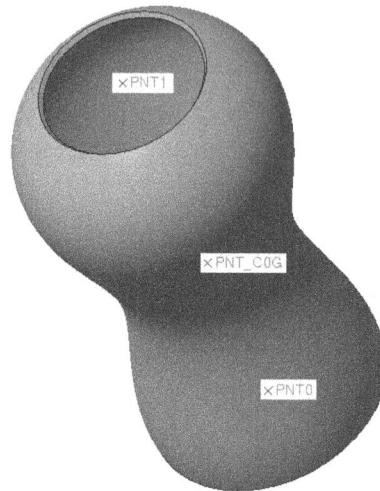

Figure 2–46

Task 6 - Create an Analysis feature that measures from the center of mass to the bottom of the flower_vase.

---

1. In the Measure group, expand ✎ (Measure) and select ⊓ (Distance).

2. Select the point at the bottom of the model, **PNT0**.

3. Press and hold <Ctrl> and select **PNT_COG**.

4. The distance from the bottom to **PNT_COG** is 112.153mm.

5. In the Measure: Distance dialog box, click 🖫 (Save).

6. Ensure that **Make Feature** is selected, set the name to **CENTER_TO_BOTTOM**, and press <Enter>.

7. Select the *Feature* tab.

8. Select the **DISTANCE** parameter, edit the name to **C_OF_G**, and press <Enter>.

9. Click **Close** in the Measure: Distance dialog box.

10. Show the **C_OF_G** feature parameters in the Model Tree.

Task 7 - Modify the part to ensure that the Analysis feature updates accordingly.

1. Increase the radius of the round (**feature id 155**) shown in Figure 2–47 to **45**. Note how the center of gravity changes. Reducing the center of mass below 1/3 of the overall height should ensure that the model remains stable when it is used.

A round size larger than 57 will cause the model to fail.

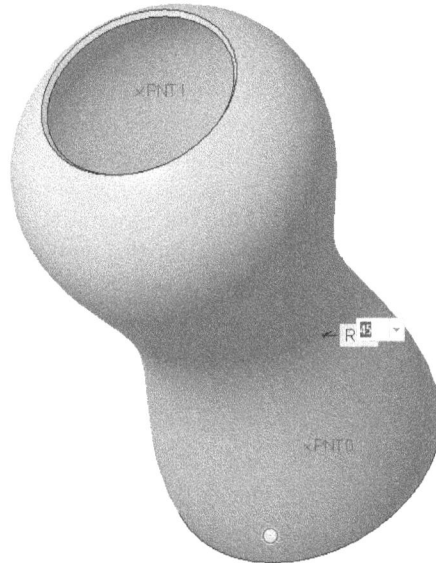

Figure 2–47

2. In the Model Tree, click ⊤ ˅ (Settings)>**Reset Tree Settings**>**Reset Tree Settings**.

3. Close the model and erase it from memory.

Practice 2c

User-Defined Analysis I

Practice Objectives

- Create a Field Point.
- Create a User-Defined Analysis.

In this practice, you will use a User-Defined Analysis (UDA) to determine the clearance between a model and its surrounding assembly components. The model analyzed is shown in Figure 2–48. The pipe connects two cold fluid containers in a top-level assembly. The underside of the pipe is surrounded by mechanical components, which produce a large amount of heat. These components are represented by the surface. The fluid must remain cool while traveling through the pipe and the heat from the other assembly components must dissipate. To achieve this goal, the pipe and components should always be separated by a minimum distance of 20 mm.

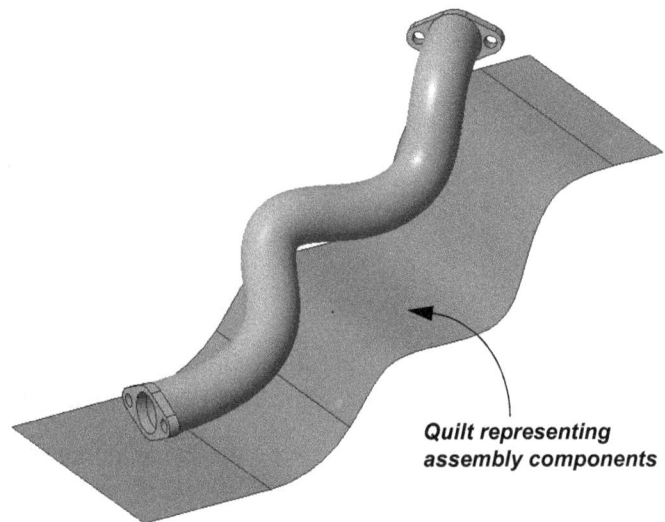

*Quilt representing
assembly components*

Figure 2–48

Task 1 - Open the pipe.prt model.

1. Set the working directory to *User-Defined_Analysis_I*.

2. Open **pipe.prt**.

3. Set the model display as follows:

- ⚡ *(Datum Display Filters)*: Only ⚡ (Point Display)
- *View* tab: ⚡ (Point Tag Display)
- ⚡ *(Spin Center)*: Off
- ⚡ *(Display Style)*: ⚡ (Shading With Edges)

Task 2 - Create a field point to measure from.

1. In the *Model* tab, expand ⚡ (Point) and select ⚡ (Field).

2. In the Selection Filter, select **Quilt**.

3. Select anywhere on the quilt (not a surface), as shown in Figure 2–49. The location does not matter because when it is used in the Analysis feature, it is permitted to move over the entire surface.

A field point is a special datum point feature that can be easily moved on the geometry on which it is placed. In this practice, the field point is constrained to the surface; however, no dimensions are rigidly constraining it to one location on the surface.

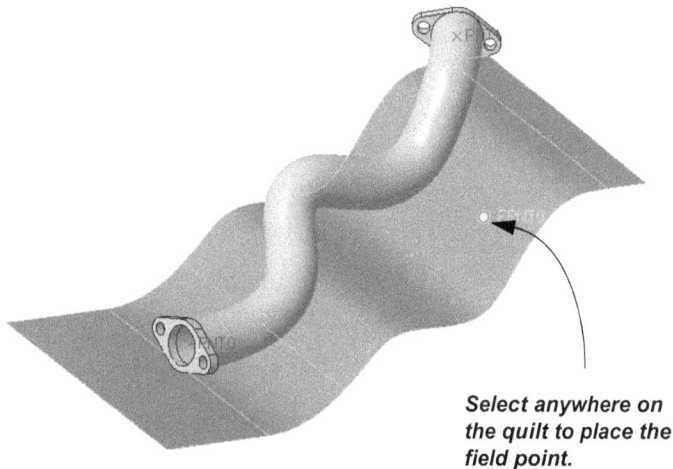

Select anywhere on the quilt to place the field point.

Figure 2–49

4. Click **OK** to complete the Field Datum Point.

Task 3 - Create a Measure Analysis feature.

1. Select the *Analysis* tab.

2. In the *Measure* group, expand ⚡ (Measure) and select ⚡ (Distance).

3. Select the field point **FPNT0**.

4. Press <Ctrl> and select the surface of the pipe.

5. The outer surface of the pipe is highlighted as shown in Figure 2–50. The resulting distance could be different than that shown, due to the placement of your field point.

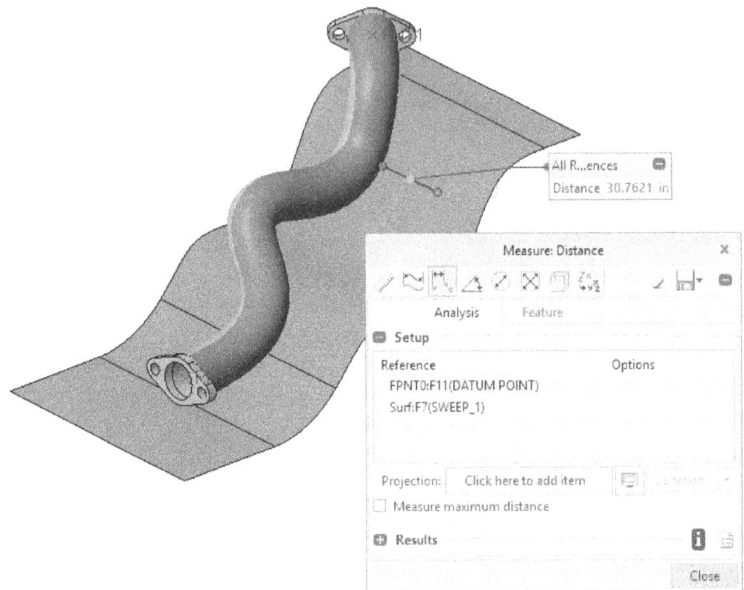

Figure 2–50

6. In the Measure: Distance dialog box, select the *Feature* tab.

7. Ensure that the **DISTANCE** parameter is selected for creation.

8. Click ⊟ (Save).

9. Ensure that **Make Feature** is selected, set the name to **DISTANCE**, and press <Enter>.

10. Click **Close** in the Measure: Distance dialog box.

Task 4 - Create a local group.

1. In the Model Tree, select **FPNT0**, press <Ctrl>, and select **DISTANCE**.

2. Select (Group) in the mini toolbar.

3. Right-click on the resulting Local group and select **Rename**.

4. Edit the name to **UDA** (after pressing <Enter> the name will read Group UDA).

Task 5 - Create a user-defined analysis.

1. In the *Custom* group in the ribbon, click ⚲ (User-Defined Analysis).

2. Note that **UDA** is selected in the Type drop-down list.

3. Accept all defaults in the *References* and *Calculation Settings* areas. The References default to those included in the UDA local group. The UDA calculates the values of the **DISTANCE** parameter. Since a field point was included in the group, this parameter is calculated for the entire field (or across the entire surface).

4. Click **Compute**. Once the analysis has completed, a fringe plot displays with a legend in the top left-hand corner of the screen. The *Results* area in the User Defined Analysis dialog box shows a minimum distance of approximately 10.38mm between the pipe and the surrounding assembly components. The fringe plot shown in Figure 2–51 indicates where this minimum occurs. This distance is lower than the 20 mm set by our design constraints; therefore, changes must be made to the design of the pipe.

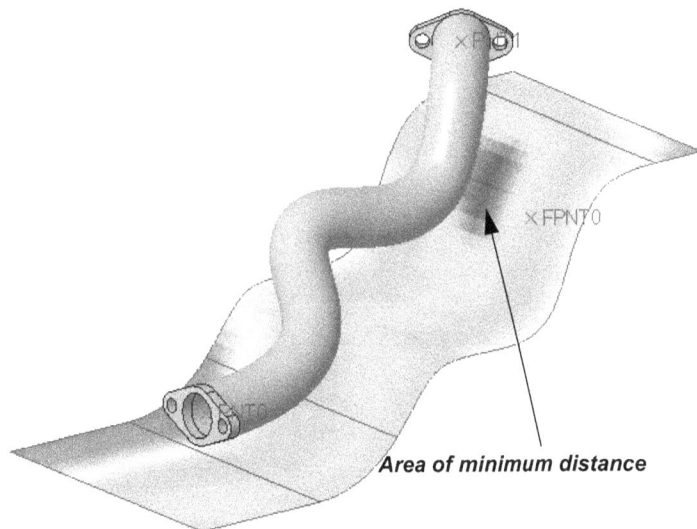

Area of minimum distance

Figure 2–51

5. Expand the *Saved Analyses* area. Set the name to
   FIELD_DIST and click ⌷ (Save) to save the analysis. By
   saving the analysis, this fringe plot can be shown on the
   model at any time without having to run the UDA again. By
   default, the fringe plot remains displayed. The display of the
   fringe can be controlled using the ⊙ ⊘ icon.

   - Leave the results displayed for the remainder of the
     practice.

6. Close the User-Defined Analysis dialog box.

Task 6 - Modify the pipe feature.

---

1. Select the **Curve id79** feature from the Model Tree and
   select ⊢d1⊣ (Edit Dimensions) in the mini toolbar. The
   dimensions display as shown in Figure 2–52.

   - If the dimensions do not display, right-click **Curve id79** in
     the Model Tree and select |↔| (Show/Hide Sketch
     Dimensions). The datum curve is used as the trajectory
     for the swept pipe.

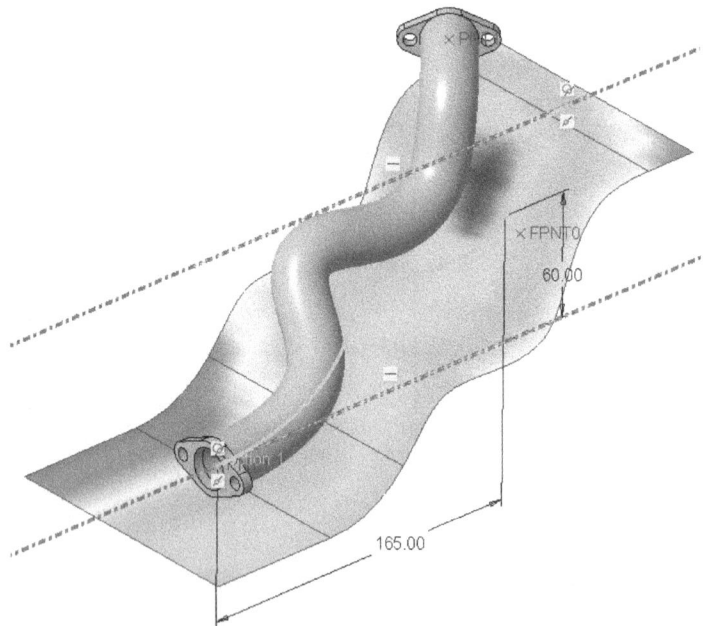

Figure 2–52

2. Change the 60 mm vertical dimension to **70** and the 165 mm
   horizontal dimension to **155**.

3. Regenerate the model. The pipe feature updates to its new location and the UDA is recalculated, as shown in Figure 2–53.

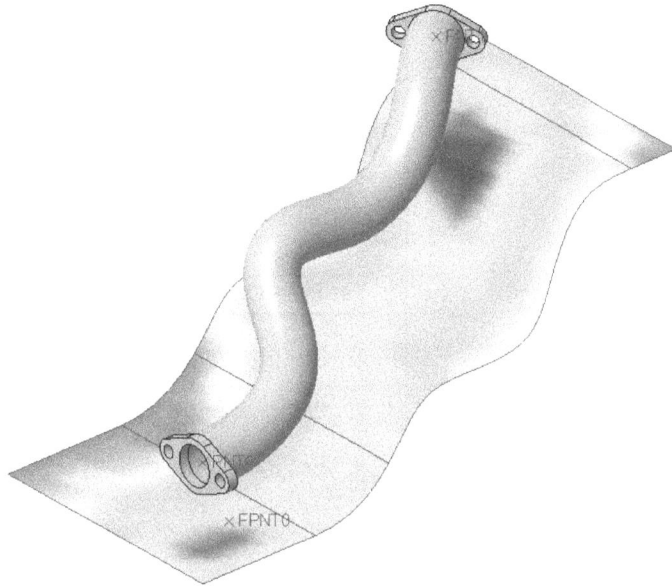

Figure 2–53

4. In the ribbon, select the *Analysis* tab.

5. Click ⌀ (User-Defined Analysis).

6. Expand the Saved Analysis area, select **FIELD_DIST** and click **Retrieve**.

7. Look at the Color Range window. The minimum value has changed to 23.3 mm. The design now meets the minimum distance constraint.

8. The exact minimum distance value can be obtained by opening the saved **FIELD_DIST** results. In the Custom group in the ribbon, click ⌀ (User-Defined Analysis) and expand the *Saved Analyses* area. Highlight the **FIELD_DIST** analysis and click **Retrieve**. The exact minimum distance is 23.314319 mm.

9. Save the model and erase it from memory.

Practice 2d | User-Defined Analysis II

Practice Objectives

- Create a Field Point.
- Create a User-Defined Analysis.

In this practice, you will use a User-Defined Analysis (UDA) to examine the cross-sectional area of internal surfaces of a model. The internal profile of the duct should vary evenly to deter turbulent flow.

Task 1 - Open the section_area model.

1. Set the working directory to *User-Defined_Analysis_II*.

2. Open **section_area.prt**.

3. Set the model display as follows:

    - *(Datum Display Filters)*: (Point Display), (Plane Display)

    - *View* tab: (Point Tag Display)

    - *(Spin Center)*: Off

    - *(Display Style)*: (Shading With Edges)

Task 2 - Create a field point to measure from.

1. In the *Model* tab, expand (Point) and select (Field).

2. Select anywhere on the curve, as shown in Figure 2–54. The **FPNT0** point displays on the curve at the location where you have made the selection.

    Note that the location does not matter because when it is used in the Analysis feature, it is permitted to move over the entire length of the curve.

A field point is a special datum point feature that can be easily moved on the geometry on which it is placed. In this practice, the field point is constrained to the curve; however, no dimensions are rigidly constraining it to one location on the curve.

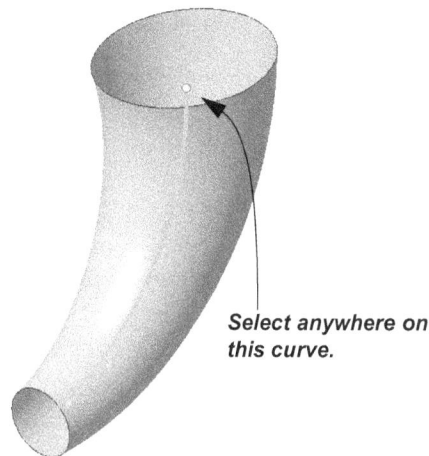

Select anywhere on this curve.

Figure 2–54

3. Click **OK** to complete the Field Datum Point.

Task 3 - Create a datum plane to be used to create a datum curve.

---

1. In the *Model* tab, click ▱ (Plane) to create a new datum plane.

2. Create the datum plane through **FPNT0** and normal to the curve on which **FPNT0** is located. The model displays as shown in Figure 2–55. If the Field Datum Point is still selected when you begin the creation of the datum plane, it is automatically selected for you. Press and hold <Ctrl> to select the datum curve to define the normal reference.

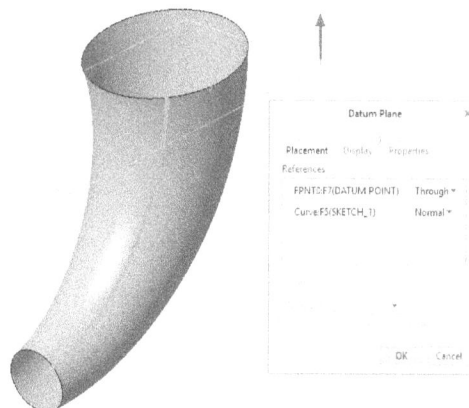

Figure 2–55

3. Click **OK** to complete the plane.

Task 4 - Create a datum curve at the intersection of the surface feature and DTM1.

1. Press and hold <Ctrl> and select **DTM1** and **Swept Blend 1** from the Model Tree.

2. In the Editing group, click ⟳ (Intersect) to create a datum curve at the intersection of these two references, as shown in Figure 2–56.

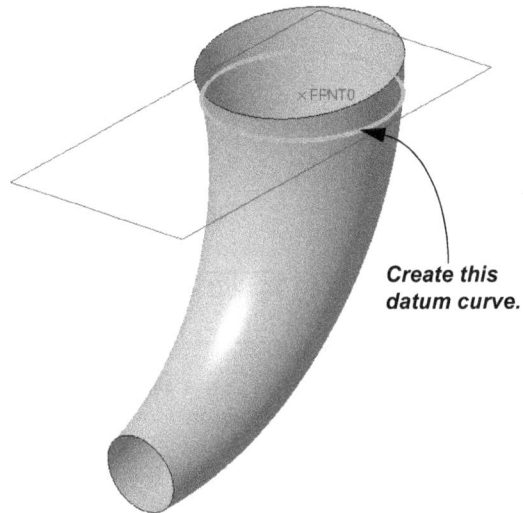

Create this datum curve.

Figure 2–56

Task 5 - Create a flat surface to represent the cross-sectional area of the model at the field point.

1. In the Surfaces group, click ☐ (Fill) to create a flat surface that references the datum curve that was just created.

2. Right-click in the graphics window and select **Define Internal Sketch**.

3. In the Sketch dialog box, select **DTM1** as Sketch Plane and **FRONT** as the Top reference plane.

4. Click **Sketch**.

5. Right-click in the graphics window and select References.

6. Select **FPNT0** as a reference for the section.

7. Click **Close** in the References dialog box.

8. Click ⌐ (Project) and select the curves created in Task 4 to define the section. The surface displays as shown in Figure 2–57.

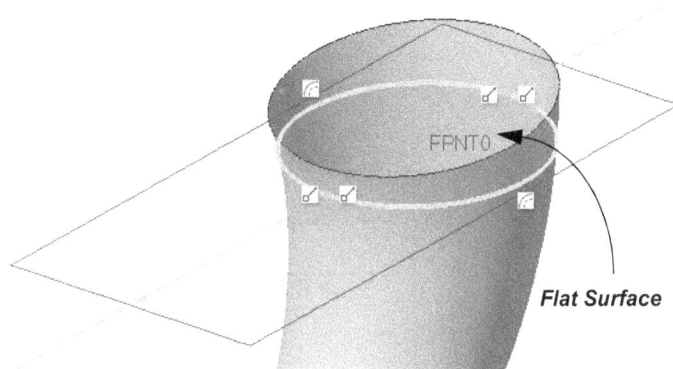

Figure 2–57

9. Click ✓ (OK)

10. Click ✓ (OK).

11. Toggle off the display of datum planes.

Task 6 - Create an Analysis feature to measure the area of the flat surface.

---

1. Select the *Analysis* tab.

2. In the Measure group, expand ⟋ (Measure) and select ⋈ (Area).

3. Select the Fill surface that you just created.

4. Click ⊟▾ (Save).

5. Ensure that **Make Feature** is selected, set the name to **FLAT_AREA**, and press <Enter>.

6. Click **Close** in the Measure: Area dialog box. The feature is added to the Model Tree.

7. Show the **AREA** parameter in the Model Tree.

Task 7 - Create a local group.

Press and hold <Shift> to select all features between the field point and the analysis feature.

1. Using the Model Tree, select all of the features between and including the field point, **FPNT0**, and the **FLAT_AREA** Analysis feature.

2. Click 🔲 (Group) in the mini toolbar.

3. Right-click on the Local group in the Model Tree and select **Rename**.

4. Edit the name to **section_area**.

Task 8 - Create a User-Defined Analysis feature to study the area at all points along the datum trajectory of the model geometry.

1. In the Custom group in the ribbon, click 🔲 (User-Defined Analysis).

   The User Defined Analysis dialog box displays as shown in Figure 2–58.

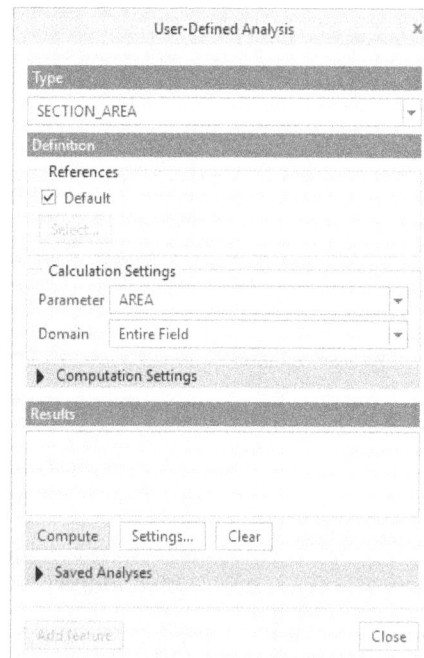

Figure 2–58

The Type drop-down list lists all UDA local groups in the model.

2. Ensure that **SECTION_AREA** is selected in the Type drop-down list.

3. Accept all defaults in the *References* area. The References options default to those included in the SECTION_AREA group. The SECTION_AREA group calculates values for the **AREA** parameter. Since a field point was included in the group, this parameter is calculated for the entire field.

4. Expand the *Computation Settings* area, as shown in Figure 2–59.

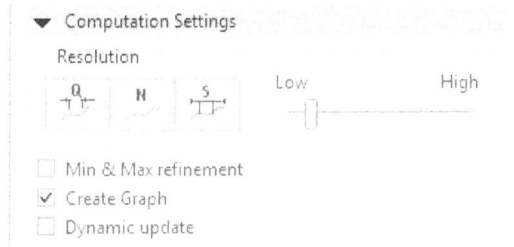

Figure 2–59

5. Drag the resolution quality slider to **High**.

6. Enable the **Min & Max refinement** option.

7. Clear the **Create Graph** option.

8. Select **Compute**. Once the analysis has been completed, it produces a porcupine plot of the surface area at each point along the model's trajectory, as shown in Figure 2–60. The porcupine plot displays the curvature progression along the trajectory. This shows that the flow in the duct is constant.

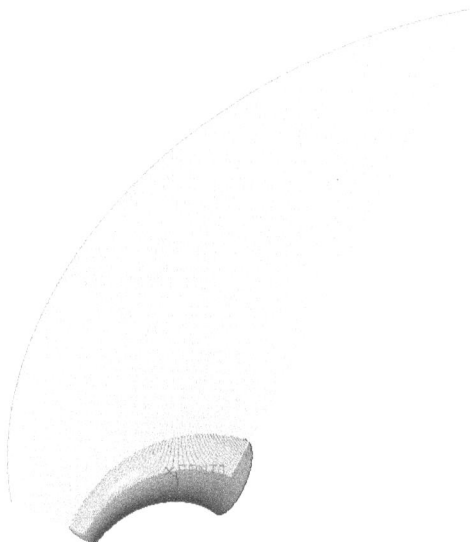

Figure 2–60

9. Clear the **Min & Max refinement** option.

10. Enable the **Create Graph** option.

11. Select **Compute**. Once the analysis has completed, a graph of the trajectory length against the sectional surface area is plotted, as shown in Figure 2–61.

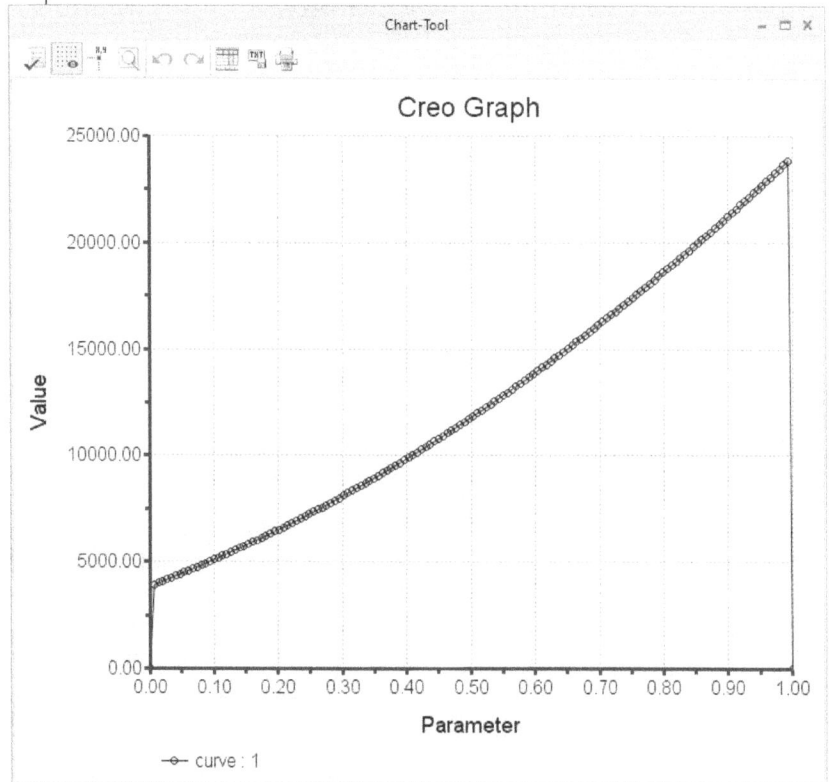

Figure 2–61

Task 9 - Customize the Chart.

1. In the Chart-Tool, click ✓ (Customize Graph). The Chart-Tool expands as shown in Figure 2–62.

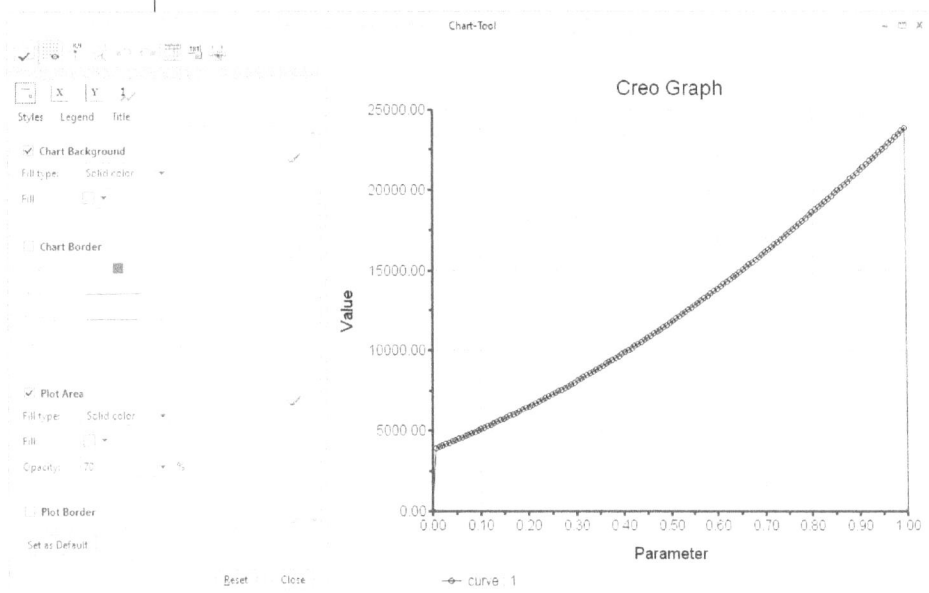

Figure 2–62

2. In the *Styles* tab, change the Fill type to **Gradient**.

3. Leave the first color swatch as white, then in the second swatch select the color **R: 28, G: 69, B: 135** as shown in Figure 2–63.

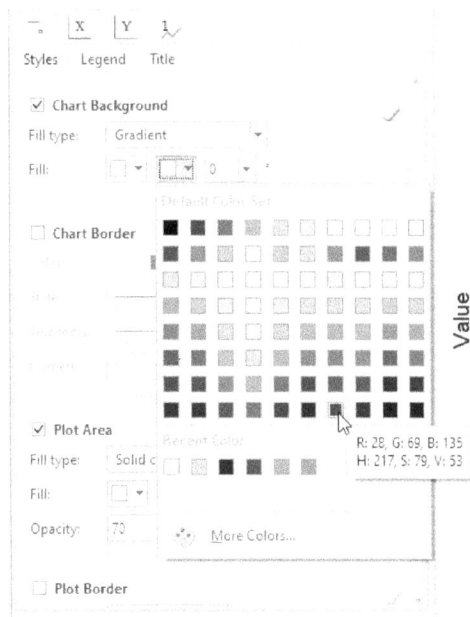

Figure 2–63

4. Edit the Fill angle to **-130**, and the chart updates as shown in Figure 2–64.

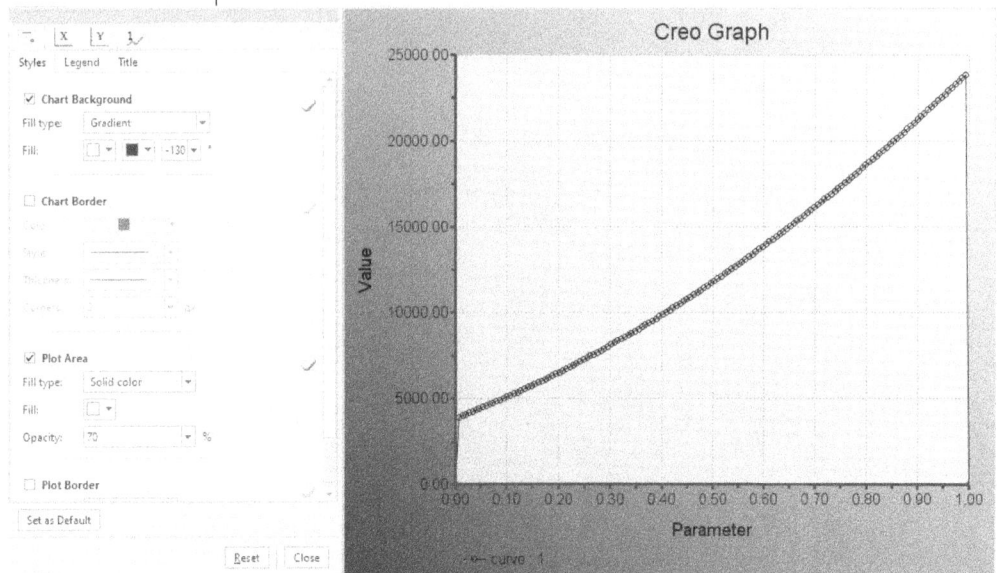

Figure 2–64

5. Select the *Legend* tab.

6. Remove the check mark next to Legend so the legend no longer displays on the chart.

7. Select the *Title* tab.

8. Click to remove the check next to Chart Title, then click to add it again.

9. The Text field activates. Change the title in the Text field to **Area vs Distance**.

10. Click the ⌐X (Format X-Axis) option.

11. Select the *Title* tab.

12. Click to remove the check next to X-axis Title, then click to add it again.

13. Change the Text field to **Distance**.

14. Change the Color to white.

15. Click the ⌐Y (Format Y-Axis) option.

16. Select the *Title* tab.

17. Click to remove the check next to Y-axis Title, then click to add it again.

18. Change the Text field to **Area**.

19. Change the Color to white.

To make this the default chart appearance, in the customization panel of the Chart-Tool, click **Save as Default**. *Note that if your changes are not saved as the default appearance, when a chart is closed and then displayed again, customizations will be reset to the standard defaults.*

20. Click **Close**. The charts updates as shown in Figure 2–65.

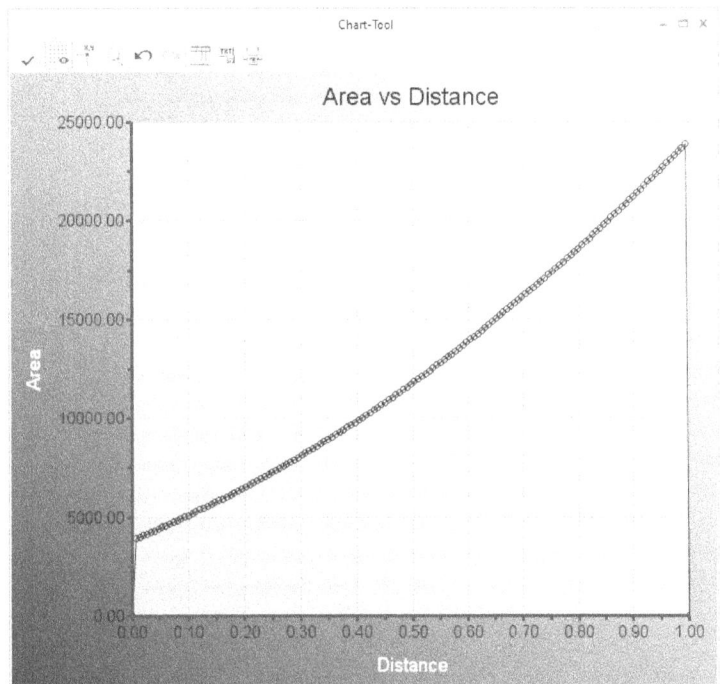

Figure 2–65

Task 10 - Save the analysis.

1. In the User-Defined Analysis dialog box, expand the *Saved Analyses* area. Set the name to **SECTION_AREA** and click

   ▣ (Save). By saving the analysis, this porcupine plot can be shown on the model at any time without having to run the UDA again. By default, the graph remains displayed. The

   display of the plot and graph can be controlled using 👁 👁.

2. Highlight the **SECTION_AREA** analysis and select 👁 👁 to toggle the results display off.

3. Click **Close** to close the dialog box.

Task 11 - Display the SECTION_AREA saved analysis.

1. In the Manage group in the ribbon, click ⊞ (Saved Analysis). The Analysis Display dialog box displays as shown in Figure 2–66.

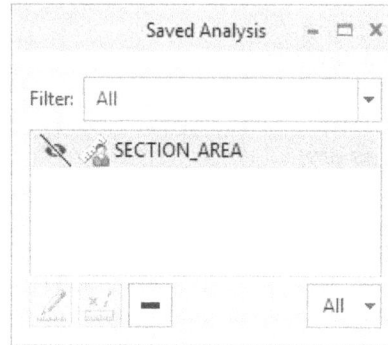

Figure 2–66

2. Highlight the **SECTION_AREA** analysis.

3. In the lower-right of the Saved Analysis dialog box, click **All>Unhide All** to display the graph and the porcupine plot.

4. Close the Analysis Display dialog box.

5. In the Model Tree, click ▌ ▾ (Settings)>**Reset Tree Settings>Reset Tree Settings**.

6. Save the model and erase it from memory.

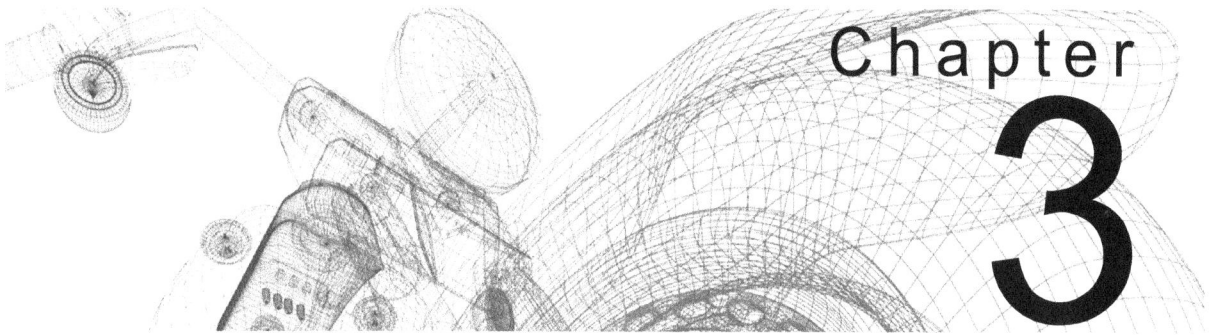

Behavioral Modeling Studies

Behavioral modeling studies enable you to test your design before manufacturing. You can assign various parameters and constraints that enable you to verify if your model reacts as intended. This chapter introduces sensitivity, feasibility, and optimization analyses.

Learning Objectives in This Chapter

- Understand how a Sensitivity Analysis shows the way in which a design parameter reacts when a design variable is changed over a specified range.
- Learn how to use a Feasibility analysis to adjust design variables to meet specific design constraints.
- Understand how to use an Optimization analysis to adjust the design variables to meet a specific goal.

3.1 Sensitivity Analysis

A Sensitivity Analysis shows how a design parameter reacts when a design variable is changed over a specified range. This analysis provides insight to an ideal start value for design variables when running a Feasibility or Optimization study. To run an analysis, in the *Analysis* tab, in the *Design Study* group, click ▣ (Sensitivity Analysis).

Example:

The design variable for the container shown in Figure 3–1 is the thickness of the shell feature.

Figure 3–1

The Sensitivity Analysis dialog box is shown in Figure 3–2.

Figure 3–2

The elements in a Sensitivity Analysis are described as follows:

Element	Description
Study Name	Enter the name of the sensitivity analysis.
Variable Selection	Define the dimension or model parameter to be analyzed. Only one variable can be changed per sensitivity analysis.
Variable Range	Specify the upper and lower range for the variable.
Parameters to Plot	Select the design parameters to plot against the design variable. More than one design parameter can be selected by pressing and holding <Shift> while selecting the parameters. Each parameter is shown on a separate plot.
Steps	Specify the number of steps for the analysis.

To generate the data, the system modifies the design variable in equal increments between the minimum and maximum value for the number of steps specified. At each modification, the model is regenerated and the value of the design parameter is stored and plotted.

The results of a Sensitivity analysis comparing the shell thickness to a design parameter for the model's solid volume are shown in Figure 3–3.

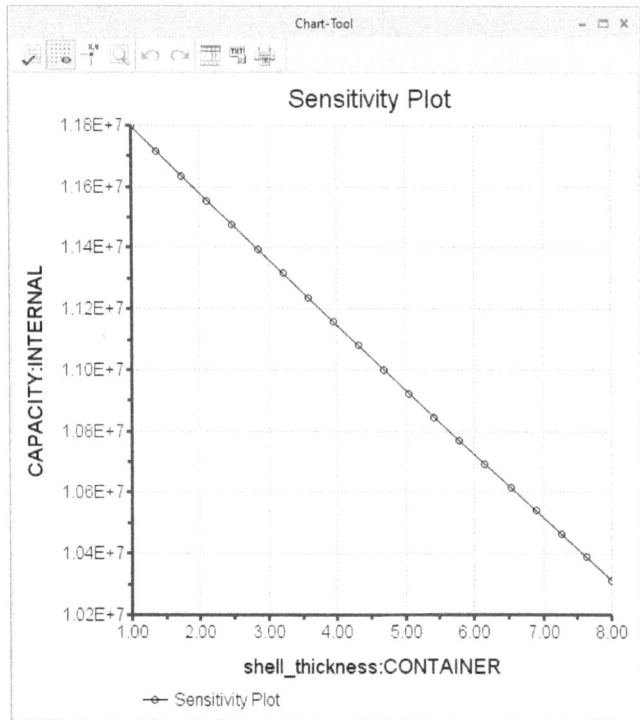

Figure 3–3

The graph begins at a wall thickness of 1.00 and makes 20 sensitivity passes to increase the thickness to 8.00. The graph shows, as expected, that an increase in shell thickness decreases the model's capacity. If the goal of your optimization is to minimize mass, an ideal start point for the shell thickness would be a low value.

3.2 Feasibility and Optimization Analyses

Feasibility

A Feasibility analysis adjusts design variables to meet specific design constraints. It tests if a feasible solution exists, given the range in which the system can adjust the design variables. If more than one parameter is varied, many solutions can exist. A Feasibility analysis stops after the first successful solution.

Design constraints have specific values. The constraint can be greater than or equal to (>=), or equal to (=) or less than (<) its current value or it can be a user-specified value.

Example:

The design constraint on the container shown in Figure 3–4 is that it must be able to hold exactly 10 L of water.

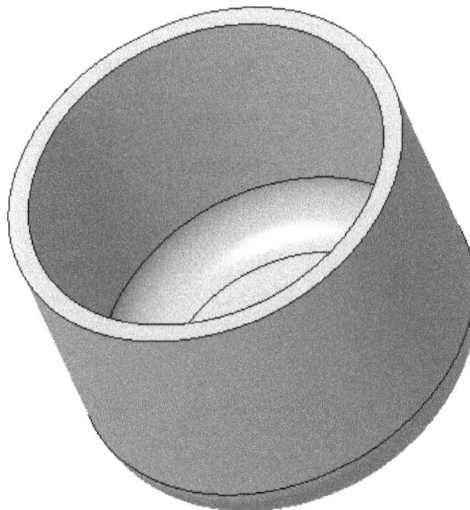

Figure 3–4

To achieve this, you can vary the design variables shown in Figure 3–5 using the minimum and maximum limits listed below.

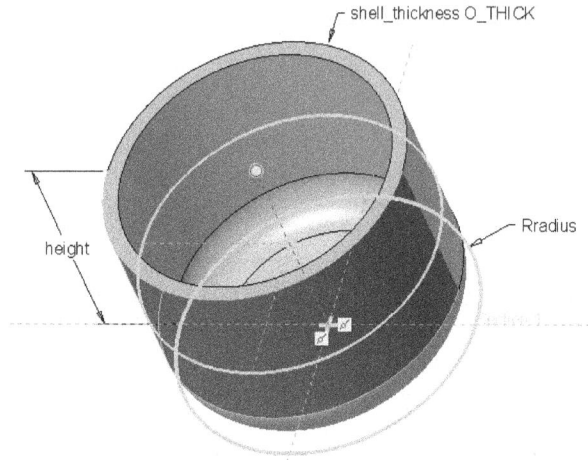

Figure 3–5

	Current Value	Minimum Value	Maximum Value
Shell_Thickness	10	2	20
Radius	100	50	300
Height	150	100	600

The Feasibility analysis determined that by modifying the dimensions to those shown in Figure 3–6, the capacity is exactly 10 L.

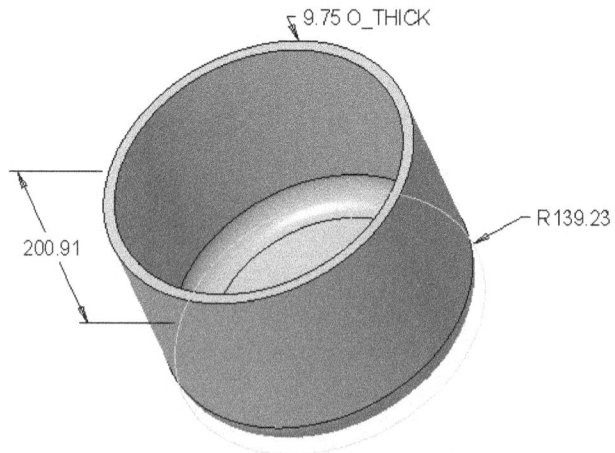

Figure 3–6

Optimization

An optimization analysis starts by adjusting the design variables to meet specific design constraints. It then makes successive passes and changes the design variables to meet a specific goal. It optimizes the model with respect to this goal while maintaining the design constraints.

A goal does not have a specific value. Goals either minimize or maximize a design parameter. It continues to improve the design until it converges on a user-specified percentage. For each pass taken, the system compares the current value of the goal to the value from the last pass. If the difference between the two values is within the convergence percentage, then the analysis is considered successful and stops. In the end, the part may not be truly optimized; the calculations stop once convergence is met, which can actually converge at a local minimum. The Multi-Objective Design Study finds the true minimum. (This topic is discussed in more detail in a later chapter.

Example:

A new design criteria has been set for the container used in the feasibility study. The container must hold exactly 10 L of water, but it must also be as light as possible. You can optimize the design to minimize mass while maintaining the original design constraint. Figure 3–7 shows the graph output of the optimization study.

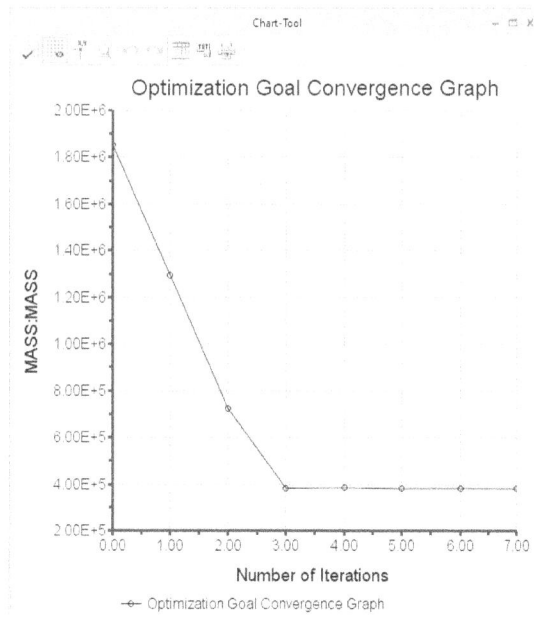

Figure 3–7

The optimization was able to reduce the weight of the container by more than 80% while still maintaining a capacity of 10 L.

Figure 3–8 shows the optimized model.

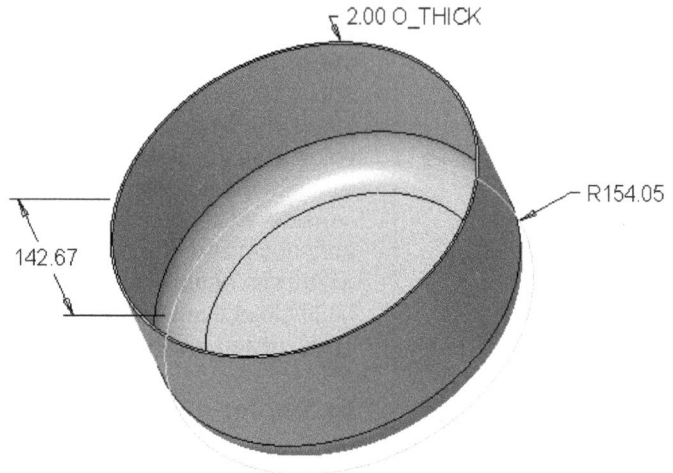

Figure 3–8

An optimization feature can be created once a study has been completed successfully. In doing so, you create a feature reflecting the settings for the optimization study. Each time the model is regenerated, the study is run and a newly optimized model is created. Once the study has completed, you can create the optimization feature by clicking ⊟ (Save Design Study) in the Optimization/Feasibility dialog box.

Both the Feasibility and Optimization studies are performed using the same dialog box. In the Design Study group, click ⬚ (Feasibility/Optimization) to open the Optimization/Feasibility dialog box shown in Figure 3–9.

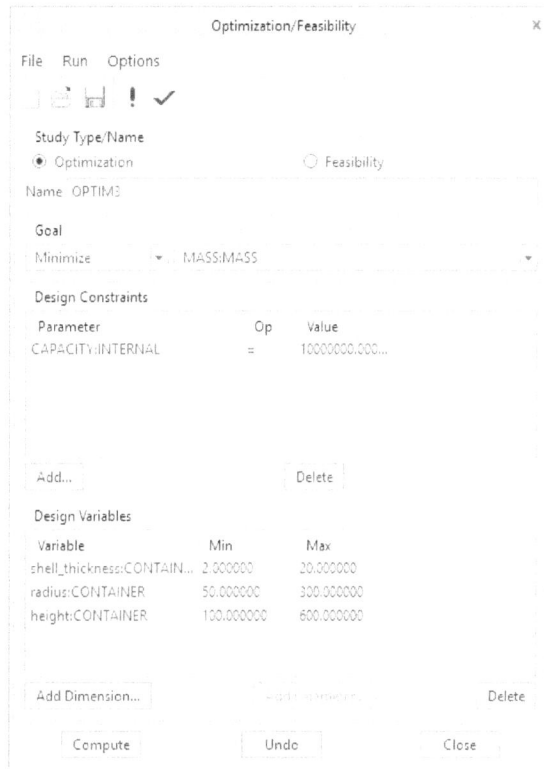

Figure 3–9

The elements required for the creation of a Feasibility or Optimization Study are described as follows:

Element	Description
Study Type/Name	Select the type of study to perform (Feasibility or Optimization) and enter a name for the study.
Goal (Optimization Studies only)	Select the optimization goal and the design parameter to optimize. The optimization criteria include: • Minimize • Maximize • Minimize Abs Val • Maximize Abs Val Only one design parameter can be selected per Optimization Study.

Design Constraints	Add one or more design parameters to optimize a specific value. The Design Constraint dialog box shown below enables you to select the parameter, its operator, and the design constraint value. 

Design Variables	Add dimensions or parameters that can be modified to achieve the design constraints and goal. Each variable requires a minimum and maximum value between which the design study can make modifications. Only include variables that have a significant effect on the design constraints or goal. Additional design variables increases the study run time. The use of the sensitivity study before hand helps determine which variables should be added.

A feasibility and optimization analysis can be customized by clicking an option in the **Options** menu in the Optimization/Feasibility dialog box. These options are described as follows:

Option	Description
Preferences	Enables you to customize the creation of graphs and how the study is run.
	The *Graphs* tab enables you to select which result graphs are created. Contains various options.
	The *Run* tab enables you to set convergence criteria and limit the number of iterations for the optimization analysis. By selecting **Animate model**, the model regenerates at each iteration.

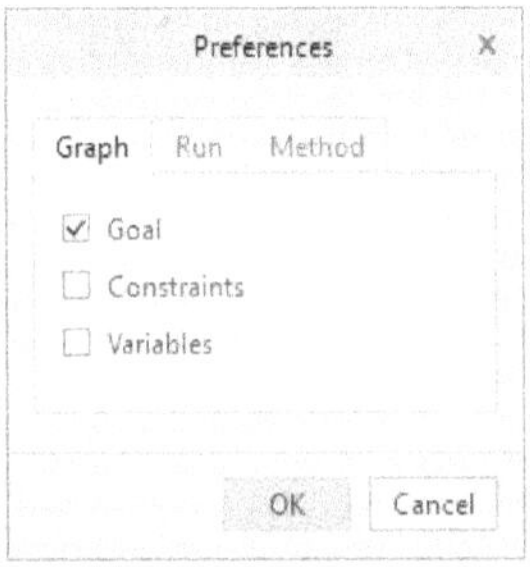

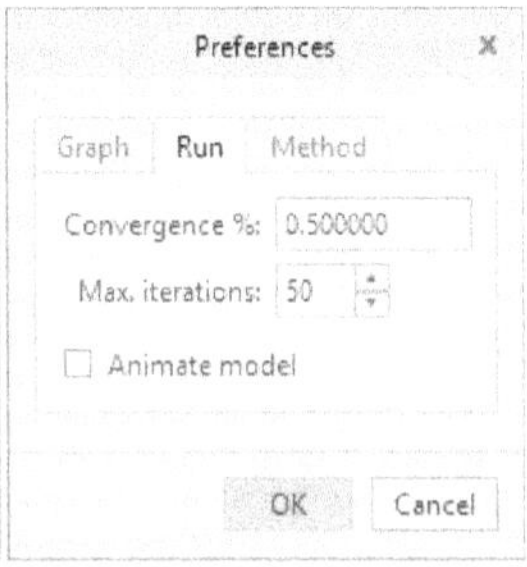

The *Method* tab enables you to select the optimization method.

- **GDP** - Use the standard algorithm (gradient-based) to optimize the model using the current model conditions as the starting point.

- **MDS** - Use the multi-objective design studies algorithm to determine the optimum starting point for the optimization. You can specify the number of starting points to compute in the *Max. Iterations* field. After the number of experiments has been filled, Behavioral Modeling uses a Paretto capability to identify the best candidates of the populated space. The best candidates are the starting points of the gradient-based optimization. This method has a higher chance of finding the overall optimum design within the design parameters and dimensions.

| **Default Range** | Enables you to control the default minimum and maximum values assigned to the design variables. |

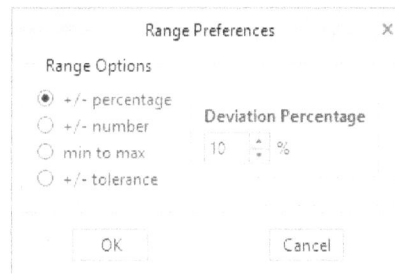

Practice 3a

Sensitivity Analysis

Practice Objective

- Set up and run a sensitivity analysis.

In this practice, you will work on a simple layout of an engine's power take-off belt system. You will create a sensitivity analysis to graph how the length of the belt and contact angle are affected by moving the location of a pulley.

Task 1 - Open the drive_train part.

1. Set the working directory to *Sensitivity_Analysis*.

2. Open **drive_train.prt**.

3. Set the model display as follows:

4. Set the model display as follows:

   - ⁺⁄₊ *(Datum Display Filters)*: All Off

   - ⋟ *(Spin Center)*: Off

   - ◻ *(Display Style)*: ◻ (Shading With Edges)

   The model displays as shown in Figure 3–10.

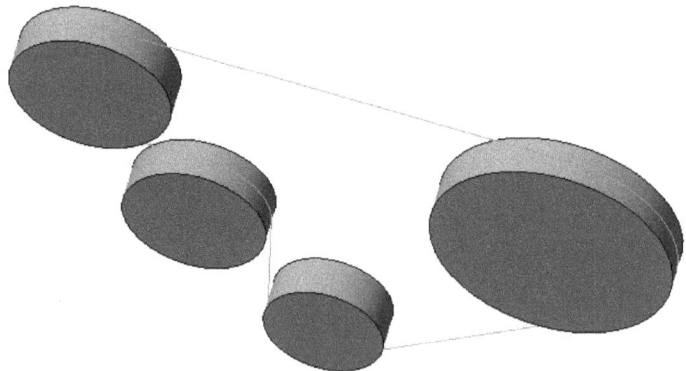

Figure 3–10

5. Investigate the model. The model is a simple layout of an engine belt system. The protrusions representing the drive, air conditioning (**AC**), power steering (**power_steer**), and the idler pulleys have been renamed for easy identification in the Model Tree. A datum curve (**BELT**) has been included to represent the belt in the system.

6. In the In-graphics toolbar, expand (Saved Orientations) and select **FRONT**.

7. Double-click on the belt datum curve directly on the model. The dimension used to create the feature displays.

8. Select the *Tools* tab and in the Model Intent group, click (Switch Dimensions) to show the dimension as a symbolic value.

9. Select the Idler pulley in the Model Tree. The dimensions associated with this feature are shown.

Figure 3–11 displays the dimension symbols for both features. This functionality is not currently available in Creo Parametric. When a feature is edited, all other dimensions are cleared from the screen.

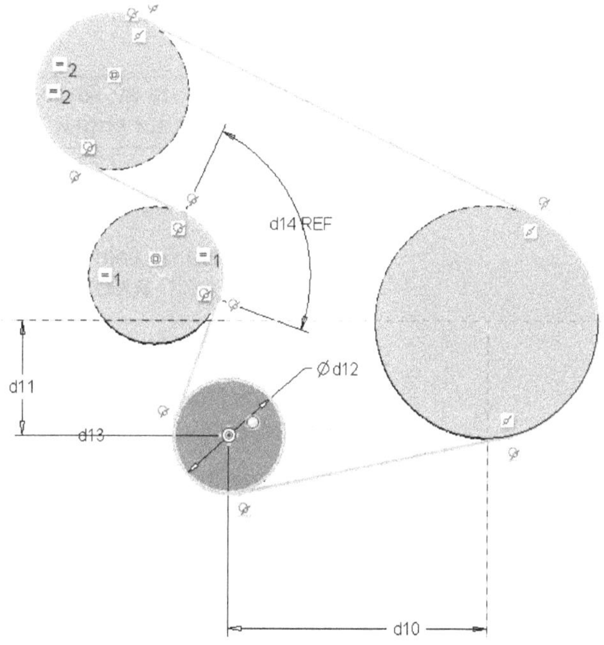

Figure 3–11

Note: For the rest of the tasks in this practice, sensitivity analysis has been used to review the results when modifying:

- The position of the idler pulley (dimension **d10**) on the overall belt length.
- The contact angle (dimension **d14**) with the power steering pulley. Note that the final design requires a contact angle of at least 120 degrees.

Task 2 - Create an Analysis feature to measure the length of the belt.

1. Select the *Analysis* tab.

2. In the Measure group, expand ✎ (Measure) and select ◪ (Length).

3. Right-click on the belt until the entire curve is highlights, then select it. The curve length should be 1135.97.

4. In the Measure: Length dialog box, select the *Feature* tab and note that the **LENGTH** parameter is selected for creation.

5. Click ▤▾ (Save), ensure that **Make Feature** is selected, and edit the name to **BELT_LENGTH** and press <Enter>.

6. Click **Close**.

Task 3 - Create an Analysis feature that calculates the contact angle.

1. In the Manage group in the ribbon, click ✕⁄ (Analysis).

2. In the Name field of the ANALYSIS dialog box, enter **CONTACT_ANGLE** and press <Enter>.

3. Select **Relation** as the analysis type.

4. Click **Next**. The Relations dialog box displays to enter the relation.

5. Enter the following relation:

   CONTACT = d14

6. Click ✓ (Verify) to verify the relation and click **OK**.

7. Click **OK** to close the Relations dialog box.

8. Click ✓ (OK) to complete the Analysis feature.

Task 4 - Run a model sensitivity analysis.

1. In the Design Study group, click ▢ (Sensitivity Analysis). The Sensitivity dialog box displays.

2. In the Sensitivity dialog box, leave the default name for the analysis.

3. Click **Dimension** and select dimension **d10** shown in Figure 3–12.

If the dimension no longer displays on the screen, double-click on the feature in the model or in the Model Tree.

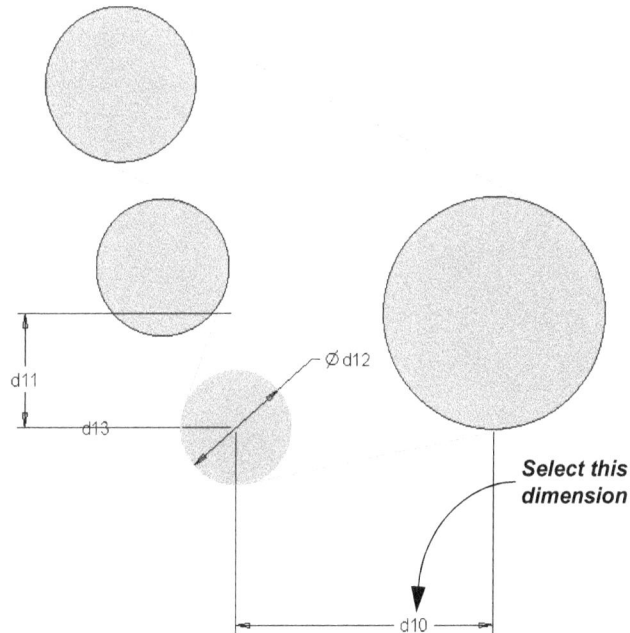

Figure 3–12

4. Enter **175** and **350** as the minimum and maximum *Variable Ranges*, respectively.

To select multiple parameters at one time, press and hold <Ctrl>.

5. In the *Parameters To Plot* area, click ⬉ (Select) and select both the **belt_length** and **contact_angle** parameters.

6. Click **OK**. The Sensitivity dialog box displays as shown in Figure 3–13.

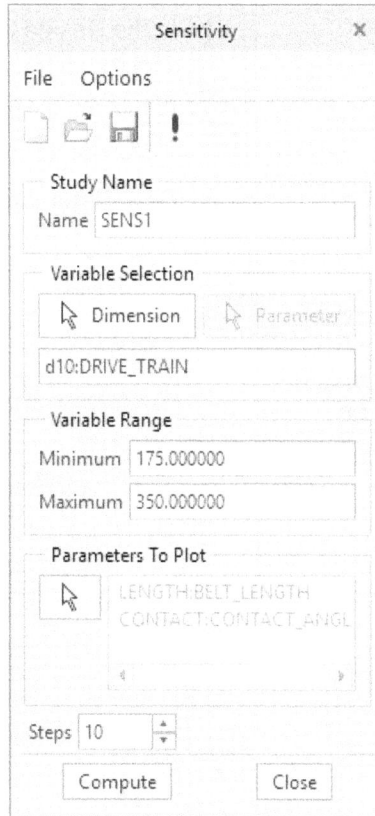

Figure 3–13

7. Click **Compute** to run the analysis. Two graphs display, showing how the belt length and contact angle change as dimension **d10** increases from *175* to **350**. These graphs are shown in Figure 3–14 and Figure 3–15.

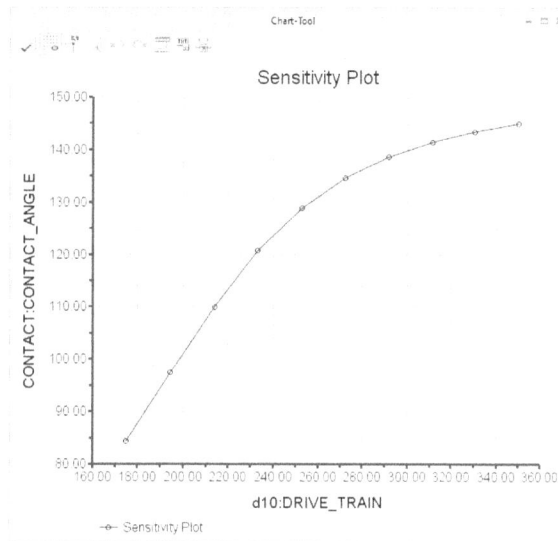

Figure 3–14

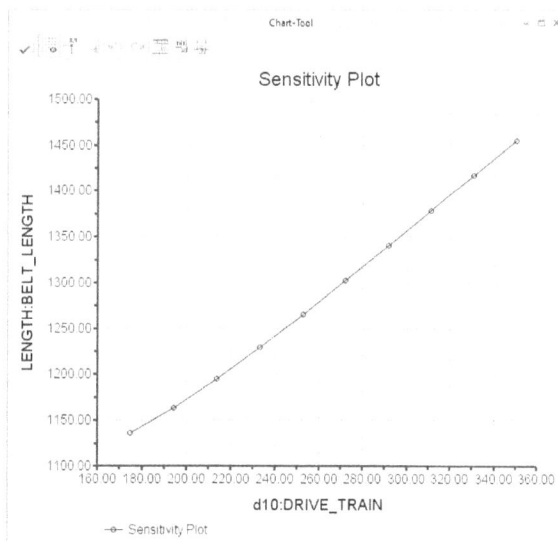

Figure 3–15

- What value must dimension **d10** be to achieve the design goal of having a minimum contact angle of 120 degrees? What should the belt length be?

By saving this design study, you can recall and rerun it without having to set it up again.

8. Save the design study.

9. Close the Sensitivity dialog box.

10. Close the model and erase it from memory.

Practice 3b

Optimization Analysis

Practice Objectives

- Create and run an optimization analysis.
- Update the model.

In this practice, you will continue to work with the canister model that you analyzed in the earlier practice. You will optimize the model with respect to the volume parameter to ensure that the fluid capacity of the canister is exactly 4L.

Task 1 - Open the canister.prt part model.

1. Set the working directory to *Optimization_Analysis*.

2. Open **canister_final1.prt**.

3. Set the model display as follows:

   - ⚹ *(Datum Display Filters)*: Only ⬜ (Plane Display)
   - *View* tab: ⬜ (Plane Tag Display)
   - ⟩ *(Spin Center)*: Off
   - ⬜ *(Display Style)*: ⬜ (Shading With Edges)

   There are three analysis features in this model:
   - **SOLID -** This model analysis feature calculates the **SOLID_VOL** parameter. This is the volume of the canister before the cut feature is added.
   - **CUT -** This model analysis feature calculates the **CUT_VOL** parameter. This is the volume of the canister after the cut feature is added.
   - **INTERNAL -** This relation analysis feature calculates the **CAPACITY** parameter. The relation subtracts **CUT_VOL** from **SOLID_VOL** to get the fluid capacity of the canister.

Task 2 - Review the values for the capacity and thickness parameters.

1. Determine the current capacity of the canister. In the Model Tree, right-click on the **INTERNAL** analysis feature and select **Information>Feature Information**. The Creo Parametric browser opens.

2. Scroll to the bottom of the browser. The **CAPACITY** parameter is listed with a current value of approximately 5.4 L.

3. Close the browser.

4. Display the **CAPACITY** parameter in the Model Tree.

   To change the capacity of the canister, you modify the overall height or wall thickness of the canister. The thickness is controlled by a model parameter called **THICKNESS**.

5. Double-click on the inside surface of the cannister. The wall thickness is approximately 4.27 mm.

6. Click anywhere on the screen.

Task 3 - Create an analysis feature for the model's mass.

1. Select the *Analysis* tab.

2. In the Model Report group, click ☐ (Mass Properties).

3. In the Quick drop-down list, select **Feature** and edit the name to **Mass**.

4. Click **Preview**. The system calculates the model mass properties based on a default density of 1.

5. Select the *Feature* tab.

6. In the *Parameters* area, remove the checkmark next to the **VOLUME** and **SURF_AREA** parameters so that they are not created.

7. Ensure that **MASS** is selected for creation.

8. Click **OK** to complete the feature.

9. Add the **MASS** parameter to the Model Tree display.

Task 4 - Optimize the model.

Design Consideration

A feasibility analysis tests the model to see if the design variables specified enable the study to meet the design constraints. For example, does changing the thickness of the canister wall between 3 mm and 6mm create a capacity of 4 L? If so, the model is regenerated to provide the first feasible solution found.

An optimization analysis runs a feasibility analysis as its first step. It then continues to change the design parameters to meet a specific goal. Minimizing the mass of the model is an example of a goal. The study continues to change the design variables over several optimization passes until it reaches an optimized value (determined by a convergence percentage), or until it runs out of passes.

In this example, the optimization analysis uses the values listed below:

	Parameter	Setting	
Goal	Mass	Minimize	
Design Constraints	Capacity	4 L	
Design Variables	Wall Thickness	2	10
	Height (d0)	300	600

1. In the Design Study group, click 🔍 (Feasibility/Optimization). The **Optimization** option is selected by default.

2. In the *Goal* area, select **Minimize** and **MASS:MASS** from the drop-down lists.

3. In the *Design Constraints* area, click **Add**. The Design Constraint dialog box displays.

4. Select the **CAPACITY:INTERNAL** parameter, as shown in Figure 3–16. The required capacity is 4,000,000 mm^3 or 4 L.

Figure 3–16

5. Click **OK**. The design constraint is added to the Optimization/Feasibility dialog box.

6. Click **Cancel** to close the Design Constraint dialog box.

7. In the *Design Variables* area, click **Add Dimension**. Select **Revolve 1** in the Model Tree and select the **400 mm** dimension, as shown in Figure 3–17.

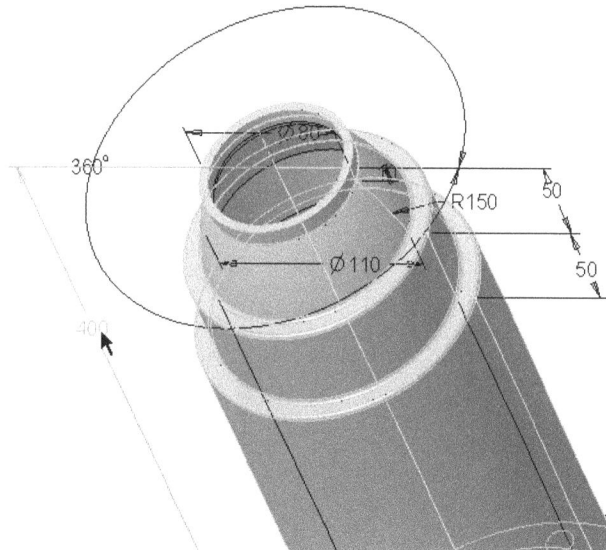

Figure 3–17

8. Click **Add Parameter**. The Select Parameter dialog box displays.

9. Select **THICKNESS:CANISTER_FINAL1** and click **OK**.

10. Click **Cancel** to close the Select Parameter dialog box.

11. Select each of the *Min* and *Max* cells for each parameter and set their values as shown in Figure 3–18.

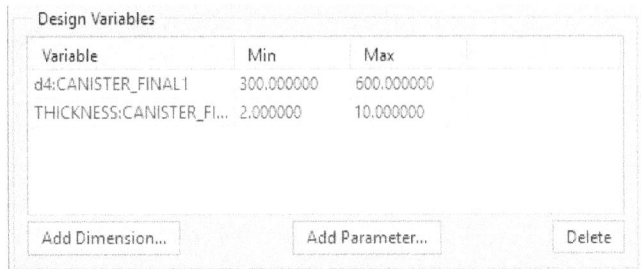

Design Variables

Variable	Min	Max
d4:CANISTER_FINAL1	300.000000	600.000000
THICKNESS:CANISTER_FI...	2.000000	10.000000

Add Dimension...   Add Parameter...   Delete

Figure 3–18

12. Click **Compute**. The optimization analysis begins and a graph displays, which updates the status of the optimization goal, **MASS**, with each pass of the study. Once complete, the phrase "The part was successfully optimized." displays in the message area. Figure 3–19 shows an optimized graph whose mass was reduced by over 40% using the optimization study.

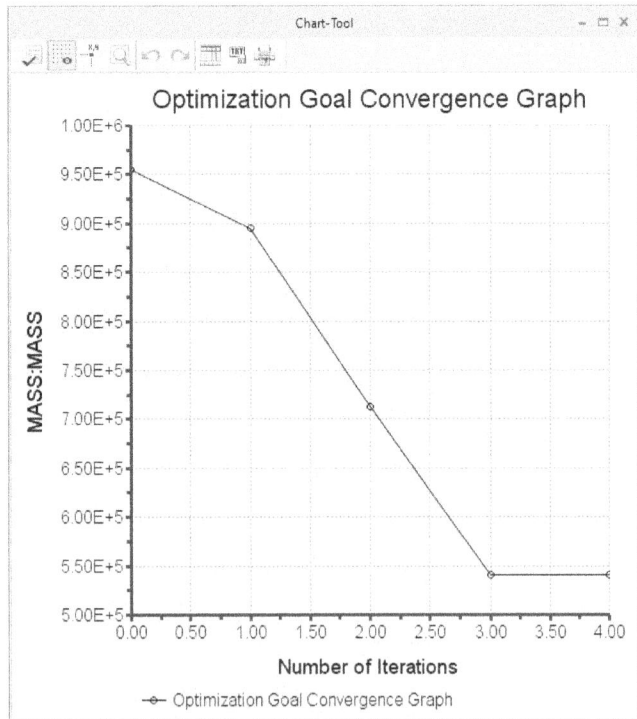

Figure 3–19

13. In the Optimization/Feasibility dialog box, select **Close** to keep the optimized values. The Confirm Model Change dialog box displays as shown in Figure 3–20.

Confirm Model Change   ✕

The model has changed as the result of Optimization.

❗ Click Reset to restore the original model.
Click Confirm to keep the changes.
Click Cancel to return to Design Study.

Reset   Confirm   Cancel

Figure 3–20

14. Select **Confirm** to keep the changes. The model displays as shown in Figure 3–21. The height of the model is 300mm and the thickness is 2.75mm.

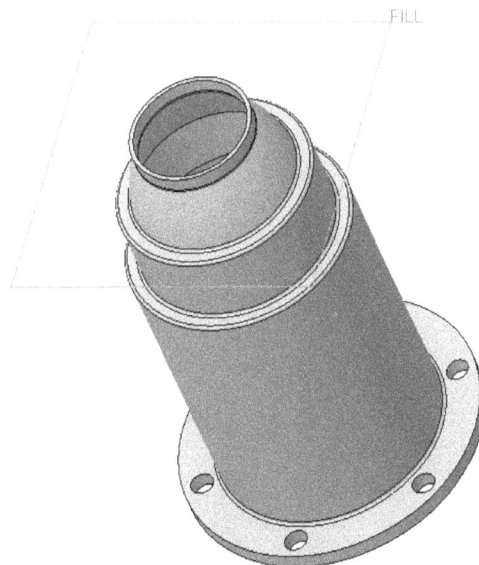

Figure 3–21

15. In the Model Tree, click 🛠 ˅ (Settings)>**Reset Tree Settings>Reset Tree Settings**.

16. Close the model and erase it from memory.

Practice 3c

Assembly Optimization

Practice Objectives

- Create assembly level analysis features.
- Create and run an optimization study.

In this practice, you will optimize a floor plan layout for a large room used as a storage area in a large airplane. The position of the center of gravity of the room is important to ensure that the airplane has good handling and is correctly balanced.

The center of gravity of the entire airplane lies at the intersection of the **CENTER_HORIZ** and **CENTER_VERT** datum planes. You will optimize the model to ensure that the center of gravity of the room also lies at the intersection of these two planes. You will then minimize the mass of the room to conserve fuel.

Task 1 - Open the floor_plan assembly model.

1. Set the working directory to *Assembly_Optimization*.

2. Open **floor_plan.asm**.

3. Set the model display as follows:

    - ⁺⁄⸲ *(Datum Display Filters)*: ˟˟ (Point Display), ↳ₐ (Csys Display)

    - ⸾ *(Spin Center)*: Off

    - ⬚⸲ *(Display Style)*: ⬚ (Shading With Edges)

4. Use the Model Tree to investigate the assembly components. The assembly consists of a floor model, two water cabinets, and three part cabinets. All five cabinets are assembled to the floor model using datum points. The points were created on curves using the **Length Ratio** option. The location of the cabinets can be modified by changing the length ratio value for each point.

Task 2 - Create a model analysis feature to create a mass parameter and a datum point at the center of gravity.

1. Select the *Analysis* tab.

2. In the Model Report group, click (Mass Properties).

3. In the Mass Properties dialog box, click **Preview**.

4. Select **Feature** from the Quick drop-down list.

5. Edit the name to **COFG**.

6. Select the *Feature* tab.

7. Do not create the **VOLUME** or **SURF_AREA** parameter.

8. Create the **MASS** parameter.

9. In the *Datums* area, enable **CSYS_COG**. Edit the name to **COG**.

10. Click **OK**. The COG coordinate system display on the model, as shown in Figure 3–22. The COG does not match the center of gravity of the airplane; therefore, an optimization study is required.

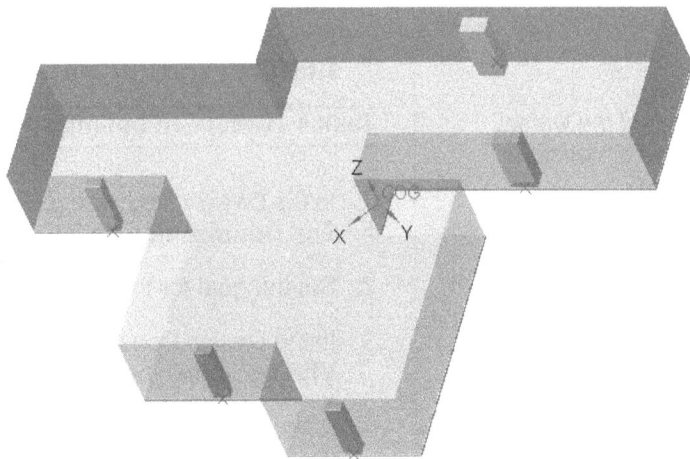

Figure 3–22

Task 3 - Create two measurement analysis features that measure the distance between the center of gravity for the room to the center of gravity for the airplane.

1. In the In-graphics toolbar, select 🖫 (Plane Display).

2. In the Measure group, expand 📏 (Measure) and select 🗂. (Distance).

3. Press and hold <Ctrl> and select the COG coordinate system and the **CENTER_HORIZ** datum plane. The distance is 612.677mm.

4. Select the *Feature* tab.

5. Edit the name of the *DISTANCE* parameter to **HORIZ**. Press <Enter> after changing the name.

6. Click 🖫 (Save), ensure that **Make Feature** is selected, and set the name to **DIST_HORIZ**.

7. Click **Close** to complete the feature.

8. Repeat the previous steps to create an additional measure analysis feature. Add the resulting parameter to the model and set the name to **VERT**. Set the name of the analysis feature to **DIST_VERT**. This feature measures the distance between the COG coordinate system and the **CENTER_VERT** datum plane.

Task 4 - Create an optimization study.

*To select the water cabinet dimensions, expand **water_cabinet.prt,** double-click on the protrusion, and select the dimensions. Do the same for the **parts_cabinet** components. To select the datum point dimension symbols, expand **floor.prt** in the Model Tree, click on **Datum Point id 469**, and select the dimensions.*

1. In the Design Study group, click 🔍 (Feasibility/Optimization). The **Optimization** option is enabled by default.

2. Set the goal for the **MASS:COFG** parameter **Minimize.**

3. In the *Design Constraints* area, click **Add**. Set the **HORIZ** and **VERT** parameters equal to zero.

4. In the *Design Variables* field, add the dimensions, and edit the *Min* and *Max* values specified in the table below. Use Figure 3–23 to locate the dimensions.

Dimension	Minimum	Maximum
d0:WATER_CABINET	200	1000
d1:WATER_CABINET	200	1000

d0:PARTS_CABINET	200	1000
d1:PARTS_CABINET	200	1000
d68:FLOOR	0.2	0.8
d76:FLOOR	0.2	0.8
d83:FLOOR	0.2	0.8
d82:FLOOR	0.2	0.8
d85:FLOOR	0.2	0.8

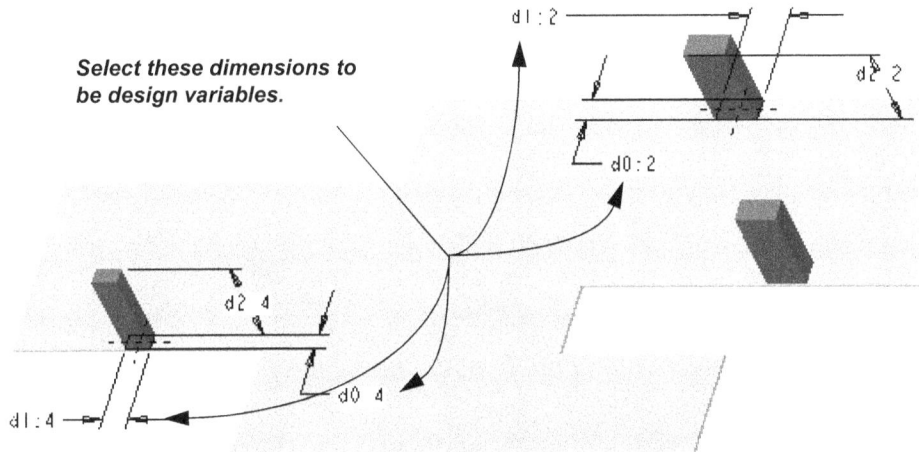

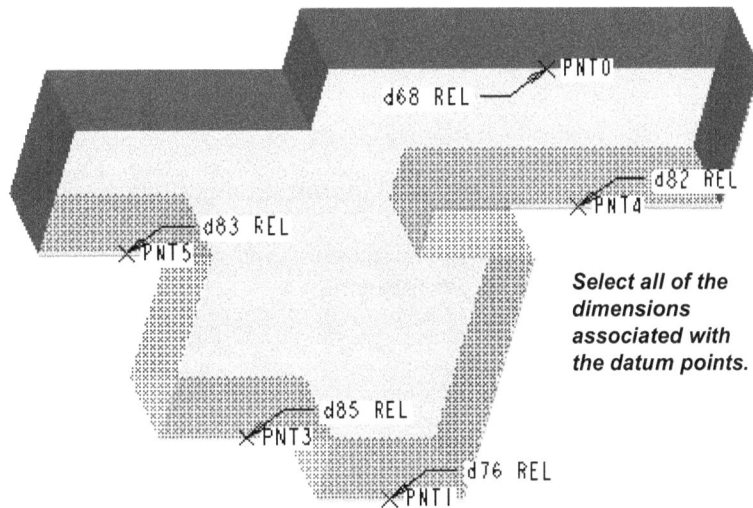

Select these dimensions to be design variables.

Select all of the dimensions associated with the datum points.

Figure 3–23

The Optimization/Feasibility dialog box displays as shown in Figure 3–24.

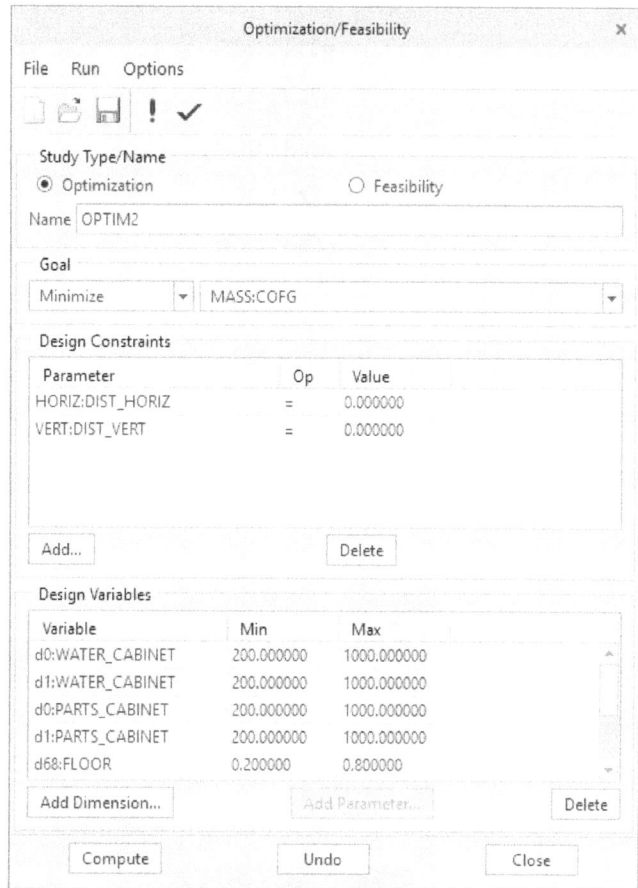

Figure 3–24

Task 5 - Customize the optimization study.

1. In the Optimization/Feasibility dialog box, click **Options> Preferences**.

2. In the *Graph* tab, select **Goal** and **Constraints**.

3. Select the *Run* tab and set the *Max Iterations* value to **10**.

4. In the Preferences dialog box, click **OK**.

5. Click **Compute** to begin the analysis. Convergence graphs for **HORIZ**, **VERT** (two design constraints) and **MASS** (the goal) display, and update with each pass. The graph for the **MASS** goal is shown in Figure 3–25.

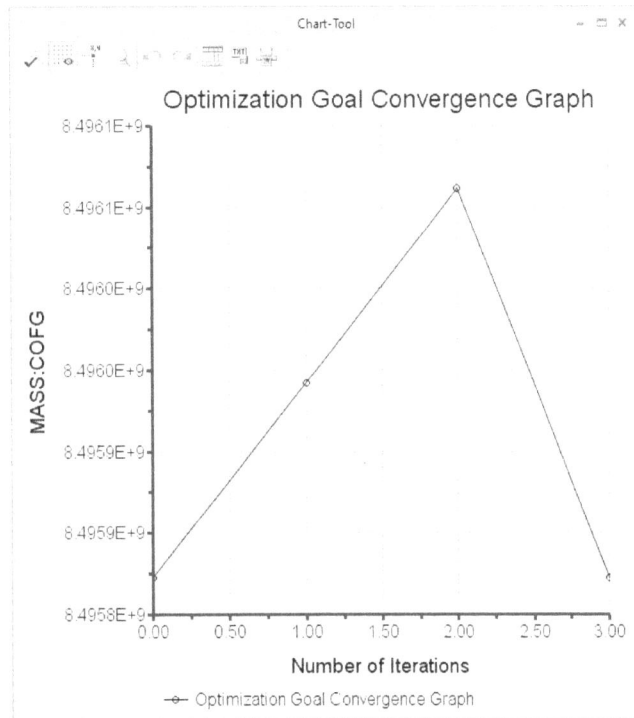

Figure 3–25

- Was the system able to minimize the mass of the model while still maintaining the design constraints? The message window reads "The part was successfully optimized."

Note that the design constraints were met, as shown in the graphs for the **HORIZ** and **VERT** parameters. With the optimized model, the position of the center of gravity is located at the intersection of the **CENTER_HORIZ** and **CENTER_VERT** datum planes.

Task 6 - Update the assembly.

1. In the Optimization/Feasibility dialog box, select **Close**.

2. Select **Confirm** to update the model. The optimized model displays as shown in Figure 3–26 and Figure 3–27. Note the new positions of the water and part cabinets.

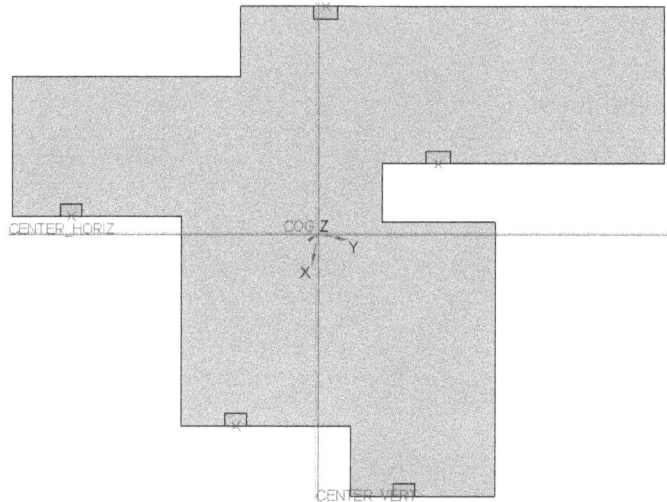

Figure 3–26

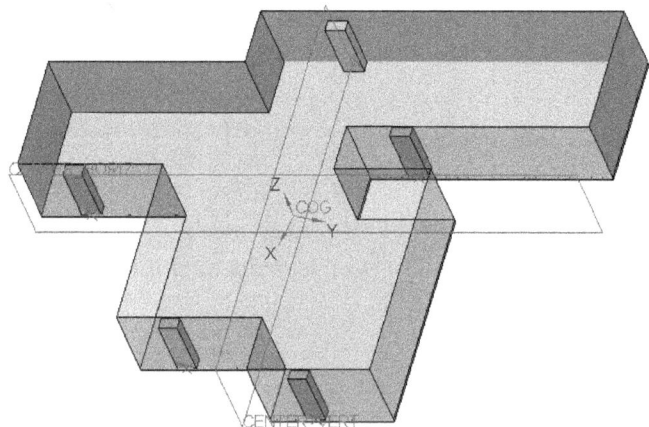

Figure 3–27

3. Close the assembly and erase it from memory.

Multi-Objective Design Studies

A Multi-Objective Design Study takes a different approach to finding an optimized solution for a design problem. A Feasibility or Optimization study checks the design parameter for each variation of the design variable. It continues to do this until the parameter meets the required design constraints. The Multi-Objective Design Study reports all values of the design parameters across a variation of the design variables. The design variables are changed within their minimum and maximum bounds in an attempt to capture all variations of the model that can possibly occur. Therefore, the Multi-Objective Design Study provides access to all permutations and variations of the model within the bounds of the design variables.

Learning Objectives in This Chapter

- Understand how Multi-Objective Design Studies are used to modify dimensions and parameters while attempting to achieve a design goal.
- Create a Multi-Objective Design Study.

4.1 Multi-Objective Design Study Methods

A Multi-Objective Design Study (MODS) enables you to find optimal solutions using multiple design goals. A multi-objective design assists you in finding an optimal range of variables for use in extracting optimal solutions. If there is more than one optimal solution, you are presented with the results so you can decide on the most appropriate the solution.

The data is stored in a master table, which lists each of the records or experiments calculated in the design study. To find the correct solution to the design problem, data is derived from the table by comparing it to design constraints that you have specified. You can specify any number of constraints to reduce the number of records down to one optimized solution.

There are two methods of deriving the optimized solution from the master table: **Constraint** and **Pareto**.

Constraint Derivation

This method allows a design constraint to be specific for any of the goals. Any records that fall out of these constraints are removed. The constraint method is accessed by selecting the **Constraint** option, as shown in Figure 4–1.

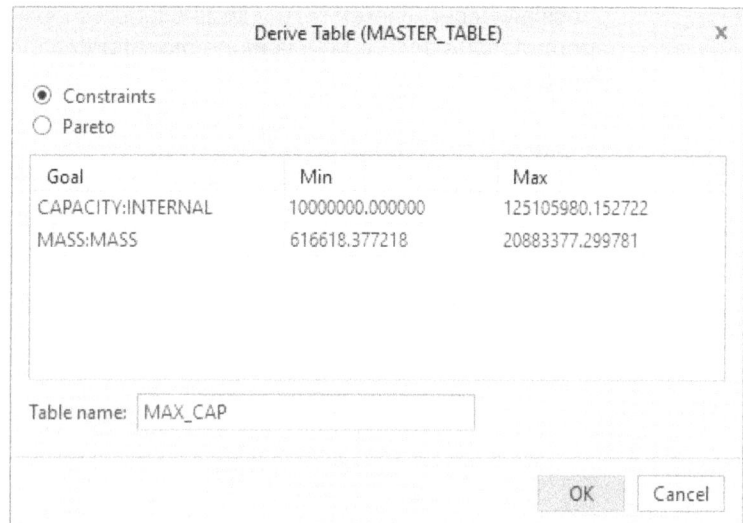

Derive Table (MASTER_TABLE)			×
⦿ Constraints			
○ Pareto			
Goal	**Min**	**Max**	
CAPACITY:INTERNAL	10000000.000000	125105980.152722	
MASS:MASS	616618.377218	20883377.299781	
Table name: MAX_CAP			
		OK	Cancel

Figure 4–1

Pareto Derivation

This method works only with minimums and maximums, rather than with constraints. If only one goal is selected to derive a table, it finds the global min/max and one solution is obtained. If more than one goal is selected, the table can have more than one solution. None of these remaining designs are necessarily better than the other. The study trades one goal at the expense of the other goal. The solutions not found in this derived table show no improvement in either of the goals and are thus excluded. Select **Pareto**, as shown in Figure 4–2. Each goal can be **Excluded**, **Minimized**, or **Maximized** using the drop-down list in the *Options* column.

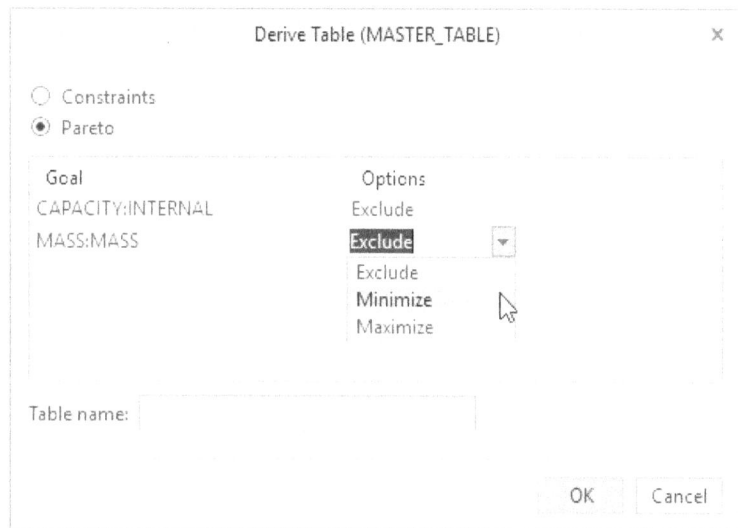

Figure 4–2

4.2 Multi-Objective Design Studies

How To: Create a Multi-Objective Design Study

1. In the *Analysis* tab, expand ⚲ (Feasibility/Optimization) and select 🌠 (Multi-Objective Design Study).
2. Click ⬜ (New Design Study) and enter a name for the study.
3. Click ⬚ (Setup Master Table) to create the master table.
4. You can select one of two options when selecting the sampling method to be used for the study: **Automatic** (default) and **Manual**.

    - The **Automatic** method evenly distributes experiments between specified minimum and maximum design variables. The Master Table for this option is shown in Figure 4–3. Click 🔲 (Add Dimension) and 🔲 (Add Parameter) to specify the design variables and enter their minimum and maximum limits. Click **Select Goals** to define the goals of the study.

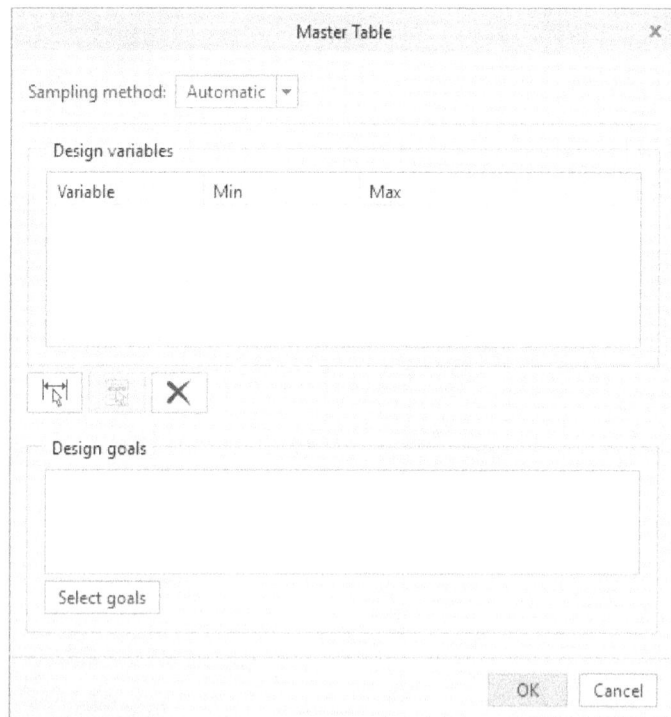

Figure 4–3

- The **Manual** method enables you to perform experiments using a table of values. You can enter values manually or import them from a file. The Master Table for this option is shown in Figure 4–4. To run experiments on all of the combinations of design variables, select **All combination** in the *Run Experiments On* area. To set the number of experiments as the number of rows that are defining the design variables, select **One per row**.

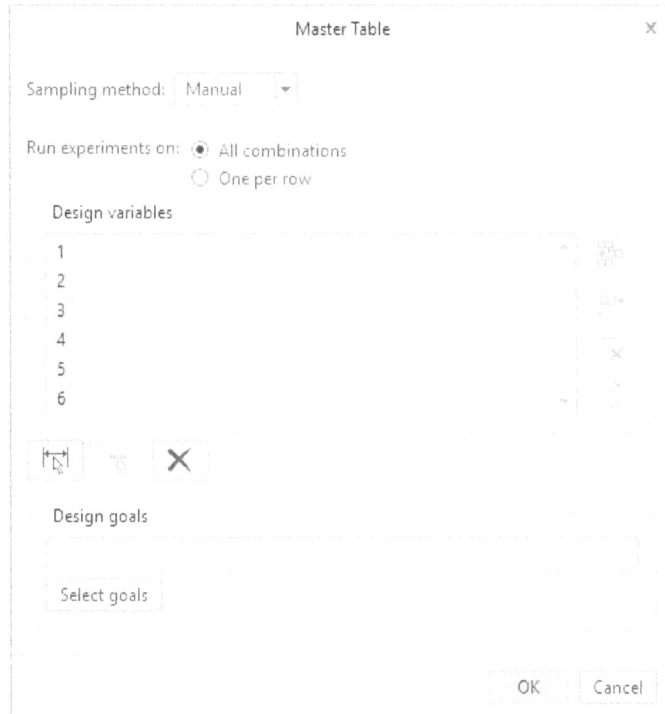

Figure 4–4

Results are more accurate and the run time longer with a higher number of experiments.

5. In the Multi-Objective Design Study dialog box, click
   ! (Compute Master Table) to run the study.
6. Specify the number of experiments to create. This is the number of records that will be calculated and listed in the master table.

7. Click ⬜ (Derive New Table) to derive further solutions from the results. Use the **Constraints** or the **Pareto** method to derive the optimized solution from the data.

Example:

Using the container shown in Figure 4–5, you can perform a Multi-Objective Design Study to optimize the model with respect to two goals: *capacity* and *mass*.

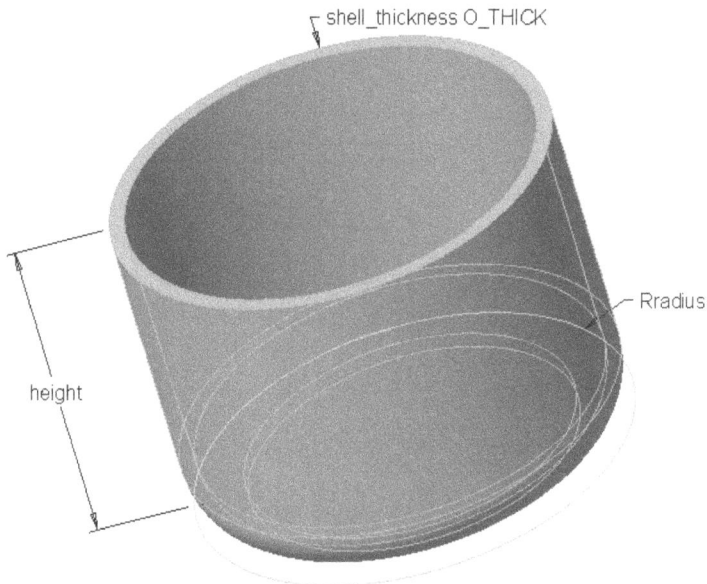

Figure 4–5

The **shell_thickness**, **height**, and **radius** design variables are added to the Master Table using the following *minimum* and *maximum* values:

	Current Value	Minimum Value	Maximum Value
Shell_Thickness	10	2	20
Radius	100	50	300
Height	150	100	600

The design goals added are mass and capacity (a relation analysis which calculates the inner capacity of the container). The Master Table dialog box is shown in Figure 4–6.

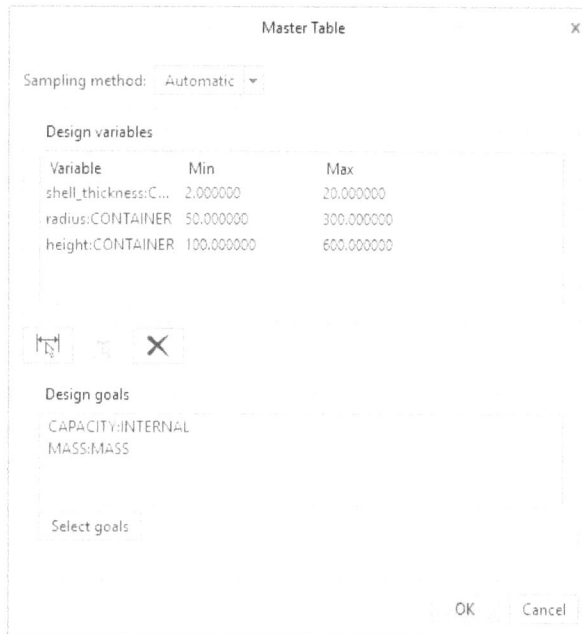

Figure 4–6

By clicking ❗ (Compute Master Table) and specifying 100 experiments, the master table data is generated. Figure 4–7 shows a subset of the 100 records that were produced.

Figure 4–7

To find the optimized solution from all this data, design constraints are applied by clicking ▢ (Derive New Table). Two derivations are used. The first design constraint is to remove all records with a capacity less than 10L. This can be done using a **Constraint** derivation, as shown in Figure 4–8, where the *minimum* for the **CAPACITY** parameter is set to **10 L**.

Derive Table (MASTER_TABLE)			×
⦿ Constraints			
◯ Pareto			
Goal	Min	Max	
CAPACITY:INTERNAL	10000000.000000	125105980.152722	
MASS:MASS	616618.377218	20883377.299781	
Table name: MAX_CAP			
		OK	Cancel

Figure 4–8

A number of records still meet this constraint. The second design criteria is to minimize mass. The **Pareto** derivation, shown in Figure 4–9, was used to select the record with the minimum mass. This derivation is performed on the reduced records to ensure that the 10L capacity constraint is met while still minimizing the mass.

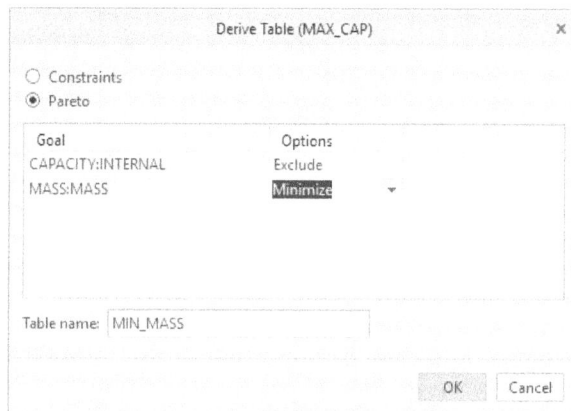

Derive Table (MAX_CAP)		×
◯ Constraints		
⦿ Pareto		
Goal	Options	
CAPACITY:INTERNAL	Exclude	
MASS:MASS	Minimize ▾	
Table name: MIN_MASS		
	OK	Cancel

Figure 4–9

A single, optimized record is the result. The model can be shown in its optimized state by right-clicking the remaining record and selecting **Show Model**. The optimized model is shown in Figure 4–10.

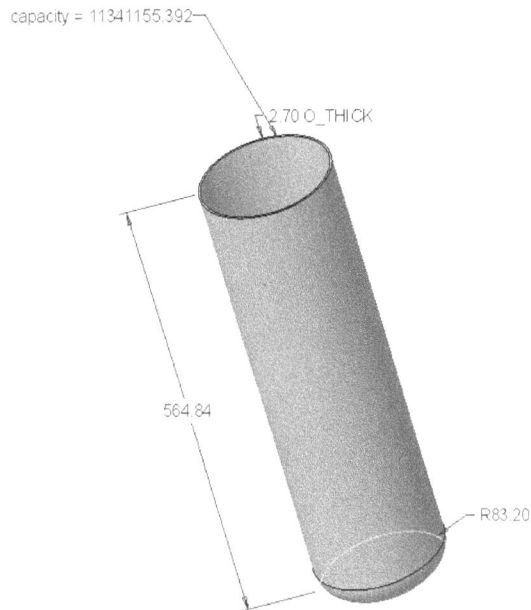

Figure 4–10

This solution differs from that found using the Optimization Study. This is because the design constraints were selected using different methods. The previous solution exists in the Master Tables records and can be extracted using different derivations. The resulting Multi-Objective Design Study dialog box is shown in Figure 4–11.

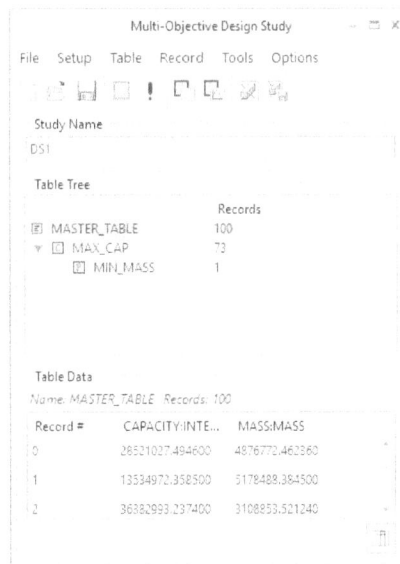

Figure 4–11

The elements of the Multi-Objective Design Study dialog box are described as follows:

Element	Description
Study Name	Specifies the name for the study.
Table Tree	Lists the tables and derivations in the study. Select the active table from the table tree when creating or modifying a derivation. The number of records contained in each table is listed in the right-hand column.
Table Data	Lists all records for the selected table. The records are listed in numeric order and provide values for all design goals and variables.

The buttons in the Multi-Objective Design Study dialog box are described as follows:

Button	Description
	Creates a new Multi-Objective Design Study.
	Opens an existing Multi-Objective Design Study.
	Saves the current Multi-Objective Design Study.
	Creates a Master Table. Selecting this button opens the Master Table dialog box.
!	Runs the Multi-Objective Design Study. Once selected, you must enter the number of experiments (records) to be created.
	Opens the Derive dialog box, which enables you to find an optimized record from the table data.
	Creates a graph of the table data. Selecting this button opens the Graph dialog box. A single variable or goal must be selected for each axis.
	Shows the regenerated model based on the parameters of the selected record.
	Saves a copy of the model with the parameter values of the selected record.

Practice 4a

Heat Sink Model

Practice Objectives

- Create and run a multi-objective design study.
- Derive optimized designs from the study.

Heat sinks are used to dissipate heat from electronic parts and small motors. In this practice, you will apply the behavioral modeling techniques to a heat sink model to meet the following four objectives:

- Minimize the mass of the heat sink.

- Maximize the surface area of the heat sink to dissipate heat.

- Determine the ratio of fin height to base thickness to accommodate manufacturing.

- Determine the ratio of fin height to heat sink width to locate the device on the part.

The results of each of these objectives can conflict with one another. You will use a multi-objective design study to provide design options.

Task 1 - Open the part heat_sink.prt

1. Set the working directory to *Heat_Sink*.

2. Open **heat_sink.prt**.

3. Set the model display as follows:

   - $\overset{\times \prime}{/}$, *(Datum Display Filters)*: All Off

   - *(Spin Center)*: Off

   - *(Display Style)*: (Shading With Edges)

The model displays as shown in Figure 4–12.

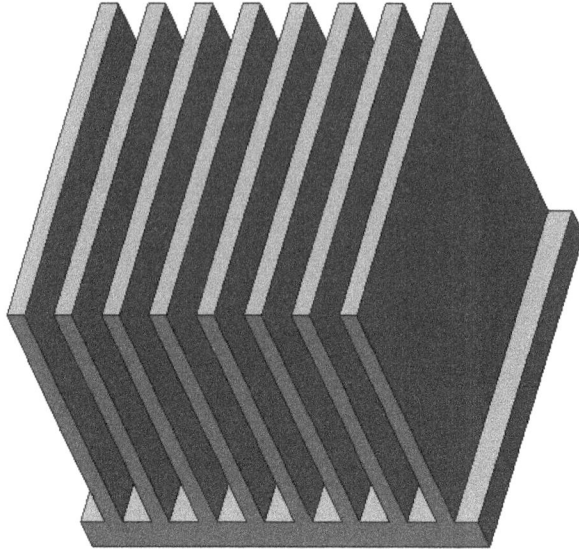

Figure 4–12

The model units are mmNs. The heat sink material density is 1e-008 tonne/mm^3.

Task 2 - Create an analysis feature for the model's mass.

---

1. Create a Mass Properties analysis feature and set the name to **MASS_PART**.

2. Click **Preview**. The heat sink properties display in the result area as shown in Figure 4–13.

The part mass is 120g = 0.26lb.

Figure 4–13

3. Select the *Feature* tab.

4. Remove the checkmark next to **VOLUME** and **SURF_AREA** in the *Parameters* area so that only **MASS** is created.

5. Edit the model mass parameter name to **HS_MASS** and press <Enter>.

6. Click **OK** to complete the feature.

Task 3 - Create a Measure analysis feature to measure the surface area of one of the fins.

---

1. In the Measure group, expand ✎ (Measure) and select ✕ (Area).

2. In the Measure: Area dialog box, click ⊕ (Expand The Dialog) if required, to display the *Analysis* and *Feature* tabs.

3. Select the surface shown in Figure 4–14. The surface area (750) should display.

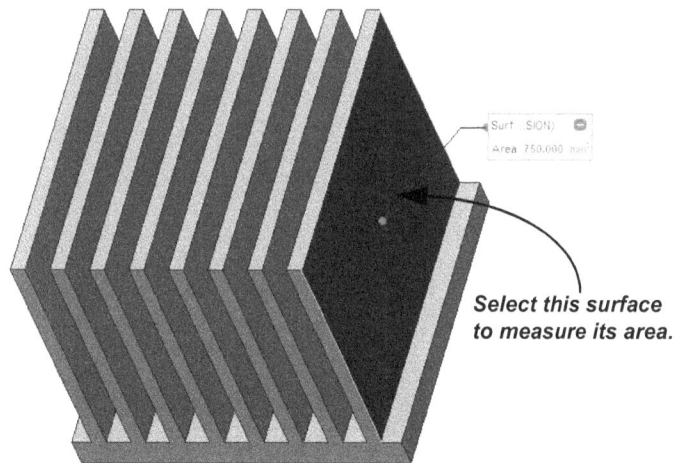

Figure 4–14

4. Select the *Feature* tab. Note that the **AREA** parameter is selected for creation.

5. Click 💾 (Save. Ensure that **Make Feature** is selected, set the name to **SURFACE_AREA**, and press <Enter>.

6. Click **Close** to complete the analysis feature.

Task 4 - Create a Relation analysis feature to calculate the height ratio.

1. In the Manage group, click ⅹ⁄ᵢ (Analysis).

2. Edit the name to **HEIGHT_RATIO** and press <Enter>.

3. In the *Type* area, select **Relation**.

4. Click **Next**.

5. Double-click on the model to display all the dimensions.

6. Enter the following relation in the relation editor:

    HEIGHT = (FIN_HEIGHT/BASE_THICK)

As an alternative to entering the symbol, click ⊢⊣ (Display Specified Dimension) and select the dimension directly on the model. The dimension symbol is automatically added at the point where the cursor was located.

7. Click ✓ (Verify) to verify the relation and select **OK**.

8. Click **OK** in the Relations dialog box.

9. Click ✓ (OK) to complete the analysis feature.

Task 5 - Create a Relation analysis feature to calculate the width ratio.

1. In the Manage group, click ⅹ⁄ᵢ (Analysis).

2. Edit the name to **WIDTH_RATIO** and press <Enter>.

3. In the *Type* area, select **Relation**.

4. Click **Next**.

5. Enter the following relation in the relation editor:

    WIDTH = (FIN_HEIGHT/BASE_THICK)

If the dimensions that were shown in the previous analysis feature were cleared, you can double-click on the model once you are in the Relations dialog box to display them again.

6. Click ✓ (Verify) to verify the relation and click **OK**.

7. In the Relations dialog box, click **OK**.

8. Click ✓ (OK) to complete the analysis feature.

Task 6 - Create a Relation analysis feature to calculate the total area of the heat sink.

1. In the Manage group, click ⅹ⁄ᵢ (Analysis).

Multi-Objective Design Studies

The smaller surfaces on each fin have not been included because their area is much smaller relative to the larger surface areas.

2. Edit the name to **TOTAL_AREA** and press <Enter>.

3. In the *Type* area, select **Relation**.

4. Click **Next**.

5. Enter the following relation in the relation editor.

   TOTAL_SURFACE=16*(AREA:FID_SURFACE_AREA)

6. Click ✓ (Verify) to verify the relation and click **OK**.

7. In the Relations dialog box, click **OK**.

8. Click ✓ (OK) to complete the analysis feature.

Task 7 - Create a Multi-Objective Design Study.

1. Select the *Tools* tab and click (Switch Dimensions).

2. Select the *Analysis* tab.

3. In the Design Study group, expand (Feasibility/ Optimization) and select (Multi-Objective Design Study). The Multi-Objective Design Study dialog box displays as shown in Figure 4–15.

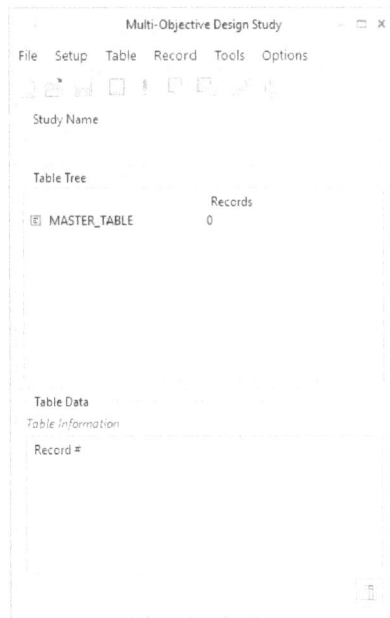

Figure 4–15

© 2021, ASCENT - Center for Technical Knowledge®   4–15

4. Click ☐ (New Design Study) to create a new design study.

5. Edit the Study name to **HEAT_SINK** and press <Enter>.

6. Click ▢ (Setup Master Table) to create a Master Table. The Master Table dialog box displays as shown in Figure 4–16.

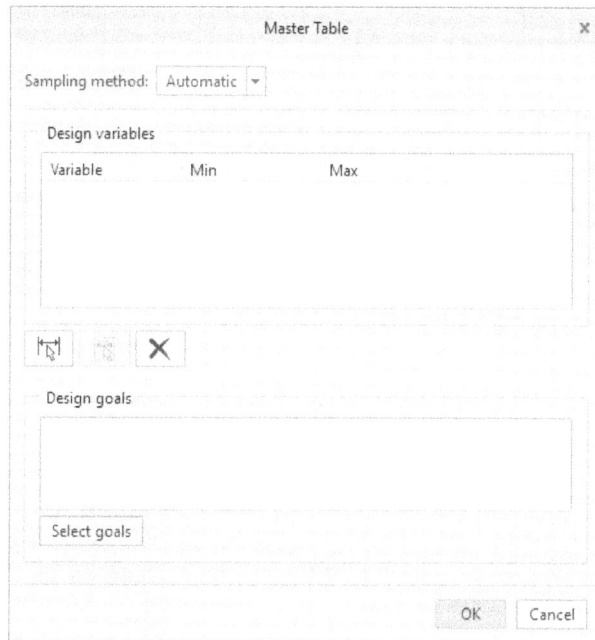

Figure 4–16

7. Click **Select Goals**. The Select Parameters dialog box displays as shown in Figure 4–17.

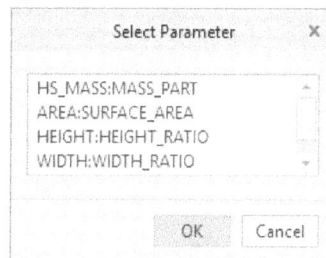

Figure 4–17

8. Press and hold <Ctrl> and select all the parameters in the Parameters dialog box. Click **OK**. The parameters display in the *Design goals* area of the Master Table dialog box.

9. Click ⌈☒⌉ (Add Dimension).

10. Select the first fin on the model and select the **FIN_HEIGHT** and **FIN_WIDTH** dimensions. Additionally, select the base and **select BASE_WIDTHTHICK** and **BASE_WIDTH** dimensions. Refer to Figure 4–18 to locate the dimensions. Press the middle mouse button to stop selecting dimensions.

*Model displayed in **No Hidden** mode for clarity.*

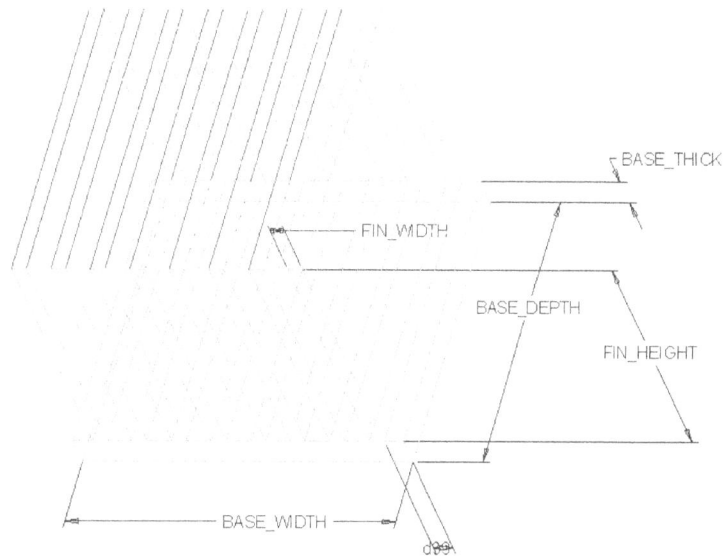

Figure 4–18

11. Select the Min and Max cells for each dimension in the Master Table dialog box. Enter the following values:

Dimension	Minimum	Maximum
FIN_HEIGHT	20	30
FIN_WIDTH	1.2	1.9
BASE_THICK	2	4
BASE_WIDTH	25	35

The Master Table dialog box displays as shown in Figure 4–19.

Note that the variables will be listed in the order in which you selected them, so be careful when entering the Min and Max values.

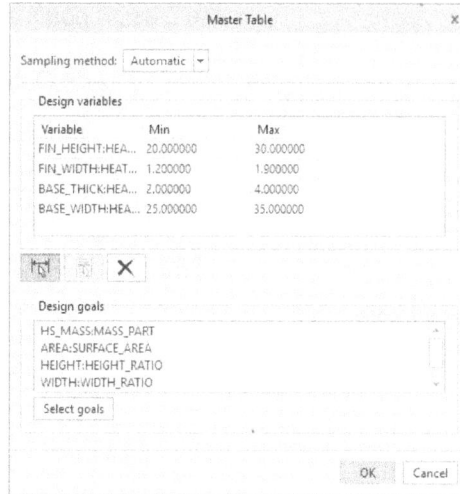

Figure 4–19

12. Click **OK** to close the Master Table dialog box.

13. Click ! (Compute Master Table) to start the design study.

Alternatively, you can click Setup>Compute/Expand to start the design study.

14. Enter **100** as the number of experiments to generate. Once complete, the Multi-Objective Design Study dialog box displays as shown in Figure 4–20.

Figure 4–20

Task 8 - Derive a solution from the results.

Design Consideration

The Multi-Objective Design Study done in the previous task shows that 100 different solutions exist for each design goal selected. The solutions were obtained by varying the design variables within their limits and recalculating the value of each parameter. Which record is the correct answer? Remember that you have multiple objectives. Focus on the total surface area. Using the Derive dialog box, you can find the record that provides the largest total surface area.

1. Click ⬚ (Derive New Table). The Derive Table dialog box displays as shown in Figure 4–21.

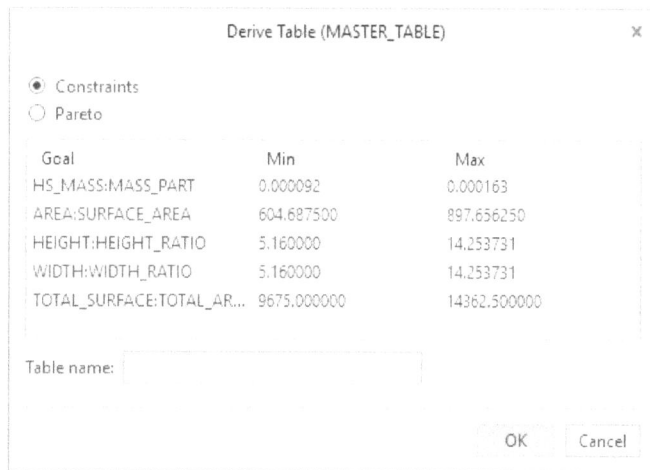

Derive Table (MASTER_TABLE)   ×

◉ Constraints
◯ Pareto

Goal	Min	Max
HS_MASS:MASS_PART	0.000092	0.000163
AREA:SURFACE_AREA	604.687500	897.656250
HEIGHT:HEIGHT_RATIO	5.160000	14.253731
WIDTH:WIDTH_RATIO	5.160000	14.253731
TOTAL_SURFACE:TOTAL_AR...	9675.000000	14362.500000

Table name:

OK   Cancel

Figure 4–21

2. Select **Pareto**.

3. Select the **Exclude** cell adjacent to the **TOTAL_SURFACE** parameter.

4. Select **Maximize** from the drop-down list. The Derive Table dialog box displays as shown in Figure 4–22.

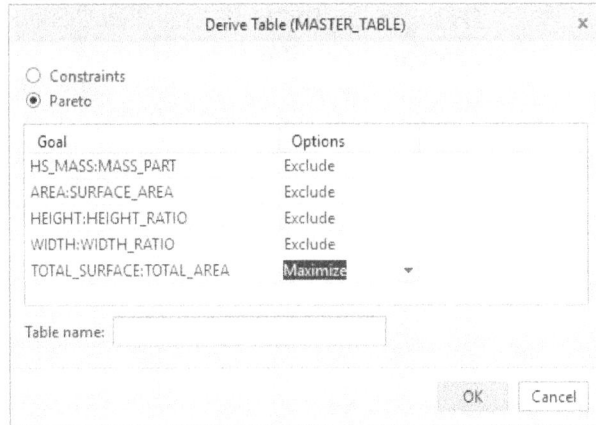

Figure 4–22

5. Set the table name to **TOTAL_AREA** and press <Enter>.

6. Click **OK**. The Multi-Objective Design Study dialog box displays as shown in Figure 4–23.

A single record exists in the Table Data field. This record is the derived version of the model with the largest total surface area.

Figure 4–23

Task 9 - Create a second derivation.

1. Select the Master Table in the *Table Tree* area.

2. Create a second derived table to Minimize the model's mass.

3. Review the records in more detail using the INFORMATION WINDOW.

Task 10 - (Optional) Create two additional derivations.

1. Create a derivation to minimize the fin height to the base thickness ratio (**HEIGHT**). Compare this to the resulting weight of the models.

2. Create a derivation to minimize the fin height to the base width ratio (**WIDTH**). Compare this to the resulting weight of the models.

Task 11 - Save all design studies.

1. In the Multi-Objective Design Study dialog box, click
   (Save Design Study) to save all of the design studies.

2. Close the dialog box.

3. Close the part and erase it from memory.

Practice 4b | Floor Plan Model

Practice Objectives

- Create and run a Multi-Objective Design Study.
- Derive optimized designs from the study.

In this practice, you will use the **floor_plan** model from a previous practice. You now have two conflicting objectives for the design of the floor plan. You will need to minimize the mass of the assembly while maximizing the storage capacity of the cabinets. It has been determined that the storage capacity constraint is your primary objective. A multi-objective design study will be used to provide a series of options for the final design.

Task 1 - Open the floor_plan_final assembly.

1. Set the working directory to *Floor_Plan*.

2. Open **floor_plan_final.asm** from the *completed_models* directory.

3. Set the model display as follows:

   - ⅍, *(Datum Display Filters)*: ↳ (Csys Display) and ⬚ (Plane Display) only

   - ⸰ *(Spin Center)*: Off

   - ⬛, *(Display Style)*: ⬜ (Shading With Edges)

   The model displays as shown in Figure 4–24.

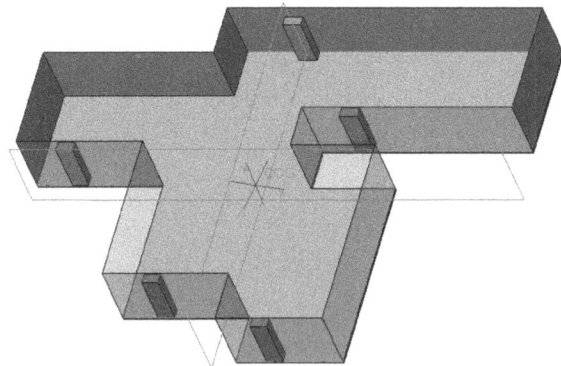

Figure 4–24

To determine the capacity of the cabinets, you must create a model analysis feature in each individual model. The parameters developed from these features can then be used in the top-level assembly.

Task 2 - Create an analysis feature in water_cabinet.prt.

1. Select **WATER_CABINET_FINAL.PRT** in the Model Tree and click ⬚ (Open).

2. Select the *Analysis* tab.

3. In the Measure group, expand ✎ (Measure) and select ⬚ (Volume).

4. In the Measure: Volume dialog box, click ⬚ (Save), ensure that **Make Feature** is selected, set the name to **WATER_VOL** and press <Enter>.

5. Select the *Feature* tab.

6. Create the **VOLUME** parameter.

7. Click **Close** to complete the feature.

8. Close the part window.

9. Open **PARTS_CABINET_FINAL.PRT**.

10. Select the *Analysis* tab.

11. In the Measure group, expand ✎ (Measure) and select ⬚ (Volume).

12. In the Measure: Volume dialog box, click ⬚ (Save), ensure that **Make Feature** is selected, set the name to **PARTS_VOL**, and press <Enter>.

13. Select the *Feature* tab.

14. Create the **VOLUME** parameter.

15. Click **Close** to complete the feature.

16. Close the part window.

Task 3 - Create relation analysis features.

Design Consideration

In this task, you create three relation analysis features. The first analysis calculates the total water cabinet volume; the second analysis calculates the total parts cabinet volume; the third analysis sums the two of these together.

1. If not already active, set **floor_plan_final.asm** as the active model.

2. Select the *Analysis* tab.

3. In the *Manage* group, click ⁙ (Analysis)**.**

4. Edit the name to **WATER** and press <Enter>.

5. Select **Relation**.

6. Click **Next**.

7. Click **Show>Session ID>Part** and select **water_cabinet_final**. The session id displays in the message window. Click **Part** and select the **parts_cabinet_final** component. These values are used in upcoming relations.

*The part level **water_vol** parameter is multiplied by two since two components exist in the assembly*

8. Enter the following relation in the relation editor. Enter the session id for **water_cabinet** in place of the # symbol in the relation.

   WATER_VOL = 2*(VOLUME:FID_WATER_VOL:#)

9. Click ✅ (Verify) to verify the relation and click **OK**.

10. Click **OK** in the Relations dialog box.

11. Click ✔ (OK) to complete the analysis feature.

12. Create a second Relation analysis feature and set the name to **PARTS**.

13. Click **Next**.

14. Enter the following relation in the relation editor. Enter the session id for **parts_cabinet** in place of the # symbol in the relation

   PARTS_VOL = 3*(VOLUME:FID_PARTS_VOL:#)

15. Click ✅ (Verify) to verify the relation and click **OK**.

16. Click **OK** in the Relations dialog box.

17. Click ✓ (OK) to complete the analysis feature.

18. Create a third Relation analysis feature named **TOTAL_VOL**.

19. Click **Next**.

20. Enter the following relation in the relation editor.

    TOTAL_VOL = WATER_VOL:FID_WATER +
    PARTS_VOL:FID_PARTS

21. Click ✓ (Verify) to verify the relation and click **OK**.

22. Click **OK** in the Relations dialog box.

23. Click ✓ (OK) to complete the analysis feature.

Task 4 - Create a Multi-Objective Design Study.

1. Select the *Tools* tab and click Ⅹ (Switch Dimensions).

2. In the *Design Study* group, expand ◈ (Feasibility/
   Optimization) and select ◈ (Multi-Objective Design Study).

3. Click ⊐ (New Design Study) to create a new design study.
   Accept the default name.

4. Click ☐ (Setup Master Table) to create the Master Table.

5. Click 🔲 (Add Dimension). Add the following dimensions and *Min* and *Max* values. Use Figure 4–25 to locate the dimensions.

Dimension	Minimum	Maximum
d0:WATER_CABINET_FINAL	200	1000
d1:WATER_CABINET_FINAL	200	1000
d2:WATER_CABINET_FINAL	300	1500
d0:PARTS_CABINET_FINAL	200	1000
d1:PARTS_CABINET_FINAL	200	1000
d2:PARTS_CABINET_FINAL	300	1500

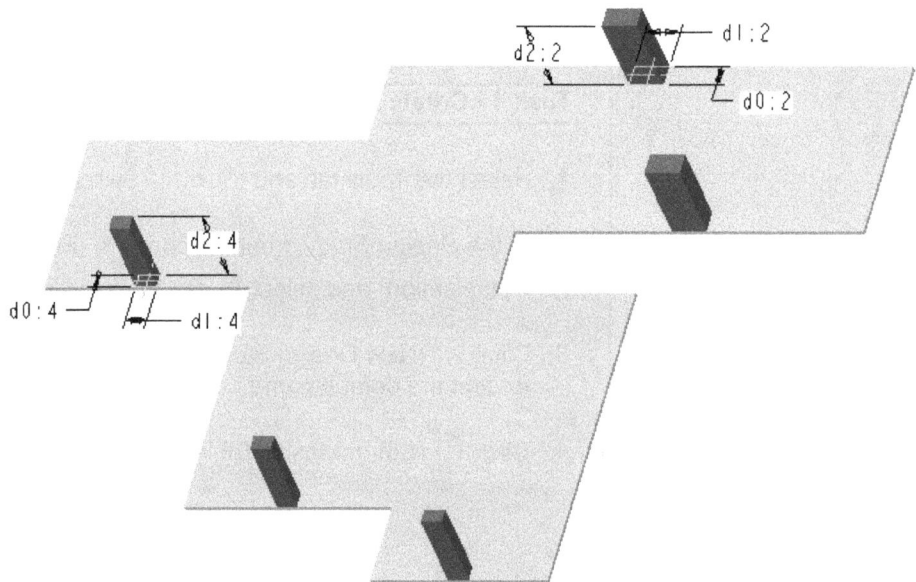

Figure 4–25

6. Click **Select Goals**. The Parameter Selection dialog box displays. Select the following parameters:

*   **MASS:COFG**
*   **WATER_VOL:WATER**
*   **PARTS_VOL:PARTS**
*   **TOTAL_VOL:TOTAL_VOL**

7. Click **OK** when complete. The Master Table dialog box displays as shown in Figure 4–26.

Note that your Variables may be in a different order, depending on how you selected them.

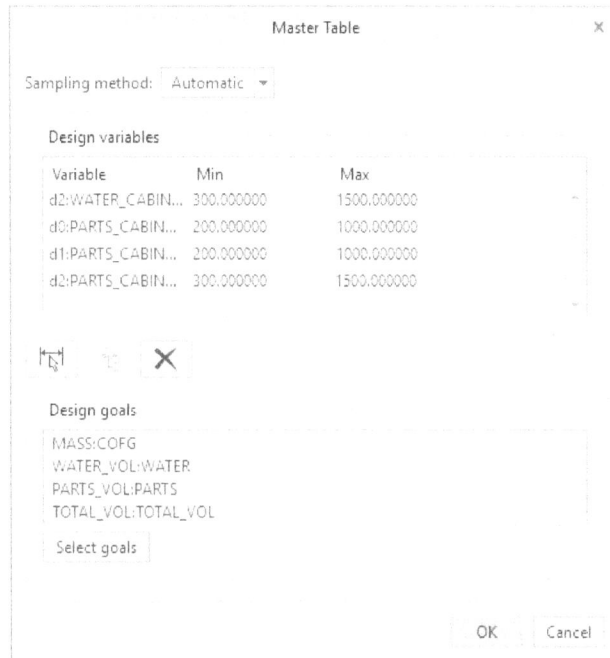

Figure 4–26

8. Click **OK**.

9. Click ! (Compute Master Table) to start the design study.

10. Enter **100** for the number of experiments to generate. The system runs through each experiment.

Task 5 - Derive a solution from the results.

Design Consideration

Based on the analysis done in the previous task, 100 different solutions exist for each design goal selected. The solutions were obtained by varying the design variables within their limits, and by recalculating the value of each parameter. Which record is the correct answer? Remember that you have multiple objectives. Focus in on mass. Using the Derive dialog box, you can find the record that provides the lowest mass.

1. Click ⌐ (Derive New Table). The Derive Table dialog box displays.

2. Select **Pareto**.

---

3. Select the **Exclude** cell, adjacent to the **MASS:COFG** parameter.

4. Select **Minimize** from the drop-down list.

5. Set the table name to **MIN_MASS**. The Derive Table dialog box displays as shown in Figure 4–27.

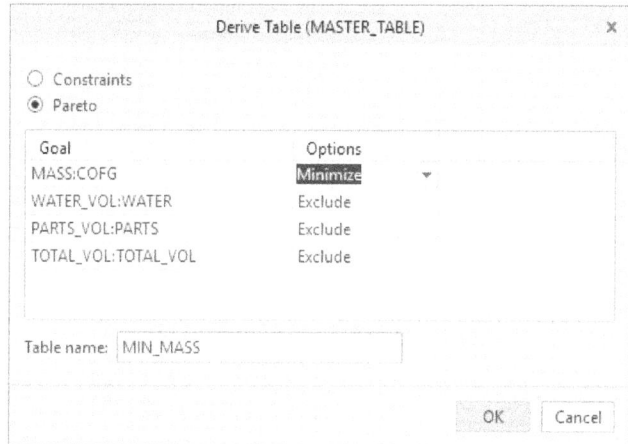

Figure 4–27

Note: If the error message "Table string is too long to be shown" displays, you can search and open the file listed at the end of the error message using a text editor instead.

6. Click **OK**. A single record exists in the *Table Tree* area. This is the derived version of the model with the least mass. It can be viewed in more detail by clicking **Table>Show Data**. The record displays as shown in Figure 4–28.

Derived minimum mass

Figure 4–28

You can continue to create several derivations of the table data and look at each version of the model. You can now focus in on your design constraints. The design requires a minimum of 800 L of water storage and 1,000 L of parts storage.

7. Create a second derivation. Highlight the Master Table in the *Table Tree* field and click ⌐ (Derive New Table).

8. Name the table **MAX_STOR**. Enter table data shown in Figure 4–29 for the **WATER_VOL** and **PARTS_VOL**. The derivation provides a list of all data that meets the design requirements of 800 L of water and 1,000 L of parts storage.

Figure 4–29

9. Click **OK**. There are a total of 10 records which meet these design constraints. Since our primary objective has been satisfied, you can create a further derivation based on mass.

10. Highlight **MAX_STOR** in the *Table Tree* area. Click ⌐ (Derive New Table).

11. Set the table name to **MIN_MASS_MAX_STOR**.

12. Use the **Pareto** method and in the MASS:COFG drop-down list, select **Minimize**.

13. Click **OK**.

*This model can also be saved to a new model name by selecting the record, right-clicking, and selecting **Save Model**.*

14. The solution to the design problem is shown in the *Table Data* area. Select the record in the *Table Data* area, right-click, and select **Show Model**. The assembly displays in a sub-window, as shown in Figure 4–30. Close the sub-window.

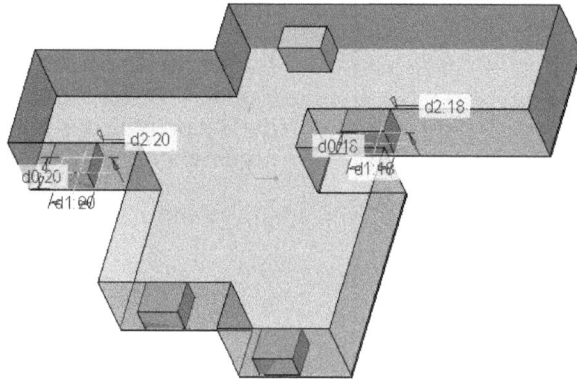

Figure 4–30

Task 6 - Save all design studies.

1. In the Multi-Objective Design Study dialog box, click

   🖫 (Save Design Study) to save all of the design studies.

2. Close the dialog box.

3. Close the assembly and erase it from memory.

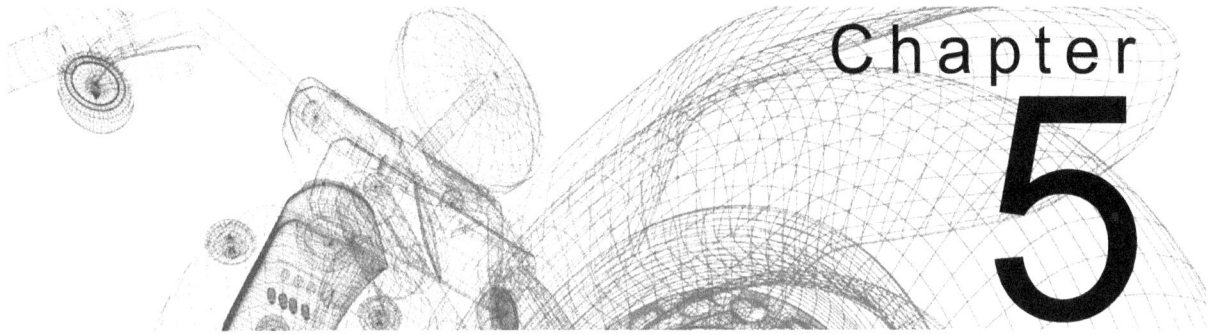

Graph Matching

A Datum Graph feature can be used to associate a graphical XY function to part geometry. Through relations, it can be used to control geometry. The graph feature must display before the feature it controls in the feature list.

Learning Objectives in This Chapter

- Understand how to use a datum graph to associate a graphical XY function to part geometry.
- Learn how to use Behavioral Modeling to compare two graphs to determine the differences in distributions of one parameter along the other parameter.
- Recognize the four methods available for comparing graphs.

5.1 Datum Graphs

A Datum Graph feature can be used to associate a graphical XY function to part geometry. Through relations, it can be used to control geometry. The graph feature must display before the feature it controls in the feature list.

To define a datum graph, in the *Model* tab, in the **Datum** group, select **Graph**. Enter a name for the graph and press <Enter>. Creo Parametric places you in the *Sketch* tab. Figure 5–1 shows an example of a datum graph sketch. This graph can be used in a relation to create the model shown in Figure 5–2.

Datum graphs must have only one x value for each y value.

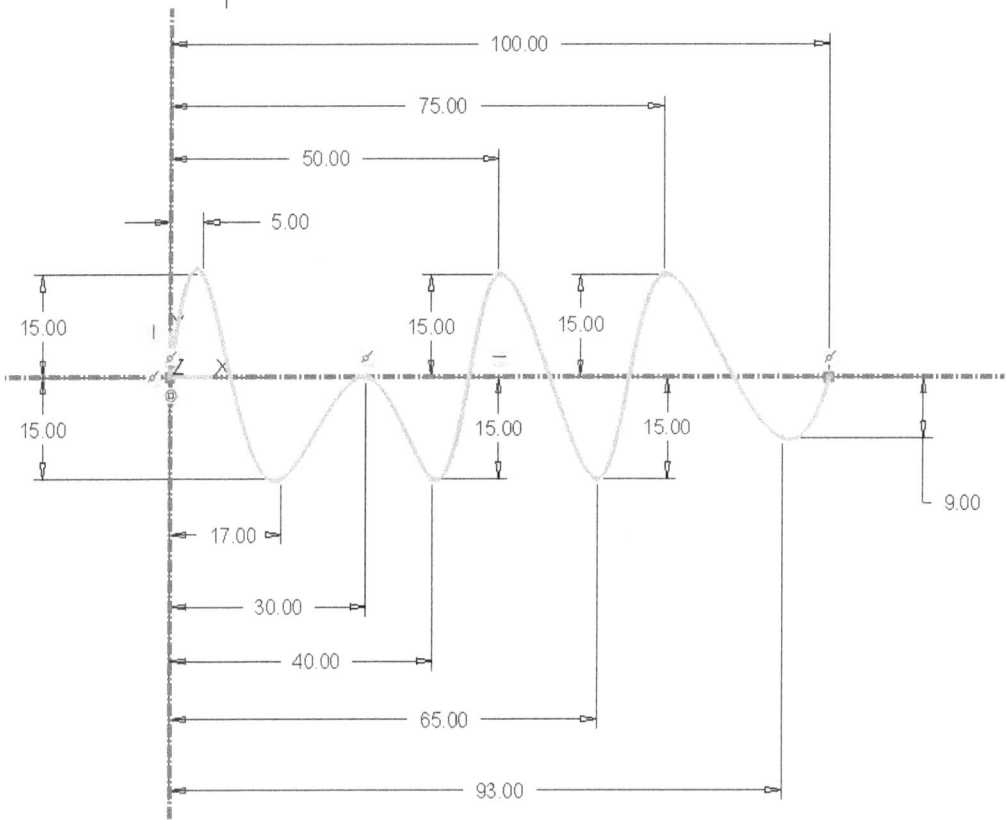

Figure 5–1

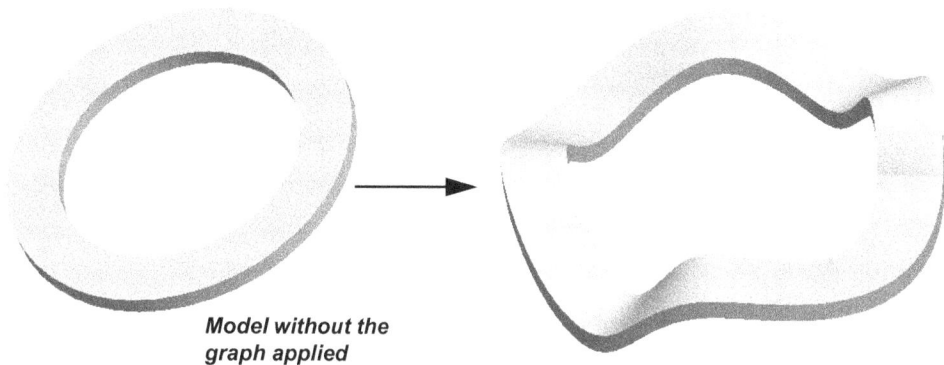

Model without the graph applied

Figure 5–2

Datum Graph sketches require the following geometry:

- Coordinate system

- Sketched entities to represent the function

- Dimensioning scheme that captures your design intent

- Horizontal and vertical centerlines (recommended)

A datum graph is stored with the model and can be used in any relation. The syntax used to reference the datum graph in a relation is as follows:

evalgraph ("graph_name", x)

Where:

evalgraph = A system-defined parameter that recognizes a datum graph feature is being referenced

graph_name = The name of the graph referenced in the relation.

x = The value along the x-axis for which the y value is returned

Consider the example in Figure 5–3. The figure shows a model before and after a relation referencing a datum graph was written.

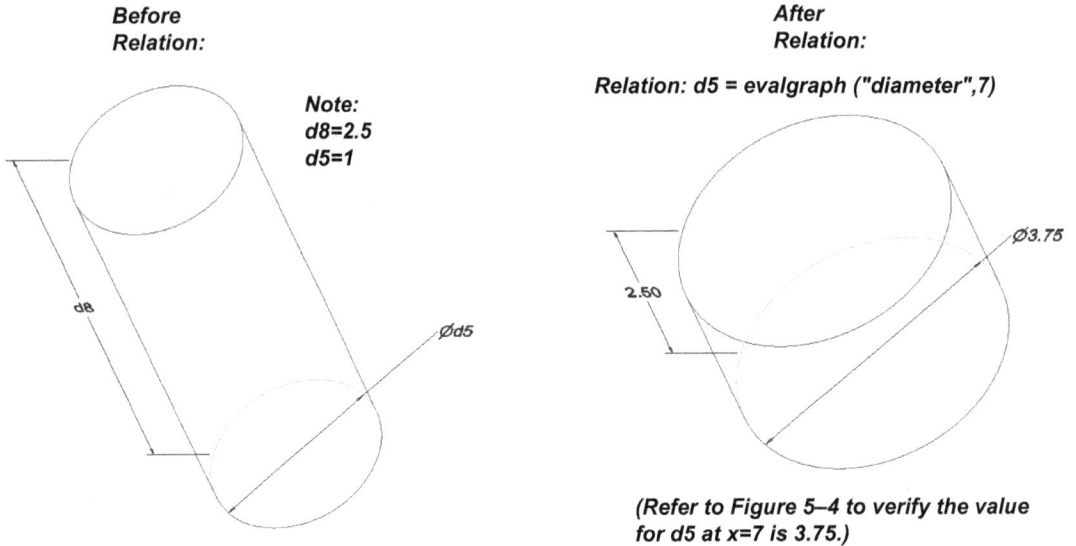

Before Relation:

After Relation:

Relation: d5 = evalgraph ("diameter",7)

Note:
d8=2.5
d5=1

Ød5

Ø3.75

2.50

d8

(Refer to Figure 5–4 to verify the value for d5 at x=7 is 3.75.)

Figure 5–3

The referenced datum graph is shown in Figure 5–4.

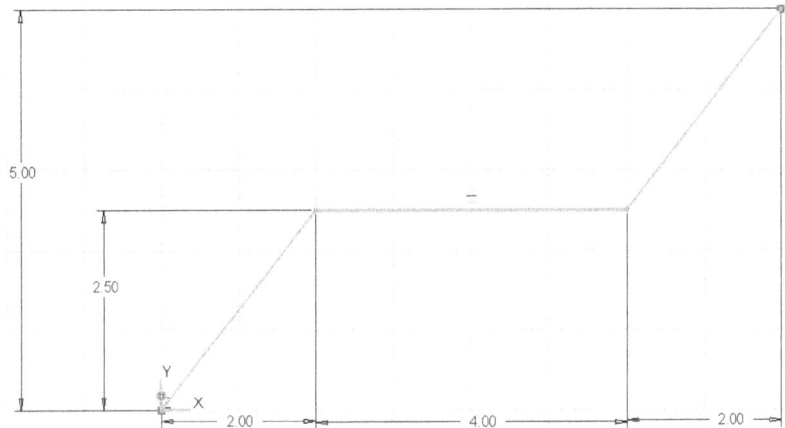

5.00

2.50

Y

X

2.00   4.00   2.00

Figure 5–4

A relation can also include functions that are performed on the evalgraph portion of the relation, d5 = evalgraph ("diameter",7) * 2, or it can use the trajpar parameter.

5.2 Comparing Datum Graphs

Using Behavioral Modeling, you can compare two graphs to determine the differences in distributions of one parameter along the other parameter.

For example, the duct shown in Figure 5–5 is created as a variable section sweep and uses the graph shown in Figure 5–6 to drive the geometry along the trajectory.

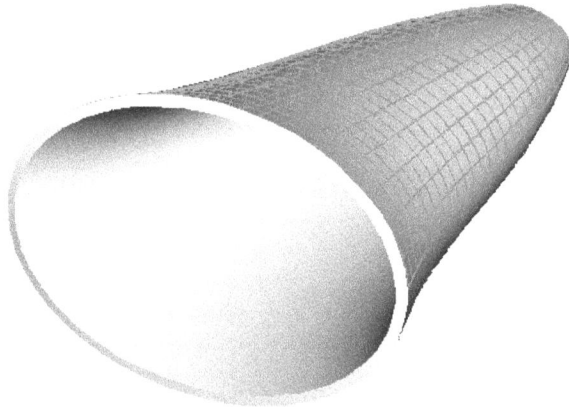

Figure 5–5

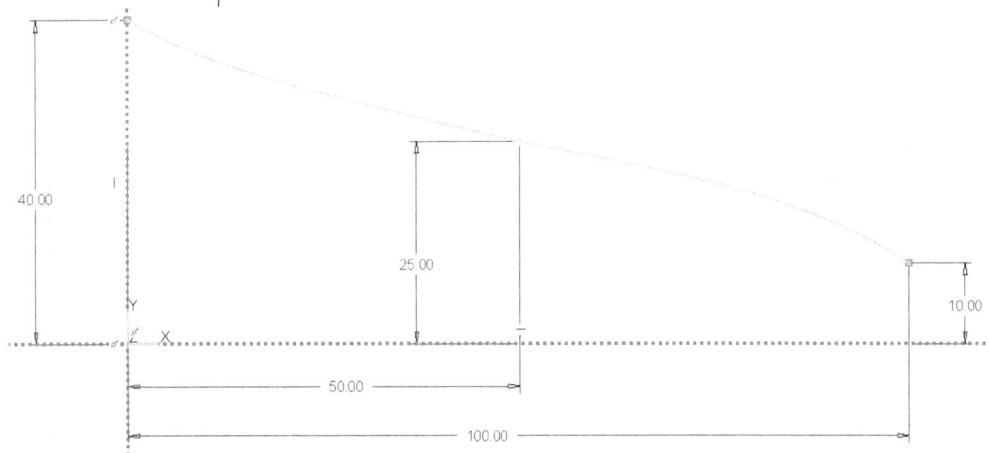

Figure 5–6

Using the compare graph functionality, you can compare the distribution of the first graph to a second graph. Once this is accomplished, you can use this parameter in Behavioral Modeler to optimize the difference and obtain the most desirable distribution.

For example, the first graph is compared with the graph shown in Figure 5–7 to obtain the graphs shown in Figure 5–8.

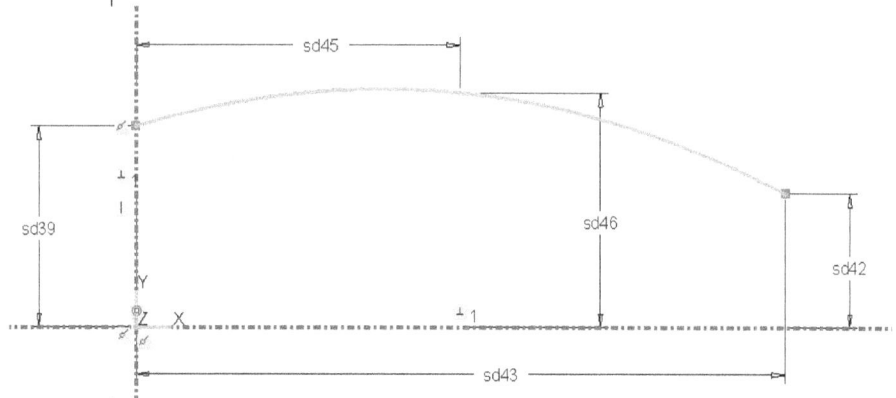

Figure 5–7

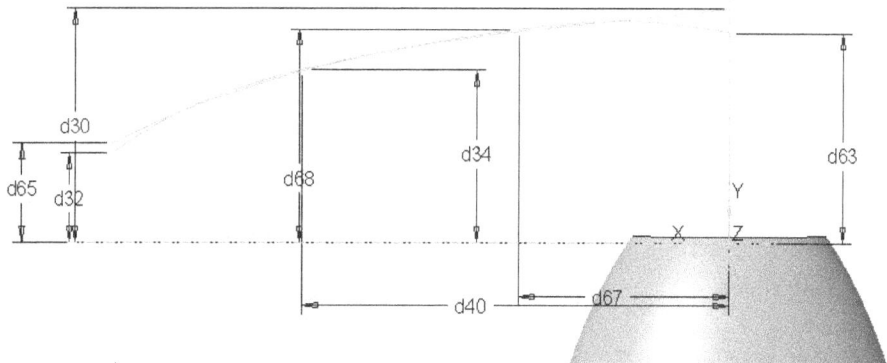

Figure 5–8

The geometry of the model updates to reflect the optimized results, as shown in Figure 5–9.

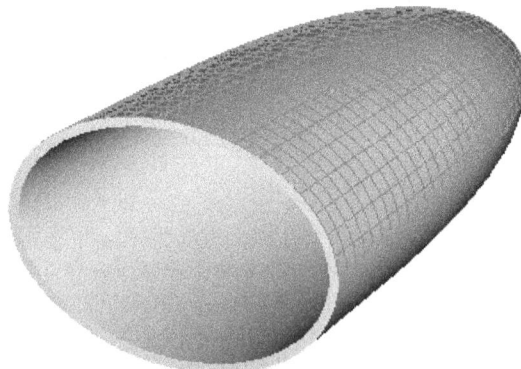

Figure 5–9

5.3 Graph Matching

Datum Graphs can be compared using one of four methods. These methods are described as follows:

Type	Based on Formula	What it measures
lone	L1norm of $f(t)-g(t)=\int|f(t)-g(t)|dt$ $-\infty<t<\infty$	Measures the area between $f(t)$ and $g(t)$.
ltwo	L2norm of $f(t)-g(t)=sqrt(\int(f(t)-g(t))^2 dt$ $-\infty<t<\infty$	Where $f(t)-g(t)$ is a measure of the error, larger values of the error have more weight on L2 norm.
linf	L∞ norm of $f(t)-g(t)=maxf(t)-g(t)$ $-\infty<t<\infty$	Measures the maximum error between two functions.
area	integral of $f(t)-g(t)=\int(f(t)-g(t))dt$ $-\infty<t<\infty$	Measures the signed area between $f(t)$ and $g(t)$.

The types are based on the concept of the norm of a vector that has been extended to functions. It assumes a function as an n-dimensional vector (where n= ∞).

How To: Match Two Datum Graph Features

1. Create both Datum Graph features in the model. The graphs must exist before the analysis feature that compares them.
2. Create a Relation analysis feature that compares the two graphs. The syntax used in the relation determines the comparison method. Add the relation using the following syntax:

   relation_name = comparegraphs("graph1", "graph2", "type", left_bound_1, right_bound_1, left_bound_2, right_bound_2)

   The relation components are described as follows:

Components	Description
relation_name	Name of the relation.
graph1	Name of first datum graph.
graph2	Name of second datum graph.
left_bound_1	Left boundaries of the first datum graph.
right_bound_1	Right boundaries of the first datum graph.
left_bound_2	Left boundaries of the second datum graph.
right_bound_2	Right boundaries of the second datum graph.
type	Comparison method (e.g., lone, ltwo, linf, area).

When adding the relation, you are permitted some flexibility. You can specify all seven components in the relation; however, you can also create the relation using either of the following methods:

- Specify the "names" only - Creo Parametric uses the lone comparison method and compares over the entire length of the graph. For example:

  RELATION=comparegraphs("GRAPH1", "GRAPH2")

- Specify the "names" and "type" only - Creo Parametric uses the specified comparison method over the entire length of the graph. For example:

  RELATION=comparegraphs("GRAPH1", "GRAPH2", "area")

3. As the final step in comparing the graphs, run an optimization study to minimize the difference.

Practice 5a

Using Graph Features

Practice Objective

- Review how a graph feature can be used to create geometry.

In this practice, you will use a graph feature to create some model geometry. The purpose of this practice is to review how graph features are used to create geometry.

Design Consideration

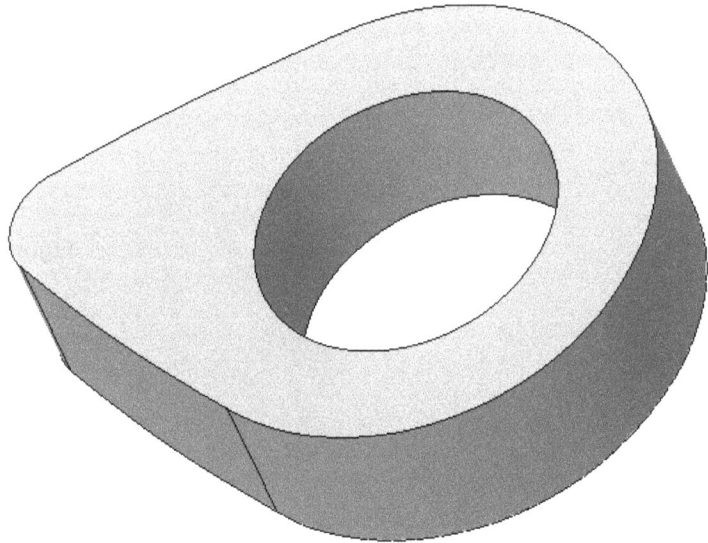

The completed model is shown in Figure 5–10.

Figure 5–10

The geometry of the cam will be created using a sweep with a variable section, where the section is controlled by a circular curve as shown in Figure 5–11 and the graph feature shown in Figure 5–12.

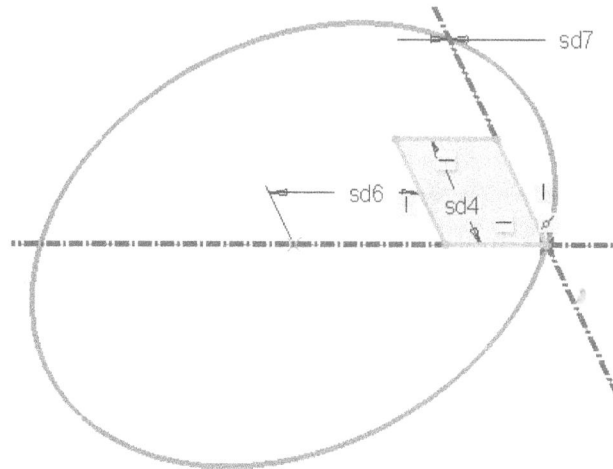

Figure 5–11

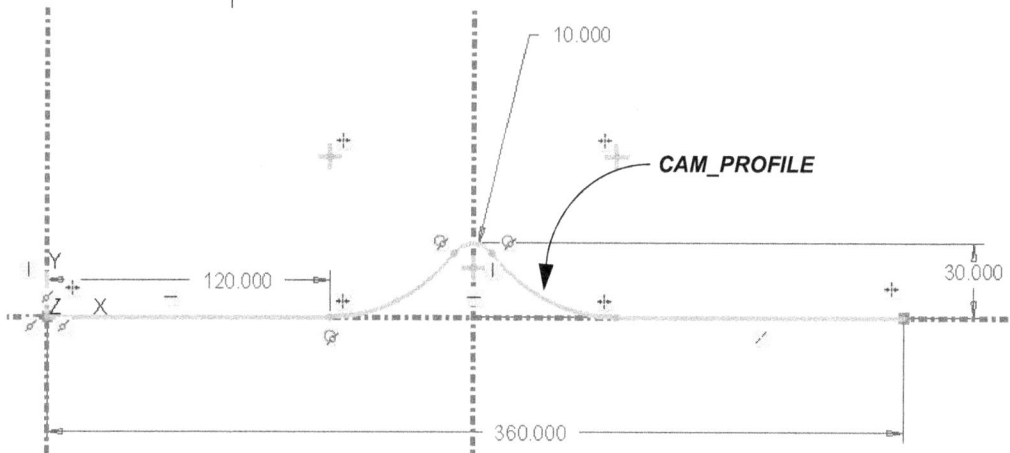

Figure 5–12

As the cam profile sweeps around the circular center, the width of the geometry is driven by the following relation:

Trajpar is a trajectory parameter that varies between 0 and 1 as the section is swept from the beginning to the end of the trajectory.

$$sd7 = evalgraph("cam\_profile", trajpar*360)/10$$

The trajpar*360 portion of the relation obtains corresponding values from the graph for X-coordinates of 0 to 360 degrees.

Task 1 - Open the cam_graph part and review the existing graph feature.

1. Set the working directory to *Using_Graph_Features*.

2. Open **cam_graph.prt**.

3. Set the model display as follows:

    - ⚘ *(Datum Display Filters)*: All On

    - ⤙ *(Spin Center)*: Off

    - ⚘ *(Display Style)*: ⬜ (Shading With Edges)

4. In the Model Tree, select **SWEEP_CIRCLE** and click

    ◉ (Show) in the mini toolbar. The part displays as shown in Figure 5–13.

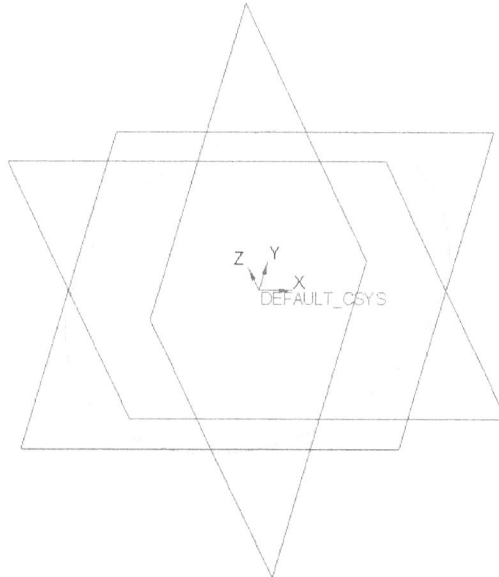

Figure 5–13

5. Toggle off the display of datum entities.

6. In the Model Tree, select **CAM_PROFILE** and select ✎ (Edit Definition) in the mini toolbar.

7. In the **REDEFINE** menu in the Menu Manager, click **Done** to edit the Section.

Note that the sketch below includes a coordinate system. The width of the cam is controlled by the height of the graph through the full 360 degree range.

8. Press <Enter> to accept the graph name. The sketch of the graph displays as shown in Figure 5–14.

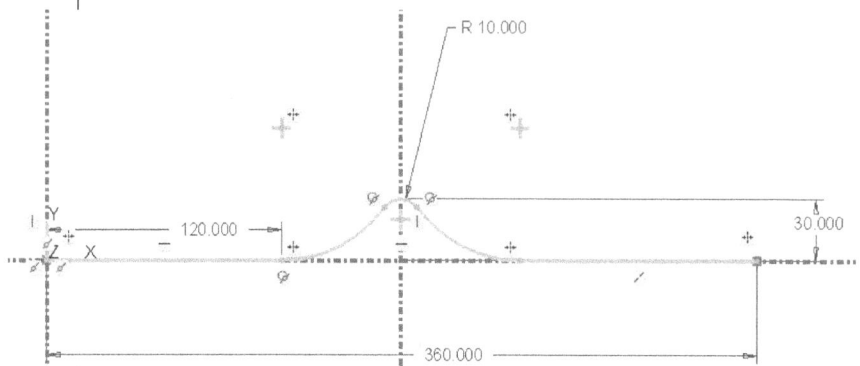

Figure 5–14

9. Click × (Cancel) to exit Sketcher.

10. Click **Yes** if prompted to confirm.

Task 2 - Create a sweep to establish the cam geometry.

---

1. In the *Model* tab of the ribbon, click 🧹 (Sweep).

2. Select the circular curve as the trajectory.

3. In the *Sweep* dashboard, click ⟋ (Variable Section) and then click ✎ (Create or Edit Section).

4. Create and dimension the sketch shown in Figure 5–15.

    • Initially, sketch the rectangle so it extends past the vertical centerline, then add the dimension and edit it to **0.00**.

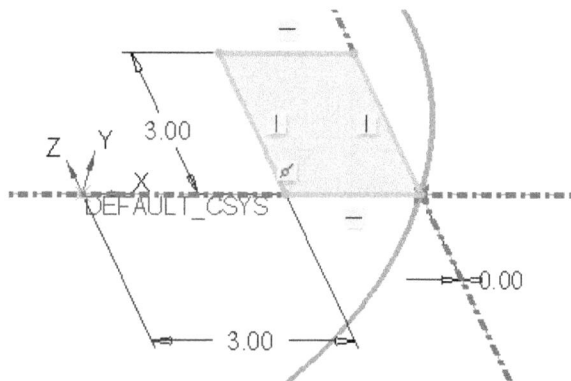

Figure 5–15

5. Select the *Tools* tab and click ⬚ (Switch Dimensions).

6. Take note of the symbol for the 0.00 dimension. In the image shown in Figure 5–16, the symbolic name is **sd7**.

   • Depending on how you created the sketch, the symbolic name may be different on your system. For the remaining steps, use the symbolic name from your sketch.

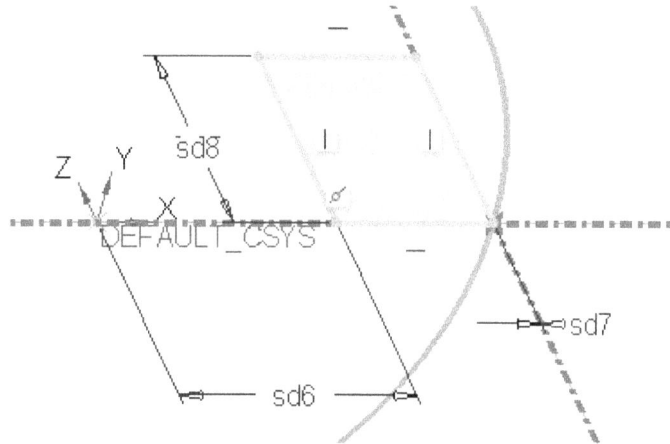

Figure 5–16

7. Ensure that the *Sketch* tab is active in the ribbon.

8. Click ✓ (OK) to complete the sketch.

9. Click ✓ (OK) to complete the sweep. The resulting geometry is shown in Figure 5–17.

The model is not yet controlled by the graph feature.

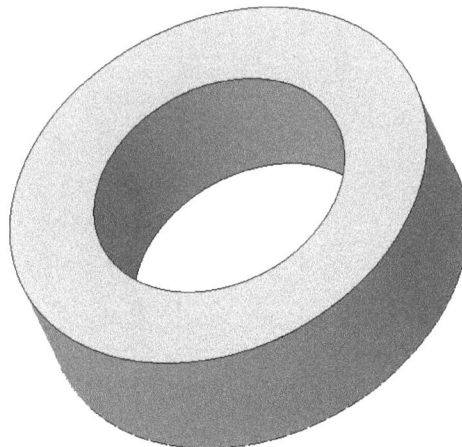

Figure 5–17

10. Select the *Tools* tab and click d= (Relations).

11. In the Relations dialog box, select **Section** from the Look In drop-down list.

12. Select **Sweep 1** in the Model Tree.

13. Select **sd7** (your number may differ), as shown in Figure 5–18.

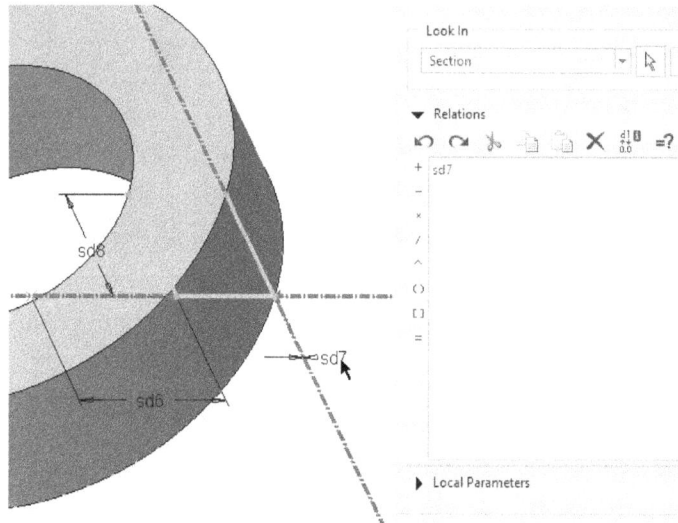

Figure 5–18

14. Type in the rest of the relation as shown in Figure 5–19.

The relation is created as a Section relation because it has to be regenerated as the sketch itself is regenerating.

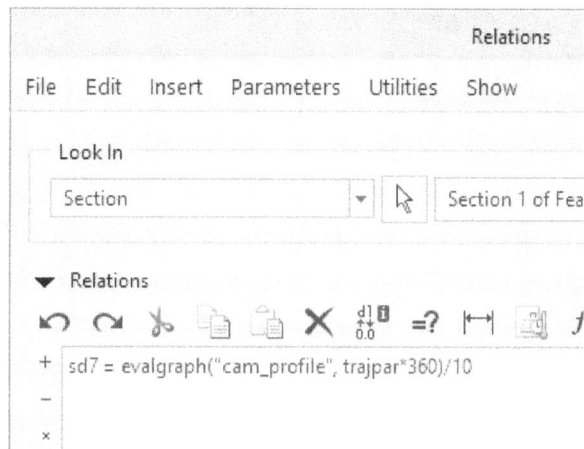

Figure 5–19

15. In the Relations dialog box, click ✓ (Verify) and click **OK**.

16. Click **OK** in the Relations dialog box.

17. If required, click ⬆ (Regenerate) in the Quick Access toolbar. The model updates as shown in Figure 5–20.

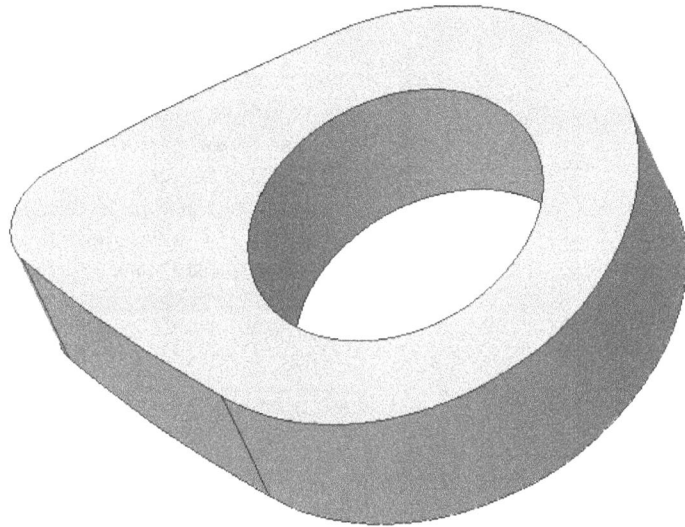

Figure 5–20

18. Close the part and erase it from memory.

Practice 5b

Comparing Graphs

Practice Objectives

- Compare two graphs.
- Optimize the distribution one along the other.

In this practice, you will use BMX functionality to compare two graphs to determine the difference in the distribution of one along the other, and to obtain the optimized distribution. The design intent requires you to change the cross-section of a duct according to a graph. To analyze it, you will compare the actual distribution of the cross-section along the length of the duct to the required distribution (defined by a graph). Once you have measured the difference, you will run the optimization study to minimize it.

Task 1 - Open the graph_matching part.

1. Set the working directory to *Comparing_Graphs*.

2. Open **graph_matching.prt**. The part displays as shown in Figure 5–21. The mesh has been added to help show the depth and shape of the model. The model represents a duct used to control air flow.

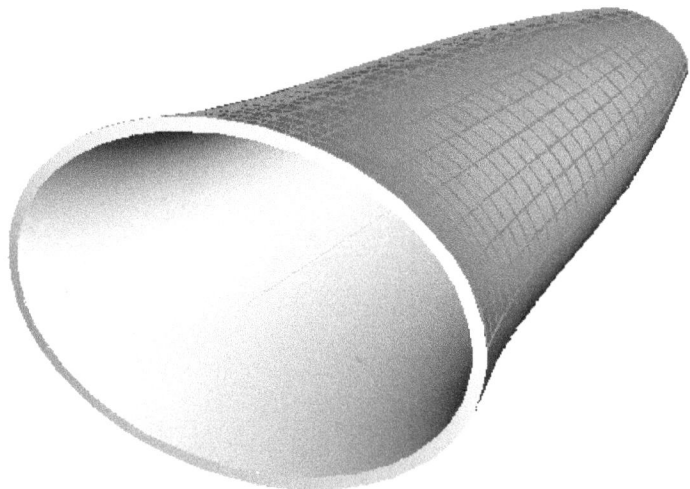

Figure 5–21

Design Consideration

The outside surface of the model is constructed as a variable section sweep with the section, as shown in Figure 5–22.

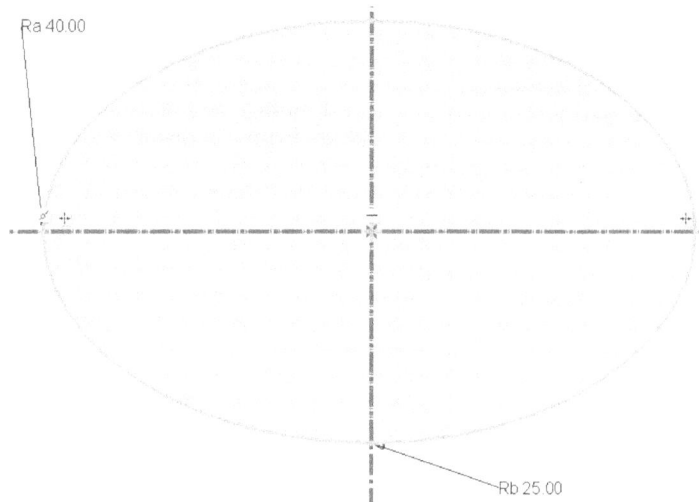

Ra 40.00

Rb 25.00

Figure 5–22

The minor radius (Rb) of the section is 0.625 of major radius (Ra. The Ra dimension (sd5) of the model is driven by a relation that references the graph feature, **GRAPH1**. This graph is shown in Figure 5–23.

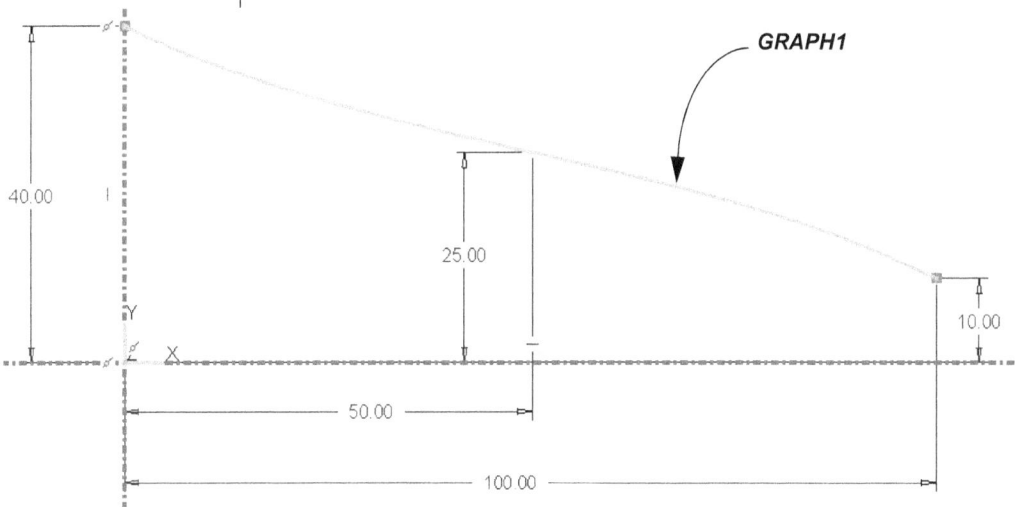

GRAPH1

40.00

25.00

10.00

50.00

100.00

Figure 5–23

The relations used for both Ra (**sd5**) and Rb (**sd6**) as the section moves along the trajectory are shown in Figure 5–24.

$$sd5 = evalgraph("graph1", trajpar*100)$$
$$sd6 = (sd5*.625)$$

Figure 5–24

The trajpar*100 portion of the relation obtains corresponding values from the graph for X-coordinates of 0 to 100.

To control the air flow through the model, the shape of the duct should be compared to the second graph feature, **GRAPH2**. This graph is shown in Figure 5–25.

Trajpar is a trajectory parameter that varies between 0 and 1 as the section is swept from the beginning to the end of the trajectory.

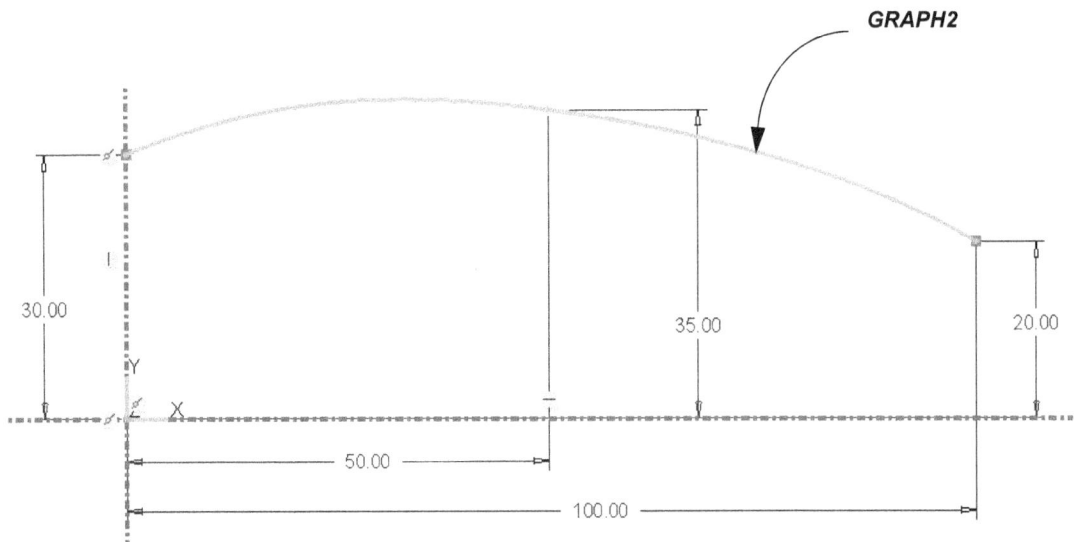

Figure 5–25

Task 2 - Create a relation analysis feature.

1. Set the model display as follows:

   - (Datum Display Filters): All Off
   - (Spin Center): Off
   - (Display Style): (Shading With Edges)

2. Select the *Analysis* tab.

3. Click ⅛ (Analysis) and create a **Relation** analysis feature and set the name to **COMPARE_GRAPH**.

4. In the ANALYSIS dialog box, click **Next**.

5. Enter the following relation in the relation editor:

   RELATION = comparegraphs("GRAPH1", "GRAPH2")

6. Click ✓ (Verify) to verify the relation and click **OK**.

7. Click **OK** in the Relations dialog box.

8. Click ✓ (OK) to complete the analysis feature.

Creo Parametric uses all values along the entire length of the graph.

Task 3 - Create an optimization study.

1. In the Design Study group, click ✐ (Feasibility/Optimization).

2. In the *Goal* area, select **Minimize** and **RELATION:COMPARE_GRAPH** from the drop-down lists.

3. In the *Design Variables* area, click **Add Dimensions**.

4. Orient the model to the saved **Back** view. Select **GRAPH1** in the Model Tree. Select the graph dimensions listed in the following table.

5. Repaint the main window. Select **GRAPH2** in the Model Tree. Select the graph dimensions listed in the following table. Refer to Figure 5–26 and Figure 5–27 to locate the dimensions.

	Dimension	Minimum	Maximum
Graph 1	d32	10	20
	d34	25	35
	d30	30	40
	d40	25	75
Graph 2	d65	10	20
	d68	25	35
	d63	30	40
	d67	25	75

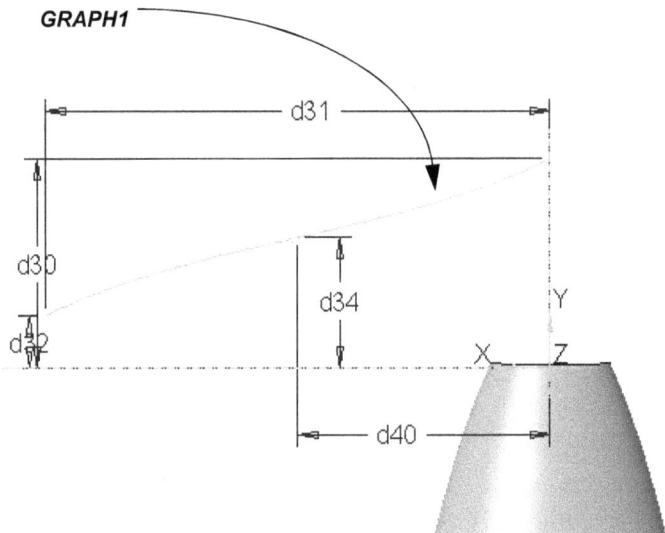

Figure 5–26

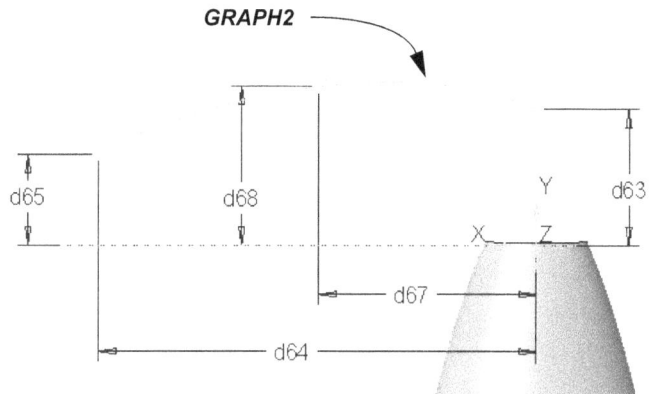

GRAPH2

Figure 5–27

6. Middle-click once you have selected all dimensions.

7. Modify the *Min* and *Max* values as shown in the table in Step 5.

8. In the Optimization/Feasibility dialog box, click **Options>Preferences** and ensure that the **Goal** option is selected in the Preferences dialog box.

9. In the Preferences dialog box, select the *Run* tab. Enter **10** in the *Convergence %* field.

10. Click **OK**. The Optimization/Feasibility dialog box displays as shown in Figure 5–28.

Your variables may display in a different order, depending on how you selected them.

Figure 5–28

11. Click **Compute**. An optimization graph displays in the GRAPH WINDOW, as shown in Figure 5–29.

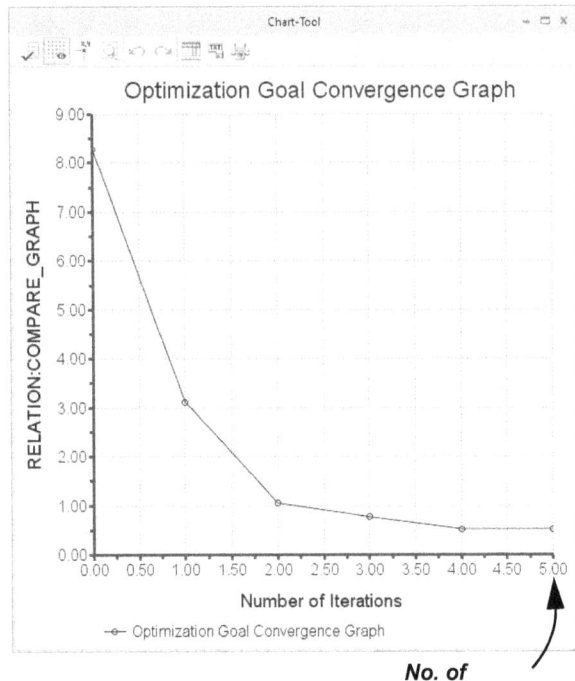

Figure 5–29

Note that the analysis is completed in five steps. The optimized graph displays on the model as shown in Figure 5–30. This graph shows the best fit result based on the optimization of the selected dimensions in **GRAPH1** and **GRAPH2**. The optimization was done using the lone type of comparison.

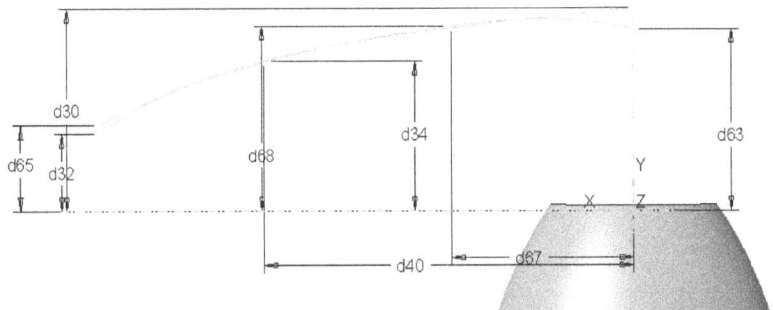

Figure 5–30

12. In the Optimization/Feasibility dialog box, click ⬛ (Save Design Study).

13. Click **Close** and **Confirm** to keep the model changes.

14. Reorient the model as shown in Figure 5–31.

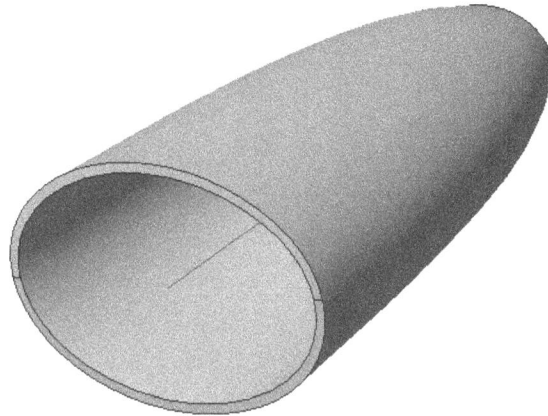

Figure 5–31

15. Close the part and erase it from memory.

Chapter

6

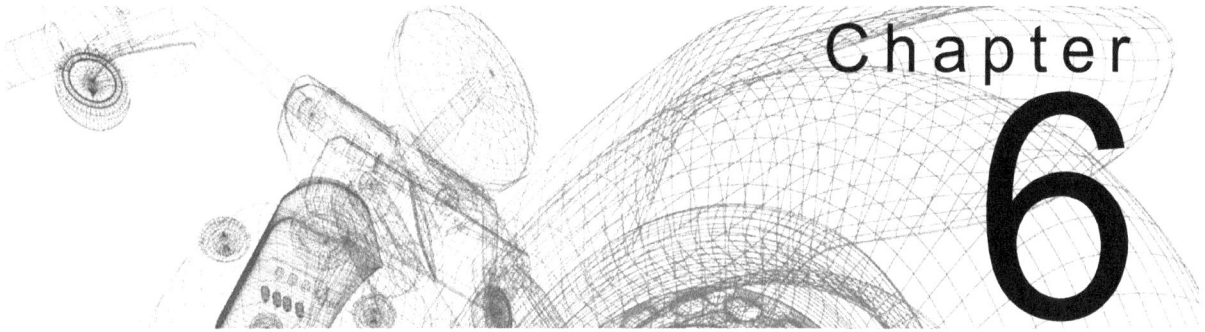

Excel Analysis

Microsoft Excel is an application that many companies use to perform calculations for their designs. BMX enables this design tool to be integrated directly into the Creo Parametric model so that the model conforms to the design requirements. This integration is accomplished using an Excel Analysis analysis feature that references an external Excel file to make calculations. Once an Excel spreadsheet is created, it can be easily referenced by multiple models.

Learning Objectives in This Chapter

- Create an Excel Analysis Feature.
- Recognize the difference between an Excel Analysis and an Excel Analysis Feature.
- Learn where Excel Files are stored.
- Review Config.pro options related to Excel Analyses.

6.1 Running Excel Analyses

Create an Excel Analysis Feature

How To: Create an Excel Analysis Feature

1. In the *Analysis* tab, in the Manage group, click ⅹ⁄ (Analysis). The ANALYSIS dialog box displays.
2. Type a new name for the analysis feature and press the <Enter> key.
3. In the *Type* area, select **Excel Analysis**.
4. Select an option from the *RegenRequest* area to define the regeneration option for the analysis feature.
5. Click **Next**. The Excel Analysis dialog box displays as shown in Figure 6–1.

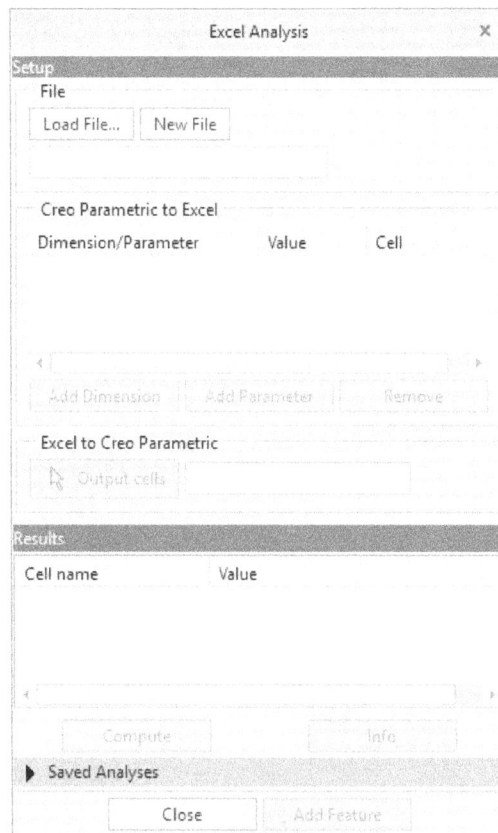

Figure 6–1

6. Click **Load File** and select the Excel file to be referenced. If an existing Excel file does not exist, click **New File** to create a new one. The Excel application displays in the background.

Use the window buttons on the bottom of the screen to switch between Excel and Creo Parametric if they do not activate automatically.

7. Select **Add Dimension** or **Add Parameter** to specify input settings (dimensions or parameters) for the feature. These input settings indicate the values that are referenced to the Excel data. As each input setting is selected, you must select a corresponding cell in the Excel spreadsheet. After each dimension or parameter and corresponding cell are selected, click **Done Sel**. Continue this procedure until all the required dimensions and parameters have been selected and cells have been assigned. Figure 6–2 shows an example of a list of Input Settings and their associated cell references.

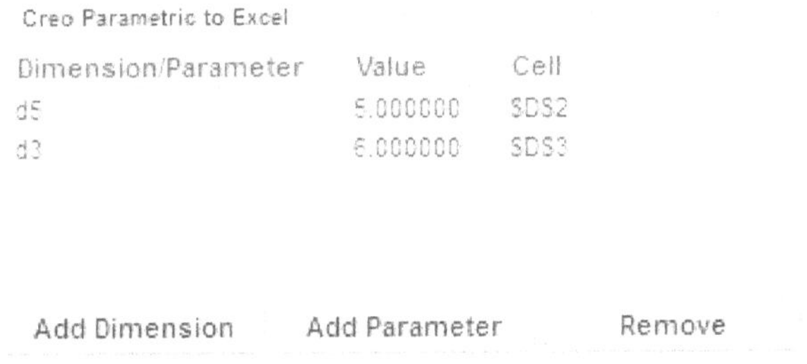

Creo Parametric to Excel

Dimension/Parameter	Value	Cell
d5	5.000000	D2
d3	6.000000	D3

Add Dimension   Add Parameter   Remove

Figure 6–2

8. Click **Output cells** and select the cell(s) to be recalculated based on the input settings. You can assign more than one cell as output cells. To select multiple cells, press and hold <Ctrl>. Once the cells are selected, click **Done Sel**. Figure 6–3 shows an example of a list of two Output cells.

9. Click **Compute** to run the analysis. The corresponding output values display in the *Results* area, as shown in Figure 6–3.

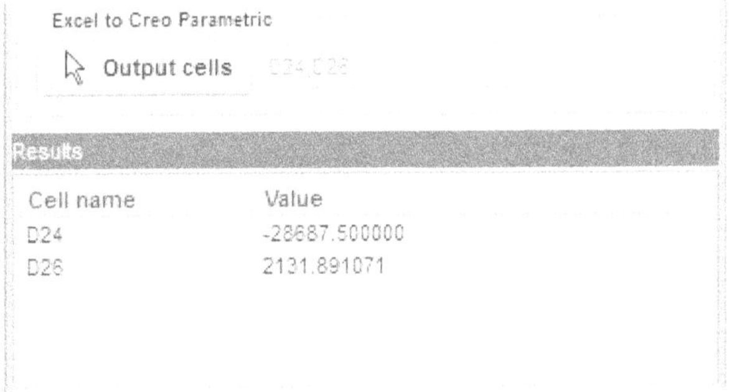

Once an analysis has been calculated, you can save the analysis using the options in the Saved Analysis area.

Excel to Creo Parametric

  Output cells   D24 D26

Results

Cell name	Value
D24	-28687.500000
D26	2131.891071

Figure 6–3

10. Click **Close** to complete the calculation. The ANALYSIS dialog box displays, enabling you to create feature parameters based on the results of the calculation.

The default name for a result parameter is XL_<rownumber>_<columnnumber>.

11. To add a result parameter to the model, select **YES** in the *Create* area and enter a *Param Name*. To prevent a result parameter from being added to the model, select **NO**. Figure 6–4 shows an example of result parameters added to the model.

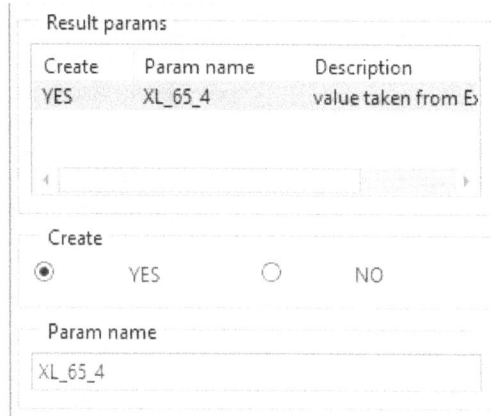

Result params

Create	Param name	Description
YES	XL_65_4	value taken from Ex

Create

⦿ YES   ○ NO

Param name

XL_65_4

Figure 6–4

12. Click ✔ (OK) to complete the Excel analysis feature.

Once used, the Excel file is not modified with the results of an analysis. The file remains a read-only file while it interacts with Creo Parametric. Each calculation is rerun based on the input settings and the equations in the cells of the file. This enables multiple analysis features and models to reference the same spreadsheet while ensuring accurate results.

Excel Analysis vs. Excel Analysis Feature

An Excel Analysis feature enables you to create parameters in the model. It also adds features to the feature list. If you are only interested in running an Excel analysis without creating a parameter, click ▦ (Excel Analysis) from the Custom group. This analysis is set up in the same way as an Excel Analysis analysis feature. You can save the results in the *Saved Analyses* area. At any time, you can use this analysis to create an Excel Analysis feature. To do this, retrieve the saved analysis, select **Add Feature** at the bottom of the Excel Analysis dialog box, and enter a name. Rerun the calculation to generate the parameters. In either situation (Excel analysis or Excel analysis feature), a change made to the model is reflected in both.

Excel File Locations

When an Excel analysis is saved or when an Excel analysis feature is created, the system saves the complete path to the .XLS file. When the saved analysis is retrieved, or when the model containing the Excel analysis feature is regenerated, Creo Parametric looks for the Excel file.

Creo Parametric searches the following locations for the Excel file:

- An Excel Analysis/Excel analysis feature's saved path.

- The working directory.

- The directory specified by the *excel_analysis_directory* config.pro option.

If the Excel file cannot be found, the feature remains at the last known values. You must redefine and set up the analysis again. As an alternative, you can close the Creo Parametric file, return the .XLS file to the correct directory and reopen the file. This prevents you from having to set up the analysis again.

Config.pro Options

The *bm_graph_tool* configuration option specifies how graphs generated by the various analyses and studies display. The options for this configuration file option are described as follows:

Option	Description
default	By default, the graphs displays in a regular Creo Parametric window.
excel_embedded	Displays the graphs in an Excel window that is embedded in the Creo Parametric screen.
excel_linked	Launches Excel and displays the graphs in Excel. Excel also shows the input and output values used to create the graphs. This Excel spreadsheet can be saved for documentation purposes or for reference.

Practice 6a

Excel Analysis

Practice Objectives

- Create Excel Analysis analysis features.
- Derive tables to find an appropriate design.

In this practice, you will analyze a model to calculate the total heat transfer in its current design. You will then perform a Multi-Objective Design Study to find configurations that meet several constraints.

The spreadsheet file is not modified through its use in Creo Parametric. This is a template containing the calculations that need to be performed to find the heat transfer. The values in this spreadsheet can be changed as required for other materials.

To calculate the total heat transfer, the practice references an Excel spreadsheet. This spreadsheet contains a number of predefined equations that are used to calculate heat transfer. This spreadsheet also contains a number of input values that are assigned from the model to perform calculations. During each analysis, the equations are used to generate the results.

The Datum Graph features in the model represent standard efficiency graphs that are available in many engineering references. Graph1 represents the efficiency values for R2c/R1=1, (Graph2 is R2c/R1=2, Graph3 is R2c/R1=3, Graph5 is R2c/R1=5). R2c is defined in the spreadsheet and R1 represents the inner diameter of a fin.

The Efficiency feature is an analysis feature that uses a relation to determine the correct efficiency value from the graphs.

Task 1 - Open the finned_cylinder.prt part.

1. Set the working directory to *Excel_Analysis*.

2. Open **finned_cylinder.prt**.

3. Set the model display as follows:

   - *(Datum Display Filters)*: All Off
   - *(Spin Center)*: Off
   - *(Display Style)*: (Shading With Edges)

4. The model consists of datum features, protrusions, and a pattern, as shown in Figure 6–5.

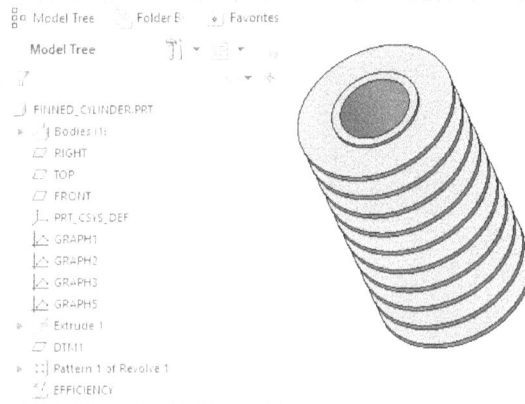

Figure 6–5

5. Examine the Model Tree and review the model.

6. In the Model Tree, right-click on **FINNED_CYLINDER.PRT** and select **Parameters**. Review the model parameters in the Parameters dialog box. The **NUMBER** parameter represents the number of fins on the model.

7. Close the Parameters dialog box.

___
Task 2 - Create a Relation analysis feature.
___

1. In the Model Tree, drag the **green line** marker so it sits immediately after the pattern.

2. Select the *Analysis* tab.

3. In the Manage group, click (Analysis).

4. Edit the name to **FINS_FOR_EXCEL** and press <Enter>.

5. Select **Relation**.

6. Click **Next**.

7. Enter the following relation in the relation editor. N is the dimensional symbol for the number of instances in the pattern.

   FINS=N

8. Click (Verify) to verify the relation and click **OK**.

9. Click **OK** in the Relations dialog box.

10. Click ✔ (OK) to complete the analysis feature.

Task 3 - Create an Excel Analysis feature.

---

1. In the Manage group, click ✕⁄ (Analysis).

2. Edit the name to **FIND_EFFICIENCY** and press <Enter>.

3. Select **Excel Analysis**.

4. Click **Next**.

5. Click **Load File** and double-click the **heat_transfer1.xls** file. Review the information; it is used to drive the analysis.

6. Select the Creo Parametric window to activate it, but do not close the Excel file.

7. In the *Creo Parametric to Excel* area, click **Add Dimension**.

8. Select both the fin at the bottom of the model and the internal protrusion, as shown in Figure 6–6.

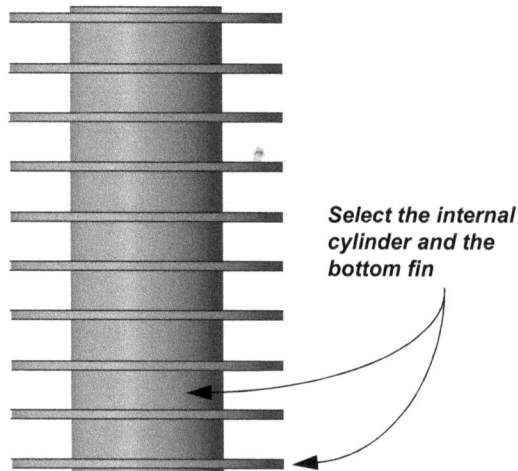

Select the internal cylinder and the bottom fin

Figure 6–6

If the dimensions display in numeric form, select the Tools tab and click ⁱ⁵⁄ (Switch Dimensions) to display their symbols.

9. Select the **THICKNESS** dimension. Excel should activate.

10. Select the cell **B4**. Activate the Creo Parametric window and click **Done Sel** from the **EXCEL SELECT** Menu Manager. The **Thickness** parameter updates in the *Input Settings* area with its *Value* and *Cell* location.

Use the window buttons on the bottom of the screen to switch between Excel and Creo Parametric if they do not activate automatically.

11. Select the **R1** dimension. Refer to Figure 6–7 to locate it. Excel should activate.

12. Select the cell **B5** and click **Done Sel**.

13. Select the **R2** dimension and select the cell **B6**. Click **Done Sel**.

14. Select the **HEIGHT** dimension and select the cell **B7**. Click **Done Sel** when finished.

15. Press the middle mouse button to stop selecting dimensions.

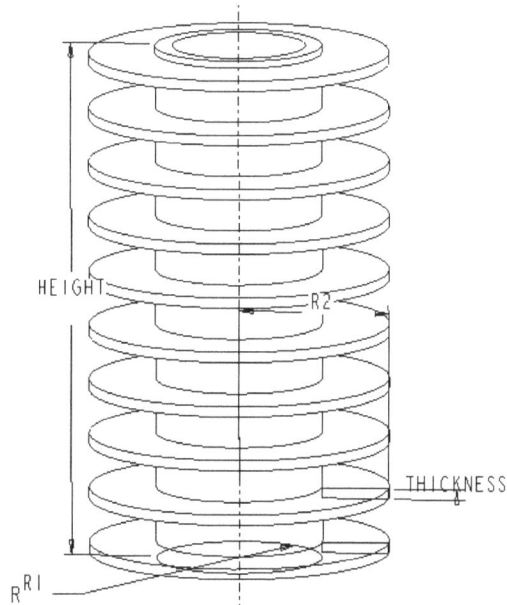

Figure 6–7

16. Click **Add Parameter**. Select **FINS:FINS_FOR_EXCEL** from the Parameters dialog box and click **OK**.

17. Select the cell **D8** and click **Done Sel**. The Input Settings are now complete.

18. In the *Output Settings* area, click **Output Cells**.

19. Select the cell **B54**, press and hold <Ctrl>, and select the cell **B57**. Click **Done Sel**. Review the *Output Cells* area and ensure that the cells **B54** and **B57** are the only output cells. If this is not the case, in the *Output Cells* area, reselect the two cells.

20. Click **Compute**. The results display in the *Results* area.

21. Click **Close** in the Excel Analysis dialog box.

22. Create both parameters. Set the Param name for the **XL_54_2** parameter to **XAXIS** and the cell name for the **XL_B57_2** parameter to **LINE**.

23. Click ✓ (OK) to complete the analysis feature.

Task 4 - Redefine the EFFICIENCY analysis feature.

---

1. In the Model Tree, right-click on the green marker and select **Exit Insert Mode**.

2. Click **Yes** to resume the EFFICIENCY analysis feature. This feature was provided to you to save you from entering extensive relations. However, the relations have errors because the reference feature is missing.

3. In the Model Tree, select **EFFICIENCY** and click ✎ (Edit Definition) in the mini toolbar.

4. Click **Next** to advance to the relations.

5. In the Relations dialog box, click **Edit>Find and Replace** to replace all instances of *1666* with **FIND_EFFICIENCY**.

6. Verify the relations and complete the redefinition of the feature.

Task 5 - Create an Excel Analysis feature to find the total heat transfer.

---

1. In the Manage group, click ×✓ (Analysis).

2. Edit the name to **TOTAL_HEAT_TX** and press <Enter>.

3. Select **Excel Analysis**.

4. Click **Next**.

5. Click **Load File** and select the **heat_transfer1.xls** file. Review the information; it is used to drive the analysis.

6. Select the Creo Parametric window to activate it.

7. In the *Input Settings* area, click **Add Dimension**.

8. Select the fin at the bottom of the model and the internal protrusion, as shown in Figure 6–8.

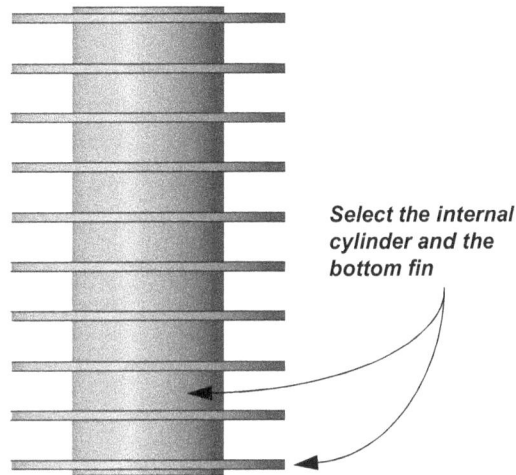

Select the internal cylinder and the bottom fin

Figure 6–8

9. Select the **THICKNESS** dimension and select the cell **B4**. Click **Done Sel**.

10. Select the **R1** dimension and select the cell **B5**. Click **Done Sel**.

11. Select the **R2** dimension and select the cell **B6**. Click **Done Sel**.

12. Select the **HEIGHT** dimension and select the cell **B7**. Click **Done Sel**.

13. Press the middle mouse button to stop selecting dimensions.

14. Select Add Parameter, add the **FINS:FINS_FOR_EXCEL** parameter and select the cell **D8**. Click **Done Sel**.

15. Add the **NF:EFFICIENCY** parameter and select the cell **D62**. Click **Done Sel**.

16. Set the cell **D65** as the only output cell.

17. Click **Compute**. The heat transfer value is **1108W**.

18. Click **Close** in the Excel Analysis dialog box.

19. Edit the name of the Result Parameter to **HEAT_W** and press <Enter>.

20. Click ✓ (OK) to complete the analysis feature.

21. Show the **HEAT_W** parameter in the Model Tree.

Task 6 - View design changes.

1. Modify the **THICKNESS** dimension to **6** and regenerate the model. Note that the heat transfer value increased from *1108W* to **1160W**.

2. Right-click on **FINNED_CYLINDER.PRT** in the Model Tree and select **Parameters**.

The NUMBER parameter is the number of fins in the model.

3. Modify the **NUMBER** parameter to **5**. Regenerate the model. Note that the heat transfer is reduced from *1160W* to **698W**.

4. Modify the **THICKNESS** dimension to **2. Regenerate if required.**

5. Modify the **NUMBER** parameter to **25**. Regenerate the model. Note that the heat transfer jumps from *698W* to **2356W**.

Task 7 - Create Analysis features to validate the design.

Design Consideration

In this task, you create Analysis features to check the following constraints:

- A maximum of 25 fins with minimum fin thickness of 2mm is permitted.

- The first and last fin must be at least 2mm from the ends.

- The minimum distance between the fins must be 4mm.

A Multi-Objective Design Study will be used. The **LEAD** dimension on the first fin is varied in the design study.

1. Create a measurement analysis feature named **DC_1** to measure the One-Sided Volume using **DTM1** as the reference. Orient the arrow as shown in Figure 6–9. Create the resulting parameter and set the name to **VOL**. Press <Enter> after typing the name.

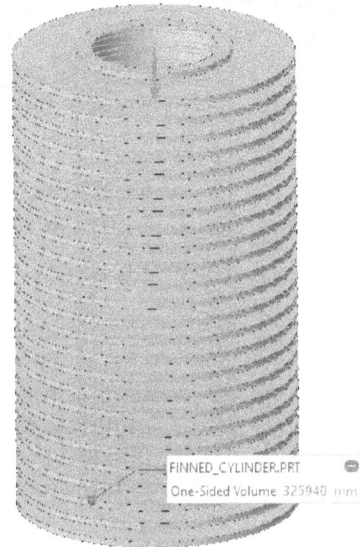

FINNED_CYLINDER.PRT
One-Sided Volume 325940 mm

Figure 6–9

2. Create a measurement analysis feature named **DC_2** to measure the distance between the first and second fins. The current distance value should be 4mm. Create the resulting parameter and set the name to **SPACING**.

Task 8 - Create a Model Analysis feature.

1. Create a measurement analysis feature named **MODEL** to calculate the Mass Properties. Create a parameter only for the Mass calculation and set the name to **MASS**.

Task 9 - Create a Multi-Objective Design Study.

1. In the Design Study group, expand ✎ (Feasibility/ Optimization) and select ⟡ (Multi-Objective Design Study).

2. Click ▭ (New Design Study) to create a new design study. Set the name to **STUDY5**.

3. Click ▢ (Setup Master Table) to create the Master Table.

4. Click **Select Goals**. The Parameter Selection dialog box displays. Select the following parameters:

   - **HEAT_W:TOTAL_HEAT_TX**
   - **VOL:DC1**
   - **SPACING:DC2**
   - **MASS:MODEL**

5. Click ⌗ (Add Dimension). Add the **THICKNESS** dimension. Enter **2** and **8** as the *Min* and *Max* values, respectively.

6. Click ⌗ (Add Parameter). Add the **NUMBER:FINNED_CYLINDER** parameter. Enter **1** and **25** as the *Min* and *Max* values, respectively.

7. Click **OK** in the Master Table dialog box.

   To capture an adequate range of design options, the study should be run to generate 200 experiments. **This can be time-consuming and can range anywhere between 5-30 minutes, depending on the hardware configuration.** This practice provides a complete design study (if you would like to run your study, please feel free to do so in your free time.)

8. Close the model and erase it from memory.

9. Open **finned_cylinder_final.prt**.

10. Select the *Analysis* tab.

11. In the Design Study group, expand ◈ (Feasibility/ Optimization) and select ⚙ (Multi-Objective Design Study).

12. Click ◷ (Open Design Study) and select **STUDY5**.

13. Click **OK**. The Multi-Objective Design Study dialog box displays as shown in Figure 6–10.

Figure 6–10

Task 10 - Derive a table to find all acceptable designs.

1. Click ☐ (Derive New Table) to derive a new table.

2. Select **Constraints** to derive the table and select **SPACING:DC_2**.

3. Enter **4.00** as the *minimum* value.

4. Set the table name to **VALID_DESIGNS**.

5. Click **OK**. There are now 133 valid design options.

Task 11 - View the Graph of this study.

1. Select **VALID_DESIGNS** in the *Table Tree* area of the dialog box.

2. Click ☐ (Graph Study).

*If the **LEAD** dimension was also varied, all designs in that **VOL:DC_1** were greater than **1414** are also filtered. Otherwise, **VOL:DC_1** does not need to be added.*

3. Select **MASS:MODEL** from the *Goals* area to define the X-axis for the graph.

4. Select the *Y-Axis* tab and select the **HEAT_W:TOTAL_HEAT_TX Goal** to define the Y-axis for the graph.

5. Click **Graph**. All design records appear on the graph, as shown in Figure 6–11.

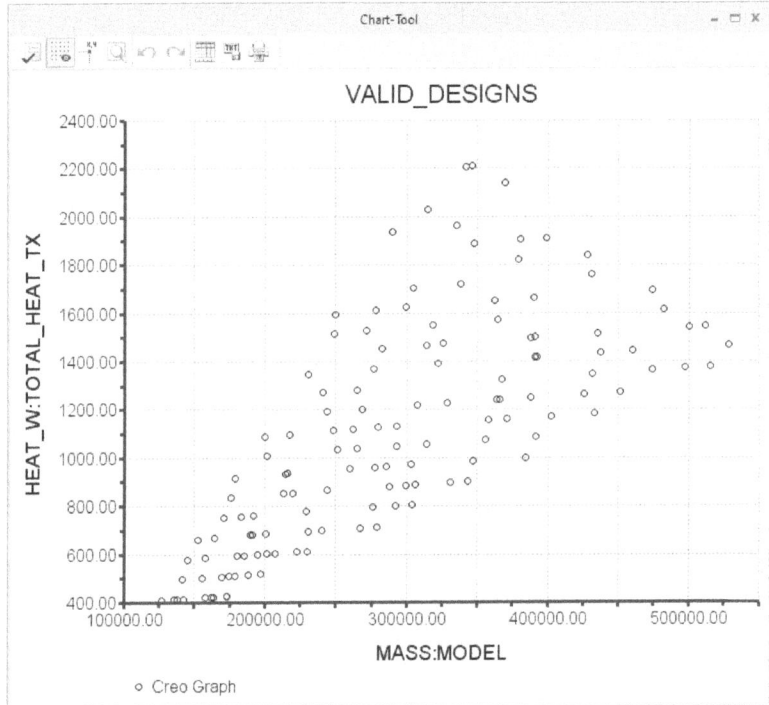

Figure 6–11

6. Close the Chart-Tool dialog box.

7. Close the Graph dialog box.

Task 12 - Derive the table to find the best design.

1. With **VALID_DESIGNS** is still selected in the Multi-Objective Design Study dialog box, click ⬚ (Derive New Table) to derive a new table.

2. Select **Pareto** to derive the table.

3. Select the **HEAT_W:TOTAL_HEAT_TX** parameter and set the option to **Maximize**.

4. Select the **MASS:MODEL** parameter and set the option to **Minimize**.

5. Set the table name to **MIN_MASS_MAX_HEAT**.

6. Click **OK**. Twenty designs now meet the criteria.

7. Select **MIN_MASS_MAX_HEAT** in the *Table Tree* area of the dialog box.

8. Click 🖳 (Graph Study).

9. Select **MASS:MODEL** from the *Goals* area to define the X-axis for the graph.

10. Select the *Y-Axis* tab and select the **HEAT_W:TOTAL_HEAT_TX Goal** to define the Y-axis for the graph.

11. Click **Graph**. The resulting graph displays as shown in Figure 6–12.

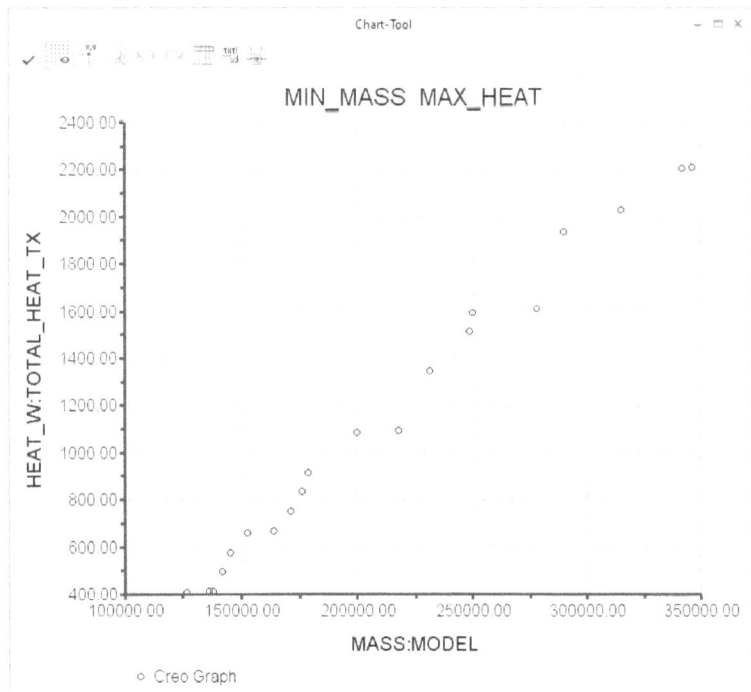

Figure 6–12

12. In the Model Tree, click ⫟ ▾ (Settings)>**Reset Tree Settings>Reset Tree Settings**.

13. Save the study and close the model.

Task 13 - (Optional) Derive additional tables.

Any of the 20 remaining models can be used as an appropriate design. Each design maximizes the heat transfer while minimizing the mass. In reaching these 20 models, one goal may be sacrificed at the expense of another. It is up to the designer to decide on a final design. If required, this table can be derived again to further refine the model.

Practice 6b

Cantilevered Plate

Practice Objectives

- Create an Excel Analysis analysis features.
- Derive tables to find an appropriate design.

In this practice, you will analyze and calculate the maximum bending stress and maximum deflection of a cantilevered plate. The plate is loaded at the free end with a single concentrated force (F=5 KN), as shown in Figure 6–13.

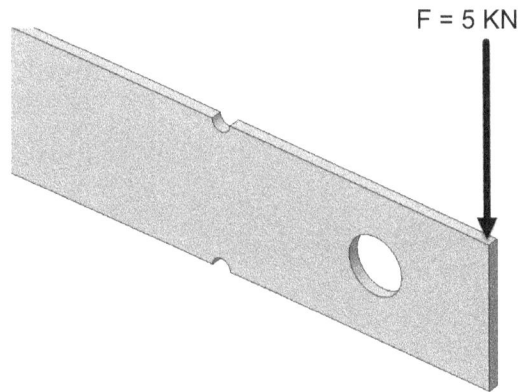

F = 5 KN

Figure 6–13

To calculate the maximum bending stress and maximum deflection, the practice references an Excel spreadsheet. This spreadsheet contains a number of predefined equations that calculate the maximum bending stress and the maximum deflection. It also contains a number of input values that are assigned to perform calculations during each analysis. You will also perform Multi-Objective Design Studies to find configurations that meet several of these constraints.

Task 1 - Open the notched_plate.prt part.

1. Set the working directory to *Cantilevered_Plate*.

2. Open **notched_plate.prt**.

3. Set the model display as follows:

   - *(Datum Display Filters)*: *(Point Display)* Only

   - *(Spin Center)*: Off

   - *(Display Style)*: (Shading With Edges)

Task 2 - Create a model analysis feature.

1. Select the *Analysis* tab.

2. Create an Mass Properties analysis feature to calculate the plate's mass and to locate the plate's center of mass. Set the analysis name to **MODEL_MASS**.

3. Click **Preview**.

4. Select the *Feature* tab.

5. Create only the mass analysis parameter and leave **MASS** as its name.

6. In the *Datums* area, enable the checkmark next to **PNT_COG**.

7. Click **OK**. The model displays as shown in Figure 6–14.

The model weight = 134.368 kg in SI units.
1 tonne = 1000kg
1lb = 0.4536kg

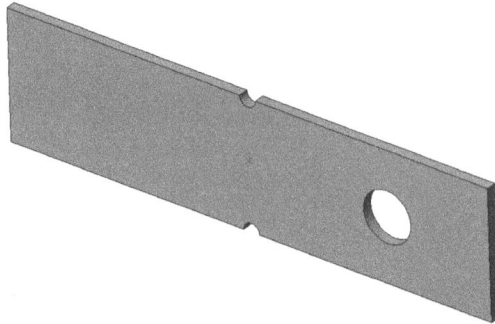

Figure 6–14

8. Display the mass parameter in the Model Tree.

Task 3 - Perform Sensitivity analyses.

Perform three sensitivity analyses that vary the **d25**, **d30** and **d37** dimensions within their permitted range. Which of these variables has the greatest effect on the plate's mass?

1. Select the *Tools* tab and click ⬚ (Switch Dimensions) to display dimensions using their symbols.

2. Select the *Analysis* tab.

3. Perform a sensitivity analysis for **d25** (width of the plate). Enter its variable range (*5mm to 6mm*) and plot it against the **MASS:MODEL_MASS** parameter. Note the change in plate mass.

4. Perform a sensitivity study for **d30** (radius of the notch). Enter the variable range *(5mm to 10mm)* and plot it against the **MASS:MODEL_MASS** parameter. Note the change in plate mass.

5. Perform a sensitivity study for **d37** (diameter of hole). Enter its variable range *(30mm to 35mm)* and plot it against the **MASS:MODEL_MASS** parameter. Note the change in plate mass.

Task 4 - Create an Excel Analysis Feature.

Design Consideration

The Excel analysis feature that is created in this task calculates the maximum bending stress and maximum deflection, then assigns these values as parameters that can be used in future studies.

1. Select the *Analysis* tab and in the Manage group, click (Analysis).

2. Set the name to **MOM_DEF and press <Enter>.**

3. Select **Excel Analysis** as the analysis feature **Type**.

4. Click **Next**.

5. Click **Load File** and select the **cantilevered_plate.xls** file.

6. Activate the Creo Parametric window and in the *Input Settings* area, click **Add Dimension**.

7. Select both the plate (**Extrude 1**) and the notch (**Extrude 2**) from the Model Tree to display the dimensions, as shown in Figure 6–15.

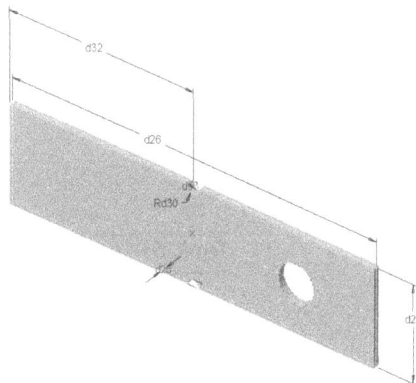

Figure 6–15

8. Select the **d30** dimension and select the cell **D2**. Click **Done Sel**.

9. Select the **d25** dimension and select the cell **D4**. Click **Done Sel**.

10. Click **Output Cells**, select the cell **D22**, press and hold <Ctrl> and select **D26**.

11. Click **Done Sel**.

12. Click **Compute**.

13. Close the Excel Analysis dialog box.

14. Create the two parameters for this analysis feature. Set the cell name for the **XL_22_4** parameter to **MOMENT** and the cell name for the **XL_26_4** parameter to **DEFLECTION**.

15. Click ✓ (OK) to complete the analysis feature.

16. Show the Excel parameters in the Model Tree. The Model Tree displays as shown in Figure 6–16.

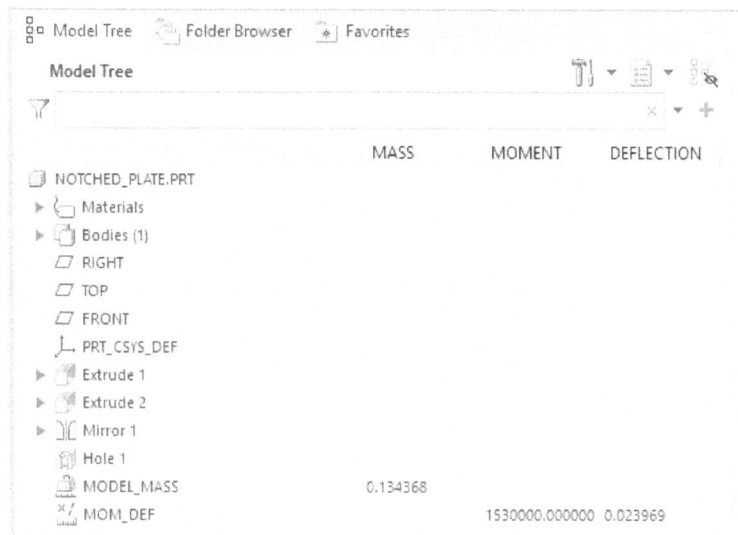

Figure 6–16

Task 5 - Create a Feasibility study.

This study analyzes the Feasibility of varying the **d25**, **d30**, and **d37** dimensions to maintain a mass of 110Kg.

d3 (5mm to 6mm)
d5 (5mm to 10mm)
d18 (30mm to 35mm)

1. Run a feasibility study with the **MASS:MODEL_MASS** design constraint set to **0.110** (110kg). Set the **d25**, **d30** and **d37** design variables using their predefined range (see the margin note located on the left). Graph the design constraints.

2. Study the effect of the weight reduction on parameters **MOMENT** and **DEFLECTION**. The values should update in the Model Tree.

3. Click **Undo** in the Optimization/Feasibility dialog box to undo the dimensional changes.

4. Click **Close** to close the dialog box.

The values may not immediately update in the Model Tree to reflect the Undo operation. To update the values, you can force a model regeneration using the Model Player.

Task 6 - Create a measure analysis feature and feasibility study that set the distance between the center of the model and center of mass at 1.5mm.

---

1. Create an ⤙ (Offset Coordinate System) datum point (**PNT0**) at the center of the model. Create the point offset from the default coordinate system 152.5; 0; 0.

2. Create a Measure analysis feature to measure the distance between **PNT_COG** and **PNT0**. Set the analysis name to **MEAS_1**. Set the distance parameter name to **DIST**. Do not create any datum features. The distance = 2.76183mm.

d39 (50mm to 150mm)
d32 (20mm to 180mm)

3. Run a feasibility study to determine values of the variable **d39** and **d32** when the design constraint **DIST:MEAS_1** is set to 1.5mm (see the margin note).

4. Click **Undo** in the Optimization/Feasibility dialog box to undo the dimensional changes.

5. Select **Close** to close the dialog box.

Task 7 - Create a Multi-Objective Design Study.

---

1. In the *Analysis* tab, expand ⬉ (Feasibility/Optimization) and select ⬙ (Multi-Objective Design Study).

2. Click ⬒ (New Design Study) to create a new design study. Set the name to **NOTCH**.

3. Click ☐ (Setup Master Table) to create the Master Table.

4. Click ⌐⊠⌐ (Add Dimension). Add the following design variables. Enter variable range as the *Min* and *Max* values.

   • hole diameter (d37) = 30mm to 35mm
   • plate thickness (d25) = 5mm to 6mm
   • notch radius (d30) = 5mm to 10mm
   • center of the hole to the free end of the plate (d39) = 50mm to 100mm
   • center of the notch to constrained end of the plate (d32) = 100mm to 170mm

5. Click **Select Goals**. The Parameter Selection dialog box displays. Select the following parameters:

   • **MASS:MODEL_MASS**
   • **MOMENT:MOM_DEF**
   • **DEFLECTION:MOM_DEF**
   • **DIST:MEAS_1**

6. Click **OK** to close the Master Table dialog box.

7. Click ! (Compute Master Table) to run the study.

8. Enter **200** as the number of experiments to run.

Task 8 - Derive tables from the results.

---

1. Derive a table to minimize the plate deflection. Set the table name to **MIN_DEFLECTION**.

2. Select the record for the **MIN_DEFLECTION** table and click **Record>Show Model**. Note the design variable values required to achieve the minimum deflection.

3. Derive another table to minimize the plate deflection and the **DIST** parameter. Set the table name to **MIN_DEFLECTION_DIST**.

4. Graph this study to view the effects of each design variable on the minimum deflection.

5. Derive a table in the **MIN_DEFLECTION_DIST** table and minimize only the deflection. Set the table name to **MIN_DEFLECTION_D1**.

6. Select the record for the **MIN_DEFLECTION_D1** table and click **Record>Show Model**. Note the design variable values required to achieve the minimum deflection.

7. Save the study.

8. In the Model Tree, click 🔧 ˅ (Settings)>**Reset Tree Settings**>**Reset Tree Settings**.

9. Close and erase the model.

This application of BMX used a spreadsheet to make multiple calculations for the maximum bending stress and deflection. These could also have been done using Creo Simulate; however, this application enabled you to easily set up the same criteria without using an FEA solution. When changes are made to the model, the maximum bending stress and deflection are easily recalculated.

Motion Analysis Features

In previous chapters, analyses were performed on static models. It is often required to evaluate parameters based on the entire range of motion for an assembly. This type of analysis can only be performed in the Assembly mode using a Motion Analysis analysis feature in the top-level assembly. The values of the analysis feature parameters are calculated at each frame throughout the motion definition.

Learning Objective in This Chapter

* Create a Motion analysis feature.

7.1 Motion Analysis Features

To run a Motion Analysis, an assembly must be created using Mechanism connections and drivers to define the required motion. Creating a mechanism in Creo Parametric requires the use of the Mechanism Design Extension (MDX).

For example, you can use MDX to set up connections and drivers, and use BMX to study the effects on the models center of gravity as it moves through its full range of motion. You can also use BMX to study the clearance of the moving assembly relative to other components. Figure 7–1 shows an example of components in a tractor assembly.

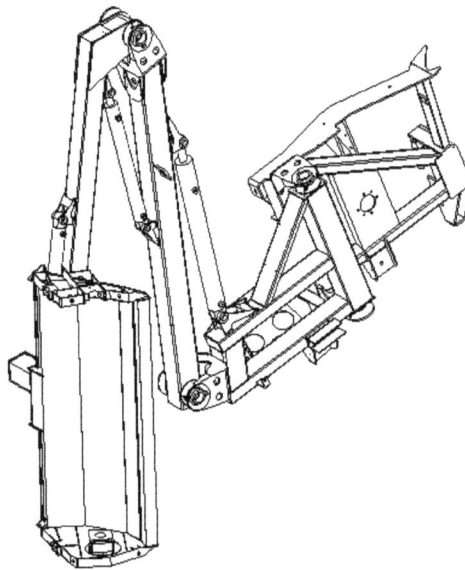

Figure 7–1

If you have a Mechanism Dynamics Option (MDO) license, you can study the effect that applied forces have on the motion of your mechanism. For example, you can set up connections and drivers and modeling entities that are not available in the kinematics-based version of Mechanism Design. These include springs, dampers, force/torque loads, and gravity. Using MDO and BMX, you can study the effects on the kinematic connections reaction force as it moves through its full range of motion.

Creating a Motion Analysis Feature

How To: Create a Motion Analysis Feature

1. In the *Analysis* tab, in the Manage group, click ⚙ (Analysis). The ANALYSIS dialog box displays.
2. Type a new name for the analysis feature and press <Enter>.
3. Select **Motion Analysis** in the *Type* area.
4. Select a *RegenRequest* option to define the regeneration option for the analysis feature.
5. Click **Next**. The Motion Analysis dialog box displays as shown in Figure 7–2.

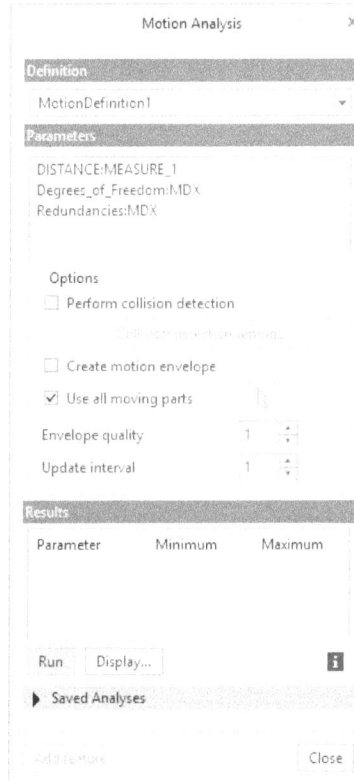

Figure 7–2

6. Select the parameters to evaluate. The parameters must exist in the top-level assembly.
7. To check for collision between components, enable the **Perform collision detection** option.
8. To create a motion envelope, select **Create motion envelope** in the *Options* area of the dialog box. A motion envelope generates a surface quilt that defines the entire range of motion. If the motion envelope is created, you can use all moving parts (select **Use all moving parts**) or select the parts that you want to include in the envelope.

Frames are the number of computation points used in the motion definition.

9. If required, specify the *Envelope quality*. The higher the number, the longer it takes to create.
10. Specify the update interval. The update interval refers to how often the display is recalculated.
11. Click **Run**. The predefined motion begins. A graph displays showing the feature parameter value through each frame.
12. When finished, the *Results* area lists the maximum and minimum value for each of the selected feature parameters along with the time at which they occurred. If a motion envelope was created, it temporarily displays on the screen as a surface.
13. Click **Close**.
14. To add a result parameter, select **YES** in the *Create* area and enter a *Param Name*. To prevent a result parameter from being added to the model, select **NO**. Figure 7–3 shows an example of result params being included and excluded.

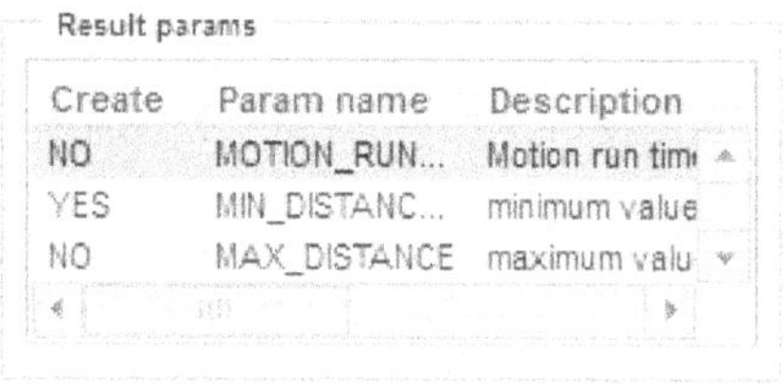

Result params

Create	Param name	Description
NO	MOTION_RUN...	Motion run tim
YES	MIN_DISTANC...	minimum value
NO	MAX_DISTANCE	maximum valu

Figure 7–3

*Next became active when **Create motion envelope** was selected in an earlier step.*

15. To control the motion envelope's display, click **Next** to advance to the result datum element. To add a result datum (motion envelope), select **YES** in the *Create* area and enter a *Datum Name*. To prevent a result datum from being added to the model, select **NO**. Figure 7–4 shows an example of result datum being added to the model. This is only available if the motion envelope was generated.

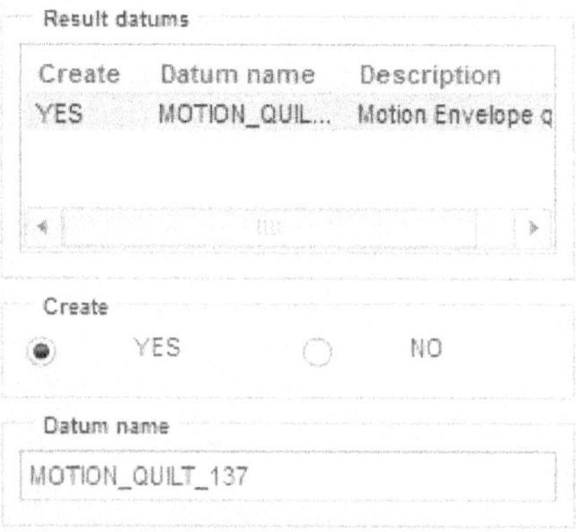

Result datums

Create	Datum name	Description
YES	MOTION_QUIL...	Motion Envelope q

Create

⦿ YES   ○ NO

Datum name

MOTION_QUILT_137

Figure 7–4

16. Click **Close** to complete the feature.

Practice 7a

Motion Analysis

Practice Objective

- Create and run a motion analysis.

In this practice, you will apply behavioral modeling techniques to analyze a doorknob assembly. The following constraints have been set for the assembly:

- The handle of the doorknob is returned to its original position using a spring. The minimum distance required for the compressed spring is 0.2 inch.

- In order for the door to open, the slider must clear the plate.

Task 1 - Open the doorknob assembly.

1. Set the working directory to *Motion_Analysis*.

2. Open **doorknob.asm**.

3. Set the model display as follows:

    - ⚡ *(Datum Display Filters)*: All Off

    - ✣ *(Spin Center)*: Off

    - ⬛ *(Display Style)*: ⬜ (Shading With Edges)

    The model displays as shown in Figure 7–5.

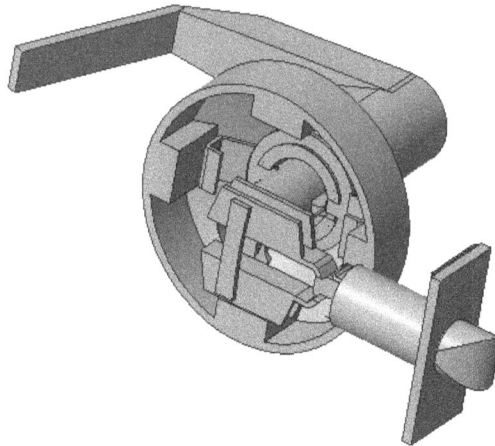

Figure 7–5

4. Assembly features should be displayed in the Model Tree by default. If features are not displayed in the Model Tree, expand 🔧 ▾ (Settings) and click **Tree Filters>Features**. This enables the display of all of the analysis features that are added to the assembly.

Task 2 - Load the MotionDefinition1.pbk file to show an animation of a predefined doorknob movement.

Design Consideration

The Mechanism Design Extension (MDX) of Creo Parametric enables you to simulate kinematic motion in your assemblies. You can drag the mechanisms through their range of motion, or create drivers to define predetermined animations. These motions permit you to examine the behavior of the mechanism. You can use the mechanism in the Behavioral Modeling Extension (BMX) to evaluate important parameters throughout its range of motion.

1. Select the *Applications* tab and click ⚙ (Mechanism). The connections are **Fixed**, **Pin**, **Slider** and **Cam**. The model driver profile type is **Cosine**.

2. In the Mechanism Tree, select **PLAYBACKS** and click ▶ (Play) in the mini toolbar. The Playbacks dialog box opens.

3. In the Playbacks dialog box, click 📂 (Restore Result Set) and open **MotionDefinition1.pbk**. The Playbacks dialog box updates as shown in Figure 7–6.

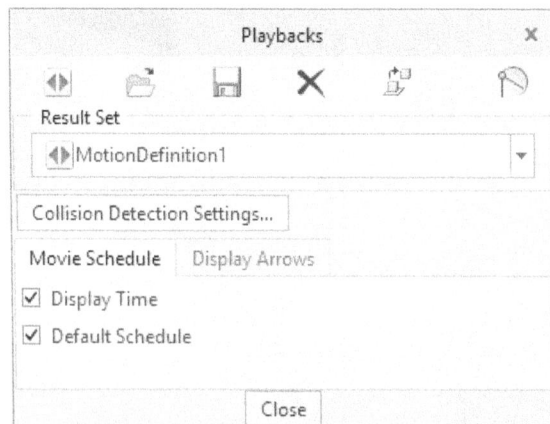

Figure 7–6

4. Click ⏮ (Play Result Set). The Animate dialog box displays as shown in Figure 7–7.

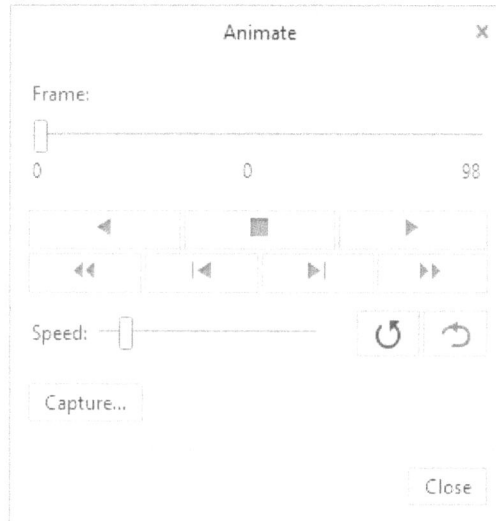

Figure 7–7

5. Click ▶ (Play) to run the animated motion of the doorknob assembly. Note that the slider does not move past the plate during the animation, as shown in Figure 7–8. The slider must clear the plate for the door to open. This is used as a design requirement later in this practice.

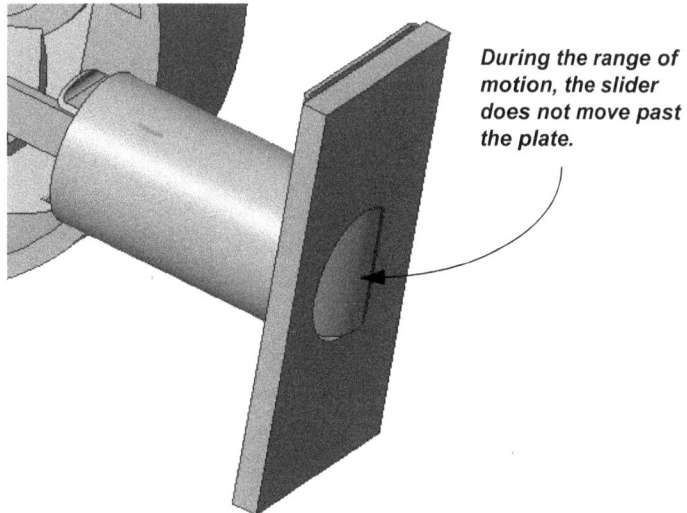

During the range of motion, the slider does not move past the plate.

Figure 7–8

6. Click ◄◄ (Reset to Beginning) to rewind the animation to the beginning once you have reviewed it.

7. Click **Close** to close the dialog box.

8. Click **Close** to close the Playbacks dialog box.

9. In the *Mechanism* tab, click ☒ (Close).

Task 3 - Create a Measure analysis feature.

---

1. Select the *View* tab.

2. In the Model Display group, click ▣ (Exploded View).

3. Select the *Analysis* tab.

4. In the Measure group, expand ⟋ (Measure) and select ⌐. (Distance).

5. Press and hold <Ctrl> and select the front surface of the **stop.prt** and cut surface of the **slide1.prt**,as shown in Figure 7–9.

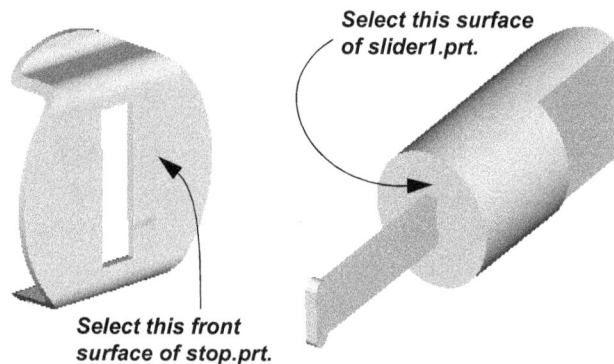

Select this surface of slider1.prt.

Select this front surface of stop.prt.

Figure 7–9

6. The distance between these surfaces displays in the Results window. The *Distance* is approximately **0.5**.

7. Click 🖫▾ (Save) and ensure that **Make Feature** is selected.

8. Edit the name to **MEASURE_1** and click **OK**.

9. Click **Confirm** when prompted to unexplode the view.

10. Select the *Feature* tab.

11. Accept **DISTANCE** as the name of the **Distance** parameter.

12. Click **Close**.

Task 4 - Create a Motion analysis feature to measure the minimum distance.

---

1. In the Manage group, click [×f] (Analysis).

2. Edit the name to **MOTION_1** and press <Enter>.

3. Select **Motion Analysis**.

4. Click **Next**. The Motion Analysis dialog box displays as shown in Figure 7–10.

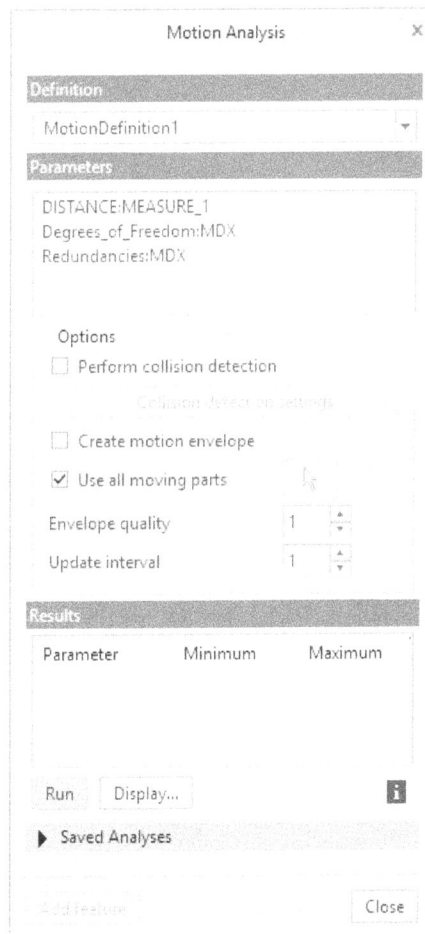

Figure 7–10

5. In the *Parameters* area, select **DISTANCE: MEASURE_1**.

6. Click **Run**. The distance against time graph displays as shown in Figure 7–11.

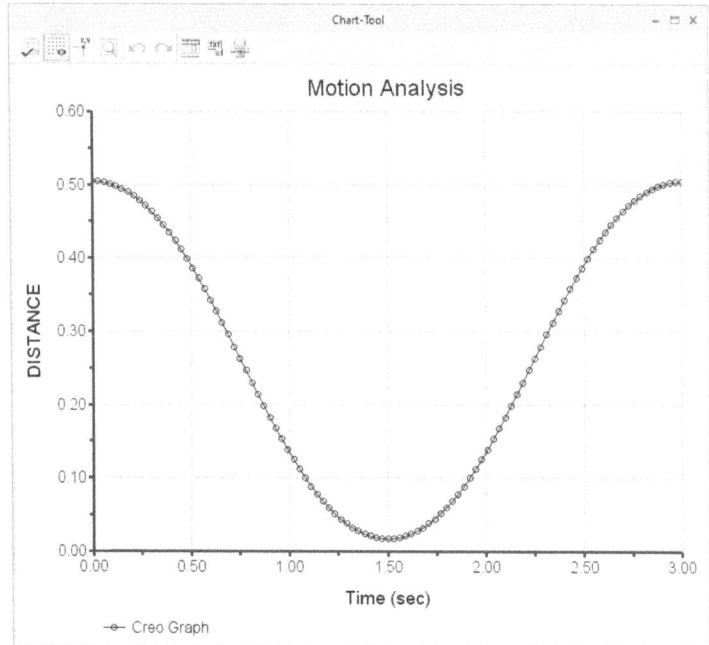

Figure 7–11

The graph in Figure 7–11 shows that the doorknob handle moves to open the door (its extreme position). The minimum distance between front surface of the **stop.prt** and cut surface of the **slide1.prt** is **0.016632 at T = 1.5sec**. You can see the same result in the Results window of the Motion Analysis dialog box, as shown in Figure 7–12.

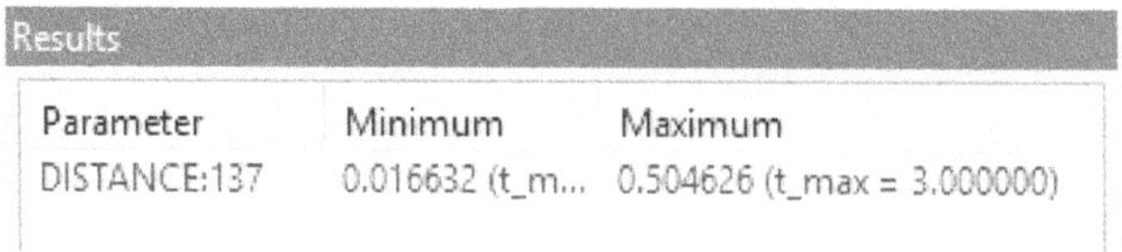

Parameter	Minimum	Maximum
DISTANCE:137	0.016632 (t_m...	0.504626 (t_max = 3.000000)

Figure 7–12

7. Close the Motion Analysis dialog box.

8. Set the **Create** cell for the **MIN_DISTANCE** parameter to **YES**.

9. Set the **Create** cell for all other parameters to **NO**.

10. Click ✔ (OK) to complete the analysis feature.

Task 5 - Create a sensitivity study.

Design Consideration

The handle of the doorknob is returned to its original position using a spring. The spring is placed inside of the slider chamber (**CYL1_LATCH.PRT**). The spring is compressed when the handle is moved to open the door. The minimum distance required for the compressed spring is 0.2 inch. In this task, you will vary the design variable **d13** of cut **id 149** in **SLIDER1.PRT** to provide insight into an ideal start for the **d13** when running a feasibility study.

The minimum distance is currently 0.016632 inch, as obtained in the motion analysis.

1. In the Design Study group, click ⬚ (Sensitivity Analysis). The Sensitivity dialog box displays as shown in Figure 7–13.

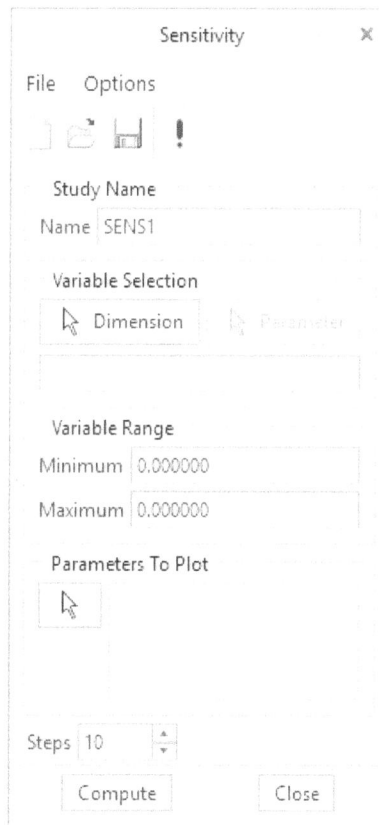

Figure 7–13

2. Maintain the default name for the analysis.

3. Explode the assembly.

4. Click **Dimension** and select dimension **.875** from cut **id 149** in **SLIDER1.PRT**, as shown in Figure 7–14.

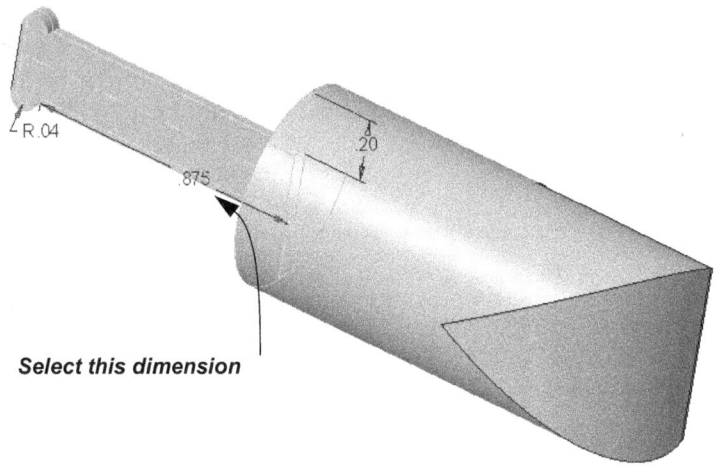

R .04

.875

20

Select this dimension

Figure 7–14

5. Enter **0.875** and **1.1** as the min and max *Variable Ranges*, respectively.

6. Press the middle mouse button to stop selecting dimensions.

7. In the *Parameters To Plot* area, click ⌨ (Select) and select **MIN_DISTANCE:MOTION_1**.

8. Click **Compute** to run the analysis. During the analysis, the graph shown in Figure 7–15 displays.

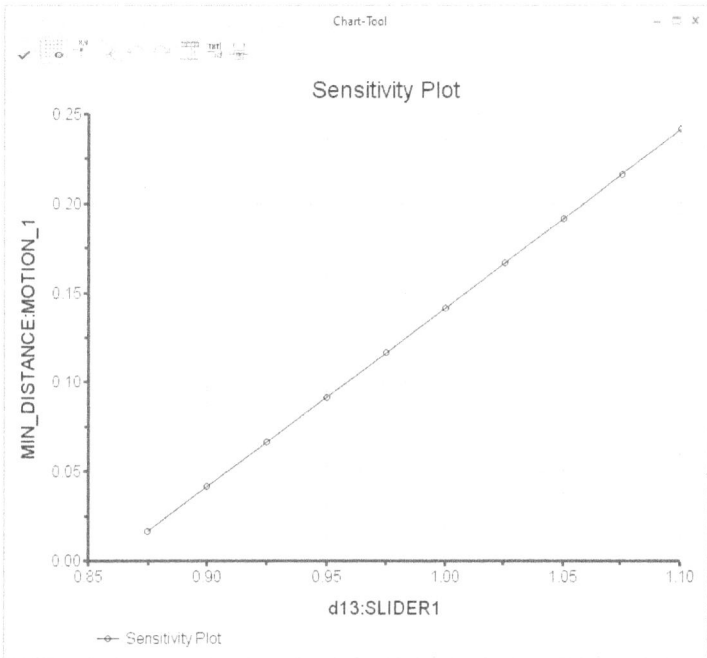

Figure 7–15

Note that the required compression distance of 0.2 (Y-axis of the graph) is within the specified range.

By saving this design study, you can recall and rerun without having to set it up again.

9. Save the design study.

10. Close the Sensitivity dialog box.

Task 6 - Create a Feasibility study.

In this task, you adjust the design variable (0.875) to meet the required compressed distance (design constraint).

1. In the Design Study group, click ✎ (Feasibility/Optimization). The Feasibility/Optimization dialog box displays.

2. Select **Feasibility**.

3. In the *Design Constraints* area, click **Add**.

4. Select the **MIN_DISTANCE:MOTION_1** parameter and set its value equal to **0.2**. Click **OK**.

5. Click **Add Dimension** and select the **.875** dimension from cut **id 149** in **SLIDER1.PRT**.

6. Set the *min* and *max* values to **0.875** and **1.1**, respectively.

7. Press the middle mouse button to stop selecting dimensions.

8. Click **Options>Preferences**.

9. In the *Graphs* tab, select **Variables**.

10. Select the *Run* tab. Enter **10** in the *Convergence %* field.

11. Click **OK**.

12. Click **Compute** to run the analysis. During the analysis, the graph shown in Figure 7–16 displays.

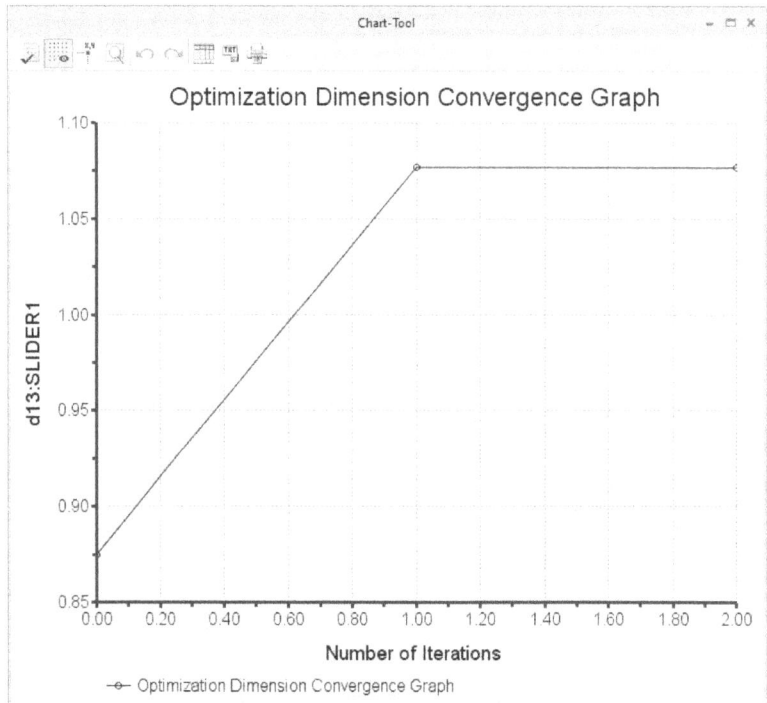

Figure 7–16

The graph shows that, after two iterations, the **dimension** needs to be modified to **1.0767** to satisfy the design constraint.

13. Close the Feasibility/Optimization dialog box.

14. Click **Confirm** when prompted regarding modification to the model.

15. Verify that the **d13** dimension is now **1.077**.

Task 7 - Create a Measure analysis feature to ensure that the slider clears the plate to permit the door to open.

1. In the In-graphics toolbar, click ×ô (Point Display) to enable the display of points.

2. In the Measure group, expand ⟋ (Measure) and select ⊓ (Distance).

3. Press and hold <Ctrl> and select the front surface of the **plate.prt** and the point shown in Figure 7–17.

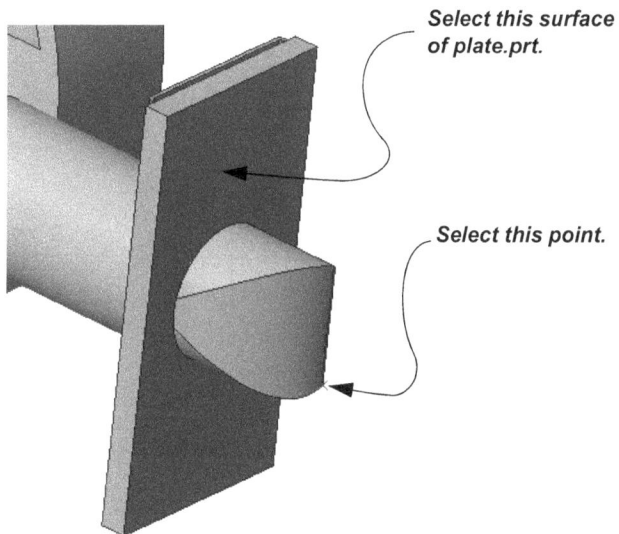

Select this surface of plate.prt.

Select this point.

Figure 7–17

The distance between these references displays in the Results window. The *Distance* is approximately **0.5**.

4. Click ⊟ (Save), ensure that **Make Feature** is selected, edit the name to **MEASURE_2**, and press <Enter>.

5. Select the *Feature* tab.

6. Leave the parameter name as **DISTANCE**.

7. Click **Close** to complete the feature.

Task 8 - Create a Motion Analysis feature to measure the minimum distance.

1. In the Manage group, click ×⟋ (Analysis).

2. Edit the name to **MOTION_2** and press <Enter>.

3. Select **Motion Analysis**.

4. Click **Next**.

5. Highlight **DISTANCE: MEASURE_2** in the Parameter window.

6. Click **Run**. The distance against time graph displays as shown in Figure 7–18.

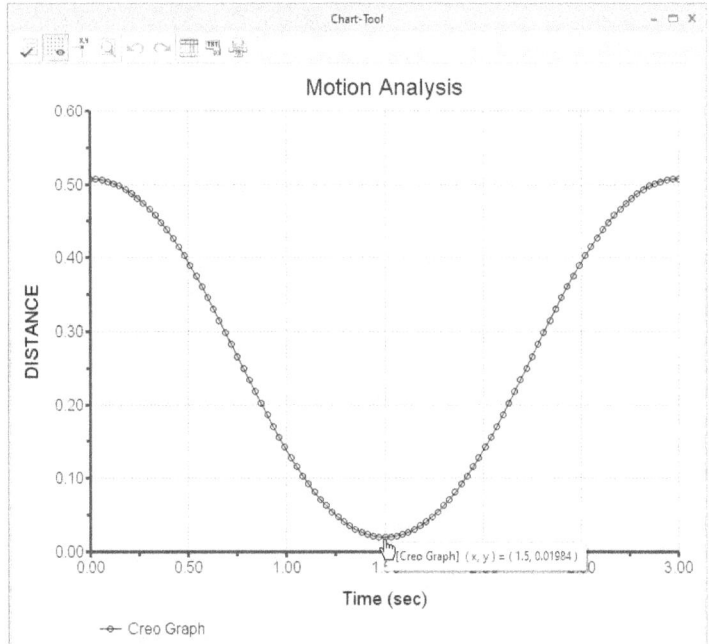

Figure 7–18

The graph in Figure 7–18 shows when the doorknob handle is moved to open the door (its extreme position). The minimum distance between front surface of the **plate.prt** and **PNT0** is **0.01984** inch at T = 1.5sec. You can see the same result in the Results window in the Motion Analysis dialog box.

7. Close the Motion Analysis dialog box.

8. Create only the **MIN_DISTANCE** parameter to **YES**.

9. Leave the parameter name as **MIN_DISTANCE**.

10. Click ✓ (OK) to complete the analysis feature.

Task 9 - Create a Feasibility study.

Design Consideration

In this task, you modify a design variable to set the minimum distance between the front surface of the plate.prt and the point to zero.

1. In the Design Study group, click ✎ (Feasibility/Optimization). The Feasibility/Optimization dialog box displays.

2. Click ▢ (New Design Study) to create a new Feasibility study.

3. Select **Feasibility**.

4. Click **Add** in the *Design Constraints* area.

5. Select the **MIN_DISTANCE:MOTION_2** parameter and set its value equal to **0**. Click **OK**.

6. Click **Add Dimension**, select **SLIDER1.PRT**, and select the **d1** dimension (**Protrusion id 39**), as shown in Figure 7–19.

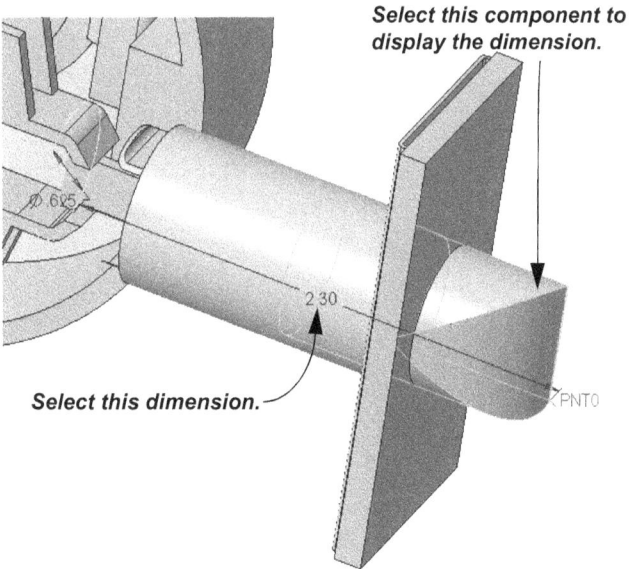

Figure 7–19

7. Set the *min* and *max* values to **2.25** and **2.3**, respectively.

8. Press the middle mouse button to stop selecting dimensions.

9. Click **Options>Preferences**.

10. In the *Graphs* tab, select **Variables**.

11. Select the *Run* tab. Enter **0.1** in the *Convergence %* field.

12. Click **OK**.

13. Click **Compute** to run the analysis. During the analysis, the graph shown in Figure 7–20 displays.

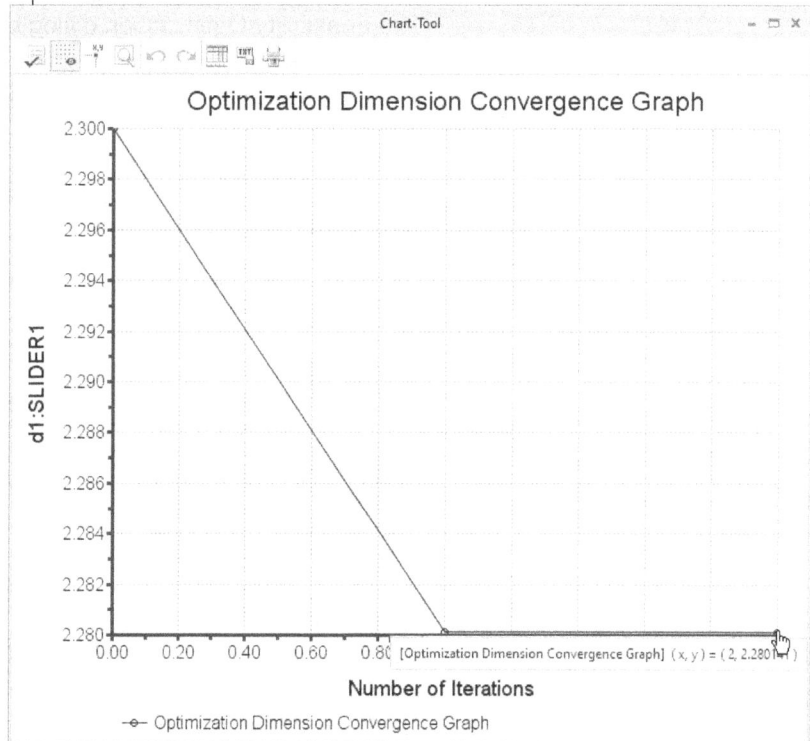

Figure 7–20

The graph shows that, after two iterations, the variable **d1** needs to be modified to **2.28014** to satisfy the design constraint.

14. Close the Feasibility/Optimization dialog box.

15. Confirm the modification to the model. Verify that the **d1** dimension is now **2.28**.

16. Close the model and erase it from memory.

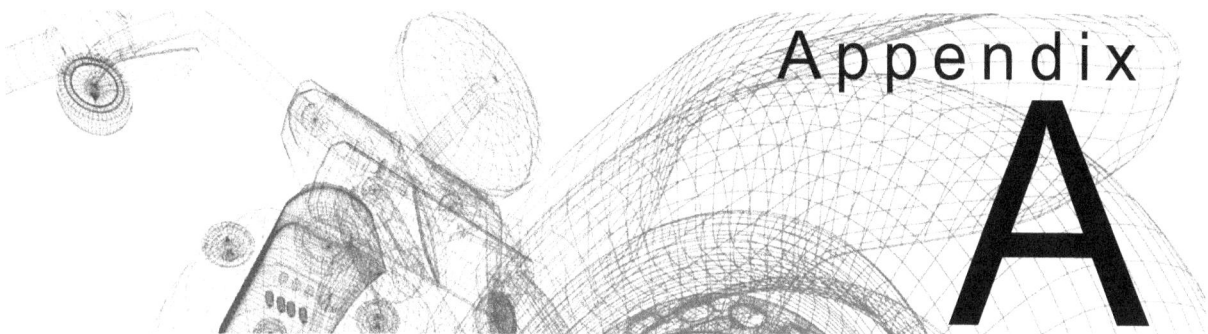

Appendix

A

Additional Practices

In this appendix, you will find additional practices.

Practice A1 | Project 1

Practice Objective

- Apply the behavioral modeling techniques to control the diameter size of cylindrical packaging surface.

In this practice, you apply the behavioral modeling techniques to control the diameter size of cylindrical packaging surface for a vase.

Task 1 - Open the part vase.prt.

1. Set the working directory to *Project_1*.

2. Open **vase.prt**. The model displays as shown in Figure A–1.

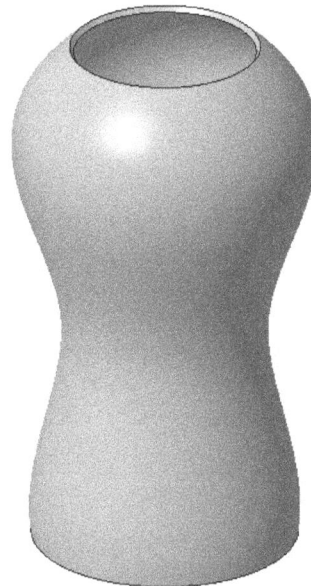

Figure A–1

Task 2 - Create features to measure the maximum vase diameter.

1. Create a field point on the outside surface of the vase.

2. Create an analysis feature to measure the distance between **FPNT0** and **A_1**. Name the analysis **MEASURE_1**. Create a distance analysis parameter and enter **DIST** as its name. Do not create any datum points.

3. Create a construction group that includes both the **FPNT0** and the **MEASURE_1** analysis feature.

4. Create a UDA analysis feature to measure the maximum value of **MEASURE_1** (maximum value of the vase diameter). Name the analysis **UDA**. Create a **UDM_max_val** parameter and enter **UDM_MAX** as its name. Do not create any datums.

Task 3 - Create a revolved surface to represent the packaging for the vase.

---

1. Create a 360° revolved surface that is one sided and has open ends. Sketch the section as shown in Figure A–2.

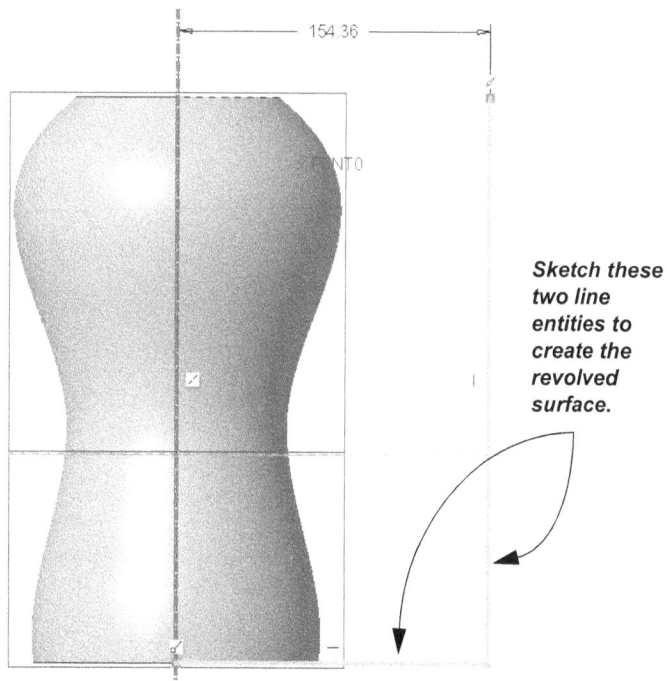

Sketch these two line entities to create the revolved surface.

Figure A–2

Relation_1 = maximum value of the vase radius +10

2. Create a relation analysis feature and name the analysis **RELATION_1**. Enter the relation d# =(UDM_MAX:FID_UDA +10) in the editor, where d# represents the radius dimension for the revolved surface, as shown in Figure A–3. The dimension symbol may vary in your sketch.

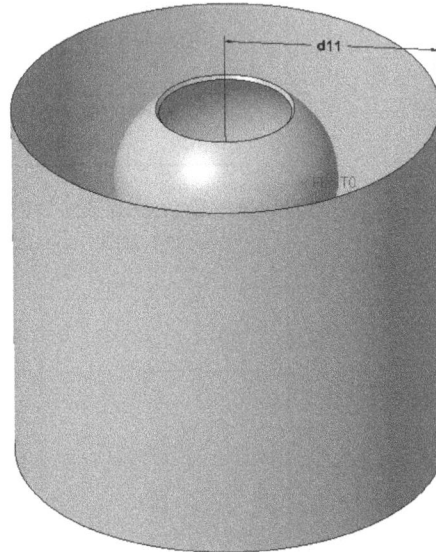

Figure A–3

3. Verify the relation and complete the analysis feature.

4. Regenerate the part. The diameter of the revolved surface updates according to the relation that you have created. The model displays as shown in Figure A–4.

Figure A–4

5. Modify the vase surface id 39 and note the effect on the revolved surface. The surface does not update automatically; therefore, select the revolved surface and click ✐ (Edit Definition) in the mini toolbar. When the dashboard displays, complete the feature. The surfaces updates to reflect the change to the vase.

6. Design a lid for the vase. Ensure that the diameter of the lid updates as changes are made to the vase.

7. Create solid geometry from the surfaces to create a solid storage container for the vase.

8. Save the model and erase it from memory.

Practice A2

Project 2

Practice Objective

- Apply behavioral modeling techniques to align the center of mass for a pulley model with a datum plane.

In this practice, you apply behavioral modeling techniques to align the center of mass for a pulley model with the default datum plane FRONT. The design variables have the following constraints:

- Tolerance on pulley flange thickness (d13, d37) is -0, +0.2

- Tolerance on pulley rounds (Rd110) is -0, +0.5

You will use the above design variable constraints to study the design and find a feasible result to meet your design intent.

Task 1 - Open the pulley part.

1. Set the working directory to *Project_2*.

2. Open **pulley.prt**. The model displays as shown in Figure A–5.

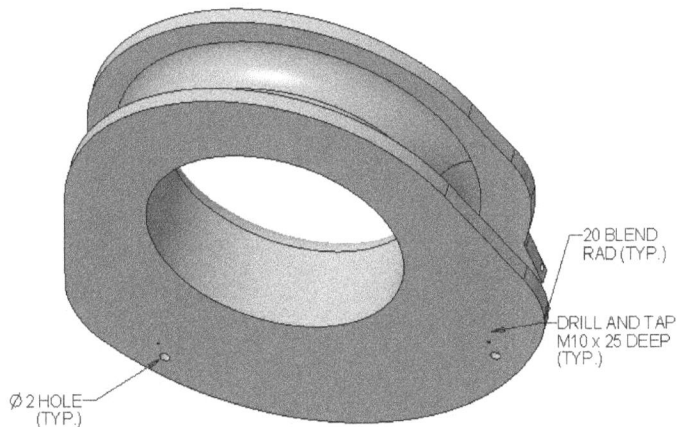

20 BLEND
RAD (TYP.)

DRILL AND TAP
M10 x 25 DEEP
(TYP.)

Ø 2 HOLE
(TYP.)

Figure A–5

3. Create a datum point through the default coordinate system for the model.

Task 2 - Create a model analysis feature to locate the center of mass for the pulley.

1. Create a model analysis feature to locate the pulley center of mass. Name the analysis **MODEL_COG**. Create a mass analysis parameter and set the name to **MASS**. Create a datum point on the center mass and set the name to **PNT_COG**. The model displays as shown in Figure A–6.

The image is shown with datum point tag display enabled.

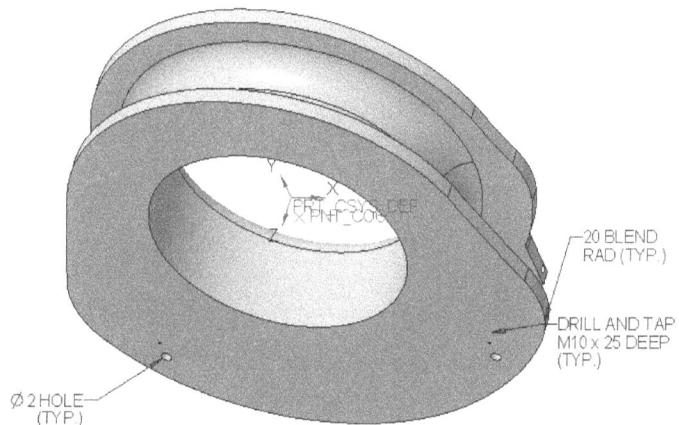

Figure A–6

Task 3 - Create a measure analysis feature.

1. Create a measure analysis feature to measure the distance between **PNT_COG** and default datum plane **FRONT**. Set the analysis name to **HORIZONTAL**. Create a distance parameter and set the name to **H_DIST**. Do not create a datum point. The computed distance equals 0.277.

Task 4 - Create a sensitivity study.

1. Create a sensitivity study on the flange thickness values (**d37**). Enter **3.2** as the maximum flange thickness and **3.0** as the minimum flange thickness. Plot this thickness against the **H_DIST** parameter. The distance between **PNT_COG** and default datum plane **FRONT** reduces to 0.057.

Task 5 - Create a sensitivity study.

1. Create a sensitivity study with **Rd110** as the variable, as shown in Figure A–7. Enter **6.5** and **6.0** as the maximum and minimum values, respectively. Plot this value against the **H_DIST** parameter. The distance between **PNT_COG** and default datum plane **FRONT** reduces to 0.235.

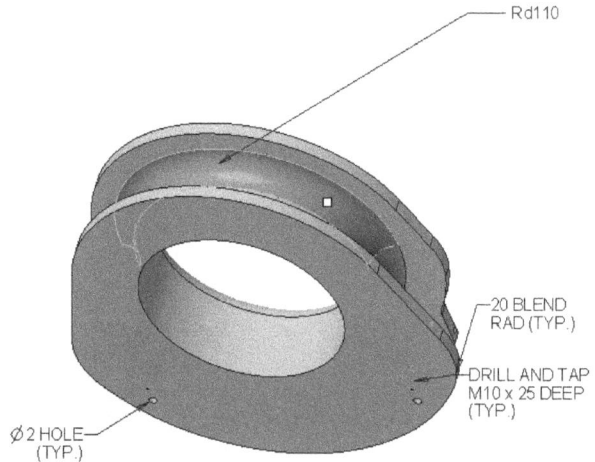

Figure A–7

Task 6 - Create a feasibility study.

Rd110 (6in to 6.5in)
d37 (3in to 3.2in)

1. Create a feasibility study with the **H_DIST** parameter set to 0, and variables **Rd110** and **d37** set to their maximum and minimum values. No feasible solution is found; however, the distance between **PNT_COG** and default datum plane **FRONT** reduces to 0.017.

Rd39 (3.6in to 4.4in)

2. Include the variable **Rd39** in your study to achieve feasibility.

3. Save the model and erase it from memory.

Practice A3

Project 3

Practice Objective

- Ensure that the center of gravity is below the waterline to increase stability.

In this practice, you work with a toy boat assembly to determine the waterline, then ensure that the center of gravity is below the waterline to increase stability. You will first create analysis features and a feasibility study to find the waterline of the boat. Once the waterline has been found, you will create a second feasibility study to position the model's center of gravity.

Task 1 - Open the boat.asm model.

1. Set the working directory to *Project_3*.

2. Open **boat.asm**. Note the toy boat assembly consists of three parts: a hull, cabin, and weight. The assembly displays as shown in Figure A–8.

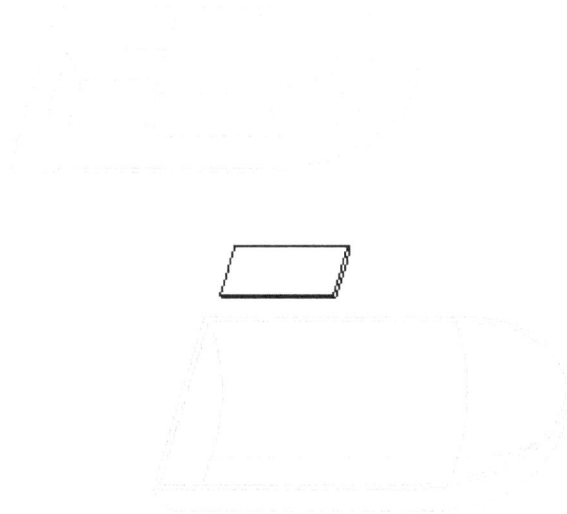

Figure A–8

Task 2 - Investigate the hull model in the assembly.

1. Display datum planes and tags.

2. Select the hull model in the Model Tree and click 🖰 (Open) in the mini toolbar. The hull part opens in a new window, as shown in Figure A–9.

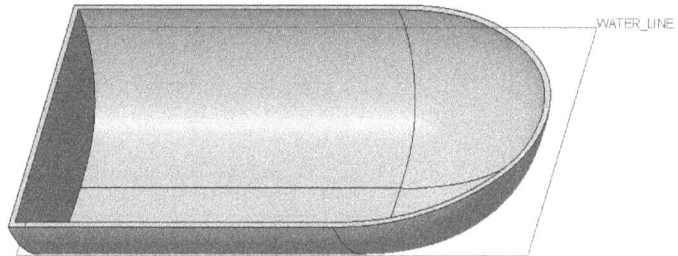

Figure A–9

Task 3 - Create an analysis feature to measure the displacement of the hull.

1. In the Model Tree, activate Insert Mode before the shell feature.

2. Create a Measure analysis feature to measure the One Sided Volume below the **WATER_LINE** datum plane. Create the **ONE_SIDED_VOLUME** parameter. Set the analysis name to **DISPLACEMENT**.

3. Cancel the Insert Mode.

4. Save **hull.prt** and close the window.

Task 4 - Measure the total mass of the assembly.

1. In the **BOAT** window, switch to the **FRONT** saved orientation.

2. Display Coordinate Systems.

3. Create a Mass Properties analysis feature to measure the assembly mass properties. Set the analysis name to **TOTAL_MASS**. Create the **MASS** parameter and a datum coordinate system at the center of gravity. The model displays as shown in Figure A–10.

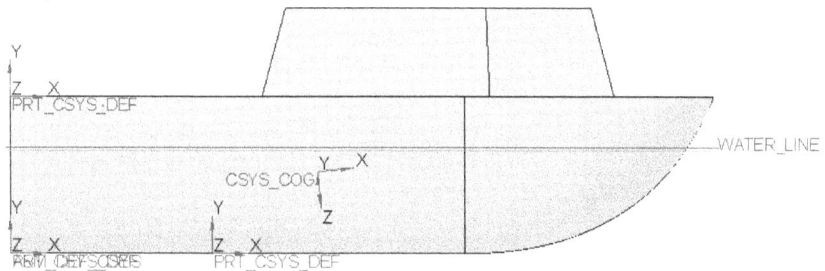

Figure A–10

Task 5 - Calculate the difference in mass using a relation analysis feature.

1. Create a relation analysis feature and name it **MASS_DIFF**.

0.04 (lbm/in^3), is the approximate density for water.

2. Enter the following relation:
   MASS_DIFF=(ONE_SIDE_VOL:FID_DISPLACEMENT:0
   *0.04)-MASS:FID_TOTAL_MASS

3. In the Relations dialog box, Select Utilities and remove the check mark next to **Unit Sensitive**.

4. Click ☑ (Verify) and click **OK**.

Task 6 - Find the waterline using a feasibility study.

1. Create a feasibility study.

2. Set the **Design Constraint** as *MASS_DIFF:MASS_DIFF* equal to **0**.

3. The only design variable is the **d57** dimension, which locates the **WATER_LINE** datum. Its range is from *0* to *5*.

4. Run the study. The model displays as shown in Figure A–11.

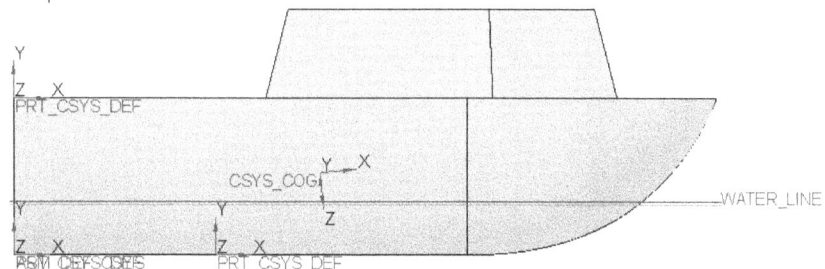

Figure A–11

The computer has found the position of the waterline by making the mass of the submerged and non-submerged portions equal. It should be noted that in this example, the waterline datum is only approximate, as you are not taking into account the slight rotation of the COG coordinate system with respect to the **WATER_LINE** datum. This rotation is insignificant and can be ignored.

Note that the COG for the boat assembly is above the waterline. For added stability, you can optimize the weight part to bring the center of gravity to be .15 below the waterline.

5. Click **Confirm** after closing the analysis dialog box.

Task 7 - Create a datum plane for the required COG position.

1. Create an Offset datum plane from **WATER_LINE**.

2. Enter a value of **-0.15** to offset below the **WATER_LINE** datum. The assembly displays as shown in Figure A–12.

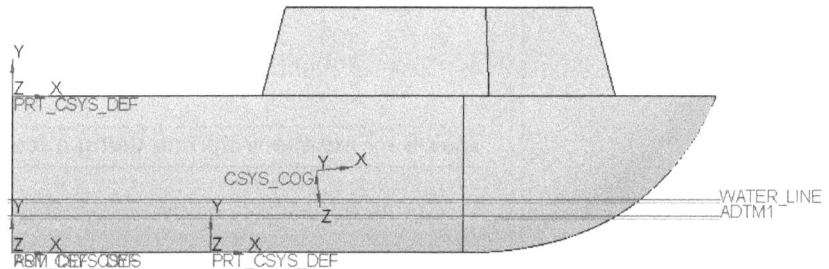

Figure A–12

Task 8 - Create another analysis feature.

1. Create a Measure analysis feature named **COG_DISTANCE** that measures the distance from the CSYS_COG coordinate system to the **ADTM1** datum plane. Create the distance parameter using the default name.

Task 9 - Position the COG on ADTM1 using a feasibility study.

1. Create a feasibility study. The constraints and variables from the previous study should still be present.

2. Add *DISTANCE:COG_DISTANCE* as a **Design Constraint** equal to 0.

3. Select the Hull component in the Model Tree and select
   ✎ (Hide) in the mini toolbar.

*The **d3** and **d2** dimensions represent the width and height of the weight component.*

4. Add the **d3** dimension from the **WEIGHT** part as a Design Variable. Vary the dimension from **0.09** to **0.25**.

5. Add the **d2** dimension from the **WEIGHT** part for an additional Design Variable. Vary the dimension from **0.90** to **2.50**.

6. Middle-click to stop adding dimensions.

7. Select the Hull component in the Model Tree and select
   ◉ (Show) in the mini toolbar.

8. Run the study. When completed, the assembly displays as shown in Figure A–13.

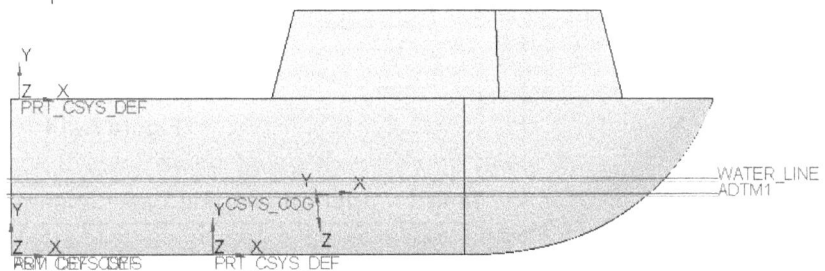

Figure A–13

9. Save the model and erase from memory.

Practice A4

Project 4

Practice Objective

- Analyze the model and make the required design changes to meet several design criteria.

In this practice, you will analyze the model and make the required design changes for **FORKB.PRT**, shown in Figure A–14, to meet the following design criteria:

- The center of gravity must lie on the **A_1** axis.

- The distance from the end of the counterweight to the **A_3** axis must be less than 350.

- Mass must be minimized.

- Try using both methods of optimization: GDP and MDS.

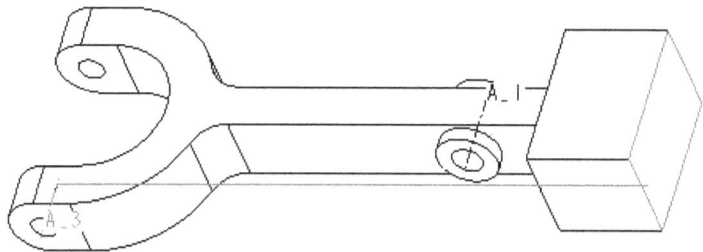

Figure A–14

Task 1 - Open the engine3.asm assembly.

1. Set the working directory to *Project_4*.

2. Open **forkb.prt**.

Task 2 - Using the above design criteria, make the required design changes without step by step instructions.

Practice A5

Project 5

Practice Objective

- Analyze a model and make the required design changes for it to meet several design criteria.

In this practice, you will analyze **SURFACEB.PRT**, shown in Figure A–15, and make the required design changes for it to meet the following design criteria:

- The revolved protrusion must follow the contours of the existing surface, while still maintaining its inherent shape.

- The protrusion should deviate from the surface by as much as **3** and as little as **0**.

The error in calculations can vary by 5%.

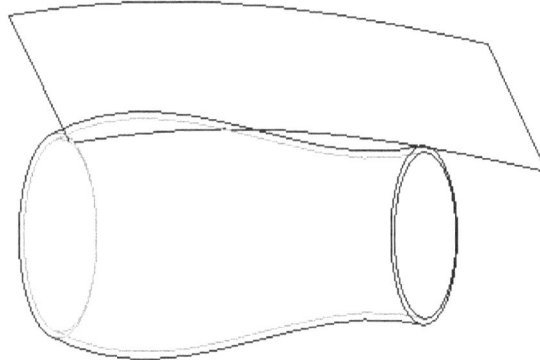

Figure A–15

Task 1 - Open the engine3.asm assembly.

1. Set the working directory to *Project_5*.

2. Open **surfaceb.prt**.

Task 2 - Using the above design criteria, make the required design changes without step by step instructions.

Practice A6

Project 6

Practice Objective

- Apply behavioral modeling techniques to a slider-crank assembly to study how crank length affects several design elements.

In this practice, you will apply behavioral modeling techniques to a slider-crank assembly to study how crank length affects the following:

- Clearance between the piston and the connecting rod.

- Distance between the crank's center line and the pin's center line.

- Velocity of the reciprocating component (piston).

The following constraint has been set for the assembly:

- Clearance between the piston and the connecting rod cannot be less than 0.0802in (2mm).

Task 1 - Open the engine3.asm assembly.

1. Set the working directory to *Project_6*.

2. Open **engine3.asm**. The model displays as shown in Figure A–16.

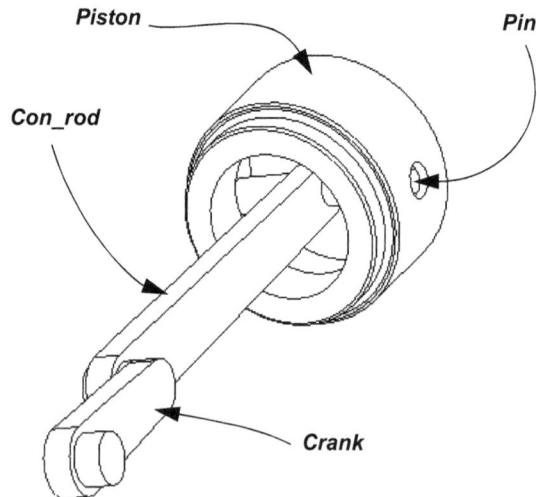

Figure A–16

3. Display features in the Model Tree (by default, they are not displayed). This enables the display of all of the analysis features that are added to the assembly.

Task 2 - Load the MotionDefinition1.pbk file to show an animation of a predefined doorknob movement.

The connections are ***Fixed***, ***Pin*** *and* ***Slider*** *The model driver profile type is* ***Cosine***.

The Mechanism Design Extension (MDX) of Creo Parametric enables you to simulate kinematic motion in an assembly. You can drag the mechanism through its range of motion or create drivers to define predetermined animations. These motions enable you to examine the behavior of the mechanism. The mechanism that is in the Behavioral Modeling Extension (BMX) is used evaluate important parameters throughout its range of motion.

1. In the *Application* tab, select 🔧 (Mechanism). Select **PLAYBACKS** from Model Tree and click ▶ (Play) in the mini toolbar. The Playbacks dialog box opens as shown in Figure A–17.

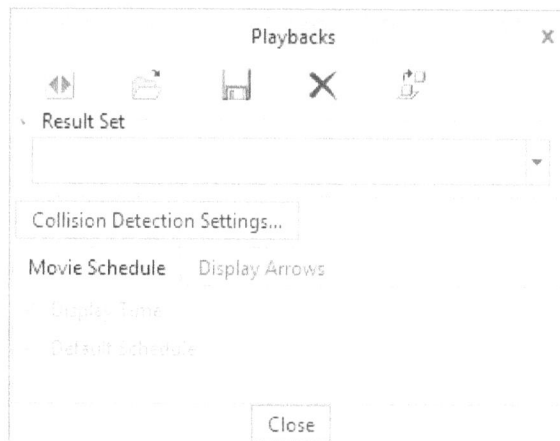

Figure A–17

2. In the Playbacks dialog box, click 📂 (Restore Result Set) and open **MotionDefinition2.pbk**.

3. Click ◄► (Play Result Set). The Animate dialog box displays as shown in Figure A–18.

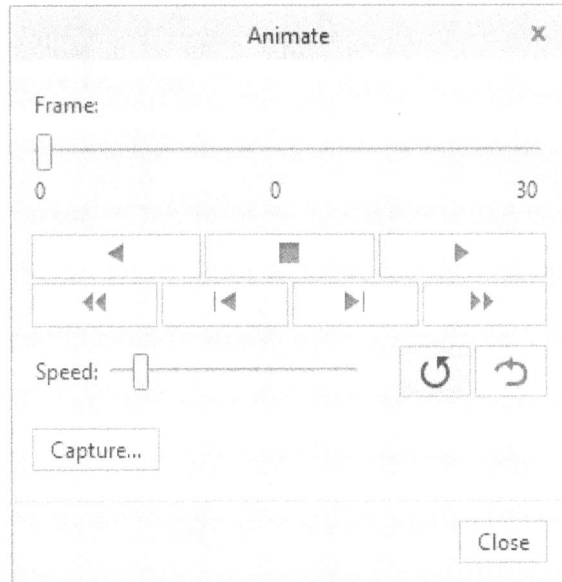

Figure A–18

4. Select the ▶ (Play) icon to run the animated motion of the slider-crank assembly.

5. Select the ◄◄ (Reset to Beginning) icon to rewind the animation to the beginning once you have reviewed it.

6. Select **Close** to close the dialog box.

7. Select **Close** to close the Results Play dialog box.

8. Return to the top-level assembly and regenerate the assembly.

Task 3 - Create a Measure analysis feature.

1. Create an analysis feature named **C_MEASURE** to measure the distance between the crank center line and pin center line. Create a distance analysis parameter named **C_to_C**. Do not create any datum points.

2. Show the **C_to_C** parameter in the Model Tree.

Task 4 - Create a Measure analysis feature.

1. Create a datum point on edge vertex, as shown in Figure A–19.

2. Create an analysis feature named **P_R_MEASURE** to measure the clearance between the connecting rod and piston. Select the surface for the connecting rod and the vertex point on the piston, as shown in Figure A–19. Create a distance analysis parameter named **P_R**. Do not create any datum points. Set the clearance to **0.82166in**.

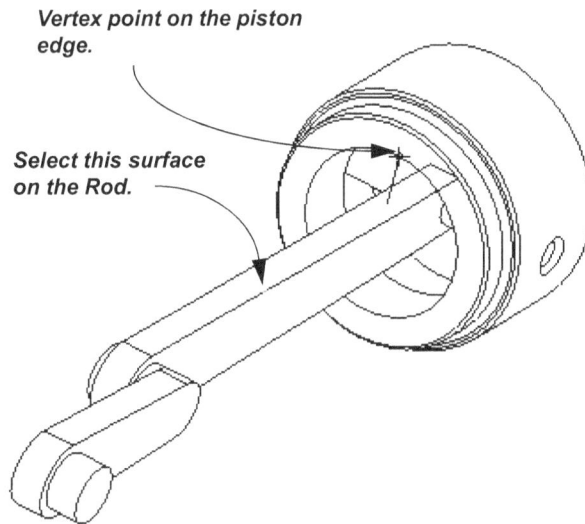

Vertex point on the piston edge.

Select this surface on the Rod.

Figure A–19

Task 5 - Create a Motion analysis feature.

Refer to Task 4 in practice 7a for reference.

The minimum clearance = 0.1573in.

1. Create and run a motion analysis feature named **MOTION** to measure the minimum clearance between the connecting rod and piston.

2. Create only the **MIN_P_R** parameter. Set the name to **P_R_DIST**.

Task 6 - Create a sensitivity study.

Refer to Task 5 in practice 7a for reference.

1. Create and run a sensitivity study to provide insight into an ideal start for the crank length **crank_length:0** when running a feasibility study. Enter **3.00** and **4.00** as the minimum and maximum variable ranges, respectively. Select the **P_R_DIST:MOTION** parameter to plot. Note that the required minimum clearance of 0.802in (Y-axis of the graph) is within the specified range.

Task 7 - Create a feasibility study.

Refer to Task 6 in practice 7a for reference.

1. Create and run a feasibility study to adjust the design variable **crank_length:0** to meet the required minimum clearance. Select the parameter **P_R_DIST:MOTION** and set its value equal to **0.0802**. Set the minimum and maximum values for **crank_length:0** to **3.00** and **3.50**, respectively.

(crank_length:0) dimension was 3in originally.

2. Verify that the **crank_length:0** dimension is now 3.30inch.

Task 8 - Create an Excel Analysis feature.

Refer to Task 5 in practice 6a for reference.

1. Create and run an Excel analysis named **VELOCITY** to find the velocity of the piston after adjustment to the crank length in Task 7. Load and open **velocity.xls**. Select the **crank_length** and cell **B4**. Select **rod_length** and cell **B5**. Select cell **B30** as the output cell and set its name to **VEL**.

Piston velocity = 0.97316in/sec

2. Show the **VEL** parameter in the Model Tree.

Task 9 - (Optional) Add piston acceleration to Excel analysis.

1. Add piston acceleration to the excel spread sheet:

   Piston acceleration = w^2*acosB + 1/q*cos2B

   Where q = b/a

2. Create and run an Excel analysis to find the acceleration of the piston after adjustment to the crank length in Task 7.

Task 10 - (Optional) Add piston total force to Excel analysis.

1. Add the total force for the reciprocating part (piston) to the spreadsheet.

   Total force (F) = m*w^2*acosB + 1/q*cos2B

   Where m = mass of the piston

2. Create and run an Excel analysis to find the total force on of the piston after adjustment to the crank length in Task 7.

3. Save the assembly and erase it from memory.

www.ingramcontent.com/pod-product-compliance
Lightning Source LLC
Chambersburg PA
CBHW082033230326

41598CB00081B/6189

The Social Psychology of the Human–Animal Bond

Laurent Bègue-Shankland

Translated by François Tharaud / Illustrations by Magali Seghetto

Routledge
Taylor & Francis Group

LONDON AND NEW YORK

Designed cover image: © Getty

First published in English 2026
by Routledge
4 Park Square, Milton Park, Abingdon, Oxon OX14 4RN

and by Routledge
605 Third Avenue, New York, NY 10158

Routledge is an imprint of the Taylor & Francis Group, an informa business

Published in French by Odile Jacob 2022

Face aux animaux: Nos émotions, nos préjugés, nos ambivalences © Odile Jacob, 2022

British Library Cataloguing-in-Publication Data
A catalogue record for this book is available from the British Library

Library of Congress Cataloging-in-Publication Data
Names: Bègue, Laurent author | Tharaud, François translator | Seghetto, Magali illustrator
Title: The social psychology of the human–animal bond / Laurent Bègue-Shankland ; translated by François Tharaud ; illustrations by Magali Seghetto.
Other titles: Face aux animaux. English
Description: Abingdon, Oxon ; New York, NY : Routledge, 2026. |
Translation of: Face aux animaux : nos émotions, nos préjugés, nos ambivalences. |
Includes bibliographical references and index. |
Identifiers: LCCN 2025017753 (print) | LCCN 2025017754 (ebook) |
ISBN 9781032912158 hardback | ISBN 9781032899602 paperback | ISBN 9781003561972 ebook
Subjects: LCSH: Human-animal relationships | Social psychology
Classification: LCC QL85 .B434 2026 (print) | LCC QL85 (ebook)
LC record available at https://lccn.loc.gov/2025017753
LC ebook record available at https://lccn.loc.gov/2025017754

ISBN: 9781032912158 (hbk)
ISBN: 9781032899602 (pbk)
ISBN: 9781003561972 (ebk)

DOI: 10.4324/9781003561972

Typeset in ITC Galliard Pro
by Newgen Publishing UK

Contents

Introduction

Illustration: Magali Seghetto

Ever since we emerged as a species, animals have surrounded us. They have inspired our religious beliefs, and some have shared our graves. Our civilizations domesticated their power, and our foundational myths never failed to include them. Is there any part of the animal body that hasn't been turned into human goods, knowledge, or symbols? The ingenious *sapiens* we have become have found uses for everything, from their droppings to their neurons, hooves, and feathers. The first books in which we gathered our knowledge about them show how omnipresent animals have been, even down to the materials from which they were made: some volumes were bound with glue made from their tendons and cartilage. If you are curious enough about bovine science to consult Buffon's original *Histoire naturelle* and its engravings,

DOI: 10.4324/9781003561972-1

not only would you learn about the anatomy of the calf as described in that 18th-century zoo-logical bible, but you could even stroke the animal's skin, of which the cover is made.

For millennia, animals have fascinated us with their differences. The sanctified boundary we have erected between us and them has surely contributed to uniting humankind. Every generation inherits the fundamental divide that codifies relations between humans and the nearly 9 million species we lump together without a moment's thought into the single category, "animals."[1] But our representations of animals have not merely been passed on unchanged. They have evolved. For the past thirty years or so, science has deeply transformed the way we look at animals. We are discovering amazing sensory abilities that had been hidden from us – kaleidoscopic worlds of ultraviolet and infrasound – and a multitude of cognitive and moral capacities we had thought they did not possess.

To find out about the place animals have held in human history, we have countless vestiges of our shared past, buried underground, out in the open, or in dark caves scattered throughout the globe. Our museums are packed with animal-related artifacts and the shelves in our libraries are brimming with encyclopaedic knowledge about animals. For whoever wishes to study our relations with them, there is no shortage of information from a variety of sources. Even something as simple as a conversation about our memories from the woods or the oceans, the contents of our childhood dreams, or the loving presence of our pets attests to the ubiquity of animals.

A different way of exploring our emotions in the face of animals is to measure the way our heart races, our pupils dilate, our skin gets clammy,[2] or our amygdala activates[3] when we are shown an onscreen image of a scorpion's raised tail with its deadly stinger, or the sharp fangs of a big cat. All these approaches and many others I describe in this book allow us to paint a panoramic picture of our relations of affection, fear, and dominance with animals.[4] They also shed light on the subterfuges that allow us to erase their identities as sentient beings in order to turn them into food or instruments while keeping a clear conscience.

Poison-control Fish at the G20 Meeting

It is November 2010 at a G20 summit in South Korea. The place is on maximum security alert, as one can tell from the impressive display of air forces, armoured vehicles, outsized barriers, and even robot weapons – not to mention tens of thousands of police officers on the lookout. To be sure, there are reasons for concern, such as the existence of global terrorist threats, the risk of an attack from North Korea, and excited crowds of anti-government demonstrators. Everything has been carefully thought out to ensure the physical safety of the world leaders gathered for two days at the convention centre in Seoul.

To guarantee and demonstrate the purity and safety of the bathrooms' drinking water, the organizers have even set up an unprecedented control system: they have introduced six fish in the water tanks on display in the basement of the building. If the animals become sluggish or show the slightest suspicious twitch, the system will go on alert! The safety of world leaders is in good hands, or rather, *good fins*, as a reporter from the Wall Street Journal joked to relax the atmosphere.

Like the ancient food tasters of royal courts, the poison-control fish were promoted to the role of aquatic sentries for the heads of States or governments of the top industrialized countries. These were not fierce piranhas, wolffish, or schools of moray eels: rather, the great powers were shielded by the colourful scales of a handful of placid, undulating goldfish. The outrage expressed by a global animal rights organization made no difference: the risks posed to these aquatic creatures left most leaders unfazed. Besides, how serious could you be about the fate of a few fish when the official menu for the summit features dishes of locally caught seafood?

Milgram's Experiment Revisited

"You can't see love in the eyes of a fish," a fifty-something participant explains in an interview after completing an experiment in my lab. That's why she's just injected it with twelve doses of a lethal substance as part of a new study design I will describe in this book. As it was presented to the participants, this unprecedented study was modelled on Milgram's experiment on submission to authority and it consisted in scientifically studying the way a large fish would react to a substance which, while stimulating its memory, could cause pain and eventually a life-threatening overdose.

Some participants stubbornly refused to give even the first injection, while others would gradually and, it seemed, unemotionally release doses that would kill the animal. But in most cases, there were signs of psychological resistance. Some participants cried when they later described the experiment. Over the course of hundreds of interviews conducted after the study, I was able to measure the sometimes-subtle manifestations of the moral dilemma participants had to face. Of course, there were visible patterns: on one side of the moral weighing scale was the suffering of the animal used for research, while on the other side was medical knowledge and the promise of new treatments. But other influences were at play. The way the equation was solved implied several psychological dimensions that will be presented in this book.

Humans Facing Animals

Humans often find it hard to understand what animals feel, because "their hearts cannot be fathomed,"[5] as philosopher René Descartes, author of the influential "animals as machines" theory, wrote in 1649. But this book is essentially about the way the human heart deals with animal lives, as I will attempt to uncover the nature of our complex and ambivalent exchanges with them.

I will explain how four major dimensions shape our relations:

1. First, the characteristics of the species: its appearance, its size, the intelligence we ascribe to it, and the morphological characteristics that make it more like us. For example, presenting dogs in a subtly more anthropomorphic way increases people's inclination to adopt a dog from a shelter or get involved in animal welfare.[6] We will also see that we perceive animals according to criteria related to our own preferences or uses. For example, we tend to regard animals as more intelligent if they move at the same speed we do. We usually consider animals as having poorer cognition if their motions are faster or slower than ours.[7]
2. Secondly, our shared evolution and the roles we have given them throughout history deeply affect our representations. The fact that some of them have long been a threat to our lives or goods while others partnered with us contributed to making us prefer some species from an emotional – or culinary – point of view. And as soon as an animal is on the menu, it is less likely to be regarded as capable of sophisticated mental states.[8]
3. Next, our cultures have given animals wildly changing assignments – from pedestals to plates. Take the cat: as the incarnation of the goddess Bastet, cats were revered for centuries in ancient Egypt. But in France, they were burned alive at summer festivals in the Middle Ages, and cat pelts were traded until the 19th century. Only in 2020 were cats taken off the list of edible animals by China's Ministry of Agriculture and Rural Affairs.[9]

    Bears used to be worshipped by the Celts, Germans, and Scandinavians, and they still are among the Ainu people of Japan, but in Europe, they were used in cruel traveling shows in the Middle Ages and were still listed as an edible species in the 1938 edition of the French food encyclopaedia *Le Larousse gastronomique*. Some religions prohibit eating pork or seafood while other cultures consider eating insects or horse meat as disgusting or immoral.

Figure I.1 "You cats may have been considered as sacred animals in ancient Egypt, but I'm certainly not impressed."
Illustration: Magali Seghetto

4. Finally, we humans vary greatly when it comes to our relations with animals. For example, if you are a woman, the likelihood of you severely beating an animal is **39** times less than it is for a man, and you are **45** times less likely to shoot one.[10] Conversely, a woman is three times more likely to participate in an animal rights protest or to be a compulsive animal hoarder (what is sometimes referred to as "Noah syndrome").[11]

Kundera's Moral Test

Our personalities and political views also influence our relations with animals. Not only can animals be a test of our identities, but our connections with them reveal the way we perceive humans who are different from us. They can reveal our conceptions of otherness.

In *The Unbearable Lightness of Being*, writer Milan Kundera wrote that, "Mankind's true moral test... consists of its attitude towards those who are at its mercy: animals." This book does not attempt to reach any conclusions on human morality in general, but it will uncover what our diverse interactions with animals say about our empathy and our connections with them as well as with other members of our own species. We will examine the mental contortions and careless or committed behaviours which characterise our heartfelt but paradoxical bond with animals.

Notes

1 For stylistic reasons, I will abstain from writing "other animals" when referring to non-human species in this book.
2 Åhs F., Rosén J., Kastrati G., Fredrikson M., Agren T., Lundström J. N. (2018). "Biological preparedness and resistance to extinction of skin conductance responses conditioned to fear relevant animal pictures: A systematic review," *Neuroscience and Biobehavioral Reviews*, 95, pp. 430–437.
3 Cao Z., Zhao Y., Tan T., Chen G., Ning X., Zhan L., Yang J. (2014). "Distinct brain activity in processing negative pictures of animals and objects: The role of human contexts," *NeuroImage*, 84, pp. 901–910.
4 Tuan Y. F. (1984). *Dominance and Affection. The Making of Pets*, Yale, Yale University Press.
5 Boyer F. (2010). "Un animal dans la tête," in J. Birnbaum (ed.), *Qui sont les animaux?* Paris, Gallimard, pp. 9–25, p. 16.
6 Butterfield M. E., Hill S. E., Lord C. G. (2012). "Mangy mutt or furry friend? Anthropomorphism promotes animal welfare," *Journal of Experimental Social Psychology*, 48 (4), pp. 957–960.
7 Morewedge C. K., Preston J., Wegner D. M. (2007). "Timescale bias in the attribution of mind," *Journal of Personality and Social Psychology*, 93 (1), pp. 1–11.
8 Bilewicz M., Imhoff R., Drogosz M. (2011). "The humanity of what we eat: Conceptions of human uniqueness among vegetarians and omnivores," *European Journal of Social Psychology*, 41 (2), pp. 201–209.
9 According to Richard Zivohlava, cats are still eaten in some northern areas of Italy and Switzerland. Richard Zivohlava A. (2019). *Dans la peau des bêtes. La vie sensible et intelligente des animaux*, Paris, Plon.
10 Herzog H. (2007). "Gender differences in human–animal interaction: A review," *Anthrozoös*, 20 (1), pp. 7–21.
11 Herzog H. (2011). *Some We Love, Some We Hate, Some We Eat*, New York, HarperCollins.

1 Humans are Animals to an Extent

Illustration: Magali Seghetto

"Plants exist for the sake of animals and... the other animals exist for the sake of human beings."
Aristotle, *Politics*[1]

Humans, the Pinnacle of Creation

We are animals who stubbornly refuse to be labelled as such. Since Aristotle and the medieval thinkers he influenced, century after century, humankind has dug an abysmal gap between itself and the other animals. This separation, an expression of the narcissism of our own species, sprang from the idea of a great chain of being in which stones, plants, invertebrates

DOI: 10.4324/9781003561972-2

and vertebrates were subordinated to one another, while Man stood at the pinnacle of creation, only surpassed by the angels and God himself.[2]

This moral divide between man, the imaginary king[3] of a hierarchical universe invented by theologians and other earthly powers, perfectly fit a biblical command that left no doubt as to the hierarchy of living beings: "…let them have dominion over the fish of the sea, and over the fowl of the air, and over the cattle, and over all the earth, and over every creeping thing that creepeth upon the earth."[4]

Darwin: One Hell of a Fall

But the grand, human-centred picture endorsed by every monotheism[5] was about to undergo a major correction. In 1859, *On the Origin of Species* was published, and it showed that the origin of our species was the mere product of biological forces. Aboard a ship named after an English dog, the Beagle, for a trip to the Galapagos islands, Darwin founded the theory of evolution. Over the next century, this new paradigm generated a relentless activity in scientific fields as diverse as palaeontology, molecular biology and cognitive science, and it permanently overturned human exceptionalism. Stunned, humans found out that they had been shaped by a multitude of random events and chance circumstances, and they were forced to accept their troubling physical and mental continuity with other species that were also created by the blind forces of chance and necessity. In 1871, in *The Descent of Man*, Darwin wrote that "there is no fundamental difference between man and the higher mammals in their mental faculties."[6] Nearly 150 years later, we learned that our genome and that of the bonobo or the chimpanzee overlapped almost entirely.[7]

The eclipse of creation theology, the new framework of evolutionary analysis and the refinement of scientific techniques brought to light facts that were hitherto neglected or invisible. These facts force us to see disturbing similarities between animals and us,[8] as well as unimagined or underestimated abilities. Old representations are spurned, and animals become subjects "because the latest scientific findings leave us no choice,"[9] acknowledges philosopher Dominique Lestel. But is this really enough for humans to relinquish their anthropocentric paradigm?

With New Perspectives Come New Biases

Now we know that animals are not entirely devoid of those sparks of mind which we thought were purely human and which we call memory, language, consciousness, or even morality.[10] But the broadening of perspectives that the scientific method allows still bears the mark of human interests. We still prefer to study those species that are most like us. This "taxonomic bias" deplored by researchers who study biodiversity[11] is evidence of an enduring, irrepressible preference for our own species. Thus, there are 20 times as many scientific papers on vertebrates than invertebrates, even though the latter are 26 times as numerous on Earth.[12]

If we really were to do justice to the quantitative significance of the 8.7 million animal species which inhabit our planet, should we not give priority to the multitude of worms, insects and fish who reside on it? They make up most of the world's biomass.[13] Worse still, science has sometimes used highly limiting frameworks of analysis, choosing to compare animals to humans in ways that disadvantaged them, like the famous test of consciousness.

The Test of Consciousness, a Mismeasure of Animals

To understand animal consciousness, what could be more tempting than using the instruments that scientists invented to study human babies? The mirror test, invented in the 1970s by

University at Albany researcher Gordon Gallup, is part of the classic battery of tests used in research on animal cognition. It consists in making a coloured, odourless, non-irritating spot on the head of an individual and then watching whether, when placed in front of a mirror, the individual shows any sign of understanding that the spot is on its own body, not on the reflection in the mirror. In human beings, before 17 months of age on average, children try to touch the spot in the mirror, not on their nose or forehead.[14]

In an animal that can recognise itself in a mirror, we are willing to acknowledge self-consciousness. But isn't this trademark of human cognition, which we marvel at finding also in wrasse fish, elephants and orca, a very poor tool for gauging animal consciousness? In a highly influential book, *The Mismeasure of Man*, paleoanthropologist Stephen Jay Gould exposed the way early intelligence tests were biased in favour of some social groups.[15] Will someone someday write *The Mismeasure of Animals*?

The spot test, which is probably suited to animals that use their vision to recognise members of their own species, seriously disadvantages animals such as dogs who prefer to use their sense of smell (which is 100,000 times better than ours)[16] or others such as moles whose eyesight is their Achilles' heel. For many species, it seems risky to infer anything from such a restrictive test. Are animals "poor in world," as Heidegger claimed,[17] or is it scientists who sometimes lack imagination?

Isn't the significance that was hitherto granted to the spot test rather a manifestation of the fact that human beings' favourite sensory modality is sight and that, even in the noble quest for objective scientific truths, our species often remains hampered by its sensory preferences? The human eye is such an admirable machine that it was often cited by theologians (or more recently, advocates of intelligent design) as evidence of a divine intelligence. Therefore, we should not be surprised by the human bias in favour of the eye, and indirectly the brain, whose development is related to the primacy of this sensory modality.[18]

What it's Like to Be an Animal

We would be mistaken if we concluded that an animal's point of view is bound to remain a mystery to us. Isn't it hasty to claim, as Wittgenstein did, that if lions could talk, we could not understand them?[19] We can approach animal worlds by paying more attention to their multiple perceptual channels – vision, of course, but also smell, taste, and the perception of waves, pressure or vibrations, and even electromagnetic sensitivity.[20]

For example, the study of fish eyes shows that, with their four types of cone cells, most of them see colours far more accurately than we do.[21] But we can also study their hearing, which has long been neglected: until the 1930s, they were thought to be deaf, probably just because they had no outer ears.[22]

Another way to understand animal intelligences is to consider the size of specialised brain areas. Philosopher Thomas Nagel is famous for asking, in a 1974 article cited over 11,000 times since, what it is like to be a bat[23] hanging upside down in the trees and equipped with aerial sonar. Neurobiologists answered that an outsized auditory cortex gifted chiroptera with the incredible virtuosity that is echolocation.[24] Among squirrels – the champions of tree acrobatics – it's the visual cortex that takes an extraordinary amount of brain space.

But there may still be something suspicious about singing the praises of the cortex: doesn't it reflect our pride as land-dwelling animals, our vanity as brain-endowed beasts? Isn't the brain, with its 80 billion neurons, our second favourite organ, as a famous humourist said? Why not decentre ourselves more radically and consider the narwhal's twisted horn, whose nerve endings allow it to perceive the salinity of water as well as its heat and pressure variations? This cetacean, also called "sea unicorn," equipped with a sonar that perceives acoustic and ultrasonic messages, has all it takes to fire our imagination![25]

The examples could be multiplied endlessly. They force us to understand that each animal embodies a way of knowing, that is has perceptive channels adapted to its survival and that it fits into the sensory environment (or *Umwelt*) that is relevant to it. We owe this idea to German biologist Jakob von Uexküll, who took the example of the tick, whose existence is essentially focused on the detection of a specific signal: the smell of butyric acid coming from the skin of mammals, on which it clings when the occasion arises by dropping from a tree. Like the tick, every animal species inhabits a world of its own.

Because animals are both near and far, it is fascinating to embrace the strangeness of their worlds. An Oxford veterinarian made the eccentric decision to live the lives of a fox, a badger, a deer or an otter, going as far as sharing their habitats and daily routines. At the beginning of his quest, he very reasonably reminded himself that they had a vast array of perceptive equipment in common: "Both mammals like me and birds, for instance, use Golgi tendon organs, Ruffini endings and muscle spindles to tell them where the various parts of their bodies are in space, and free nerve endings to scream 'Horrid!' or 'Hot!'"[26] He was right to remember that, despite obvious differences, many species have similar perceptual channels. To go back to Thomas Nagel's example of the bat, echolocation is also used by other animals, like dolphins, and even humans are capable of it. Blind people commonly use acoustic reverberation to find their way around, and sighted people can use it with a little training.[27]

But let's go back to our English vet. What did he learn from months of animal otherness, feeding on worms, wandering almost naked through icy river water or sleeping in muddy holes? That each animal in its own way is at one with its natural habitat and that if a human wants to get close to this, he hits the limits of his own senses.[28]

Evolving Representations

The ontological gap we have created between animals and ourselves has long been a source of philosophical satisfaction as well as an excuse to use animals as tools and resources for millennia. Have the changes in perspective imposed by new scientific findings challenged this instrumentalization of animals for our own benefit? Recent history shows that scientific knowledge by itself is not enough to deeply transform our relations with animals. Several recent studies have confirmed that the growth of our knowledge about animals does not automatically change the way we behave towards them.[29]

Since the 19th century, the industrialisation of farming and the rise of the use of animals on a large scale in human activities show that knowing about our biological relatedness did not do much to change our unbalanced relationships. After all, didn't Darwin himself sacrifice thousands of animals in his research, including mammals of which he knew how close they were to him?[30] However, new trends are emerging today. They might be due to a civilizing process which makes the sight of blood and violence increasingly unbearable,[31] as well as the development of scientific knowledge that transforms our representations of animals.

Humans living in the 21st century are more willing than their predecessors to question their values when interacting with animals.[32] Meat eating has become a moral issue.[33] In France, since an amendment introduced in January 2015, animals have been legally recognized as sentient beings.[34] In November 2021, the National Assembly adopted a law prohibiting the use of wild animals in traveling circuses and in dolphinariums as well as the sale of puppies and kittens in pet stores. Penalties for animal abuses have been increased. This progress in animal rights can only erode the indifference which might have been the common response, a few decades ago, to this graphic depiction of the animal condition by a philosopher:

Their blood clarifies our wines. Their dried blood and their feathers are our fertilizer. So is their manure. Their fat is in our soaps and in our walls, in the paint and in the biofuel used in cement plants. Their skin is on our shoes, our armchairs and our bags. Their bladders filter our fruit juices. Their bones whiten the sugar for our coffee. Their flesh is our meat. They are organ donors, testers and tasters for every molecule introduced on the market. Every act of human life features portions, traces, or scents from their cadavers and their byproducts.[35]

Today, there is a conflict between, on the one hand, the practices of domination we inherited from past ages (and which were taken to extremes with the intensification of animal exploitation in the 20th-century food industry and scientific research) and on the other hand, the discovery of our shared nature and fate with animals, accompanied by a growing sensitivity to their plight. This gap generates contradictory phenomena. This dissonance can be mitigated by the evolution of laws, social norms, or changes in individual behaviours (for example, food habits). But it can also be solved psychologically by resorting to representations that legitimize our practices by rationalizing them.

Let us take a very concrete example in the food domain. In his lab, a researcher at the University of Kent made participants eat either beef jerky or the same amount of cashew nuts, then he assessed their representations of various animals such as fish, kangaroos or cows. He noted that, compared to the ones who had received cashews, the participants who had had jerky downplayed the cognitive abilities of ruminants and thought they were less deserving of moral consideration.[36]

Thus, denying (or ignoring) the sensory and cognitive abilities of animals, as well as the establishment of a strict hierarchy between us and them, are ordinary responses to situations that challenge our usual practices.

To better grasp everything that has been connecting us with animals for millennia, let us start with a quick visit through the countless imaginary and material spaces in which they have been dwelling with us.

Notes

1 Aristotle (1984). *Politics*. Translated by Carnes Lord. Chicago and London, Chicago U.P.
2 Brandt M. J., Reyna C. (2011). "The chain of being: A hierarchy of morality," *Perspectives on Psychological Science*, 6 (5), pp. 428–446.
3 The expression comes from Montaigne's *Essays*, Book 2, chapter 12.
4 Genesis 1:26 (King James version).
5 See Baratay É. (2015). *Des bêtes et des dieux. Les animaux dans les religions*, Paris, Cerf; Baratay É. (1996). *L'Église et l'animal. France, xviie -xxe siècle*, Paris, Cerf; Preece R., Fraser D. (2000). "The status of animals in biblical and Christian thought: A study in colliding values," *Society and Animals*, 8, pp. 245–263. According to Frans de Waal, the boundaries drawn by *sapiens* between their world and that of other primates are strongly related to their cultural representations of the sacred and the divine. The primatologist observes that the religions that developed in regions without anthropoid animals are more likely to put humans on a pedestal, while in India, China or Japan, where monkeys and apes expose humans to animals that look like them, the human–animal divide is not drawn as sharply. They have apelike deities like the monkey god Hanuman.
6 Darwin (1871). *The Descent of Man, and Selection in Relation to Sex*. London, John Murray, chapter 2.
7 Prüfer K. et al. (2012). "The bonobo genome compared with the chimpanzee and human genomes," *Nature*, 486, pp. 527–531. Humans share 98.7% of their DNA with these apes.
8 Those similarities sometimes trigger defensive cognitive mechanisms through which people deny that humans are determined by natural forces. See for example Deconchy J.-P. (2000). *Les Animaux surnaturés*, Grenoble, PUG.

9 Lestel D. (2003). *Les Origines animales de la culture*, Paris, Flammarion, p. 10.

10 Le Neindre P., Dunier M., Larrère R., Prunet P. (2018). *La Conscience des animaux*, Versailles, Éditions Quæ.

11 Troudet J., Grandcolas P., Blin A. et al. (2017). "Taxonomic bias in biodiversity data and societal preferences," *Scientific Reports*, 7, 9132.

12 Chansigaud V. (2019). "Domestication et peur du sauvage," in K. L. Matignon (éd.). *Révolutions animales*, Paris, Les Liens qui libèrent, pp. 31–43.

13 The human species only accounts for 0.01% of earthly biomass. Bar-On P. R., Milo R. (2018). "The biomass distribution on earth," *PNAS*, 115, p. 25.

14 Brooks-Gunn J., Lewis M. (1984). "The development of early visual self-recognition," *Developmental Review*, 4, pp. 215–239.

15 Gould S. J. (1996). *The Mismeasure of Man*. Revised and expanded edition, Norton.

16 Cyrulnik B., Lou Matignon K., Fougea F. (2010). La Fabuleuse Aventure des hommes et des animaux, Paris, Hachette, Pluriel, p. 17.

17 Heidegger M. (1996) *The Fundamental Concepts of Metaphysics*, 2nd ed., Indiana U. P.

18 Chapouthier G. (2020). *Sauver l'homme par l'animal*, Paris, Odile Jacob, p. 50.

19 Wittgenstein L. (1994). *The Wittgenstein Reader*, Oxford, Blackwell.

20 Grison B., Raffaellan A. (2021). *Les portes de la perception animale*, Paris, Delachaux et Niestlé.

21 Balcombe J. (2018). *À quoi pensent les poissons?* Paris, La Plage, p. 44.

22 Balcombe 2018, p. 57.

23 Nagel T. (1974). "What is it like to be a bat?" *The Philosophical Review*, 83 (4), pp. 435–450.

24 Le Neindre P., Deputte B. L. (2020). *Vivre parmi les animaux, mieux les comprendre*, Versailles, Éditions Quæ, pp. 48–54.

25 Grison B. (2021). *Les portes de la perception animale*, Lausanne, Delachaux et Niestlé, p. 20. See also Pouydebat E. (2017). *L'Intelligence animale. Cervelles d'oiseaux et mémoires d'éléphants*, Paris, Odile Jacob.

26 Foster C. (2016). *Being a Beast: Adventures Across the Species Divide*, London, Metropolitan Books.

27 Schwitzgebel E., Gordon M. S. (2000). "How well do we know our own conscious experience? The case of human echolocation," *Philosophical Topics*, 282 (2), pp. 235–246.

28 Foster (2016). *Being a Beast*.

29 Hazel S. J., Signal T. D., Taylor N. (2011). "Can teaching veterinary and animal-science students about animal welfare affect their attitude toward animals and human-related empathy?" *Journal of Veterinary Medical Education*, 38 (1), pp. 74–83; Jamieson J., Reiss M. J., Allen D., Asher L., Wathes C. M., Abeyesinghe S. M. (2012). "Measuring the success of a farm animal welfare education event," *Animal Welfare*, 21 (1), pp. 65–75.

30 Herzog H. (2011). *Some We Love, Some We Hate, Some We Eat*, New York, Harper, p. 207.

31 Elias N. (2000). *The Civilizing Process*. Revised ed, London: Blackwell.

32 Auberger J., Keating P. (2009). *Histoire humaine des animaux*, Paris, Ellipses.

33 Rozin P. (1997). "Moralization," in A. M. Brandt, P. Rozin (eds.), *Morality and Health*, Taylor & Francis/Routledge, pp. 379–401. Many books show this evolution. Ricard M. (2014). *Plaidoyer pour les animaux*, Paris, Allary; Gibert M. (2015). *Voir son steak comme un animal mort*, Montréal, Lux; Caron A. (2013). *No steak*, Paris, Fayard; Page M. (2017). *Les animaux ne sont pas comestibles*, Paris, Robert Laffont; Vieille Blanchard E. (2018). *Révolution végane*, Paris, Dunod; Giroux V., Larue R. (2017). *Le Véganisme*, Paris, PUF; Larue R. (2020). *La Pensée végane. 50 regards sur la condition animale*, Paris, PUF.

34 Article 515-14 of the French Civil Code uses the definition common to the Criminal Code and the Rural Code.
    Article 521-1 of the Penal Code punishes with two years' imprisonment and a 30,000 euro fine for serious abuse of animals. Article L 214-1 of the Rural Code requires that they live "in conditions compatible with the biological requirements of their species."

35 Utria E. (2016). *Essai sur les droits des animaux*, PhD dissertation, University of Rouen, p. 13, quoted in F. Burgat (2018). *Être le bien d'un autre*, Paris, Rivages poche, p. 9.

36 Loughnan S., Haslam N., Bastian B. (2010). "The role of meat consumption in the denial of moral status and mind to meat animals," *Appetite*, 55 (1), pp. 156–159.

2 The Role of Animals in Human Cultures

Illustration: Magali Seghetto

The reason why animals have played such different roles in human cultures is probably because we have never stopped using them as mirrors. Animal worship was humankind's original religion,[1] and our totems, which we erected in their images in Africa, North America and Australia, materialise our early tribal lives. They served to unite human groups but also to designate their members, as French historian Éric Baratay reminds us:

> In Rome, among every citizen's three names, the *nomen* and the *cognomen* were often derived from the name of an animal: *porcus* (pig) became *porcius* or *porcina*, *aper* (wild boar) became *apricius*, and so on. This habit was even more widespread in the Celtic and Germanic worlds. In the latter, the animals most commonly referred to, such as the

DOI: 10.4324/9781003561972-3

eagle, the snake, the boar, the horse, and particularly the bear and the wolf, stand for the strength, speed and bravery warriors needed for battle. The names they inspired (first names for the French) were used until the 12th century in France... Some are still around, like *Bernhard*, from *Bern* (bear) and *hart* (strong), or *Wolfgang* (wolf).[2]

Animals are an inexhaustible source of metaphors and symbolism, and anthropologists regard them as *food for thought*.[3] So much so that, among the shapes people spontaneously come up with when taking the famous Rorschach test (which is scientifically obsolete but still informative to us),[4] animal figures are the most frequently mentioned,[5] especially by younger subjects. For example, in a study conducted in France with 360 children aged 2 to 9, no less than 4,009 spontaneous references to animals were counted, out of a total of 8,435 perceived shapes.[6] Animals are the creatures onto whom we project our inner worlds. When we ask guilt-prone people to ascribe emotions to a dog that has just been briefly described to them, they say the dog feels guilty.[7] And people who value submission to authority have a slight preference for a breed of dogs that is valued for its obedience.[8]

Analysing mentions of animals in the written press reveals that they are overabundant in pop culture as objects of affection, but also as saviours, threats, victims, utilitarian objects, imaginary and mythological beings, surrogate humans, or sources of wonder.[9]

Ancestral Companionship

When our ancestors shared their natural environment and every hour of their days and nights with animals, long before they could experience, as they do today, being separated from most species by urbanisation, they were probably struck by their resemblance with many of them: animals also had ears, eyes, teeth, legs, hair, and other features they shared with humans. People could not fail either to notice disturbing behavioural similarities for, like us, the animals we pay the most attention to tend to move around, sleep, play, communicate, run, mate, give birth to offspring, sometimes form hierarchical groups, fight, and make up.[10]

Despite those striking similarities, one anthropological constant appeared, and in every climate, animals are defined by it: they are not like *us humans*.[11] Here we have a universal law: humans are the animal that claims not to be one. But this persistent need to distinguish oneself from animals comes with another tendency we find in every culture: humans are fascinated by animals. According to University of Pennsylvania anthropologist Pat Shipman, no mammal has such lasting and intimate relationships with other animals as the human species.[12]

The compelling coexistence of differences and similarities between humans and animals, and the magnetic appeal of the latter, are probably the reasons for the central place animals have had in primitive art, myths and rituals.[13] As early as the Upper Palaeolithic (45,000 BP), animals abound in cave paintings. For example, the Pyrenean cave of Niaux is home to an incredible bestiary of bison, horses, ibexes, deer, a sketch of a weasel, and even fish. In a study on the presence of animals in 62 painted caves, French palaeontologist André Leroi-Gourhan counted no less than 1,386 mammals (lion, bear, mammoth, rhinoceros, horse, wild boar, deer, hind, Irish elk, reindeer, bullock, bison, chamois, and ibex).[14]

According to archaeologists, even though they were sources of food (and clothing),[15] these animals were painted mainly because they fascinated our ancestors.[16] The totemism of North America, Australia or Africa is abundant evidence for this veneration. Sometimes it's the threat in them that concerned humans. In the French department of Ardèche, among the 420 highly realistic animal paintings that have adorned the Chauvet cave for 30,000 years, 64% are particularly fearsome animals such as big cats or mammoths.

Mutual Attraction

The sense of danger caused by some animals in the past is just one aspect of our relations with them. Mutual attraction brought us closer with several species, including wolves, the wild species that left the deepest mark in Western civilisation.[17] Their canine descendants stand out as the oldest domesticated species, with at least 14 millennia of companionship with humans.[18] Like several other species (e.g., wild pigs, monkeys, or lambs), wolf cubs were sometimes breastfed by women (as other animals still are today[19]) or given food that had been chewed by humans.[20] This physical connection ushered in a long history shared by our species and theirs – a bond so strong that not even death could break it. It is now known that the loss of an animal can be one of the most heart-breaking experiences in someone's life[21] – especially for children,[22] whose attachment to pets starts out deep and then fades with adulthood.[23] People who have a strong bond with their pet go through similar stages of grief than those experienced when losing a relative: their daily routines are upset, they call in sick, and they experience depressive episodes.[24]

Everyday life with pets has been a hallmark of the human condition throughout history[25] Huge amounts are spent on pets: the turnover for the pet market was close to 5 billion euros in 2019. The importance we give them cannot be simply explained by the "petishism" of our era, nor is it just a trend in affluent societies like ours. Particularly strong bonds between people and their pets also exist in poorer and non-Western societies, or among the underprivileged or even homeless people.

Ancient Greek historian Herodotus reported that in ancient Egypt, people formally mourned their family cat, and those closest to the animal manifested this by shaving their eyebrows.[26] If a cat was deliberately killed, the culprit was liable to be stoned. In his *Natural History*, Pliny reports that Alexander the Great held a solemn funeral for his horse Bucephalus, mortally wounded in battle. A city, Bucephalia, was even built around his tomb. Ethnologist Jacqueline Milliet notes that in New Guinea "women cut off one of their phalanxes when their favourite animal dies – a custom usually reserved for the death of a child".[27] No need to go as far as antiquity or the Antipodes to gauge this attachment at every level of society. Veterinarian Claude Béata says "the bond between [former French President] François Mitterrand and his dog Baltique was so strong that he had requested that she should fly along with his coffin in the Falcon jet that brought her master's remains to his hometown, Jarnac. Back there, because she was not allowed inside the church, Baltique waited outside without a leash, and the pictures of her looking at the coffin moved a lot of French men and women."[28] This emotional bond sometimes takes the form of outpourings on social networks, as happened when Mishka – a hugely popular husky dog – died: her Facebook page received over 17,000 comments after she passed away.[29] The pain of grieving for an animal is also evidenced in a more permanent way in the epitaphs.[30]

Grieving goes both ways: not only are some animals upset by the death of their peers,[31] but they can also be upset when their human companions pass away. In his *Natural History*, Pliny describes how Jason's dog let itself starve to death after its master was murdered. Another deeply moving sign of cross-species bonding was this tomb discovered by archaeologists on an Israeli palaeolithic site, which contained the skeleton of an elderly person and that of a five-month-old dog. The bodies, which were interred twelve thousand years ago, had been laid out in such a way that the left hand of the deceased rested on the shoulder of her four-legged companion.[32] In 2007, a French team from the National Museum of Natural History found a nearly ten-thousand-year-old tomb on the island of Cyprus: it was decorated with seashells and polished stones and in it rested a human in his or her thirties with a cat by their side.[33]

Death is also what humans will sometimes risk in order not to abandon their pets. Research on the circumstances that prevent the evacuation of residents in the event of a natural or industrial disaster shows that refusal to abandon a pet is one of the main causes. One study shows that after an evacuation due to a train accident in Wisconsin, 40% of pet owners came back to the disaster area illegally to rescue them.[34]

From Oracles to Religions

With the advent of domestication, farm animals played an increasingly important role in the daily lives of humans and in their artistic creations.

During the neolithic era, cows frequently appeared on earthenware, on jewels, and on the walls of the temples of great civilisations. Egyptian culture gave prominence to animals through its religious belief system (Hathor was a cow, Horus a falcon, Anubis a jackal, and so on), its animal worship, its animal-headed mummies and even in its writing, which includes 180 animal hieroglyphics – nearly one in four signs.[35]

In celestial space, ancient Greek gave its name to the zodiac – a word meaning "the circle of small animals." Greek civilisation was always a cornucopia of sacred beasts and hybrid creatures (minotaur, centaur, sphinx, mermaid, griffin, hippogriff, phoenix, Cerberus), half-animal deities (such as the god Pan) or gods taking animal forms (as when Zeus turned into an eagle, a swan, or a bull) or accompanied by animals (Athena's owl, Dionysus's panther).

Humans also used animals to try to tame the future. In Rome, the divinatory rites of *ornithomancy* drew sophisticated omens from the songs or flights of birds. Under different skies and in other eras, the movements and tracks of the tarantulas of Cameroon, the jackals of Mali, and the mice of Burkina Faso were also interpreted as omens. After a ritual slaughter, an animal's entrails, especially the liver, were the object of bloody consultations by seers trying to predict future events.

Figure 2.1 "You've got to put the eye before the beetle, unless the past participle comes before the snake."

Illustration: Magali Seghetto

Figure 2.2 Chiron, a centaur from Greek mythology.
Photo: Wellcome Collection gallery (2018-03-28): https://wellcomecollection.org/works/gusvmwhg CC-BY-4.0

Throughout the world, religious buildings have honoured animals on their tympanums, columns and stained-glass windows. In Europe, the medieval era abundantly represented the lamb, a symbol of Christ, and used animals to evoke the evangelists (the lion for Mark, the ox for Luke, the eagle for John), but there were also plenty of pictures of imaginary animals like dragons and unicorns. Animals are prominent in every literary genre, and they abound in visual art. Especially since the 15th century, pets and wild or exotic animals have been constantly represented in countless paintings and sculptures.

Finally, they adorned seals and shields, flags and coats of arms, espoused opposite political views and personified entire nations. Think about the bees, which first symbolised royal hierarchy and empire, but were later turned by Proudhon into an emblem of collectivism. With some variation from one period to another, 30 to 60% of the symbols on banners represent

Figure 2.3 "There can be no peace until they renounce their Rabbit God and replace him with our Duck God!"

Illustration: Magali Seghetto

animals (with a predominance of bears and wild boars from the 5th to the 11th century, and later eagles and lions).[36] Today, about 40 countries display an animal on their flags.

From Representation to Mimicry

Animals sometimes play unexpected roles. Joachim-Raphaël Boronali, who painted *Sunset Over the Adriatic*, which was exhibited in 1910, did so with a paintbrush that was tied to his tail. The artist was a donkey.[37] Other mammals – monkeys, horses, dogs, elephants – delighted humans with their naked creativity, unsettled critics, and sometimes even drew their masters' attention. Before depicting himself as a monkey in his late self-portraits, Picasso had been seduced by the painting style of Congo, a chimpanzee studied and made famous by zoologist Desmond Morris. Like Miro and Dali, Picasso even acquired abstract expressionist canvases painted by the talented primate.

If we limited the representation of animals to two-dimensional works, we would be forgetting about the major role of animal choreographies in many human cultures that have always imitated animal motions. They are omnipresent in martial arts and traditional dances. Was not music originally inspired by the animals' buzzes, stridulations, chirps, bellows and trumpeting? Were not their rhythms the metronomes of our inspiration? Not to mention our instruments, like those flutes crafted over 20 thousand years ago out of the ulnae of vultures and discovered in 1920 in the cave of Isturitz, in the Basque Country, or our pianos, whose keys were layered with ivory until the mid-20th century, or double bass strings made from sheep guts.

From Camille Saint-Saëns's zoological, carnivalesque fantasy to traditional music, from Mozart's concerto evoking a starling to Oliver Messiaen's *Réveil des oiseaux* ("Awakening of the birds"), animals reside with lightness and intensity within the rhythms and melodies that tug at our heartstrings.[38] Some unlikely musical encounters can overwhelm us, as does that of classical cellist Beatrice Harrison playing with a nightingale, or international rockstar Peter

Gabriel accompanied by the melancholy notes played by bonobo Kanzi on the keyboard. This mosaic of examples, which could be made infinitely richer with more examples from Asian, African or Oceanian cultures, reminds us that animals pervade our representations, continually summon our senses and inspire every art form.

Animals as Tools and Resources

There is no doubt about the role animals played in the building of civilisations. They pulled the ploughs in our fields, the barges on our canals, the stagecoaches on our roads, the carriages, omnibuses and hearses in our cities and countryside. They hauled the lumber for our houses and the building blocks of our sacred monuments, spun our millstones, and were enlisted in our hunts.[39] They warned us of our enemy's approach: when crickets stopped singing or dogs started barking, we knew our foes were close. They were sentries, but also proud and faithful fighters: think about Hannibal's elephants, Napoleon's horses, and the millions of four-legged First World War soldiers – horses that were sacrificed on the battlefields.[40] It is estimated that on the Western front, eight million horses, three million mules, and two hundred thousand pigeons were used as carriers, mounts or messengers.[41] In wartime, these animal aides shared our hell on earth, and their blood and screams mingled with ours. Later, land armies widely used anti-tank dogs (who exploded under the machines) or mine-detecting rats – and at sea, dolphins still perform that function.

Countless animals were also enrolled in the merciless war against another internal enemy – diseases – with more haphazard effects. Medicine and magic, barely distinguishable from one another until the 17th century,

> used animals rather than plants or minerals because animated creatures seemed endowed with a stronger vital force that had to be captured to achieve a healing effect... Everything was used: secretions (milk, blood, fat, excrements), organs, which were often cooked or burned, then ground, or whole bodies (like those of insects, frogs, or snakes) – agonising

Figure 2.4 The US army uses dolphins to detect mines.
Illustration: Magali Seghetto

or cooked. Treatments followed the rules of imitation and contact. It was believed that "like cures like" – that was how the life force could restore health: liver cured the liver, eyesight was cured with an animal famed for its perception, like the bat...[42]

In the 1st century, no less than a hundred animals belonged in the famous pharmacopeia of Greek doctor Pedanius Dioscorides, which was largely retained during the Middle Ages,[43] and over 1,500 different animal species are used in traditional Chinese medicine (pangolin scales, bear bile, tiger bone liquor, and so on).[44] Out of a list of 150 prescription drugs available in the United States, 27 are made from animal products. The search for new molecules in living organisms is essential for bioprospecting, an activity that is both controversial and increasing[45] in several industrial sectors like pharmacology, cosmetology, and agriculture.[46]

Finally, raising and using large herbivores for food deeply shaped the economies of human civilisations once those species were domesticated during the neolithic era.[47] Capitalism, which has thrived on the labour and exploitation of animals, is immensely indebted to "the paws, hooves, and claws of animals."[48] Animals have been treated like "an underclass that was exploited to build the economy."[49] Domestication was a deep transformation, changing the living conditions of animals and humans both. It also shaped the relations between humans: they became more inegalitarian,[50] favouring accumulation and the institutionalisation of wealth gaps.[51]

In the future, animals will not stop inspiring scientific research – notably through the development of new technologies imitating natural adaptations. Following in the footsteps of the Wright brothers, whose first motorised aircraft was designed in the early 19th century after observing vultures, aeronautics is taking an interest in the common crane, whose flight is exceptionally energy efficient. A lot of cutting-edge technology is and will be forged in the crucible of biomimicry, which innovates by drawing inspiration from living organisms.

The brief overview I have just proposed illustrates how humankind developed thanks to an incessant *extraction of animality*:[52] we have made our own every kind of animal material one can think of –eggs, flesh, fat, skin, hair, excrement, bone and ivory. We have channelled animal energy and strength for traction, transport and combat. Our religions, cultures and science have revolved around animal resources and our fascination for animals.

The Beneficial Presence of Animals

According to biologist E. O. Wilson, human evolution has favoured an innate tendency to bond with other life forms.[53] This fundamental affinity is called *biophilia*. A growing body of work suggests that immersion in the natural environment provides us with a sense of well-being[54] which is amplified by the presence of animals, whose enchantment has been felt since the dawn of humanity and manifests itself as early as infancy. This predilection has been the subject of studies showing that, within hours of birth, infants gaze with greater attraction and curiosity at light patterns that simulate the movement of a chicken than they do with random figures or ones that reproduce the same movement in reverse.[55] At the age of 7 months, photographs of dogs or lizards activate neural networks that are distinct from those mobilised by pictures of familiar objects like furniture.[56] When children aged 18 to 33 months are given the opportunity to interact with attractive toys or animals (even if the animals are not very mobile), they show more interest in the latter. Careful analysis of their behaviour shows that they perform more gestures directed at the animals and ask more questions about them. Animals sustain the visual attention of children, encourage and facilitate their interactions with other children as well as adults, stimulate affiliation (the child makes an effort to communicate with and understand the animal), encourage children to improve their motor skills so they can interact physically with the animal, stimulate vocal and physical imitation, and boost the imagination.[57]

When parents step in, they become active mediators and direct children's attention towards animals more than toys.[58] It is therefore hardly surprising that among the first 100 words children know, many refer to the animal world, or that the ads they best remember are those involving animals.[59]

This is also true for children who are learning sign language or a spoken language.[60] French psychologist Hubert Montagner observed that, when it comes to animals, the vocabulary used by children is broader than it is in other domains, which is certainly related to the fact that in language-learning books and arithmetic books for children, nine characters out of ten are animals.[61] They are also prevalent in several psychological tests designed for children.[62]

It is often with animals that children first witness childbirth and death. The ubiquity of animals is not limited to daytime life, as evidenced by studies on children's dreams,[63] and this privileged place does not fade away with adolescence.[64]

Later in life, pets will occupy an essential place for older children, who say they appreciate the comfort and faithfulness they provide. The importance of animals is also confirmed in adults, who are quicker to detect animals than plants in scenes presented to them,[65] and who recall animals more accurately than plants when both have been shown to them shortly before – even when they have studied botany![66]

Animals have a soothing, calming effect on people who live close to them on a daily basis.[67] According to a study conducted in 26 European countries, the larger the number of bird species present in their surroundings were, the higher the residents' subjective well-being was.[68] Pets also play an important role: children who have had a strong attachment to an animal develop more self-confidence and better psychological balance.[69] Hugging an animal lowers one's blood pressure,[70] as does the act of simply contemplating a swimming fish.[71] Pets ease the moral pain one may feel after being socially rejected.[72] Sometimes the presence of animals seems even more effective than that of humans when it comes to relieving stress. In one study, participants had to perform a challenging task in the lab in the presence of their dog or someone close to them, and the results indicated that canine company had a more beneficial effect on their heart rate and blood pressure than the presence of a human friend.[73] In the same vein, a survey conducted after the March––April 2020 lockdown suggested that people who stayed home with a pet had a 16% higher morale than others.[74]

Finally, while pets are not always harmless (for example, they increase the risk of accidents among the elderly),[75] their presence is beneficial in the case of several somatic or psychological pathologies.[76] An Australian study of a representative sample showed that pet owners had to see a doctor 12% less often than people who did not have a pet.[77] This result was confirmed by a study that followed a cohort of participants for five years.[78] More broadly, a synthesis of studies including a total of 3 million people indicated that dog owners enjoyed a significant increase in life expectancy.[79]

Psychological care also benefits greatly from the participation of animals. Their introduction into psychotherapies (albeit in a more active way than was practiced by Freud, who let his dog Jofi lie at the foot of his famous couch during sessions)[80] provides multiple benefits, for several reasons: they stimulate verbal exchange,[81] promote touch and care, focus attention, encourage exercise (for example people with dogs walk twice as far every day as people who don't have a dog[82]), elicit laughter, alleviate loneliness, and facilitate social contact.[83] On this last point, research shows that 83% of dog owners claim that their pet gives them opportunities to talk to people.[84] In one study, a researcher counted the number of social interactions he had over five days, either walking with a Labrador retriever or without an animal. The

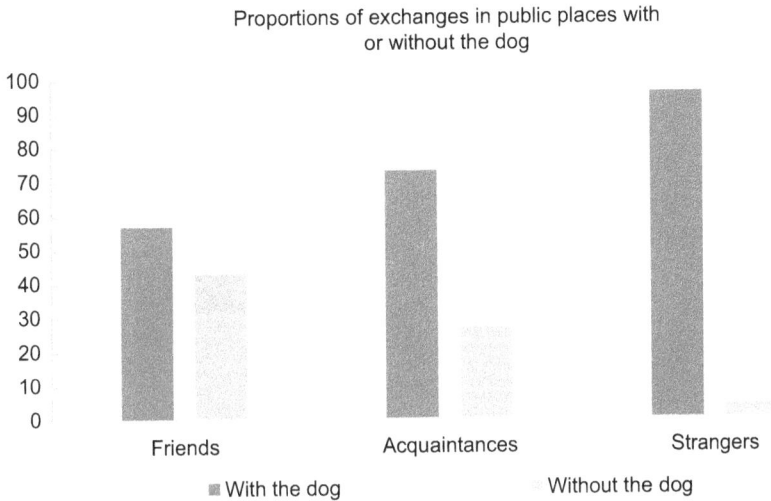

Proportions of exchanges in public places with
or without the dog

Figure 2.5 The mere presence of a dog increases the number of exchanges, especially with people who are unknown to the dog owner.

results confirmed the facilitation of social interactions by the dog: exchanges with passers-by significantly increased in its presence, especially with strangers.[85]

Partisan Zoology

With rare exceptions, Western philosophers have perpetually opposed man to animal.[86] Animals were denied a host of higher human faculties like consciousness, empathy or cultural transmission – an error that was later corrected by researchers.[87] This is the undeniable privilege of science, which, although it once claimed that humankind was the only species that buried its dead, was able to put that mistaken idea to rest when it found that even such small insects as ants had a special way of tending to their dead.[88]

From childhood onward, we rank animals according to their significance for us. While some are dismissed as repulsive or dangerous creatures (for example centipedes, bats, or moles), others, like cats or giraffes, get all our admiration. The birth of baby pandas now makes the headlines.

The consideration given to different animals is the result of several influences like their zoological similarity with humans,[89] how familiar they are, but also how cute[90] and childlike their faces are[91] (this is known as *neoteny*, which inspires spontaneous protective behaviours and vocalisations like those elicited by our own babies), their beauty,[92] but also the attractiveness or rarity[93] of the species and even its size.[94]

The linguistic and cultural environment also indicates the way animals are valued. Language profoundly shapes the boundaries of empathy – distinguishing for example between "cattle" and "pets," the latter being gifted with individuality, personality, and preferences that we acknowledge, while other animals are treated like objects, tools or materials.

Apart from animal exploitation, there are dozens of expressions that impart positive or negative value to animals and use them to describe human behaviours: we call one another

Figure 2.6 "It feels like the whole world is pressuring us to have baby pandas."
Illustration: Magali Seghetto

sheep, chicken, hawks or doves, we eat like pigs and work like dogs, we are sly as foxes, and we like to horse around.[95]

As you can see, in everyday usage, the words "animal" or "beast" do not refer to zoological realities – they most often express value judgements on things and people. As soon as it is applied to humans, the word "animal" become derogatory.[96] Thus, most synonyms of the word "animal" have negative connotations.[97] Our lack of consideration for animals is also expressed in more subtle ways. For example, the range of vocabulary used to refer to animal noises is very narrow – it is often limited to one term – contrary to our vocabulary for human sounds.[98] Most often, using a word for an animal noise such as *barking*, *howling*, or *growling* to refer to a sound made by a human voice is demeaning.[99] Another sign of disrespect is that the terms used to describe the suffering of killing of animals are often euphemisms. Linguist Catherine Kerbrat-Orecchioni noted some of them:

> When an animal that is no longer profitable alive gets sent to the slaughterhouse, it is said to be *harvested*; force-feeding geese or ducks is called *assisted feeding*; and on French rabbit farms, eliminating excess babies by smashing their skulls against a hard surface is called *balancing the nests*; the word for the same operation on pig farms – *wall therapy* – is more honest (it is the technique recommended by the *Institut du porc* because it is quick, painless, and most of all, cheap); there are also *nurseries* and *maternity wards* (buildings where sows give birth in iron cages) – the cutest invention being *piglet care*, which consists in cutting their tails off, grinding their teeth, and castrating them without anaesthesia.[100]

Finally, the history of religion in the West reminds us that Evil is primarily embodied by animals. The devil has horns and hooves, and witches are recognisable by the animals they keep company with: owls, bats, spiders, snakes, and the like.[101] An extravagant etymology was even invented to better condemn the Cathar heretics, whose name was (falsely) derived from the Latin *cattus* – that most devilish animal, the cat.[102] In the 15th century, the seven deadly sins were also personified by animals: "The lion, the mole, the goat, the boar, the pig, the dog, and the donkey were the respective emblems of the seven deadly sins: pride, greed, lust, anger, gluttony, envy, and sloth."[103]

From Aesop to Disney

Moralists have often used animal tropes to educate and mock humans. In the wake of Aesop and Pliny the Elder, Jean de La Fontaine conjured over 450 scaled, furry, or feathered animals in his mischievous tales. Through animal representations, it is primarily humans and social groups that are portrayed and sometimes fiercely ridiculed for their gullibility, greed, or cruelty.

The analysis of children's literature is very instructive. A Purdue University psychologist examined the contents of ten randomly selected books for young children published between 1988 and 1992. Nearly 90% of them included animals, and in 40% of them, animals were anthropomorphized: they wore clothes, and they ate and slept in houses like humans.[104] Cartoon animals express human preferences. A systematic analysis of all 56 animated films made by Disney between 1937 and 2016 shows that the dogs usually have human-like features,[105] rats tend to be villains (as do eagles and bats), and swans play altruistic characters. As for cows: when they appear, it is most often as meat or leather. Working animals like draught horses are given human features sparingly, and when an animal dies, music is more likely heard if the animal was human-like.[106]

Fictional representations of animals contribute to the transmission of values and social norms. Through the story of Babar, author Jean de Brunhof conveys a worldview in which plants must be "tamed and useful,"[107] and he embellishes colonialism.[108] Animal representations prescribe gender roles in children's magazines and Disney cartoons.[109] Their characters also shape animal and human stereotypes. For example, Disney's anthropomorphic animals – whether foxes, cats, lions, or frogs – almost always take on White characteristics[110] and they tend to be vegetarians.[111] Their voices also tend to be recorded by white actors, even when the animals are African like lioness Nala in *The Lion King* (1994).

Furthermore, the representation of animals in Disney productions has also evolved in the direction of decreasing biodiversity. A fine-grained analysis of 51 films over a period of 70 years has shown that the number of animal species depicted (except for the main characters) had been gradually decreasing as well as the screentime devoted to natural environments including vegetation.[112]

As we can see, the minimal scientific definition of animals according to which they are living beings with complex cell nuclei (*eukaryotes*) that feed on vegetable or animal matter (*heterotrophs*) contrasts, through its conciseness and coherence, with the anthropocentric perspective that underlies ordinary language.[113] Talking about animals also means introducing a category that expresses our attitudes to strangeness and difference, sometimes even among humans: "our behaviour with animals often reveals our conceptions of the Other."[114] The opposition between humanity and animals seems to foreshadow all those that human groups erect between them.

Notes

1 Nobrega Alves R. R., Barboza D. (2018). "The role of animals in human culture," in R. R. Nobrega Alves, U. P. Albuquerque (eds.). *Ethnozoology. Animals in our Lives*, New York, Academic Press, pp. 277–301.

2 Baratay É. (2003). *Et l'homme créa l'animal*, Paris, Odile Jacob, p. 239.

3 Lévi-Strauss C. (2017). *Le Totémisme aujourd'hui*, Paris, PUF.

4   Lilienfeld S. O., Wood J. M., Garb H. N. (2000), "The scientific status of projective techniques," *Psychological Science in the Public Interest*, 1 (2), pp. 27–66.
5   Shepard P. (1978). *Thinking Animals: Animals and the Development of Human Intelligence*, New York, Viking Press.
6   Beizman R. (1970). "Étude du contenu des réponses animales dans le Rorschach," *Psychologie clinique et projective*, 24, pp. 5–43.
7   Brown C. M., McLean J. L. (2015). "Anthropomorphizing dogs: Projecting one's own personality and consequences for supporting animal rights," *Anthrozoös*, 28 (1), pp. 73–86
8   Serpell J. (1986). *In the Company of Animals*, Oxford, Blackwell, pp. 28–29.
9   Herzog H. A., Galvin S. L. (1992). "Animals, archetypes, and popular culture: Tales from the tabloid press," *Anthrozoös*, 5 (2), pp. 77–92.
10 de Waal, F. (1989). *Peacemaking Among Primates*. Harvard University Press.
11 Russell N. (2011). *Social Zooarcheology*, Cambridge, Cambridge University Press.
12 Shipman P. (2019). "Sans les animaux, le monde ne serait pas humain," in K. L. Matignon (ed.). *Révolutions animales*, Paris, Les Liens qui libèrent, pp. 22–27.
13 Mason J. (2007). "Animals. From soul and the sacred in prehistoric times to symbols and slaves in antiquity," in L. Kalof (ed.). *A Cultural History of Animals in Antiquity*, London, Bloomsbury, chapter 1, pp. 17–45.
14 Leroi-Gourhan A. (1958). "Répartition et groupement des animaux dans l'art pariétal paléolithique," *Bulletin de la Société préhistorique française*, 55–59, pp. 515–528.
15 Gilligan I. (2019). *Climate, Clothing, and Agriculture in Prehistory*, Cambridge, Cambridge University Press.
16 Mason J. (2007). "Animals. From soul and the sacred in prehistoric times to symbols and slaves in antiquity."
17 Delort R. (1984). *Les animaux ont une histoire*, Paris, Seuil.
18 Digard J.-P. (1999). *Les Français et leurs animaux*, Paris, Fayard, p. 9.
19 Milliet J. (2007). "L'allaitement des animaux par des femmes, entre mythe et réalité," in E. Dounias, E. Motte Florac, M. Dunham (eds.). *Le Symbolisme des animaux: l'animal, clef de voûte de la relation entre l'homme et la nature?* Paris, IRD, pp. 881–911.
20 Matignon K. L. (2000). "L'allaitement des animaux par des femmes. Jacqueline Milliet," in K. L. Matignon (ed.). *Sans les animaux, le monde ne serait pas humain*, Paris, Albin Michel, pp. 151–157.
21 Adams C. L., Bonnett B. N., Meek A. H. (2000). "Predictors of owner response to companion animal death in 177 clients from 14 practices in Ontario," *Journal of the American Veterinary Medical Association*, 217 (9), pp. 1303–1309.
22 Cowling D., Isenstein S., Schneider M. (2020). "When the bond breaks: Variables associated with grief following companion animal loss," *Anthrozoös*, 33, pp. 693–708.
23 Albert A., Bulcroft K. (1988). "Pets, families, and the life course," *Journal of Marriage and the Family*, 50 (2), pp. 543–552.
24 Cowling D., Isenstein S., Schneider M. (2020). "When the bond breaks: Variables associated with grief following companion animal loss," *Anthrozoös*, 33, pp. 693–708.
25 Nobrega Alves R. R., Albuquerque D. (2018). "Introduction: Animals in our lives," in R. R. Nobrega Alves, U. P. Albuquerque (eds.). *Ethnozoology. Animals in our lives*, New York, Academic Press, pp. 1–7.
26 De Mello M. (2012). *Animals and Society. An Introduction to Human–Animals Studies*, New York, Columbia University Press, p. 34.
27 Milliet J. (1998). "La part féminine dans le phénomène animal de compagnie," in B. Cyrulnik (ed.). *Si les lions pouvaient parler. Essais sur la condition animale*, Paris, Gallimard, p. 1089.
28 Béata C. (2015). *Au risque d'aimer. Des origines animales de l'attachement aux amours humaines*, Paris, Odile Jacob, p. 290.
29 Parkinson C. (2020). *Animals, Anthropomorphism and Mediated Encounters*, London, Routledge, p. 97.
30 See Desmond J.-C. (2016). *Displaying Death and Animating Life. Human-Animal Relations in Art, Science, and Everyday Life*, Chicago, University of Chicago Press.

31 About the new field of comparative thanatology, see for example Anderson J. R. (2020). "Responses to death and dying: Primates and other mammals," *Primates*, 61, pp. 1–7.

32 Serpell J. (1986). *In the Company of Animals*, p. 58.

33 Vigne J.-D., Guilaine J., Debue K., Haye L., Gérard P. (2004). "Early taming of the cat in Cyprus," *Science*, 304 (5668), p. 259.

34 Irvine L. (2009). *Filling the Ark. Animal Welfare in Disasters*, Philadelphia, Temple University Press.

35 Classical Egyptian includes 800 hieroglyphics.

36 Baratay É. (2003). *Et l'homme créa l'animal*, Paris, Odile Jacob, p. 250.

37 Example drawn from Despret V. (2013). *Que diraient les animaux si on leur posait les bonnes questions?* Paris, La Découverte, p. 9.

38 Patterson-Kane E. M. (2007). "Music as a shared trait among humans and animals," in M. Bekoff (ed.). *Encyclopedia of Human-Animal Relationships*, Westport, Greenwood Press, vol. 4., pp. 1227–1231.

39 Baratay É. (2008). *Bêtes de somme. Des animaux au service des hommes*, Paris, La Martinière.

40 For a brief biography of Warrior, one of the most famous British war horses, see Baratay É. (2017). *Biographies animales*, Paris, Seuil, p. 57–82.

41 Baratay É. (2019). "Les chevaux dans les guerres, héros oubliés," in K. L. Matignon (ed.). *Révolutions animales*, pp. 57–63; Voir aussi Baratay É. (2003). *Et l'homme créa l'animal*, Paris, Odile Jacob.

42 Baratay E. *Et l'homme créa l'animal*, Paris, Odile Jacob, p.116

43 Delort R. (1984). *Les animaux ont une histoire*, p. 65.

44 Nobrega Alves R. R., Policarpo I. S. (2018). "Animals and human health: Where do they meet? in R. R. Nobrega Alves, U. P. Albuquerque (eds.), *Ethnozoology*, pp. 233–259. This traditional pharmacopeia is very profitable: it grossed 34 billion euros in 2018 (Lacaze J. [2019]. " Les croyances de la médecine chinoise à l'origine d'un important trafic d'animaux," *National Geographic*, 232, January.)

45 George A. E. (2011). "Bioprospecting and biopiracy," in D. K. Chatterjee (ed.). *Encyclopedia of Global Justice*, Dordrecht, Springer.

46 Nobrega Alves R. R., Albuquerque D. (2018). "Introduction: Animals in our lives," in R. R. Nobrega Alves, U. P. Albuquerque (eds.), *Ethnozoology*,, pp. 1–7.

47 Norwood F. V., Lusk J. (2011). *Compassion by the pound: The economics of farm animal welfare*, Abingdon, Oxford University Press.

48 Murray M. (2011). "The underdog in history: Serfdom, slavery and species in the creation and development of capitalism," in N. Taylor, T. Signal (eds.), *Theorizing Animals: Re-Thinking Human-Animal Relations*, Boston, Brill Academic Press, pp. 87–106.

49 Baratay É. (2008). *Bêtes de somme. Des animaux au service des hommes*, Paris, La Martinière.

50 Serpell J. (1986). *In the Company of Animals*, op. ct.

51 Nibert D. (2013). *Animal Oppression and Human Violence. Domesecration, Capitalism, and Global Conflict*, New York, Columbia University Press.

52 Armengaud F. (1998). " Au titre du sacrifice: l'exploitation économique, symbolique et idéologique des animaux, " in B. Cyrulnik (ed.). *Si les lions pouvaient parler*, p. 856–887.

53 Wilson E. O. (1984). *Biophilia*, Cambridge, Harvard University Press; see also Wilson E. O. (1993). La Diversité de la vie, Paris, Odile Jacob.

54 Bell P. A., Greene T. C., Fisher J. D., Baum A. (1996). *Environmental Psychology*, New York, Harcourt, 4th ed.; Keniger L. E., Gaston K. J., Irvine K. N., Fuller R. A. (2013). "What are the benefits of interacting with nature?," *International Journal of Environmental Research and Public Health*, 10 (3), pp. 913–935.

55 Simion F., Regolin L., Bulf H. (2008). "A predisposition for biological motion in the newborn baby," *PNAS USA*, 105 (2), p. 809–813.

56 Elsner B., Jeschonek S., Pauen S. (2013). "Event-related potentials for 7-month-olds' processing of animals and furniture items," *Developmental Cognitive Neuroscience*, 3, pp. 53–60.

57 Montagner H. (2002). *L'Enfant et l'Animal. Les émotions qui libèrent l'intelligence*, Paris, Odile Jacob, see p. 262 and following.

58 Lobue V., Bloom Pikard M., Sherman K., Axford C., Dreloache J. (2013). "Young children's interest in live animals," *British Journal of Developmental Psychology*, 31, pp. 57–69.

59 Arluke A. (2007). "The appeal of animals to children," in M. Bekoff (ed.). *Encyclopedia of Human–Animal Relationships*, Westport, Greenwood Press, vol. 1., pp. 205–207.

60 Caselli M. C., Bates E. et al., (1995). "Cross-linguistic lexical development," *Cognitive Development*, 10, pp. 159–199.

61 Kellert S. (1993). "The biological basis for human values of nature," in S. Kellert, E. O. Wilson (eds.). *The Biophilia Hypothesis*, Washington, Island Press; Montagner H. (2002). *L'Enfant et l'Animal*.

62 Rossant L., Villemin V. (1998). "L'animal et le développement de l'enfant," in B. Cyrulnik (ed.). *Si les lions pouvaient parler*, p. 1306–1325.

63 Sándor P., Szakadát S., Kertész K., Bódizs R. (2015). "Content analysis of 4- to 8-year-old children's dream reports," *Frontiers in Psychology*, 6, p. 534.

64 Montagner H. (1995). *L'Enfant, l'animal et l'école*, Paris, Bayard.

65 Balas B., Momsen J. L. (2014). "Attention 'blinks' differently for plants and animals," *CBE Life Sciences Education*, 13 (3), pp. 437–443.

66 Schussler E. E., Olzak L. A. (2008). "It's not easy being green: Student recall of plant and animal images," *Journal of Biological Education*, 42 (3), pp. 112–119.

67 Melson G. (2001). *Les Animaux dans la vie des enfants*, Paris, Payot.

68 Methorst J., Rehdanz C., Mueller T., Hansjürgens B., Bonn A., Böhning-Gaese. A. (2021). "The importance of species diversity for human well-being in Europe," *Ecological Economics*, 181, p. 106917.

69 Paul E. S., Serpell J. A. (1996). "Obtaining a new pet dog: Effects on middle childhood children and their families," *Applied Animal Behaviour Science*, 47 (1–2), pp. 17–29.

70 Allen K. (2003). "Are pets healthy pleasure? The influence of pets on blood pressure," *Current Directions in Psychological Science*, 12 (6), pp. 236–239.

71 Herzog H. (2011). *Some We Love, Some We Hate, Some We Eat*, New York, Harper.

72 McConnell A. R., Brown C. M., Shoda T. M., Stayton L. E., Martin C. E. (2011). "Friends with benefits: On the positive consequences of pet ownership," *Journal of Personality and Social Psychology*, 101 (6), pp. 1239–1252.

73 Campo R. A., Uchino B. N. (2013). "Humans' bonding with their companion dogs: Cardiovascular benefits during and after stress," *Journal of Sociology & Social Welfare*, 40, pp. 237–259. A similar result was found with children suffering from an attachment disorder: see Beetz A., Julius H., Turner D., Kotrschal K. (2012). "Effects of social support by a dog on stress modulation in male children with insecure attachment," *Frontiers in Psychology*, 3, p. 352.

74 Assessfirst 2020 survey, quoted by Dombreval L. (2021). *Barbaries*, Paris, Michel Lafon, p. 120.

75 Kurrie S., Day R., Cameron I. (2004). "The perils of companion animal ownership: A new fall-injury risk factor," *Medical Journal of Australia*, 181, pp. 682–683.

76 Amiot C. E., Bastian B. (2015). "Toward a psychology of human–animal relations," *Psychological Bulletin*, 141 (1), p. 6–47. Voir aussi Michalon J. (2013). *Panser avec les animaux. Sociologie du soin par le contact animalier*, Paris, Presse des Mines.

77 Headey B. (1998). "Health benefits and health cost saving due to pets: Preliminary estimates from an Australian national survey," *Social Indicators Research*, 47, pp. 233–243.

78 The observed were independent of the health status of the participants at the beginning of the study. Voir Headey B., Grabka M. (2007). "Pets and human health in Germany and Australia: National longitudinal results," *Social Indicators Research*, 80, pp. 297–311.

79 Murray J. K., Gruffydd-Jones T. J., Roberts M. A., Browne W. J. (2015). "Assessing changes in the UK pet cat and dog populations: Numbers and household ownership," *Veterinary Records*, 177, p. 259.

80 It is still not known whether he was trying to cure the "Rat Man" or the "Wolf Man".

81 Taylor N. (2013). *Humans, Animals, and Society. An Introduction to Human-Animal Studies*, New York, Lantern Books.

82 Brown S. G., Rhodes R. E. (2006). "Relationships among dog ownership and leisure-time walking in Western Canadian adults," *American Journal of Preventive Medicine*, 30 (2), pp. 131—136.

83 Eddy J., Hart L. A., Boltz R. P. (1988). "The effects of service dogs on social acknowledgments of people in wheelchairs," *The Journal of Psychology: Interdisciplinary and Applied*, 122 (1), pp. 39–45.

84 McNicholas J., Collis G. (2000). "Dogs as catalysts for social interactions: Robustness of the effect," *British Journal of Psychology*, 91 (1), pp. 61–70.

85 McNicholas J., Collis G. (2000).

86 Fontenay É. de (1998). *Le Silence des bêtes. La philosophie à l'épreuve de l'animalité*, Paris, Fayard.

87 De Waal F. (2001). *Quand les singes prennent le thé. De la culture animale*, Paris, Fayard.

88 Pull C. D., Cremer S. (2017). "Co-founding ant queens prevent disease by performing prophylactic undertaking behaviour," *BMC Evolutionary Biology*, 17, p. 219.

89 According to a study by Sarah Batt, biological classification explains 25% of human preferences for any given animal. Sarah Batt (2009). "Human attitudes towards animals in relation to species similarity to humans: A multivariate approach, *Bioscience Horizons: The International Journal of Student Research*, 2, pp. 180–190. See also Miralles A., Raymond M., Lecointre G. (2019). "Empathy and compassion toward other species decrease with evolutionary divergence time," *Scientific Reports*, 9, p. 19555.

90 This perception reflects the choices in selective breeding that lead to the creation of anthropized races.

91 Borgi M., Cogliati-Dezza I., Brelsford V., Meints K., Cirulli F. (2014). "Baby schema in human and animal faces induces cuteness perception and gaze allocation in children," *Frontiers in Psychology*, 5, 411.

92 Klebl C., Luo Y., Bastian B. (2021). "Beyond aesthetic judgment: Beauty increases moral standing through perceptions of purity," *Personality and Social Psychology Bulletin*, in press. (https://doi.org/10.1177/01461672211023648).

93 In a study carried out by University of Arizona researcher Anna Gunnthorsdotti, participants were presented with a leaflet that was supposed to come from a conservation organisation pleading for the protection of bats or monkeys. On the leaflet were pictures of the animals – sometimes attractive, sometimes unattractive. The results showed that in both cases, the attractiveness of the animal increased public support for its protection. Support for the monkey was higher than support for the bat. Voir Gunnthorsdottir A. (2001). "Physical attractiveness of an animal species as a decision factor for its preservation," Anthrozoös, 14, pp. 204–215; Colleony A., Clayton S., Couvet D., Saint Jalme M., Prevot A. C. (2017). "Human preferences for species conservation: Animal charisma trumps endangered status »," *Biological Conservation*, 206, pp. 263–269.

94 Ward P., Mosberger N., Kistler C., Fischer O. (2008). "The relationship between popularity and body size in zoo animals," Conservation Biology, 12, pp. 1408–1411; see also Kellert S. (1993). "Attitudes, knowledge, and behavior toward wildlife among the industrial superpowers: United States, Japan, and Germany," *The Journal of Social Issues*, 49, pp. 53–69.

95 Brunet S. (2018). *Verser des larmes de crocodile et 99 autres expressions animalières*, Paris, First.

96 Marsolier M.-C. (2020). *Le Mépris des bêtes*, Paris, PUF.

97 https://www.collinsdictionary.com/dictionary/english-thesaurus/animal.

98 Kerbrat-Orecchioni C. (2021). *Nous et les autres animaux*, Paris, Lambert-Lucas.

99 Marsolier M.-C. (2020). *Le Mépris des bêtes*, p. 50.

100 Kerbrat Orecchioni C. (2021). *Nous et les autres animaux*, p. 242.

101 Serpell J. A. (2007). "Witchcraft and animals," in M. Bekoff (ed.). *Encyclopedia of Human–Animal Relationships*, pp. 622–626. See also Muchembled R. (2000). *Une histoire du diable*. xiie–xxe siècle, Paris, Seuil, Points.

102 Delort R. (1984). Les animaux ont une histoire, p. 432.

103 Vincent-Cassy M. (1984). Les Animaux et les péchés capitaux: de la symbolique à l'emblématique, Actes des congrès de la Société des historiens médiévistes de l'enseignement supérieur public, 15e congrès, Toulouse, 1984: "Le monde animal et ses représentations au Moyen Âge" (xie–xve siècle), pp. 121–132.

104 Black C. N. "Animals in picture books for children," unpublished study quoted in Melson G. (2001). *Les Animaux dans la vie des enfants*, p. 197.

105 There is one exception, however: when they are cast as villains, like the dogs in Bambi. See Stanton R. R. (2021). *The Disneyfication of Animals*, Cham, Palgrave Macmillan, p. 43.

106 Stanton (2021). *The Disneyfication of Animals*.

107 Zask J. (2020). *Zoocities. Des animaux sauvages dans la ville*, Paris, Premier Parallèle, p. 40.

108 De Mello M. (2012). *Animals and Society*, p. 331.

109 For example, 91% of hunters are men in these magazines and cartoons.

110 Wrenn C. (2017). "The Disney nonhuman princess, sex and gender news," cité par Dardenne E. (2020). *Introduction aux études animales*, Paris, PUF, p. 215.

111 Stanton R. R. (2021). *The Disneyfication of Animals*.

112 Prévot-Julliard A. C., Julliard R., Clayton S. (2015). "Historical evidence for nature disconnection in a 70-year time series of Disney animated films," *Public Understanding of Science*, 24 (6), pp. 672–680.

113 I am using a distinction made by Chapouthier G. (2019). "Réflexions sur la manière de classer les animaux et sur ses conséquences juridiques," Revue semestrielle de droit animalier, 1–2, pp. 509–515.

114 Cyrulnik B. (2010). *Mémoire de singe et paroles d'homme*, Paris, Fayard, Pluriel, p. 71.

3   Interwoven Relationships Between Animals and Humans

Illustration: Magali Seghetto

"Humans first drew the boundary between who deserved rights (i.e., humans) and other living species, and they eventually found themselves moving that boundary within the human species."[1]

Claude Lévi-Strauss

Not only are animals the universal metaphor for otherness, but they also very often embody the very essence of insignificance or degradation.[2] For anthropologist Claude Lévi-Strauss, the binary distinction that humanity has created between its species and all others is doubly detrimental. First, it creates an injurious distinction between humans and the rest of the animal world. Then, within the crucible of that duality, it forges a "vicious circle," for that condition "serves to cast some people aside, claiming for an ever-smaller minority the privilege of a humanism that was corrupted at the onset for having borrowed its main principle and notion from self-love."[3]

Thus, the principle of a hierarchy of beings may be hard-wired in the human brain, like a pernicious divide allowing us to degrade our fellow human beings by merely associating

DOI: 10.4324/9781003561972-4

them with animals. In a study conducted in 11 countries in which volunteers were asked to indicate how they would react if someone bumped into them without apologizing, a plethora of animal insults came up (*bitch*, *cow*, *jackass*, *pig*, *rat*, and so on), as if one could not insult a fellow human being without some derogatory reference to animals.[4] In France, when journalist Sandra Muller started a broad social movement denouncing sexual abuse in 2017, it was the hashtag *balance ton porc* ("call out your pig") which forged solidarity among victims. The tendency to use pig-related insults in French even includes references to pork-based foods: a pig-headed person can be called a "lard-head" (*tête de lard*), an idiot an *andouille* (a type of pork sausage), and an unattractive woman a *boudin* (blood sausage or pudding). In 2018, the Paris public transport operator RATP launched a campaign against harassment, and on each of the three different posters that were displayed in the Paris metro, a lone woman was portrayed being threatened either by a bear, a pack of wolves, or a shark.[5]

Outsiders are the universal target of choice for animalisation. In his essay *Race et Histoire*, Claude Lévi-Strauss noted that the history of humankind is full of examples showing that all kinds of animal insults are used to strip Others of their dignity: *lice, monkeys, dogs, pigs, rats, parasites, insects*…[6] From the Greek and Roman world, which already animalised subordinated social groups, to the genocides of the 20th century which exemplified the phenomenon on a terrifying scale with Armenian, Jewish, Tutsi and other victims, these logics intensify in times of intergroup conflict: "Conflict between pagans and Christians in the Roman empire, between Christians and heretics in the 12th century, witches in the 15th and 16th centuries, etc. From the Renaissance onwards, the process took on a new dimension with the printing press, which added books and engravings to oral discourse. The 19th century was also a

Figure 3.1 From 1870 to 1918, Germans were the targets of bestialising caricatures.
Illustration: Magali Seghetto

Figure 3.2 Man's head inspired by an owl.
Illustration: Charles Le Brun, 1670, Official painter of King Louis XIV
Source: https://parkstone.international/2016/05/17/charles-le-brun-ce-que-vous-allez-apprendre-sur-lartiste-star-du-xviie-siecle-va-surement-vous-etonner/

climactic moment because of strong political, nationalistic, and social tensions, and because of the rise of unprecedented means of communication such as newspapers and posters."[7]

One still encounters animalising racism today in such places as sports arenas[8] or courts of law.[9] In a study on the media coverage of 153 capital trials, University of Pennsylvania scholar Philip Goff found that a bestialising designation was four times as likely when the accused was Black. Regardless of the economic status of the accused, the circumstances or the seriousness of the crime, Black people who were tried for homicide were more likely to be executed if they had been described as ape-like in newspaper columns. In another study, participants were presented with a series of photos of faces of people from traditional or industrial societies. The researchers would then measure to what extent these faces were associated with various categories of words. The faces of people who seemed to belong to traditional societies were more often described as animal-like or child-like and more likely to be attributed features that were not specifically human.[10]

This animalisation of outsiders also manifested in many pseudoscientific works which purported to quantify how animal-like people were by analysing their facial features. Measuring the angles in people's faces allegedly allowed the father of physiognomy, Kaspar Lavater, to determine how human a face was:

[According to this system, a]ll creatures which we comprehend under the name of man, with all their anomalies, are included between sixty and seventy degrees...What is below seventy degrees gives the countenance of the negro of Angola and the Calmuc; and by a further diminution loses all trace of resemblance to humanity.[11]

Dehumanising a Group by Animalising it

Animalising (or bestialising) means denying the humanity of an individual or a group by assigning primitive traits to them, sometimes in a surprisingly abrupt manner. This is shown by a series of studies conducted by a researcher from Northwestern University,[12] which consisted of showing volunteers the following scale and asking them "how evolved" each group was by moving a cursor on a line.

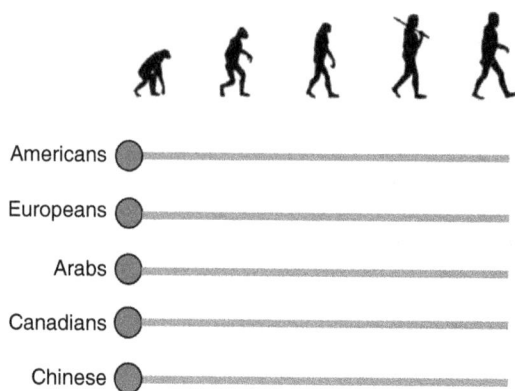

Figure 3.3 A measure of intergroup prejudice. Participants move a cursor to express their judgement on various social categories.

In a study that used this method with American respondents, participants estimated that South Koreans, Chinese people and Mexican immigrants were "less evolved." It also transpired that the more participants dehumanised Arabs (by placing them closer to the left end of the spectrum), the more they opposed their being accepted as immigrants to the United States and the more they tolerated their being subjected to discrimination on the job market or from the police, or even torture. In another study, American participants who were informed during an experiment that Americans were considered less evolved by Arabs then tended to express negative judgements towards that group.[13]

Part of the job of historians is to show to what extent the use of bestialising representations declines when intergroup tensions diminish. In France, this happened during the second half of the 20th century, when nationalism and antisemitism declined after peaking during WWII.[14] But dehumanisation never goes away completely – it keeps ebbing and flowing depending on national circumstances. After a terrorist attack in the United States (an explosion that killed three people and injured 140 during the 2013 Boston marathon), the dehumanization of Arabs intensified.[15] Conversely, when foreigners are involved in constructive exchanges, they are less likely to be dehumanised.[16]

Can referring to individuals or groups as animals make them more likely to come to harm? This was suggested by philosopher Theodor Adorno, who theorised about the psychological foundations of fascism[17] and who, in his essay *Minima Moralia*, claimed that "The constantly encountered assertion that *savages, blacks, Japanese are like animals, monkeys for example, is the key to the pogrom*."[18] A Stanford University study put this reasoning to the test.[19] Participants were recruited and gathered into teams of three supervisors whose role was to analyse collective decision-making. The supervisors could hear the verbal exchanges between members of the group who were in an adjacent room. At the end of each decision-making session, when a mistake was found (those mistakes had been planned in advance by the experimenters; also, there was no decision-making team but only recordings designed to pretend there was one), the supervisors had to sanction it with an electric shock ranging from an intensity of 1 to 10 for every member of the group that had just performed poorly. While they were sitting for the experiment, the supervisors could hear an intercom exchange between the research assistant and the experimenter: the assistant would either say that the members of the group seemed to be "full of humanity" or, conversely, that they were a team of "animals." In the last condition (the neutral one), no judgement was expressed about the group.

The results fit Adorno's hypothesis: with every session, the subjects who had been called "animals" would get ever stronger electric shocks, and those who had been described in favourable terms received the weakest possible shocks, while the neutral-condition participants received mid-range shocks.[20]

Are People Who Care More about Animals Also More Compassionate with Humans?

The philosophical claim that the basis for the dehumanisation of minorities is the boundary drawn between humans and animals did not remain in the realm of pure speculation. Two Canadian researchers, Kimberly Costello and Gordon Hodson, carried out a series of studies which demonstrated this provocative theory. In a study on a sample of Canadian children aged 6 to 10, the researchers brought to light several particularly interesting phenomena. First, the children whose parents subscribed to the idea of a sharp divide between animals and humans took over the same hierarchical representation. It was strongest in those children who had experienced predominantly punitive parenting,[21] and it decreased as children's cognitive abilities improved. Finally, the more children adhered to the idea of a hierarchy between humans and animals, the more prejudiced they were and the more they dehumanised black people.

Those results were confirmed in a sample of adult participants:[22] the more they supported a sharp distinction between animals and humans, the more reluctant they were to ascribe specifically human features to immigrants. Conversely, people who felt solidarity with animals were also less likely to display demeaning attitudes towards minorities.[23]

As a whole, these results are reminiscent of an old hypothesis by one of the founders of prejudice studies, psychologist Gordon Allport. For this Harvard researcher, there is a link between expressing prejudices against a given minority (for example Jews or homosexuals) and expressing similar prejudices against other minorities.[24] This phenomenon is particularly marked when it comes to low-status groups,[25] and it is amplified in people who score high for personality traits like authoritarianism[26] or social dominance orientation,[27] to which we will return.

A Framing Effect

Since the use of animal labels leads to the denigration of certain identities, is it conceivable that a positive view of animals benefits human groups through a kind of drying up of the "well of contempt" that is animalisation? Although one might doubt that a change in the representation of animals would suffice to solve hostility and violence between human groups (after all, one can still use foul language, or plant-based[28] rather than animal-based insults to refer to those one hates), some studies show that the conceptual opposition between animals and humans plays a deep, systemic role. One might therefore ask whether a redrawing of those boundaries might not benefit humans as well as other species.

That much is suggested by a study in which the experimenters presented the participants with scientific information that emphasised some similarities between humans and animals. This blurring of the boundary with animals had two consequences: it decreased the dehumanisation of immigrants, and it ultimately produced a more favourable attitude towards them.[29]

In another study, a group of volunteers was asked to write an essay on similarities between humans and animals, while others were asked to write about similarities between animals and humans. Despite appearances, the two instructions are not equivalent. Classic research in cognitive psychology shows that, when reference to oneself is emphasized in a context of comparison with another, perceived similarity is higher than it is when reference to the other is emphasized.[30] For example, if we are asked "To what extent do you think you are like your neighbour William?" our perception of similarity will be higher than if we are asked "To what extent do you think your neighbour William is like you?" Following this instruction, it was noted that, when participants subsequently completed a questionnaire on the cognitive abilities of animals, those who had compared them with humans granted them more mental abilities. Furthermore, this increase in ascribed abilities strengthened the feeling of moral obligation towards animals.

The same researchers then hypothesised that the widening of the moral circle caused by the idea of proximity to animals strengthened support for certain discriminated groups. Indeed, their results confirmed that people who had been asked to write an essay emphasising similarities between animals and humans were more likely to commit to helping victims of social rejection.

Categorising Animals and Depriving Them of Individuality

We saw that the category "animal" is used to denigrate human groups and might even be considered as "the gold standard of human discrimination."[31] We could add that the cognitive mechanisms at work when we think about human groups or interact with them also apply to animals as a group. The simplifying process that consists in erasing complexity or variation between individuals in a category is one of these mechanisms. The most obvious one is the very use of the category "animal," which is not only artificially opposed to "human," but also lumps together creatures as dissimilar as the amoeba and the blue whale.

The animal is "that which is on the other side, inside the cage," explains philosopher Patrice Rouget.[32] This undifferentiated perception of (other) animals is the result of a very general identity mechanism through which individual humans differentiate themselves from other categories of living organisms well before they can specifically identify them. Could this kind of self-centred cognition be found in all species, as Plato suggested?

> This is what another thinking animal (if there is such a thing) – say, a crane – would do… It would probably assign names as you do, taking first of all a single genus, the crane, to oppose it to other living creatures and to glorify itself, and it would reject all the rest, including men, for whom it would probably use no other name than "beasts."[33]

This inclination goes hand in hand with a tendency to demean the animal world more directly by designating it in a homogeneous and monolithic way. The very use of the word *animal* to refer to a multitude of different species is revealing not only of human self-centeredness, but also of a certain disregard for animals.[34] *Animal* is an oppressive word chosen by humans in order to "enclose a huge number of living beings within that single concept,"[35] deplored Jacques Derrida. This complete undifferentiation is the most obvious expression of a downgrading of the animal world, the philosopher adds:

> The confusion of all nonhuman living creatures within the general and common category of the animal is not simply a sin against rigorous thinking, vigilance, lucidity, or empirical authority, it is also a crime. Not a crime against animality, precisely, but a crime of the first order against the animals, against animals.[36]

Another form of denigration consists in considering that, within a given species, individuals are perfectly interchangeable.[37] The animal only exists as a manifestation of a species, not as an individual, claimed Augustine in *The City of God*[38] – an idea that was later taken over by Thomas Aquinas.[39] This perception is enough to affect our representation of their abilities, as was demonstrated in the case of human groups.

Thus, in a study, people were presented as individuals ("20 employees working in a small business") or simply as a group ("a small business") having experienced a cyberattack that caused the company to go bankrupt. The participants then had to comment on the victims' ability to feel pain and suffering and to have intentions and goals. Then they would indicate how much sympathy they felt for them. The results showed that this simple linguistic framing was enough to have a significant influence on measured outcomes: the respondents showed more empathy towards the "25 employees" than towards the members of the "small business."[40] The relevance of this study seems obvious when it comes to understanding the possible consequences of the deindividuation of animals.

When animals belong to species subjected to human exploitation, using a mass noun to refer to them expresses a further degree of denial of their individuality, as when one wears *chinchilla* or *mink* and eats *duck* or *beef*.[41] The animal disappears entirely when it is referred to as a material quantity. According to the same logic, fish are not counted but designated in tonnage. The deindividuation of animals seems especially inevitable when they are destined to become food for humans, since this offers the comfort of their complete disappearance before they are consumed. Of course, individuating an animal does not mean one can no longer make a meal out of it, but making the living animal completely invisible secures the consumer's moral comfort.

As soon as animals are perceived in a less utilitarian way, one can start to notice differences between members of a species. This is what happens in experiments which highlight behavioural variation between individuals in unexpected domains. For example, ethologist Cédric Sueur and his team at the University of Strasbourg analysed 749 drawings made by female orangutans in a Japanese zoological garden. He observed that each one of them had a pictorial style of her own, as shown by her choice of colours, the shapes that were drawn or the space that was used.[42] In some instances, the psychological dimensions used to describe human personality are appropriate for animals.[43] Scientific observation in their natural environment or in the lab confirms the existence of stable differences between individuals in many vertebrates, including fish.[44] It also allows us to avoid misinterpretations of their behaviour such as mistaking a chimpanzee's fearful expression for one of joy because it looks like a human smile, or thinking that a dolphin trained to do somersaults is really smiling in its little pool, or that the swaying of an elephant in the spotlight is natural when it is actually a sign of stress or boredom.[45]

Since the scientific data on the individuality and complexity of animals as evidenced by their psychology and behaviour is known, how is it that we have retained so many prejudices and blind spots?

Notes

1 Lévi-Strauss C. (1979). Interview with Jean Marie Benoist, "L'Idéologie marxiste, communiste et totalitaire n'est qu'une ruse de l'histoire," *Le Monde*, January 21–22, p. 14, quoted in Legrand S. (2010). "Figures du monstrueux. Entre l'humain et l'inhumain," in J. Birnbaum (ed.), *Qui sont les animaux?* Paris, Gallimard, pp. 225–240.

2 The "animal = evil" equation is an old one, and anthropologists say it is a universal one. Our animal nature is the heritage that Freud, in *Civilisation and Its Discontents*, wanted us to replace with the social order by conquering our instincts, and sociologist Norbert Elias noted that one of the characteristics of the civilizing process was precisely the effort to rid oneself of any animal features.

3   Lévi-Strauss C. (1973). *Anthropologie structurale deux*, Paris, Plon, p. 53.

4   Van Oudenhoven J.P., et al. (2008). "Terms of abuse as expression and reinforcement of cultures," *International Journal of Intercultural Relations*, 32, pp. 174–185.

5   Bègue-Shankland,L. (2018). " 'Balance ton transport' ": comment la RATP diabolise les animaux pour lutter contre le harcèlement sexuel," *The Conversation*, 16 March.

6   Originally, the word *barbarian* referred to birdsong, as opposed to meaningful human language. Lévi-Strauss C. (1961). *Race et Histoire*. Paris, Albin Michel, p. 20; see also Bain P., Vaes J., Leyens J.-P. (2014). *Humanness and Dehumanization*, New York, Routledge; Roberts M. S. (2008). *The Mark of the Beast. Animality and Human Oppression*, West Lafayette, Purdue University Press; Smith D. L. (2011). *Less than Human: Why we Demean, Enslave, and Exterminate Others*, New York, St Martin's Press; Le Bras-Chopard A. (2000). *Le Zoo des philosophes. De la bestialisation à l'exclusion*, Paris, Plon.

7   Baratay É. (2003). *Et l'homme créa l'animal*, Paris, Odile Jacob, p. 242.

8   https://www.lemonde.fr/sport/article/2019/11/19/racisme-face-aux-cris-de-singe-et-auxinsul tes-la-prise-de-conscience-des-footballeurs_6019666_3242.html.

9   Goff P. A., Eberhardt J. L., Williams M. J., Jackson M. C. (2008). "Not yet human: Implicit knowledge, historical dehumanization, and contemporary consequences," *Journal of Personality and Social Psychology*, 94, pp. 292–306. The animalising of the Other sometimes expresses itself in very paradoxical ways – for example when an animal rights activist and former film star denouncing the use of dogs or cats as bait for shark fishing called the Reunion Islanders she was criticizing a "degenerate population" that still had "savage genes." Talpin J. (2021). "Bardot, les Réunionnais, et leurs gènes de sauvages," *Le Monde*, October 9, p. 15.

10 Saminaden A., Loughnan S., Haslam N. (2010). "Afterimages of savages: Implicit associations between 'primitives,' animals and children," *British Journal of Social Psychology*, 49, pp. 91–105.

11 Lavater, J. K. (1850). *Essays on Physiognomy: Designed to Promote the Knowledge and the Love of Mankind*. W. Tegg. Quoted in Fontenay, Elisabeth de. (2012). *Without Offending Humans: A Critique of Animal Rights*. University of Minnesota Press.

12 Kteily N., Bruneau E., Waytz A., Cotterill S. (2015). "The ascent of man: Theoretical and empirical evidence for blatant dehumanization," *Journal of Personality and Social Psychology*, 109 (5), pp. 901–931.

13 Kteily N., Hodson G., Bruneau E. (2016). "They see us as less than human: Metadehumanization predicts intergroup conflict via reciprocal dehumanization," *Journal of Personality and Social Psychology*, 110 (3), pp. 343–370.

14 Baratay É. (2003). *Et l'homme créa l'animal*, Paris, Odile Jacob, p. 243.

15 Kteily N., Bruneau E., Waytz A., Cotterill S. (2015). "The ascent of man: Theoretical and empirical evidence for blatant dehumanization."

16 Bruneau E., Hameiri B., Moore-Berg S. L., Kteily N. (2020). "Intergroup contact reduces dehumanization and meta-dehumanization: Cross-sectional, longitudinal and experimental evidence from 16 samples in 5 countries," *Personality and Social Psychology Bulletin*, 47 (6), doi.org/10.1177/0146167220949004.

17 Adorno T. W., Frenkel-Brunswik E., Levinson D. J., Sanford R. N. (1950). *The Authoritarian Personality*, New York, Harpers.

18 Adorno T. (1978). *Minima Moralia: Reflections from Damaged Life*, Verso, p. 105. In the same vein, Poliakov wrote: "Interspecific barriers eventually found their counterpart in hierarchical 'interracial' barriers." Poliakov L. (1975). *Hommes et bêtes. Entretiens sur le racisme*, Paris, Mouton.

19 Bandura A., Underwood B., Fromson M. E. (1975). "Disinhibition of aggression through diffusion of responsibility and dehumanization of victims," *Journal of Research in Personality*, 9 (4), pp. 253–269.

20 Less overt ways of demeaning are sometimes used against outsiders by refusing to grant them feelings that are considered specifically human, such as shame or happiness (so-called "secondary" emotions), while acknowledging that they experience "primary" emotions that are not distinctly human, such as fear or pleasure. Thus individuals ascribe more secondary (subtle) emotions to members of their ingroup than they ascribe to members of a lower status group. Leyens J.-P.,

Paladino M., Rodríguez-Torres R., Vaes J., Demoulin S., Rodríguez-Pérez A. et al. (2000). "The emotional side of prejudice: The attribution of secondary emotions to ingroups and outgroups," *Personality and Social Psychology Review*, 4, pp. 186–197. For an overview, see also Leyens J.-P. (2015). *L'Humanité écorchée. Humanité et infrahumanisation*, Grenoble, PUG.

21 This parenting style is evidenced by test answers like "I scold and criticize my child to that he or she can improve."

22 Costello K., Hodson G. (2010). "Exploring the roots of dehumanization: The role of animal–human similarity in promoting immigrant humanization," *Group Processes & Intergroup Relations*, 13 (1), pp. 3--22.

23 Amiot C. E., Bastian B. (2017). "Solidarity with animals: Assessing a relevant dimension of social identification with animals," *PLoS One*, 12 (1), p. e0168184.

24 Allport G. W. (1954). *The Nature of Prejudice*, Boston, Addison-Wesley.

25 Bergh R., Akrami N., Sidanius J., Sibley C. G. (2016). "Is group membership necessary for understanding generalized prejudice? A re-evaluation of why prejudices are interrelated," *Journal of Personality and Social Psychology*, 111 (3), pp. 367–395.

26 Altemeyer B. (1996). *The Authoritarian Specter*, Boston, Harvard University Press.

27 Sidanius J., Pratto F. (1999). *Social Dominance: An Intergroup Theory of Social Hierarchy and Oppression*, Cambridge, Cambridge University Press.

28 Historian Eric Baratay notes that political caricatures from the French Revolution to the Dreyfus affair were full of regression to animal but also vegetable states. See Baratay É. (2003). *Et l'homme créa l'animal*, Paris, Odile Jacob, p. 242.

29 However, this phenomenon was not observed in the population of children studied by the researchers. See Costello K., Hodson G. (2014). "Explaining dehumanization among children: The interspecies model of prejudice," *The British Journal of Social Psychology*, 53 (1), pp. 175–197.

30 Codol J.-P. (1984). "La perception de la similitude interpersonnelle: influence de l'appartenance catégorielle et du point de référence de la comparaison," *L'Année Psychologique*, 84, pp. 43–56.

31 Bimbenet E. (2011). *L'Animal que je ne suis plus*, Paris, Gallimard, p. 131.

32 Rouget P. (2014). *La Violence de l'humanisme*, Paris, Calmann-Lévy, p. 17.

33 Platon, *Le Politique*, 263c-e, ed. L. Brisson et J.F. Pradeau. Paris, Flammarion, 2003, cited in Marsolier M.-C. (2020). *Le Mépris des bêtes*, Paris, PUF, p. 19.

34 See Marsolier M.-C. (2020). *Le Mépris des bêtes*, p. 11.

35 Derrida J (2006). *L'Animal donc que je suis*, Paris, Galilée, p. 54. To rebel against this prejudice, the philosopher coined "a chimerical word that sounded as though it contravened the laws of the French language, *l'animot*" (a combination of *animal* and *mot*, which is French for "word"). *The Animal That Therefore I Am*, Fordham UP, 2009.

36 Derrida J. (2006) *L'Animal donc que je suis*, *The Animal That Therefore I Am*, Fordham UP, 2009.

37 Burgat F. (1995). *L'Animal dans les pratiques de consommation*, Paris, PUF, p. 4.

38 See Rouget P. (2014). *La Violence de l'humanisme*, Paris, Calmann-Lévy, p. 128.

39 Thomas Aquinas, *Summa Contra Gentiles*, quoted in Fontenay É. de (1998). *Le Silence des bêtes*, Paris, Fayard, p. 249. According to linguist Emile Benvéniste's research, animals are usually referred to with plural forms, which makes them seem undifferentiated. Benvéniste É. (1969). *Le Vocabulaire des institutions indo-européennes, tome 1: Économie, parenté, société*, Paris, Minuit, p. 39.

40 Hodson G., Doucher C. (2020). "Language framing shapes dehumanization of groups: A successful replication and extension of Cooley et al. (2017)," *Journal of Experimental Psychology: General*, 149 (8), pp. 1603–1607.

41 See Marsolier M.-C. (2020). *Le Mépris des bêtes*, p. 112 and following.

42 Pelé M., Thomas G., Liénard A., Eguchi N., Shimada M., Sueur C. (2021). "I wanna draw like you: Inter- and intra-individual differences in orang-utan drawings," *Animals*, 11, p. 320.

43 Gosling S. D., John O. P. (1990). "Personality dimensions in nonhuman animals: A cross-species review," *Current Directions in Psychological Science*, 8, pp. 69–75.

44 Castanheira M. F., Herrera M., Costas B., Conceição L. E., Martins C. I. (2013). "Can we predict personality in fish? Searching for consistency over time and across contexts," *PLoS One*, 8 (4), p. e62037.

45 People who spend a lot of time with animals are not necessarily the best informed. Recently, circus artist André-Joseph Bouglione confessed after deciding to keep animals out of his shows: "To me, the gentle swaying of elephants when they're at rest meant that they were relaxed. But what I thought was a sign of relaxation was actually a disorder due to being locked in." Bouglione A.-J. (2018). *Contre l'exploitation animale*, Paris, Tchou.

4   The Origins of Our Prejudices Against Animals

Illustration: Magali Seghetto

"What we think we know is actually based on a series of highly questionable prejudices, most of which are due to our lack of attention."[1]

Vinciane Despret

Our prejudices against animals are part of a shared ancestral history.[2] What is the origin of those representations? The main explanation, the most obvious one, goes back to our primitive fear of animals, and sometimes it stems from our mutual hostility. Before ruling the animal world and becoming the "dominant ecological force on the planet,"[3] humans had to find ways to protect themselves against the predators that terrorised them. According to historian Éric Baratay, it

DOI: 10.4324/9781003561972-5

was only in the late 19th century that the fears elicited by certain dangerous animals began to decrease in Europe: wolves and bears were decimated, and insect pests were controlled.

Since we have long-standing antagonisms with several species, it is no wonder that our representations were shaped by these multimillennial feuds. The danger posed by some animals may even have shaped our basic perceptive abilities. According to the "snake-detection theory," the primate visual system evolved under pressure from dangerous reptiles: those individuals who could spot them faster than the others increased their chances of survival and passed this ability on to their offspring.[4]

The universal fear of snakes (*ophiophobia*) or spiders (*arachnophobia*) crosses the veil that separates our dreams from our waking hours. Children's nightmares are full of frightening beasts.[5] The fears caused by some animals also cross the fragile boundary between normality and mental illness, as in the case of zoopsia, those visual hallucinations of repulsive animals that torment victims of alcoholism when they experience delirium tremens.[6]

Where Animals and Humans Meet

Some geographers argue that our cities were initially built to protect us from the real or imagined dangers of the wild,[7] and one may suppose that this distancing has reinforced our ambivalent representations of the animal world.[8]

To understand the conflicts that pit us against animals, Philip Nyhus, a professor of environmental studies at Colby College, categorises our interactions with animals along three dimensions.

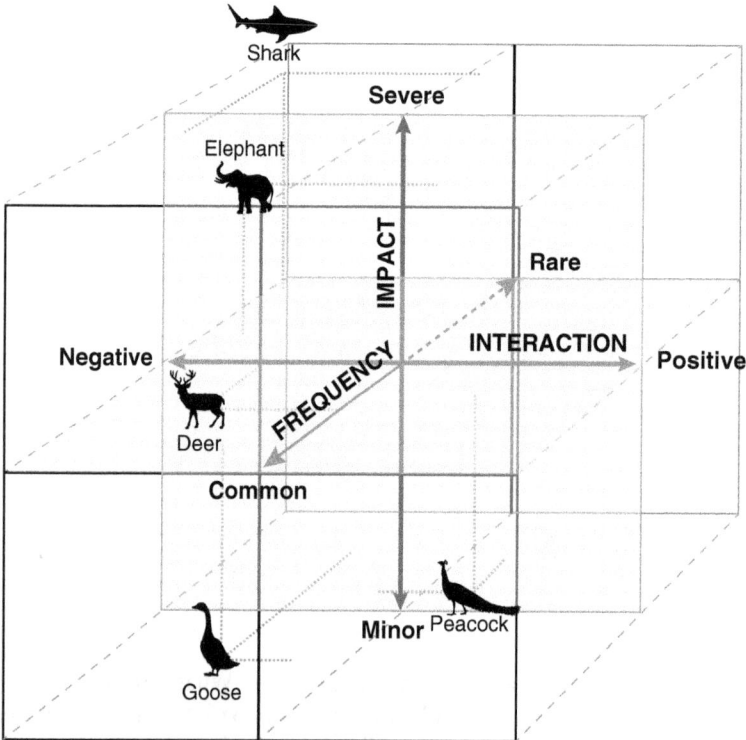

Figure 4.1 Types of conflicts between humans and wild animals: a three-dimensional model
Philip Nyhus (2016).

- *The first dimension* concerns the polarity of our mutual contacts. When their appearance fills us with wonder or even awe,[9] or when we are soothed by their company, we are at the gratifying and positive pole. Conversely, if their numbers or their appetites threaten our harvests or if their fangs kill our livestock, we are at the negative pole. According to a recent international study, 20 to 60% of European and American city dwellers are irritated by conflicts with wild animals, which they blame for causing damage or nuisance.[10] According to a study in Singapore, inhabitants come across two monkeys per hour on average, and in 20% of those encounters, the monkeys attack people.[11] The more the behaviour of a given species is considered unpredictable or uncontrollable, the more it causes a sense of threat.[12]
- *A second dimension* which describes our contacts with animals corresponds to the extent of their occurrence in the human sphere. We consider this occurrence benign when pigeons defecate on our monuments or when we are charmed by squirrels racing in the trees, but it becomes worrying or even deadly in the case of car accidents, physical attacks or illnesses caused by animals.
- *A third and last dimension* concerns the frequency of our contacts with them. These daily encounters with many familiar species are sometimes absolutely unique events, as was the sublime appearance of a snow leopard for travel writer Sylvain Tesson.[13]

The history of civilisations suggests that conflicts over material resources are a powerful influence on the relations between human groups.[14] The same kind of rivalry can occur among animals. It is probably not the first image that comes to mind when we think about our present relations with other species. However, for most of their evolutionary history, humans were not the irresponsible "apex predators"[15] they are often accused of being today. Our ancestors very often became the meals of animals who had the advantage of more powerful jaws and imposing statures.

Three Types of Animal Threats

Animals pose three types of risks for humans: direct physical attacks or indirect ones (against crops or pets), accidental collisions with vehicles, and parasitism or zoonoses (diseases transmitted by animals).[16]

Physical Attacks

There is plenty of historical evidence of conflict between humans and animals: human skulls dented by the teeth of big cats,[17] the development of herd-management techniques to counter predators ten thousand years ago,[18] written witness accounts from 300 BC describing the destruction of crops by elephants, medieval trials of pigs who had devoured babies or the excommunication of insects that had devastated harvests,[19] laws prescribing the eradication of wolves or other species in several countries, not to mention techniques such as hunting, trapping or poisoning with strychnine or DDT which have only continued to improve. Recently, several Japanese cities have deployed robots that look like terrifying wolves whose blinking red eyes, lateral head movements and loud growls (over sixty different kinds) are meant to keep bears away from people's homes.

Animals may attack humans when they are motivated by territorial or predatory instincts, but they are often defending themselves when they perceive a threat to their offspring or to themselves, as was probably the case in Ariège when a man was attacked by a female bear and he shot her. According to witnesses, the 70-year-old hunter "first encountered two cubs,

Figure 4.2 In 1457, this sow was put on trial for killing an infant.

Illustration: "Trial of a sow and pigs at Lavegny," *The book of days: a miscellany of popular antiquities*, 1869. https://en.wikipedia.org/wiki/Animal_trial

then the mother violently attacked him from behind and dragged him by the legs for more than 15 meters."[20]

This type of conflict notably concerns large herbivores or predators which may endanger people, cattle or crops. For instance, in four southern provinces of China, ten thousand people were allegedly injured or killed by tiger attacks over the last two millennia, which started a "war against nature" and the eradication of tigers under Mao Zedong.[21] It has been recorded that the sharp fangs of about two dozen species of carnivores threatened nine different species of animals that typically make up the world's herds.[22] That is why on every continent, countless wolves, jaguars, lions, tigers and wild dogs have been exterminated without mercy.[23]

A rigorous count, however, forces one to recognise that humans are more often physically threatened by large herbivores than predators.[24] Elephants and hippopotamuses also cause significant crop damage.[25] It is also worth mentioning bears, who endanger livestock, crops and beehives in many parts of the world[26] and occasionally attack humans. One Indian study found that over a 5-year period, 735 people had been injured or killed by bears,[27] while an estimate for North America put the annual number of people killed at 30.[28]

The picture would be very incomplete if we neglected the deadly danger posed by formidable reptiles such as crocodiles or caimans,[29] not to mention the 600 smaller species of venomous reptiles whose bites still cause tens of thousands of deaths every year.

Animals	Number of humans killed every year
Mosquito	725,000
Human	475,000
Snake	50,000
Dog	25,000
Tsetse fly	10,000
Triatoma (insect transmitting Chagas disease)	10,000
Freshwater snail	10,000
Roundworm (ascaris)	2,500
Tapeworm	2,000
Crocodile	1,000
Hippopotamus	500
Lion	100
Elephant	100
Wolf	10
Shark	10

Number of humans killed by various species[30]

Although less studied, the risks posed by marine animals should not be overlooked. According to the International Shark Attack File,[31] nearly 5,800 shark attacks have been recorded in 88 countries since the 16th century. Currently, there are about 90 attacks a year on the surface of the globe. About ten of these are fatal.

Finally, the damage caused to seedlings or crops usually implicates far less intimidating but particularly voracious animals such as sparrows, starlings or pigeons, which are sometimes subject to brutal measures. In 2014, nearly three million of these birds were exterminated by the US Department of Agriculture.[32] We should include the fearsome insect species that were part of the ten biblical plagues of Egypt, such as the locusts that mercilessly ravage crops and are a centuries-old cause of food insecurity and famine, and the mosquitoes that continue to cause nearly 750,000 annual deaths from the viral and parasitic diseases they spread.

Land and Air Collisions

This is the second type of contact and threat: on land, the intensification of transport over the past century has caused countless accidents as roads have segmented habitats and forced animals to cross them to access food and water, or to breed or migrate. Moreover, the accumulation of food waste and roadkill on roadsides attracts wildlife. In the United States, no less than a million vertebrates are killed on fast lanes every day.[33] Another study counted 700,000 deer and hinds killed by traffic, 29,000 injuries and 200 human deaths in one year from the same cause.[34] In Europe, it is estimated that there are about half a million traffic accidents involving deer or hinds every year. These collisions injure 30,000 drivers and kill over 200 of them every year.[35] In France, accidents involving large ungulates cause 50 deaths and 2,500 injuries every year.[36]

In airspace, collisions between birds and planes can also endanger humans during their flights. Such an event was brought to the screen by the film *Sully*, which recounts a tragic accident: in 2009, a flock of Canadian geese collided with an Airbus A320, nearly costing the lives of all 150 passengers. From 1988 to 2013, 229 collisions between birds and planes were recorded, killing countless birds and 250 humans. But many accidents are not recorded. According to another study, nearly 130,000 bird–plane collisions took place between 1990 and 2012. Although they are far less documented, collisions at sea certainly cause many animal deaths and a significant but smaller number of human casualties. Those involving whales are reported to have caused 1,762 human deaths worldwide over a period of 40 years.[37]

Zoonoses

The worms and other parasites carried by some animals pose a third type of animal threat, and not the least if one considers the vast number of deaths caused by the plague, yellow fever, Ebola, or severe acute respiratory syndrome. For example, dogs are held responsible for nearly all 55,000 cases of rabies cases recorded throughout the world every year.[38] Animals that are evolutionarily closer to us, like macaques, are hardly more reassuring, with their "mouths full of bacteria that are potentially lethal to humans. They carry diseases like rabies and herpes virus B. They may even carry Ebola and monkeypox."[39]

At the time of writing, over 5 million people worldwide have died from coronavirus – a pandemic that is most likely animal in origin. Nearly 60% of infectious diseases affecting humans can be transmitted by animals[40] (9 in 25 for the most dangerous diseases[41]) and, as we saw earlier, mosquitoes contribute disproportionately. I should add that the risk of zoonoses is amplified by concentration farming for human consumption.[42]

Conflicts Over Resources Influence Representations

Conflicts over material resources often turn their protagonists into opponents whose conflictual interactions fashion their mutual representations. When riches are at stake, we vilify those who might deprive us of them. This is evidenced in laboratory studies in which human groups are made to compete against each other for small amounts of money, but also in field observations.[43] For example, in a classic ethnographic study on 30 African ethnic groups, it was found that nearly all of them perceived themselves more positively than others, and that the closer the other ethnic groups lived and were therefore the more likely to covet the same territory or the same resources, the more they were denigrated.[44]

A similar phenomenon occurs with different animal species. All it takes is a picnic ruined by a few hornets,[45] a lawn ravaged by moles, longhorn beetles eating at the wooden framework of a house or a collision between a car and a wild boar to make us realise that any physical threat of interference with our goals degrades our representation of the animals involved. Without thinking for a second that there might be other ways of viewing the conflict (for example, who ran into whom on the road?), in these situations, we immediately perceive a conflict in which the animals are opponents to be subdued or eliminated. In some cases, the overabundance of some species is also seen as a sign of human social and sanitary failing, as is the case in Malaysia with crows, whose presence is concentrated in slums.[46]

Usually, people who live in urban environments have more positive attitudes towards wildlife than country people, as it is very rare for city dwellers to have encounters with wild animals.[47] Farmers and hunters have more negative views of wolves and bears than the general public, who are far less concerned with the threat they pose to farm animals or to prey that is also coveted by hunters.[48] These perceptions have also fluctuated throughout history. Essayist Jeffrey Masson reminds us that, in Native American cultures, wolves were particularly respected and even referred to as "scouts." Farming irreversibly turned wolves (as well as bears, foxes and birds of prey) into enemies of humankind, and the struggle became a merciless one. As a threat to livestock,[49] the wolf was called *varka* (thief) by the Indo-Europeans.[50]

Thus, our emotional responses to any given species are shaped by the way it threatens our resources or benefits us. This also applies to insects. An experimental study showed that people had less consideration for a beetle presented as being useless to humans or as a threat to their resources than they had when it was presented as useful to humans and harmless to their crops. Similarly, pigeons, who were once celebrated in France as air messengers of the Great War, are now fought as urban pests. Conversely, foxes and stone martens have been redeemed to some extent since a 2017 study published in the Proceeding of the Royal Society showed how they help to decrease the spread of the dreaded Lyme disease by eating the rodents that are its main carriers.[51]

From a human perspective, not only do animals covet our crops or threaten us physically, but they are also obviously resources themselves. The divergence between human and animal interests is insoluble when what we are after is their very bodies. Raised for meat, or caged for their skin, they become *capital* (a Latin word that gave us *chattel* and *cattle*, just as the Latin word for herd, *pecus*, came from *pecunia*, money) and they move from the status of adversary or threat to a further level of degradation by becoming property. According to the FAO, 65 to 100 billion animals are killed for human consumption every year.

The Two Dimensions of our Perception of Animals

The social representations of different species emerge through our contact with animals, and we pass them on to our children. Animal symbolism and everyday beliefs about animals' abilities contribute to the elaboration of mental patterns which are organised along two dimensions – as is also the case for human groups. For example, just as there are shared, stable representations of Italians or Swedes, there are also stereotypes of dogs or cows. Thus,

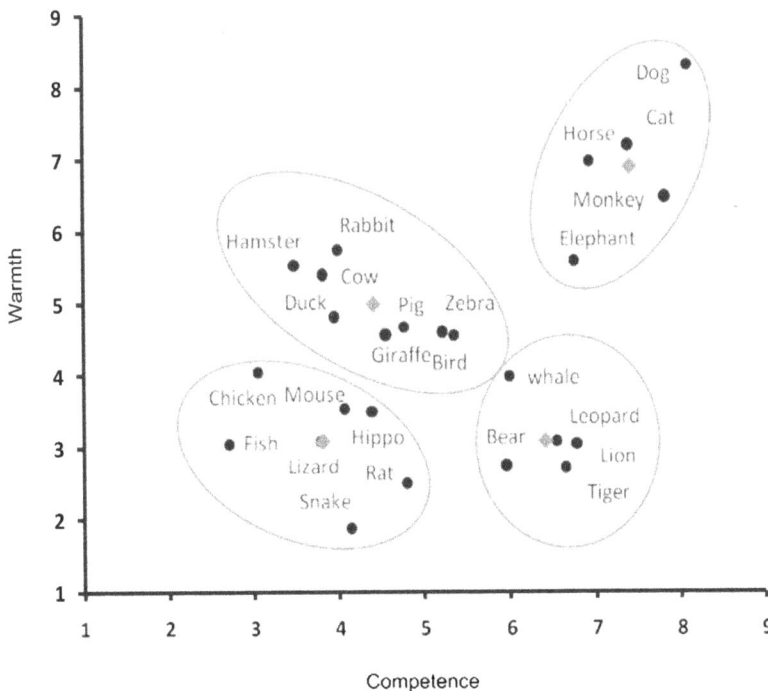

Figure 4.3 Animal stereotypes along two fundamental dimensions of social perception.[55]

to describe the social representations of different animals, it is enlightening to mobilise two major dimensions of social perception, which have so far been applied to the analysis of relations between human groups.[52] The first one, *warmth*, concerns the extent to which the species involved is friendly to humans (roughly, its ability to elicit human affection), while the second refers to its ability to act upon its environment and alter it (its *competence*).

The various combinations of these two dimensions refer to very different kinds of perceptions and predispositions for interactions with animals. For example, a human group that is seen to have a strong ability to elicit affection and a high level of competence is always preferred. Conversely a group with low competence eliciting little affection becomes an object of contempt. By transposing this model to our perception of animals, researchers have observed that the category "low warmth, high competence" included animals like bears or tigers; the category "high warmth, high competence" included "companion" animals like dogs and horses; the category "high warmth, low competence" included cows and ducks, and finally the category "low warmth, low competence" included animals like snakes or rats.[53]

If participants are asked to match human groups with animal species (they are told that in the context of developing a video game, characters must be represented by animal avatars), it appears that the suggested matches do correspond to the same two dimensions of warmth and competence. For example, an elderly person is often matched with a low-competence animal, while a businessman tends to get a high-competence animal as an avatar. An outsider will often get represented by a low-warmth animal like a lizard, while our first choice for an ingroup member will tend to be a friendly animal, like a dog.

In the same way as human categories, animal categories are invested with social value. Some animals are "good," like the ones we allow into our homes, while others are regarded as useful, weird, harmful or even evil. The emotions and behaviours they elicit result from their place on the *sociozoological scale*.[54] These representations manifest the changing nature of our relations with animals while justifying their status in a specific order of things – that of *might makes right*.

Notes

1   Despret V. (2020). *Quand le loup habitera avec l'agneau*, Paris, Les Empêcheurs de penser en rond, p. 105.
2   See Delort R. (1984). *Les animaux ont une histoire*, Paris, Seuil.
3   Nyhus P. J. (2016). "Human–wildlife conflict and coexistence," *Annual Review of Environmental Resources*, 41, pp. 143–171, p. 144.
4   Isbell L. A. (2006). "Snakes as agents of evolutionary change in primate brains," *Journal of Human Evolution*, 51 (1), pp. 1–35. In children as in adults, snakes are detected by the visual system faster than other animals; see LoBue V., DeLoache J. S. (2008). "Detecting the snake in the grass: Attention to fear-relevant stimuli by adults and young children," *Psychological Science*, 19 (3), pp. 284–289.
5   Schredl M., Blagrove M. (2021). "Animals in dreams of children, adolescents, and adults: The UK Library Study," *Imagination, Cognition and Personality*, 41 (1), pp. 87–104.
6   Platz W. E., Oberlaender F., Seidel M. L. (1995). "The phenomenology of perceptual hallucinations in alcohol-induced delirium tremens," *Psychopathology*, 28, pp. 247–255.
7   Magle S. (2019). "Human–animal relationships in the urban wild," in G. Hosey, V. Melfi V. (eds.). *Anthrozoology: Human–Animal Interactions in Domesticated and Wild Animals*, Oxford, Oxford University Press, pp. 119–141.
8   This distancing remains very limited, as Joëlle Zask shows in her work on the presence of animals in urban environments.
9   Bethelmy L. C., Corraliza J. A. (2019). "Transcendence and sublime experience in nature: Awe and inspiring energy," *Frontiers in Psychology*, 10, p. 509.
10 Soulsbury C. D., White P. C. L. (2015). "Human–wildlife interactions in urban areas: A review of conflicts, benefits and opportunities," *Wildlife Research*, 42, p. 54.

11 Zask J. (2021). *Face à une bête sauvage*, Paris, Premier Parallèle, p. 111.

12 Johansson M., Karlsson J. (2011). "Subjective experience of fear and the cognitive interpretation of large carnivores," *Human Dimensions of Wildlife*, 16 (1), pp. 15–29.

13 Tesson S. (2019). *La Panthère des neiges*, Paris, Gallimard. English translation by Frank Wynne: *The Art of Patience: Seeking the Snow Leopard in Tibet*, Penguin, 2021.

14 Campbell D. T. (1965). *Ethnocentric and Other Altruistic Motives*, Lincoln, University of Nebraska Press.

15 Foster C. (2018). *Dans la peau d'une bête*, Paris, Plon, p. 266.

16 This threefold categorisation comes from Nyhus P. J. (2016). "Human–wildlife conflict and coexistence."

17 Kruuk V. (2002). *Hunter and Hunted. Relationships between Carnivores and People*, Cambridge, Cambridge University Press.

18 Freitas Torres D., Oliveira E. S., Nobrega Alves R. E. (2018). "Understanding human-wildlife conflicts and their implications," in R. R. Nobrega Alves, U. P. Albuquerque (eds.), *Ethnozoology*, New York, Academic Press, pp. 421–445. See also Delort R. (1984). *Les animaux ont une histoire*, pp. 20–122.

19 Weiss K. J., Fromm L., Glazer J. (2018). "Assignment of culpability to animals as a form of abuse: Historical and cultural perspectives," *Behavioral Sciences & the Law*, 36 (6), pp. 661–674.

20 Gagneret P. (2021). "Dans les Pyrénées, un accident inédit relance le débat sur l'ours," *Le Monde*, 23 November, p. 9.

21 Tilson R., Nyhus P. J. (2010). *Tigers of the World: The Biology, Politics, and Conservation of Panthera Tigris*, San Diego, Academic/Elsevier; Nyhus P. J. (2016). "Human–wildlife conflict and coexistence."

22 Inskip C., Zimmermann A. (2009). "Human–felid conflict: A review of patterns and priorities world-wide," *Oryx*, 43, pp. 18–34.

23 Gittleman J. L., Funk S. L., Macdonald D. W., Wayne R. K. (2001). *Carnivore Conservation*, Cambridge, Cambridge University Press.

24 Conover M. R. (2002). *Resolving Human–Wildlife Conflicts: The Science of Wildlife Damage Management*, Boca Raton, CRC Press.

25 Hoare R. (2012). "Lessons from 15 years of human elephant conflict mitigation: Management considerations involving biological, physical and governance issues in Africa," *Pachyderm*, 51, pp. 60–74.

26 Can O. E., D'Cruze N., Garshelis D. L., Beecham J., Macdonald D. W. (2014). "Resolving human–bear conflict: A global survey of countries, experts, and key factors," *Conservation Letters*, 7, p. 501–513.

27 Rajpurohit K. S., Krausman P. R. (2000). "Human–sloth–bear conflicts in Madhya Pradesh, India," *Wildlife Society Bulletin*, 28, pp. 393–399, quoted by Freitas Torres D., Oliveira E. S., Nobrega Alvers R. E. (2018). "Understanding human–wildlife conflicts and their implications," in R. R. Nobrega Alves, U. P. Albuquerque (eds.), *Ethnozoology*, p. 426.

28 Conover M. R. (2002). *Resolving Human–Wildlife Conflicts: The Science of Wildlife Damage Management.*

29 Conover M. R. (2002).

30 Hosey G., Melfi V. (2019). *Anthrozoology: Human-Animal Interactions in Domesticated and Wild Animals.*

31 Freitas Torres D., Oliveira E. S., Nobrega Alves R. E. (2018). "Understanding human–wildlife conflicts and their implications," in R. R. Nobrega Alves, U. P. Albuquerque (eds.), *Ethnozoology*, p. 424.

32 Nyhus P. J. (2016). "Human–wildlife conflict and coexistence."

33 Lalo J. (1987). "The problem of road-kill," *American Forests*, 50, pp. 50–52.

34 Romin L. A., Bissonette J. A. (1996). "Deer–vehicle collisions: Status of state monitoring activities and mitigation efforts," *Wildlife Society Bulletin*, 24, pp. 276–283.

35 Langbein J., Putman R., Pokorny B. (2011). "Traffic collisions involving deer and other ungulates in Europe and available measures for mitigation," in R. Putman M. Apollonio, R. Andersen (eds.). *Ungulate Management in Europe: Problems and Practices*, Cambridge (UK), Cambridge University Press, pp. 215–259.

36 Bruinderink G. W., Hazebroek E. (1996). "Ungulate traffic collisions in Europe," *Conservation Biology*, 10, pp. 1059–1067.

37 Van Der Hoop J. M., Moore M. J., Barco S. G., Cole T. V., Daoust P.-Y. et al. (2013). "Assessment of management to mitigate anthropogenic effects on large whales," *Conservation Biology*, 27, pp. 121–133.

38 Hughes J., Macdonald D. W. (2013). "A review of the interactions between free-roaming domestic dogs and wildlife," *Biology of Conservation*, 157, pp. 341–351.

39 Zask J. (2021). *Face à une bête sauvage,*, p. 111.

40 Conover M. R., Vail R. (2015). *Human Diseases from Wildlife*, Boca Raton, CRC Press.

41 Curtis V., Biran A. (2001). "Dirt, disgust, and disease. Is hygiene in our genes?" *Perspectives in Biology and Medicine*, 44 (1), pp. 17–31.

42 Espinosa R., Tago D., Treich N. (2020). "Infectious diseases and meat production," *Environmental Resource Economy*, 76, pp. 1019–1044.

43 Brown R. (1995). *Prejudice*, London, Blackwell.

44 Brewer M. B., Campbell D. T. (1976). *Ethnocentrism and Intergroup Attitudes: East African Evidence*, London, Sage.

45 In France, 15 annual deaths are caused by bees, wasps or hornets.

46 See Zask J. (2021). *Face à une bête sauvage*, p. 23.

47 Adams C. E., Lindseay K. L. (2010). *Urban Wildlife Management*, Boca Raton, CRC Press.

48 Ericsson G., Heberlein T. A. (2003). "Attitudes of hunters, locals and general public in Sweden now that wolves are back," *Biology of Conservation*, 111, pp. 149–159.

49 Historian Eric Baratay estimates that nearly 10% of farm animals were killed by wild animals like wolves in the Pyrenees in the 19th century; see Baratay É. (2003). *Et l'homme créa l'animal*, Paris, Odile Jacob, p. 205.

50 Delort R. (1984). *Les animaux ont une histoire*, p. 322. On representations of wolves and their evolution, see Baratay É. (2003). *Et l'homme créa l'animal*, Paris, Odile Jacob, chapter 11.

51 Hofmeester T. R. et al. (2017). "Cascading effects of predator activity on tick-borne disease risk," *Proceedings of the Royal Society*, 284, p. 20170453.

52 Fiske S. T., Cuddy A. J. C., Glick P., Xu J. (2002). "A model of (often mixed) stereotype content: Competence and warmth, respectively, follow from perceived status and competition," *Journal of Personality and Social Psychology*, 82, pp. 878–902.

53 Sevillano V., Fiske S. T. (2016). "Warmth and competence in animals," *Journal of Applied Social Psychology*, 46 (5), pp. 276–293.

54 Arluke A., Sanders C. (1996). *Regarding Animals*, Philadelphia, Temple University Press.

55 Fiske et al. (2002).

5   The Paradoxes of Might Makes Right

Illustration: Magali Seghetto

In ancient Greece, domestic animals were sacrificed according to rituals where nothing was left to chance. Well-defined codes precisely regulated the way ceremonies were to unfold: how the animals were chosen, how the blood should flow, and even the smells. Rigid rules governed everyone's place and role, how space was divided, the chants and prayers, the preparation of the altar with water or grains of barley. Historians of ancient Greece have written about a key moment in the ritual: when the victim was supposed to give consent to its sacrifice.[1] The slightest movement of the animal's head as it was sprinkled with holy water was interpreted as consent for its killing.[2]

For eight centuries, the way in which blood was spilled onto Greek altars was a crucial practice, and it is still the subject of much scholarship in contemporary Hellenistic circles. Did the imagined consent of the animal manifest the approval of the gods? Was the blade that

DOI: 10.4324/9781003561972-6

was used for the sacrifice hidden away in a basket until the fatal moment? What really matters here is that there was an arrangement through which the victim, with its gesture of consent, no longer really seemed like a victim.

This expectation of the animal's acquiescence might lead one to believe that, although humanity knows it reduces animals to insignificance, the ritual slitting of an animal's throat is still a significant act, a disturbing form of bloodshed for the "empathetic predators" that we are.[3] Because it restores harmony in the human mind, any kind of presumed consent from the victim seems welcome.[4]

It is not only in ancient times that people imagined that animals consented to being killed. The Yakut hunters of Russia have a traditional saying: "You came to me, Lord Bear, you wish me to kill you,"[5] and the bullfighting world still presents the bull as a "partner" in a sacrificial choreography.[6] The discourse on livestock farming sometimes refers to the "gift animals make of their work and their lives."[7] Destined for the abattoir, they are alleged to consent to a cycle of "give, receive, and give back."[8]

In the book *Experimentation: A User's Guide*, published by French research institutions Inserm and CNRS, researchers are reminded that the animal is their "partner."[9] So, transgenic mice and docile beagles are considered willing participants,[10] and sometimes even, as one commercial insert put it, seem "eager to serve."[11] The squirrel monkeys or cats that are subjected to harsh experimental procedures are called "colleagues."[12] This notion of animals consenting to or even eagerly anticipating human use, can be found in its most egregious form in the "suicide food"[13] advertising genre, where merry pigs, laughing cows and jovial hens volunteer for human consumption.

Cognitive Dissonance

Harmonising one's thoughts and actions is a human concern that a Stanford University researcher, Leon Festinger, placed at the heart of an important theory of cognitive balance.[14] The theory of cognitive dissonance was developed to account for the psychological processes that allow us to reconcile incompatible thoughts and restore a subjectively acceptable sense of coherence when we experience psychological discomfort. According to one study, a European meat consumer eats 1,094 animals over a lifetime, including 4 bovines, 4 lambs, 46 pigs and 945 chickens.[15] The problem is that the animals we eat the most are also the ones that are treated the worst,[16] and it is regularly pointed out that abattoirs fail to meet sanitary standards and cause levels of animal suffering that blatantly contradict the "happy meat" marketing fairy tale.[17] Thus, so many consumers could feel some degree of guilt towards slaughtered animals[18] that we might expect them to engage in processes of cognitive appeasement.

The experience of cognitive dissonance may stem from a contradiction between two opposing thoughts: "I'm harming animals" and "I don't want to hurt animals". Sometimes, it also results from a desire for coherence, which can lead individuals to recognise that their behaviour (e.g., attending a bullfight) is incompatible with the image of a caring person they wish to project. A radical way of overcoming dissonance can be to reduce or even eliminate actions that involve harming animals. For instance, since meat eating is a major cause of animal suffering,[19] abstaining from it can be a way of aligning one's thoughts and actions. Surveys of European consumers show that this decision is not on the agenda for most of them:[20] in France, meat consumption had doubled since the 1950s, and those who voluntarily abstain from it make up less than 5% of the population in most countries. Although there has been significant change among the younger generations, there are only 2.2% of vegetarians or vegans in France today,[21] and many of them eventually give up.[22] Surveys show that 40 to 75% of vegetarians end up eating meat or fish again.[23] However, there are other ways of resolving the cognitive dissonance known as the *meat paradox*.[24]

How to Solve the Problem of Meat Consumption?

Avoidance

One way of mitigating cognitive discomfort is avoidance.[25] In order not to experience the unpleasant feeling of dissonance between the principle of non-violence and meat eating in a psychologically economical way, why not simply avoid situations that might cause this feeling? With the rise in human sensitivity and the growing rejection of cruelty towards animals,[26] recognisable animal bodies had to disappear from our shelves and tables, as sociologist Norbert Elias analysed:

> The manner in which meat was served changed considerably between the Middle Ages and the modern era. The nature of these changes is most instructive. The upper echelons of medieval society had whole animals or quarters of meat brought to the meal table. This was the usual way of serving fish, birds – sometimes unplucked –, hares, sheep and calves. Large game, pigs and oxen would be roasted whole on a spit… The orientation of this change was very clear: the original norm, whereby the sight of a dead animal being carved up at the meal table was regarded as agreeable, or at least in no way unpleasant, was replaced by another norm which dictated that the connection between a plate of meat and a dead animal should, as far as possible, be forgotten.[27]

The distancing and concealment of abattoirs, the disappearance of whole animal bodies from stalls, dinner tables and cookery books (a historic French medieval cookbook was called *Le Viandier* – "The Meat Book"), the elimination of body parts from plates, such as eyes or ears that are too reminiscent of the actual animal, the depictions of happy rural life for farmed animals – all of this allows us to avoid the moral unease that may come with meat eating.

However, when one can no longer conceal the crude reality of animal flesh, the distorting properties and plastic virtues of language come in handy. The designation of animal substance borrows from a lexicon that dissociates it from its species and places it in a food category. Thus, a pig is transubstantiated into *pork* before it is transformed into ham, and a cow is converted into anatomical segments, like fillet or rump steak, and perfectly concealed by the geometrical shapes that are superimposed on its flesh. This dissociation, which the meat industry knows to be a necessity, allows them to thwart any form of empathy and to make the act of eating more comfortable. A study by two researchers at the London School of Economics showed that, conversely, after an experimental manipulation in which consumers were made to perceive a pig as more human, the participants anticipated that they would feel guilty if they ate it, and said they were less likely to do so.[28]

In a study that quite literally illustrates the phenomenon of "de-animalization," participants were presented with pictures of lambs or pigs that had been cooked and laid out on a tray. Some of them were shown animals without their heads, while others were presented with whole animals. Then the researchers measured the participants' empathy for the animals and the disgust they felt at the thought of eating them. The results showed that intact animals elicited more empathy than decapitated ones and that the idea of eating them caused more revulsion.[29]

Over 30 studies have delved into the phenomenon of "de-animalization." Women and younger consumers from industrialized countries are more affected than others when presented with a dish containing a whole animal body as opposed to one that no longer looks like an animal.[30]

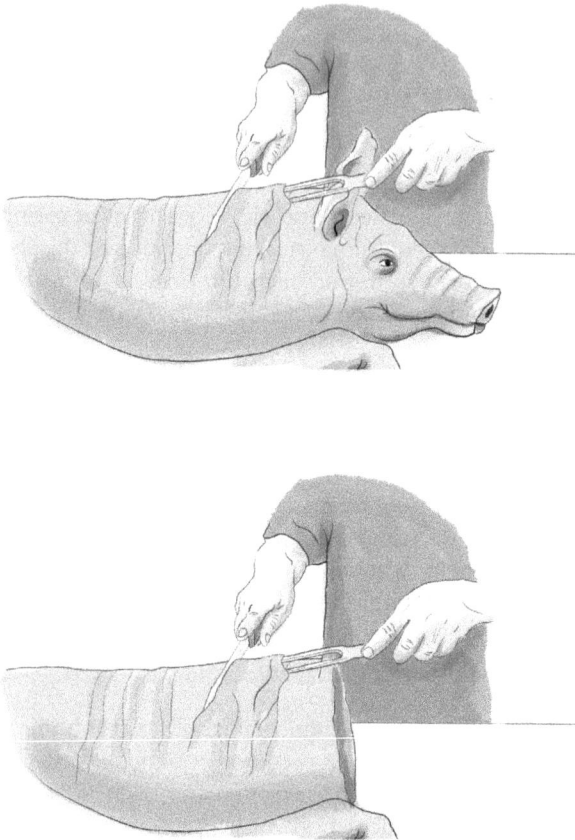

Figure 5.1 Animals destined for human consumption and presented with their heads cause more disgust and empathy than intact ones, especially among women and younger participants.
Illustration: Magali Seghetto

Easing Responsibility

If, despite avoiding the explicit form of meat and euphemising its presentation, omnivorous eaters are still disturbed by the living origin of the food they consume, several cognitive adjustments can still occur. In this regard, the cultural justifications of meat eating identified by Jared Piazza and his colleagues are compelling, albeit to varying degrees.[31] Indeed, while it may be difficult to justify animal consumption – at least from an ethical perspective – merely on the basis of majority practice or the gustatory pleasure of grilled meat (the famous, succulent Maillard reaction[32]), individuals can still invoke imperious biological necessity or deep evolutionary determinism ("we've always eaten meat") to convince themselves that meat eating is demanded by human nature.

If one believes that abstaining from meat eating is a threat to one's health or a violation of some deep anthropological constraint, why persist in playing the angel and renouncing animal flesh? If one persists in (wrongly) thinking that meat is a vital necessity,[33] one does not have the option of abstaining from it. And the feeling of not having a choice alleviates the experience of dissonance.[34]

Downplaying Meat Consumption

Studies on nutrition in the general population show surprising inconsistencies in how people report their diets in consumer surveys. Many meat or fish eaters still describe themselves as vegetarians.[35] It is unclear whether they know too little about vegetarianism or whether this is because they use the term loosely.

However, there are also active mechanisms that lead individuals to downplay their meat consumption. In one study, female participants who were asked to fill an anonymous question-naire reported lower levels of meat consumption if they were led to believe that they would later watch a documentary about animal abuse in industrial farming.[36] Research also reports a downplaying of self-reported meat consumption among omnivores who describe their eating habits immediately after learning about those of a vegetarian, whose mere mention seems to increase their cognitive dissonance.[37]

The Denial of Animal Abilities and the Moral Exclusion of Animals

Downplaying the sensory abilities, intelligence or value of consumed animals is a universal mechanism[38] that is part of a desire to reduce cognitive discomfort. This idea is illustrated by observations made by Yvonne Verdier, an ethnologist who specializes in rural life:

> As it grows fatter, the pig becomes a *Monsieur* ("Sir"). He gets called that way because he is "nice and clean, lovely, white and pink, and he does us good, especially once he's dead." But you start to like him and it's heart-breaking when you have to kill him. So, one morning, you decide the animal has gone bad, as if to make the crime less serious (thus the farmer, when she chooses which barn animal she will kill, chooses the one that is "too old," who is "no longer any good" or who "bothers the other ones").[39]

Ethnologist Catherine Rémy has studied this "negative subjectivity" among abattoir workers when they discuss how dangerous an animal is if it does not "cooperate" in its own slaughter. These phenomena of dissonance reduction have also been studied in a more systematic way. In a laboratory setting, for example, one study showed that merely knowing one was about to eat a piece of meat was enough to lower the emotional and mental abilities one would attribute to slaughtered animals. Moreover, presenting animals as intended for human con-sumption was shown to facilitate access to narratives that justified eating them. For example, participants rated the mental abilities of 32 different animals, and it turned out that their assessment of how edible they were was negatively correlated with the abilities that were attributed to them: cows or pigs were considered to be far less intelligent than cats, lions and antelopes. This confirmed the findings of another study which showed that, when shown a picture of a cow on its way to the abattoir, participants were more likely to downplay its mental abilities and capacity for suffering than they were if the same cow was not about to be killed.[40]

The simple fact of putting an animal in a food category is enough to influence the way one thinks about its mental abilities. In one study, participants were presented with a docu-ment about a mammal, Bennett's tree-kangaroo. They were informed that the mammal only lived in New Guinea, that its population was significant and stable, and that it had a rapid reproductive cycle. Various pieces of information were then introduced. For example, it was mentioned that the animal's meat was consumed by New Guineans – or on the contrary, nothing was said about its consumption. Participants then had to say to what extent they thought this type of kangaroo would suffer if it was injured, and if it deserved to be protected from abuse. It was found that the mere fact of categorising the animal as edible was enough for people to minimise the sensory abilities they attributed to it.[41] Conversely, all it takes for a consumer to feel disgust at the thought of eating an animal is to think about its mental abilities.[42]

Meat-eating humans therefore actively use their reasoning skills to justify their food preferences. These cognitive processes can support established practices in myriad ways. In some cases, the motives are transparent – they stem from economic interests or corporate norms.[43] Thus, when the head of the Nîmes bullfighting arena claims that "there is no evidence that [the bull] suffers in the arena"[44] or when an expert says that overfed ducks "easily get used to force-feeding,"[45] these are public statements whose authors do not necessarily need to believe deeply. But more often than not, the mechanisms of justification are more subtle, non-verbal and sincere. We want to convince ourselves that we are morally decent and consistent people.

However, the well-oiled justifications that organise the world according to modalities that fit our practices must overcome one possible form of resistance, a substantial one. It springs from the emotional and moral dispositions that are constantly at play in our relationships with members of our own species, and that must be controlled when it comes to considering how much empathy we should grant other animals. We harbour several moral codes rooted in our history[46] and some of them prohibit the abuse of other living beings. However, many of us condone this abuse, because the boundaries of empathy are extremely fluid.

Notes

1 Carrin-Bouez M. (1978). "Le sacrifice consenti à regret," *Systèmes de pensée en Afrique noire*, 3, pp. 135–149; Mehl V., Brulé P., 2008 (eds.), *Le Sacrifice antique. Vestiges, procédures et stratégies*, Rennes, PUR; Burkert W. (1983). *Homo Necans. The Anthropology of Ancient Greek Sacrificial Ritual and Myth*, Berkeley, University of California Press, p. 4.

2 In ancient Greece, one could also transfer guilt onto the instrument of the sacrifice: the knife. See Voir Serpell J. (1986). *In the Company of Animals*, Oxford, Blackwell, p. 164. This cultural pattern was not limited to the Greeks. For example, among the Santals in the East of India, you can also find the idea of an exchange or transaction between the victim and the priests.

3 Stépanoff C. (2021). *L'Animal et la Mort. Chasse, modernité et crise du sauvage*, Paris, La Découverte.

4 See Playoust-Braure A., Bonnardel Y. (2020). *Solidarité animale*, Paris, la Découverte, pp. 79–80.

5 Foer J. S. (2010). *Faut-il manger les animaux?* Paris, Éditions de l'Olivier, p. 132.

6 The belief which leads hunters to see their practice as an animal gift is not a universal one. A study on the native peoples of Australia showed that none of them subscribed to this belief. See Hayden B. (2013). "Hunting on heaven and earth: A comment on knight," *Current Anthropology*, 54, pp. 495–496.

7 Porcher J. (2014). *Vivre avec les animaux. Une utopie pour le xxie siècle*, Paris, La Découverte, p. 35. For a critique of this thesis, see Lepeltier T. (2017). *L'Imposture intellectuelle des carnivores*, Paris, Max Milo.

8 Porcher J. (2014). *Vivre avec les animaux*, p.34.

9 Brugère H. et al. (1992). *Expérimentation animale, mode d'emploi*, Paris, Inserm, p. 13.

10 See especially Arluke A. (1994). " 'We build a better Beagle': Fantastic creatures in lab animal ad," *Qualitative Sociology*, 17, pp. 143–158.

11 Arluke A. (1994).

12 Dunayer J. (2000). "In the name of science: The language of vivisection," Organization & Environment, 13 (4), pp. 432–452, particularly p. 444.

13 See Parkinson C. (2020). *Animals, Anthropomorphism and Mediated Encounters*, London, Routledge, p. 73; Playoust-Braure A., Bonnardel Y. (2020). *Solidarité animale*, pp. 79–80.

14 Festinger L. (1957). *A Theory of Cognitive Dissonance*, Palo Alto, Stanford University Press.

15 French survey by CREDOC, quoted by Curtay J.-P., Magnin V. (2018). *Moins de viande. Vers une transition au profit de notre santé, du monde vivant et de l'environnement*, Paris, Solar, p. 23.

16 For example, according to official data provided by the French farming sector and governmental organisations, intensive farming where animals have no access to the outdoors in concerns 83% of chicken, 97% of turkeys, 99% of rabbits and 95% of pigs.

17 Pilgrim K. (2013). "'Happy cows,' 'happy beefs': A critique of the rationale for ethical meat," *Environmental Humanities*, 3, pp. 111–127.

18 Digard J.-P. (1999). *Les Français et leurs animaux*, Paris, Fayard, p. 148.

19 Norwood B., Lusk J. (2011). *Compassion by the Pound: The Economics of Farm Animal Welfare*, New York, Oxford University Press; Gancille J.-M. (2020). *Carnage*, Paris, Rue de l'Echiquier.

20 Hartmann C., Siegrist M. (2017). "Consumer perception and behaviour regarding sustainable protein consumption: A systematic review," *Trends in Food Science Technology*, 61, pp. 11–25.

21 France Agrimer (2020). *Végétariens et flexitariens en France en 2020*, Enquête IFOP pour France Agrimer.

22 On a vegetarian's profile, see Rosenfeld D. L. (2018). The psychology of vegetarianism: Recent advances and future directions. *Appetite*, *131*, pp. 125–138; Rosenfeld, D. L., Burrow, A. L. (2017). Vegetarian on purpose: Understanding the motivations of plant-based dieters. *Appetite*, *116*, pp. 456–463; Allès, B., Baudry, J., Méjean, C., Touvier, M., Péneau, S., Hercberg, S., Kesse-Guyot, E. (2017). Comparison of sociodemographic and nutritional characteristics between self-reported vegetarians, vegans, and meat-eaters from the NutriNet-Santé study. *Nutrients*, *9* (9), p. 1023; Bègue, L. & Vezirian, K. (2023). "Analytic cognitive style is inversely related to meat consumption," *Personality and Individual Differences*, 212, 112269; Bègue, L. & Vezirian, K. (2025)/ Meatless but not mindless: Cognitive style, meat exclusion and the role of underlying motives, *Food and Quality Preference*, 105496.

23 Ruby M. B. (2012). "Vegetarianism. A blossoming field of study," *Appetite*, 58 (1), pp. 141–150; Cooney N. (2014). *Veganomics*, New York, Lantern Books.

24 Loughnan S., Haslam N., Bastian B. (2010). "The role of meat consumption in the denial of moral status and mind to meat animals," *Appetite*, 55 (1),. See also Rothgerber H., Rosenfeld D. L. (2021). "Meat-related cognitive dissonance: The social psychology of eating animals," *Social and Personality Psychology Compass*, 15, p. e12592. A cross-cultural perspective is introduced by Tian Q., Hilton D., Becker M. (2016). "Confronting the meat paradox in different cultural contexts: Reactions among Chinese and French participants," *Appetite*, 96, pp. 187–194.

25 Rothgerber H. (2020). "Meat-related cognitive dissonance: A conceptual framework for understanding how meat eaters reduce negative arousal from eating animals," *Appetite*, 146, p. 104511.

26 Pinker S. (2011). *The Better Angels of Our Nature*, New York, Viking Books, chapter 7.

27 Elias N. (1969). *The Civilizing Process*, Oxford, Blackwell.

28 Wang F., Basso F. (2019). "'Animals are friends, not food': Anthropomorphism leads to less favorable attitudes toward meat consumption by inducing feelings of anticipatory guilt," *Appetite*, 138, pp. 153–173.

29 Kunst J. R., Hohle S. M. (2016). "Meat eaters by dissociation: How we present, prepare and talk about meat increases positivity to eating meat by reducing empathy and disgust," *Appetite*, 105, pp. 758–774.

30 Benningstad N. C., Kunst J. R. (2020). "Dissociating meat from its animal origins: A systematic literature review," *Appetite*, 147, p. 104554.

31 Piazza J., Ruby M. B., Loughnan S., Luong M., Kulik J., Watkins H. M., Seigerman M. (2015). "Rationalizing meat consumption. The 4Ns," *Appetite*, 91, pp. 114–128.

32 Mottram D. S. (1998). "Flavor formation in meat and meat: A review," *Food Chemistry*, 62 (4), pp. 415–424.

33 According to health authorities, meat consumption is not a vital necessity for humans: Melina V., Craig W., Levin S. (2016). "Position of the Academy of Nutrition and Dietetics: Vegetarian diets," *Journal of the Academy of Nutrition and Dietetics*, 116 (12), pp. 1970–1980; Mariotti F. (2017). *Vegetarian and Plant-Based Diets in Health and Disease Prevention*, New York, Academic Press.

34 Cooper J. (2007). *Cognitive Dissonance: Fifty Years of a Classic Theory*, London, Sage.

35 Rothgerber H. (2014). "A comparison of attitudes toward meat and animals among strict and semi-vegetarians," *Appetite*, 72, pp. 98–105.

36 Rothgerber H. (2019). " 'But I don't eat that much meat': Situational underreporting of meat consumption by women," *Society and Animals*, 27, pp. 150–173.

37 Rothgerber H. (2014). "A comparison of attitudes toward meat and animals among strict and semi-vegetarians."

38 On the universality of the degradation of animals before slaughtering, see Dalla Bernardina S. (1991). "Une personne pas tout à fait comme les autres. L'animal et son statut," *L'Homme*, 31 (4), pp. 33–50.

39 Verdier Y. (1977)." Le langage des cochons," *Ethnologie française*, 7 (2), pp. 143–154.

40 Loughnan S., Haslam N., Bastian B. (2010). "The role of meat consumption in the denial of moral status and mind to meat animals."

41 To analyse the meat paradox, one can draw upon the sociology of deviant behaviour, which shows that, when transgressing norms, individuals use "neutralizing techniques" which allow them to morally distance themselves from behaviour that could be considered problematic. See for example Graça J., Calheiros M. M., Oliveira A. (2016). "Situating moral disengagement: Motivated reasoning in meat consumption and substitution," *Personality and Individual Differences*, 90, pp. 353–364.

42 Ruby M. B., Heine S. J. (2012). "Too close to home. Factors predicting meat avoidance," *Appetite*, 59 (1), pp. 47–52.

43 Hannan J. (2020). *Meatsplaining. The Animal Agriculture Industry and the Rhetoric of Denial*, Sydney, Sydney University Press.

44 Jeangène Vilmer J.-B. (2011). *L'Éthique animale*, Paris, PUF, pp. 11–12

45 Guéméné D., Guy G. (2004). "Foie gras, gavage et bien-être animal: vers un peu d'objectivité!" actes des 5e et 6e Journées de la recherche sur les palmipèdes à foie gras, *Filières avicoles*, 670, quoted in Faracchi A. (2012). *Les poules préfèrent les cages*, Paris, Éditions Yves Michel, p. 104.

46 Graham J., Nosek B. A., Haidt J., Iyer R., Koleva S., Ditto P. H. (2011). "Mapping the moral domain," *Journal of Personality and Social Psychology*, 101 (2), pp. 366–385. They are the harm principle and the principles of fairness, loyalty, authority, and purity. See Haidt J. (2012). *The Righteous Mind: Why Good People are Divided by Politics and Religion*, New York, Pantheon; Haidt J. (2007). "The new synthesis in moral psychology," *Science*, 316 (5827), pp. 998–1002.

6   The Fluid Boundaries of Empathy

Illustration: Magali Seghetto

> *"The animals that inhabit the sea are a species alien and separate from us, as if they were born and lived in some other world."*
>
> Plutarch[1]

If empathy is indeed the foundation of human morality, as many philosophers and neuroscientists claim, do all animals benefit? Experiencing the world the way we think another being does – a common definition of empathy[2] – requires some effort of imagination. But our own imagination is so limited that it breaks like a ray of light when it hits the surface of the water.

DOI: 10.4324/9781003561972-7

Are Fish Outside the Scope of our Empathy?

Identifying with marine animals seems too difficult for us. Fish do not shed tears, much less scream. The physical signs that would usually elicit our emotional responses are simply not there. They do not have the kind of face[3] that we terrestrial bipeds have erected as the temple of individuality.[4] Theirs seems devoid of any expression and almost undifferentiated from the rest of their body. Flanked with flat eyes, strangely devoid of eyelids,[5] somewhat repulsive with their slimy, oblong bodies, they live apart from us, in a distant, silent world at the outer limits of human consideration. Finally, their small size and the fact that they often move around in large numbers makes it hard to see them as individuals.[6] For all these reasons, the verdict on fish expressed by the famous 18th-century naturalist Louis Buffon has lost none of its relevance:

> Animals such as fish, whose body is covered with scales... must be the most stupid of all animals... Their sensations must be very weak and obscure since they can only feel through their scales.[7]

The example of fish is quite compelling when it comes to exploring the fragility and limits of our empathy for animals. The latter seems to be selective and easily influenced by the particular signals that trigger it and determine its level. Fish do not elicit much empathy, but that is hardly surprising as they are barely considered to be animals in everyday thinking! This was demonstrated by a study conducted at Johns Hopkins University, in which participants were asked to make a list of every animal that spontaneously came to mind for ten minutes. The results showed that, among those that were quoted by over half of the participants, 90% were mammals.[8] Fish were only a fraction of the inventory even though there are over 33,000 species and they make up 60% of vertebrates.[9] In another study, participants were shown photos of animals perceived as closer to humans, like a gorilla, or more distant animals, like a catfish. The volunteers were then asked to express their solidarity with animals in general.[10] The results showed that a solidarity with animals was expressed much more strongly after having considered large mammals.

When portrayed in films, fish are often over-simplified and look like the paper replicas that French children happily hang on our backs on April Fools' Day. A study of 56 Disney animated films released between 1937 and 2016 found that only 21 different species were represented and that, in one third of the films, it was impossible to tell what species of fish was being portrayed – which was not the case for mammals.[11] While the hunting of mammals and birds is denounced in *Brother Bear*, fish, on the contrary, are depicted as a festive food that brings people together – and, one might add, even connects them with the divine realm. When Christ reappears in front of his disciples, does he not make broiled fish as his meal on the shore of Lake Tiberias?[12]

Thus, fish are not spontaneously perceived as individuals. Farmed mammals are counted in heads, but fish are recorded in tons and are referred to as "fish stocks." We find it so hard to see them as individuals that many people who refer to themselves as vegetarians keep gulping them down as though they were merely aquatic plants.[13] Fish do not really touch us – or only literally so, during "fish therapy" sessions! (This consists in having fish eat the dead skin of patients with eczema, dermatitis or psoriasis. Patients immerse their epidermis in the water, and sometimes contact with the fish cures them.)[14]

Fish Culture

Still, fish did not go unnoticed in early human cultures. The fish is a major symbolic figure, already present in prehistoric caves, in Roman mosaics, and even in Egyptian hieroglyphs.

Figure 6.1 Blenders containing goldfish at the mercy of visitors at the Trapholt Art Museum exhibition.
Illustration: Magali Seghetto

Fish are at the heart of foundational religious books and in the mythologies of indigenous peoples. *Icthus* (the fish) was the Greek acronym for "Jesus Christ, God's son, saviour"[15] and the fish became a symbol of Christianity. It is also widespread in medieval and renaissance art, as well as in the romantic, neoclassical, realist and impressionist movements, and finally in modern art (e.g., Matisse, Picasso, Klee, Soutine and Magritte). It is abundant in Asian visual art. Whether depicted in motion or stillness, in pleasant, violent or allegorical representations, it is part of a varied and prolific imagery.[16]

Artists glorify fish but may also use them as mere props left at the mercy of the audience. In a 2000 exhibition at the Trapholt Art Museum in Denmark, a Chilean artist provided visitors with 10 blenders, each containing a goldfish. The visitors could press the "on" button – and two of them did. For the artist, Marco Evaristti, the purpose of the installation was to test people's moral sense. The director of the museum was sued but he was not convicted, as the court considered that the lightning speed of the blades ensured a painless death for the fish.

The omnipresence of fish in human cultures was strongly related to their status as food. No deep compassion seemed possible for an animal that was captured with an instrument – the fishing rod – that seems like the perfect symbol of innocent, bucolic leisure. Many families do have fish as pets (60 million families worldwide are reported as having fish in an aquarium),[17] but their place may be more decorative than emotional. Historian of symbols Michel Pastoureau noted that stuffed fish are rarely hugged by children, who prefer to hug toys with arms or legs.[18]

This emotional distance is perfectly consistent with the use of fish as food. Sixteenth- and seventeenth-century theologians claimed that the reason schools of fish swam close to the shores was because they were destined for human consumption.[19] This argument was ridiculed by Voltaire in his novel *Candide*, in which metaphysician Pangloss asserts that the ultimate cause of animals is none other than the human stomach. Today, nearly 15% of animal proteins consumed throughout the world come from fish,[20] and according to a United Nations report on agriculture, 1,000 to 2,700 billion fish are killed every year.[21] That represents almost 98% of all animals killed for human consumption.

Not many people are upset about the fate of fish. Surveys on the abilities people attribute to fish, such as their capacity for pleasure or pain, show that most people think they are almost entirely devoid of them.[22] Economic studies of people's willingness to pay more for a food item if it means better animal welfare confirm that while consumers are sometimes willing to spend more to improve the fate of cows or chickens, they remain stingy when it comes to fish.[23]

Fish are also prime candidates for scientific research, which intensified in the late 19th century with the invention of modern aquariums with sophisticated filtering, heating, and lighting systems. Today, nearly 1,500 fish species are sold as pets worldwide, which means over 20 million fish per year.[24] Fish have become some of the most frequent "guests" in research laboratories (along with rats and mice), especially in comparative genomics, developmental biology, ethology and behavioural neurobiology.[25] One of them, the zebrafish, has become a bit of a scientific superstar: there are now almost 25,000 scientific papers about it. The reason researchers are so interested in this small, 3- to 4-centimetre-long fish from Indian rivers is the striking similarity between its genome and that of the human species. Moreover, the development of the zebrafish embryo outside its mother's body allows for precise observation of developmental stages due to its relative transparency during this period. Since the development of organs such as the heart, kidney or brain of the fish is influenced by the same genes as in humans, its observation is irreplaceable.

Human–animal similarities are one of the paradoxes of animal experimentation. We think they are good biological models for understanding and treating human diseases because we have similar physiologies,[26] but this also makes them forced candidates for experiments that no human would like to be subjected to. Marine biologist Jonathan Balcombe reminds us that they – like other vertebrates – have a skeleton as well as muscular, nervous, cardiovascular, respiratory, sensory, digestive, reproductive, endocrine, and excretory systems.[27] The evolutionary history and comparative anatomy of fish and other vertebrates cause a strange impression of similarity:[28] to quote the title of a palaeontologist's book, we all have an "inner fish." But that may not be enough to trigger our empathy, which is anything but disinterested.

Conditions for Empathy

"Too many legs or not enough legs and it's a deal-breaker,"[29] says one specialist of human–animal relationships, summing up a fundamental aspect of the empathy we have for them. When it comes to human groups, the key to our consideration of them is how similar they seem to us.[30] An obvious sign of our collective egocentrism is that our empathy towards strangers or minorities is largely modulated by the traits we think we share with them. Laboratory studies show that when people are shown a video of someone suffering, their empathy is greater if they are made to perceive a point in common with the victim. The criteria for empathetic inclusion can be their membership in a valued group or an attribution of belief: we are more willing to take an interest in strangers if they share our ideas, beliefs or behaviours.[31]

The iron law of similarity of abilities is at play in exactly in the same way when it comes to our relations with animals: it is reminiscent of the famous "Speak and I shall baptise you!" said by the 18th-century Cardinal of Polignac to an orangutan he came across in the king's garden,[32] and completed by Vercors' cruel aphorism in his novel *Les Animaux denaturés*: "If he speaks, baptise him, but if he doesn't, cook him."

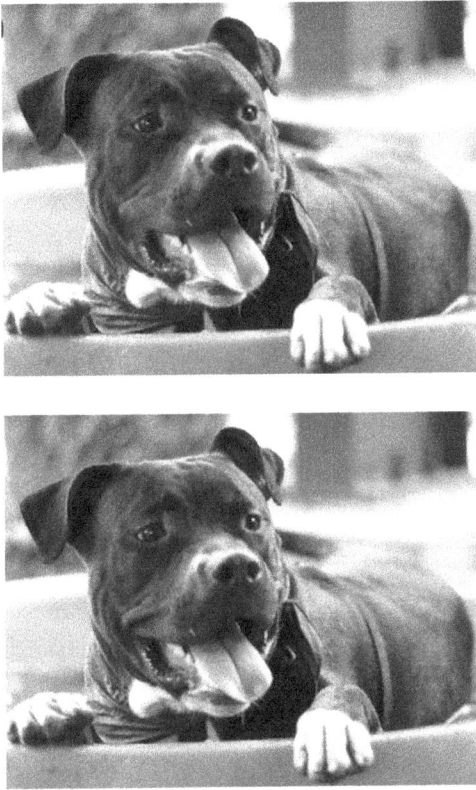

Figure 6.2 A study shows that the more smiling dog in the bottom photo is preferred by observers.

Short of language, physical resemblance can suffice. In one study, participants were asked to respond to a series of statements like "I feel a strong bond with animals" or "I feel solidarity with animals" after being shown two kinds of photos of animals, some of which had human-like expressions. The results showed that participants who had seen anthropomorphic (i.e., human-like) animal faces expressed a stronger emotional bond with animals in general.[33]

In another study, participants were asked to comment on 80 photos of dogs whose appearance had been subtly altered. It appeared that the dogs with the most human-like faces – the ones with large, well-spaced eyes and coloured irises, or those with an expression that looked like human smiles – were preferred.[34]

The relationships we form with animals facilitate our perception of similarities – even with fish. To explain the effects of this bond, one researcher gave each participant a Siamese fighting fish and he found that those who became attached to their fish over time also tended to see it as less dissimilar from themselves.[35]

Our resemblance with the millions of species that surround us is largely the result of our respective places on the evolutionary timeline. According to a study by Sarah Batt, species membership predicts 25% of our preference for any given animal.[36] More recently, a team from the Paris Museum of National History mapped the empathy-inducing potential of species. The researchers showed 3,500 participants pictures of 52 species representing the phylogenetic diversity of life on Earth. (There were 47 animal species, 4 plants and 1 mushroom.) They were shown pairs of photos representing two different species each time. They had to pick the species they thought they were most likely to feel emotions for, and the one

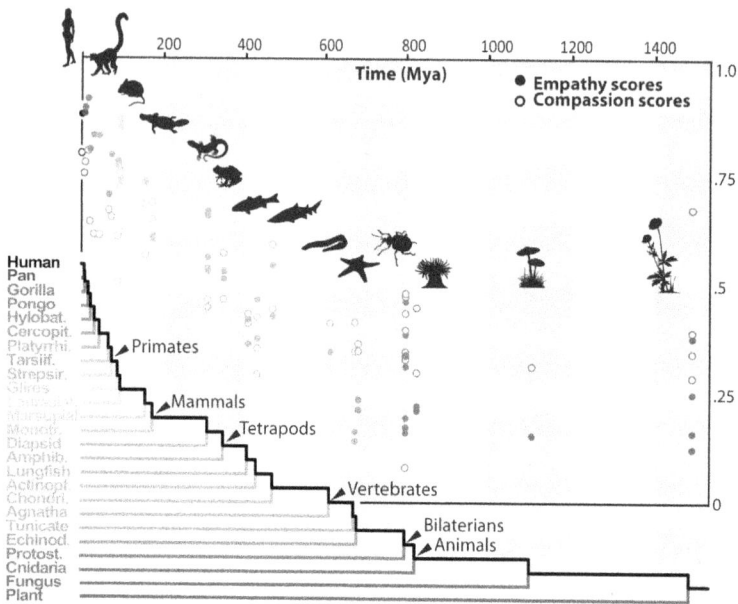

Figure 6.3 Empathy and compassion for animal species are related to their evolutionary distance from humans.

Source: Miralles *et al.*, 2019, with permission.

they would save first in a life-threatening emergency. The results showed that the older our evolutionary separation with any species was, the less empathy it elicited. Since there is a correlation between evolutionary distance and morphological likeness, empathy seemed to result from the existence of physical traits suggesting similarity with humans.

It is therefore the physical characteristics that enable us to identify with animals, allowing empathy to develop:[37] since we feel closer to great apes than anemones, we feel more empathy for them. Conversely, morphologically very distant animals leave us almost completely indifferent.

Another study reveals that the severity of punishment sought by participants against people who committed violent acts against animals increased the closer animals seemed to be to the human species.[38] Moreover, the sanctions requested to punish violence against very human-like species like primates were more severe among participants with very high levels of empathy.[39] Such a hierarchy between animals based on their anatomical, behavioural and ecological proximity with humans is easily confirmed in zoos, where mammals are clearly over-represented[40] and attract more visitors.[41]

Proximity to the human species also accounts for concern for endangered animals: the more human-like they seem, the more we worry about their fate.[42] The same hierarchy explains why, after the flooding of a research laboratory in Texas, a newspaper summarised the response of a veterinarian from the centre as follows: "We abandoned them, and it's terrible; 78 monkeys and 35 dogs drowned" – not a single word about the mice that had also died.[43] This oversight also reflects another reality: in the United States, mice have the same status that fruit flies (drosophila) or nematode worms have in France: they are simply not counted in official research statistics and are not protected by animal welfare laws. Even though they are the most commonly used animals in research laboratories, mice are experimented on in the US without any ethical constraints: legally speaking, they do not exist.

Our empathy for most animals is therefore highly conditional. The well-known failings of this moral disposition in our relations with fellow humans[44] seem to be exacerbated when it comes to other species. Empathy often reflects systematic in-group preference, and its priorities are easily and disproportionately influenced by signals such as tears, facial expressions of sadness, or cries of pain.[45] Humanity's lack of consideration for fish confirms the fact that our own species is the centre of our moral circle. We are willing to show consideration for animals that are close to us, but the fate of fish leaves us indifferent.

Philosopher Francis Wolff expressed the same bias when he stated that the pain of a gudgeon caught by a fisherman's hook could not be equated with that of a dog beaten by its master.[46] However, an additional dimension may be involved in the case of the abused dog: the apparent wantonness of the violence inflicted on an animal that will not be eaten later. Our indifference towards fish shows that human empathy may be water-soluble, but what can we learn from violence against land animals?

Notes

1   Plutarque, "Propos de table," IV, dans *Œuvres morales*, tome 3, p. 303, cited in Fontenay É. de (1998). *Le Silence des bêtes*, Paris, Fayard.

2   See Bloom P. (2016). *Against Empathy. The Case for Rational Compassion*, London, The Bodley Head, p. 16. For a more in-depth approach of empathy and an introduction to its different forms, see Hoffman M. (2008). *Empathie et développement moral: les émotions morales et la justice*, Grenoble, PUG.

3   Marc Bekoff (2009) notes that this is also the case with birds and reptiles. *Les Émotions des animaux*, Paris, Payot.

4   Philosopher Emmanuel Levinas wrote striking pages about the human face, but he seems to have been less impressed with animals: "I cannot tell you at what point something can be called a face. The human face is absolutely different and it's only after a while that you discover the face of an animal. I don't know if a snake has a face." Quoted in Derrida J. (2006) *L'Animal que donc je suis*, Paris, Galilée, p. 149. English translation: *The Animal That Therefore I Am*, Fordham U P, 2008.

5   For a witty yet scientifically informed introduction to the lives of fish, see Moro S., Vaucher F. (2018). *Les Paupières des poissons*, Paris, La Plage.

6   Wadewitz L. (2011). "Are fish wildlife?" *Environmental History*, 16 (3), pp. 423–427.

7   Buffon G. L. (1818). *Œuvres complètes, tome V: De l'homme*, pp. 192–193, quoted in Cervellon C. (2020). *L'Animal*, Paris, Belin Éducation, p. 58.

8   Henley N. (1979). "A psychological study of the semantics of animal terms," *Journal of Verbal Learning & Verbal Behavior*, 8, pp. 176–184.

9   Froese R., Proelss A. (2010). "Rebuilding fish stocks no later than 2015: Will Europe meet the deadline?," Fish and Fisheries, 11 (2), pp. 194–202.

10 Amiot C. E., Bastian B. (2017). "Solidarity with animals: Assessing a relevant dimension of social identification with animals," *PLoS One*, 12 (1).

11 Stanton R. R. (2021). *The Disneyfication of Animals*, Cham, Palgrave Macmillan.

12 Luke, 24:42.

13 Cooney N. (2014). *Veganomics*, New York, Lantern Books.

14 Nobrega Alves R. R., Policarpo I. S. (2018). "Animals and human health: Where do they meet," in R. R. Nobrega Alves, U. P. Albuquerque (eds.), *Ethnozoology*, New York, Academic Press, pp. 233–259.

15 In ancient Greek: *Iēsoús Khristós, Theoú Huiós, Sōtér*.

16 Moyle P. B., Moyle M. M. (1991). "Introduction to fish imagery in art," *Environmental Biology of Fishes*, 31, pp. 5–23.

17   Zupanc G., Zupanc M. (2007). "Fish and humans," in M. Bekoff (ed.). *Encyclopedia of Human–Animal Relationships*, Westport, Greenwood Press, vol. 4., pp. 1118–1122.

18   Pastoureau M. (2002). *Les Animaux célèbres*, Paris, Bonneton, p. 206.

19   Serpell J. (1986). *In the Company of Animals*, Oxford, Blackwell, p. 124.

20   Troadec J.-P., article "Pêche," *Encyclopédia Universalis*.

21   Balcombe J. (2018). *À quoi pensent les poissons?* Paris, La Plage, p. 12. Every human eats 13 kilos of fish per year on average in the world. Fish make up 15% of animal protein (Zupanc G., Zupanc M. (2007). "Fish and humans," in M. Bekoff (ed.). *Encyclopedia of Human–Animal Relationships*, vol. 4., pp. 1118–1122.

22   Ormandy E. H., Schuppli C. A., Weary D. M. (2012). "Factors affecting people's acceptance of the use of zebrafish and mice in research," *Alternatives to Laboratory Animals*, 40 (6), pp. 321–333.

23   Clark B., Stewart G. B., Panzone L. A., Kyriazakis I., Frewer L. J. (2017). "Citizens, consumers and farm animal welfare: A meta-analysis of willingness-to- pay studies," Food Policy, 5 (68), pp. 112–127.

24   Nobrega Alves R. R., Albuquerque U. P. (eds.) (2018). *Ethnozoology*.

25   Zupanc G., Zupanc M. (2007) "Fish and humans."

26   However, that correspondance is far from perfect. One of the most common critiques of animal experimentation is that the result do not apply to humans. See Akhtar A. (2015). "The flaws and human harms of animal experimentation," Cambridge Quarterly of Healthcare Ethics, 24 (4), pp. 407–419; Van Norman G. A. (2020). "Limitations of animal studies for predicting toxicity in clinical trials. Part 2: Potential alternatives to the use of animals in preclinical trials," *JACC. Basic to Translational Science*, 5 (4), pp. 387–397.

27   Balcombe J. (2018). *À quoi pensent les poissons?*, p. 19.

28   Neil Shubin made a very compelling case in *Your Inner Fish. A Journey into 3.5-Billion-Year History of the Human Body*, New York, Vintage, 2009.

29   Herzog H. (2011). *Some We Love, Some We Hate, Some We Eat*, New York, Harper, p. 38.

30   Tajfel H., Turner J.C. (1986) "The social identity theory of intergroup behavior," in S. Worchel, W. G. Austin (eds.). *Psychology of Intergroup Relation*, Chicago, Hall Publishers, pp. 7–24.

31   Milton Rokeach's work on belief congruence demonstrates this psychological principle. See Rokeach M., Rothman G. (1965). "The principle of belief congruence and the congruity principle as models of cognitive interaction," *Psychological Review*, 72 (2), pp. 128–142. The powerful influence of similarity has also been observed in capuchin monkeys, who are more likely to watch or approach humans who imitate their gestures with a ball (for example by imitating a capuchin who takes a ball in its mouth) compared with human experimenters who make different gestures with the object. See Paukner A. et al. (2009). "Capuchin monkeys display affiliation toward humans who imitate them," *Science*, 325 (5942), pp. 880–883.

32   Vercors (1975). *Les Animaux dénaturés*, Paris, Le Livre de Poche.

33   Amiot C. E., Bastian B. (2017). "Solidarity with animals: Assessing a relevant dimension of social identification with animals."

34   Hecht J., Horowitz A. (2015) "Seeing dogs: Human preferences for dog physical attributes," *Anthrozoös*, 28 (1), pp. 153–163.

35   Kiesler S., Lee S.-l., Kramer A. D. I. (2006). "Relationship effects in psychological explanations of nonhuman behavior," *Anthrozoös*, 19 (4), pp. 335–352.

36   Amiot C. E., Bastian B. (2017). "Solidarity with animals: Assessing a relevant dimension of social identification with animals."

37   The authors of the study call this phenomenon the *anthopomorphic stimulus hypothesis*.

38   Allen M. W., Hunstone M., Waerstad J., Foy E., Hobbins T., Wikner B., Wirrel J. (2002). "Human-to-animal similarity and participant mood influence punishment recommendations for animal abusers," *Society and Animals*, 10 (3), pp. 267–284.

39   On the connections between measures of individual empathy and attitudes towards animals, see Kasperbauer T. J. (2015). "Rejecting empathy for animal ethics," *Ethic Theory Moral Practice*, 18, pp. 817–833.

40   Surinova M. (1971). "An analysis of the popularity of animals," *International Zoo Yearbook*, 11, pp. 165–167.

41 Moss A., Esson M. (2010). "Visitor interest in zoo animals and the implication for collection planning and zoo education programmes, *Zoo Biology*, 29, pp. 715–731.

42 Gunnthorsdottir A. (2001) "Physical attractiveness of an animal species as a decision factor for its preservation," *Anthrozoös*, 14 (4), pp. 204–215.

43 Irvine L. (2009). *Filling the Ark. Animal Welfare in Disasters*, Philadelphia, Temple University Press.

44 Bloom P. (2016). *Against Empathy. The Case for Rational Compassion.*

45 For example, one researcher presented the story of a 10-year-old girl who suffered from a serious disease and needed treatment to relieve her pain. The participants were informed that she was on a waiting list and that the people who came before her on the list needed the treatment even more. When asked about what should be done, the participants acknowledged that she had to wait. However, all it took was for the expérimenter to ask them to put themselves in her shoes and they recommended that she be moved up the list. Batson C. D., Klein T. R., Highberger L., Shaw L. L. (1995). "Immorality from empathy-induced altruism: When compassion and justice conflict," *Journal of Personality and Social Psychology*, 68 (6), pp. 1042–1054.

46 Wolf F. (2010). "Libérer les animaux? Un slogan immoral et absurde," in J. Birnbaum (ed.), *Qui sont les animaux?* Paris, Gallimard, pp. 180–193, particularly p. 192.

7   Cruelty Towards Animals and Deviance

Illustration: Magali Seghetto

Brutality towards animals was commonplace in mid-18th century London. The harshness of the mores of his time undoubtedly inspired William Hogarth when he created his famous pictorial fable entitled *The Four Stages of Cruelty* (1751). In this series of engravings, Hogarth wanted to chronicle the fall of a young Londoner named Tom Nero. Sold for a shilling and widely distributed, these pictures became very popular: Kant himself is said to have mentioned them in his teachings.[1]

In the first engraving, one can see Tom Nero holding and torturing a dog by sticking an arrow in its backside. Around him, young people compete in their perversity, committing the worst acts of cruelty on their unfortunate victims, a bird, cats, a dog, a rooster...

As an adult, Tom Nero is then depicted as a brutal cart driver abusing his workhorse in the middle of a London street. In the next stage, Nero has just committed murder and his victim,

DOI: 10.4324/9781003561972-8

Figure 7.1 The first stage of cruelty.
Illustration: William Hogarth, 1751, **https://en.wikipedia.org/wiki/The_Four_Stages_of_Cruelty**

a pregnant young woman dressed like a servant, lies at his feet. He is surrounded and arrested by a small crowd. In the next etching, which ends Nero's life of depravity, the scoundrel has been hanged. He lies lifeless on a dissection table in a medical amphitheatre. His abdomen is wide open to the incisions of the surgeons, who are using their scalpels on his disgusting innards during a public dissection. Under the operating table, a dog is eating the heart of the repulsive corpse.

THE REWARD OF CRUELTY.

Figure 7.2 The Reward of Cruelty.
Source: William Hogarth, 1751, **https://en.wikipedia.org/wiki/The_Four_Stages_of_Cruelty**

By depicting the progression from a teenager's abuse of animals to the femicide that form part of this sinister quadriptych, William Hogarth wanted to condemn the animal cruelty he saw all too often in his own city. In a book he wrote about his art, he discussed the *Four Stages*:

The Prints were engraved with the hope of in some degree correcting that barbarous treatment of animals, the very sight of which renders the streets of our Metropolis so distressing to every feeling mind.

This indictment of animal cruelty, which regards it as a symptom or even a prodrome of bloody crime, has lost none of its relevance. The high-profile stories of serial killers like Ted Bundy, who committed at least 37 homicides, and of many other criminals[2] whose killing of animals preceded their other crimes, keep resurfacing. "Some serial killers started with animals," a woman worried in a village in the East of France in 2019, when her area was confronted with the disappearance of several cats[3] and the main suspect confessed to having tortured and killed four of them. The same kind of panic spread the following year when an unprecedented wave of horse mutilations occurred in France and Germany.

Is there a Connection between Animal Abuse and Violence against Humans?

However, the facts linking animal and human abuse seem to be tempered by contradictory evidence which seems to suggest that a particular mass murderer was, on the contrary, a great friend of animals.[4] Some forms of attachment to animals do not seem to make one less likely to commit violent crimes, as can be seen in the complex relationship between the Nazis and the animal world. During the Third Reich, unprecedented animal welfare laws were passed. Promulgated as early as 1933 and extended five years later, they were the most advanced in the world at the time.[5] For example, the German government requested that fish be anaesthetized before they were slaughtered.[6] One of the Reich's most influential dignitaries, Hermann Göring, outraged by the unbearable torture of animal experimentation (which did not stop during the Nazi period,[7] while horrendous human experimentation was developing),[8] even contemplated "sending those who still thought they could treat animals like inanimate property to concentration camps."[9]

To go beyond scattered and anecdotal evidence, we must turn to a very comprehensive synthesis on the correlations between cruelty towards animal and human victims.[10] The journal *Research in Veterinary Science*[11] found 96 publications on this issue since 1960. In 98% of the articles, violence against humans was positively correlated with violence against animals.

The permanence of this statistical connection led several public authorities to take an interest in the way people treated animals in order to detect or predict violence against humans. Since 2015, US police forces have been gathering data on acts of cruelty against domestic animals and the data has been correlated with domestic abuse and homicide.[12] In psychiatry, the reference manual used to categorise mental disorders has included animal abuse in its diagnosis of behavioural problems since 1987. Recently, Cambridge professor Simon Baron-Cohen introduced a measurement of animal abuse in the calculation of his empathy coefficient.[13] In several countries, social workers are trained in this area, and they include signs of animal abuse in their indicators of family dysfunction. Finally, there are countless studies on the links between psychiatric issues and animal abuse,[14] some of which are on serial killers. What do these studies say?

Serial Killers and a Norman Peasant

In 1838, Pierre Rivière, a 20-year-old man with black hair and eyebrows, a narrow forehead and shifty gaze was tried and sentenced to death for the triple murder of his mother, sister and brother. In the archives of the trial collected by philosopher Michel Foucault, we discover that he brutally and senselessly mistreated his horses, and abused all sorts of other animals:

> I would crucify frogs and birds, and I had also devised another kind of torture to make them perish. It consisted in nailing them to a tree with three nails. I called it "enuepharing," I took children with me to do this and sometimes I would do it on my own.[15]

Today, when tragedies as striking and rare as serial or mass murders[16] occur, the background of the perpetrators is thoroughly scrutinised, especially if they're young. Were there any warning signs? Domestic violence? Weapons in the home? Was the family dysfunctional? Political officials and sometimes journalists like to mention factors they consider to be relevant: social adversity, ultraviolent video games, single-parent families and nihilistic culture are among of the usual suspects. This entails the risk of overlooking more subtle, seemingly negligeable indicators that could act as warning signs.

Cruelty towards animals is one of the signs that should have alerted the people around Eric Harris and Dylan Klebold, who shot twelve students and a teacher in cold blood on April 20, 1999, at a high school in Columbine before taking their own lives. Background analysis revealed that the teenagers, aged 17 and 18, had bragged about mutilating animals. Was it an isolated incident? A careful analysis of the background of 23 school shooters who committed their crimes between 1998 and 2012 confirmed that 43% of them had committed violence against animals before the massacre.[17] However, some studies come to different conclusions.[18]

Children's abuse of animals has been regarded by many thinkers since antiquity as an alarming vice, which educational authorities and society as a whole should resolutely combat. After Pythagoras, theologian Thomas Aquinas and philosophers Montaigne, Kant and Locke[19] suspected that it was a concerning sign of callousness and a portent of future crimes – an idea that was later endorsed by psychologist Anna Freud and anthropologist Margaret Mead.

One of the earliest attempts to understand this phenomenon from a scientific perspective was made by psychiatrist John Macdonald during the second half of the 20th century.[20] He found a pattern, now commonly referred to as the "Macdonald triad," which predicts future acts of violence. This was based on his analysis of a hundred patients in a hospital in Colorado, all of whom had issued death threats. According to Macdonald, patients who had been diagnosed with enuresis after the age of 5 or who had set fires or been cruel to animals as children were more likely to engage in criminal violence as adults.

Although psychiatry no longer uses this framework to analyse problematic behaviour in children and adolescents (the three facets of the triad turned out not to be as clearly related as was initially suggested),[21] it has alerted many psychiatrists and social workers to the underlying problems that may lie behind animal abuse.[22]

Violence and the Sociozoological Scale

When looking at the criminal records of people who are incarcerated for violent crimes, it appears that each inmate has usually victimised several people over their lifetime. In the succession of misdemeanours that make up a "criminal career," there is often more than one victim for each offender. This grim ratio would be even more disproportionate if the animal victims who had the misfortune of crossing the criminals' path were included. One could even claim that the violence of these criminals is not speciesist, since it does not discriminate between individuals according to their species: humans and non-human animals are victimised equally.

For example, Linda Merz-Perez and her colleagues interviewed a sample of 45 violent offenders in a high security prison in Florida, which they compared with a group of non-violent offenders. The researchers found that 56% of violent offenders reported having abused animals during childhood, as opposed to 20% of non-violent offenders.

These are retrospective studies of animal abuse in the perpetrators' personal histories, but sometimes the same crimes are used to predict the future. In a study based on FBI data on a sample of 150 men charged with active animal abuse (physical or sexual assault) or passive animal abuse (i.e. criminal negligence), no less than 96% of the men had been previously charged with or committed similar crimes over the following six years.[23] Similar analyses were carried out with mass or serial killers and they confirmed that some criminals had a childhood history of cruelty to animals.

These studies also show the polymorphism of animal abuse and the diversity of the species that are victimised. This is a significant fact. From a psychological point of view, tearing the legs off a spider is hardly comparable to putting a cat in a plastic bag and beating it up. Regardless of the biological proximity of other species, humans categorise animals according to anthropocentric criteria, which means that they are influenced by human interests, whether material or emotional, and culture contributes to spreading those criteria. For example, as we have seen, while fish enjoy much lower recognition than large anthropoid animals throughout the world,[24] the value of creatures such as dogs and pigs varies widely in different contexts. Cherished in the West for their affectionate and sociable nature, dogs are valued for their meat in at least 42 cultures around the world.[25] In the aftermath of a Western campaign that aimed to get people to treat our canine friends more humanely, dog soup is now called "Bardot" in Korea.[26]

In France, violence against animals such as dogs, who enjoy a high rank on the sociozoological scale (which reflects the value a culture ascribes to different animal species), seems more serious than violence against lower-ranking species. Therefore, when looking for clues that might predict serious violence against humans, abuse of sociozoologically close animals such as cats or dogs is the most relevant indicator. It has also been observed that proximity in an even more literal sense could also be relevant: teenagers who abuse animals living close to them at home are less likely to engage in serious antisocial behaviour than those who actively seek animals to abuse outside their homes. The latter are clearly more motivated in their search for victims to satisfy their violent urges.[27]

Who by Fire, Who by Water?

Not all acts of cruelty are equal. Some violent methods demand greater proximity to the victim, and sometimes even close physical contact. In an American study conducted on 314 prison inmates who had abused animals, the most common method – as is often the case in American studies – was using a firearm (in 77 cases), which allows a certain physical distance between the perpetrator and the animal and may have a facilitating effect. Other methods included hitting (43 cases), poisoning (17 cases), throwing the animal against a wall or an object (9 cases), strangling or suffocation (6 cases), stabbing (6 cases), drowning (5 cases) and burning (5 cases).[28] In another study, violent perpetrators were more likely than others to engage in acts involving greater physical proximity, such as hitting, kicking, trampling, stabbing, pouring irritating chemicals, burning, and dismemberment.[29] Another retrospective study conducted on 257 American inmates found that two indicators were especially predictive of violence against humans. The first was purely quantitative: having committed multiple acts of cruelty against animals. The second was qualitative: having stabbed an animal (which implies physical contact) was found to be highly predictive of violence against humans.

One of the limitations of many existing studies is the small size of their samples (rarely more than 100 people) and the absence of a control group allowing for rigorous comparison. Indeed, when we learn that 21% of the 354 serial killers in a reference study had committed acts of cruelty against animals,[30] or that 46% of perpetrators of sexual homicide had abused animals when they were teenagers,[31] a crucial piece of information is missing: how common are these acts in the general population?

Another problem is that animal abuse is very often not reported (or less reported in some cultural contexts) or it is not recorded by the authorities. In the largest study on mass murderers in the US from 1982 to 2018, evidence of animal abuse was found for only 10% of them. However, for other types of homicide, such as serial murders, the data seems very different, perhaps because the acts are spread over a longer period, while in the case of mass murderers each death occurs during the same event. Thus, in a study on serial killers who committed sadistic acts, there was evidence that in almost 90% of cases, the perpetrators had also abused animals.[32]

What We Learn from General Population Studies

Self-reported crime studies, which ask people directly about their own transgressions, overcome several limitations that plague other studies based on public data. They assume that respondents will confess to past misconduct if they are guaranteed that the study is anonymous and confidential. There are validation studies of this methodology that give it some credence. For example, if we get respondents to take part in the study for a second time, fitting them with physiological sensors that can measure the slight stress associated with a dishonest answer, the answers overlap in a satisfactory way.[33]

The best studies are based on representative samples in which participants use secure response collection devices. In a study conducted by Michael Vaughn at the University of Saint Louis in the United States, a sample of 43,000 participants answered 31 questions about delinquent behaviour such as hitting someone, setting a fire, using a weapon during a fight, etc. When the researcher compared people who had abused animals with people who had not, he found that animal abusers had higher rates of *every* type of delinquent behaviour.

Cruel Teenagers

Studies on adolescent or child populations are less frequent. Sonia Lucia, of the University of Geneva, and Martin Killias, of the University of Zurich, interviewed more than 3,600 Swiss children and teenagers aged 13 to 16.[34] The results showed that 12% of them (17% of boys and 8% of girls) admitted to having deliberately mistreated an animal.[35] Of those admitting their cruelty, 5% of boys and 1.5% of girls had abused an animal more than once. The animal victims were cats or dogs (29%), fish, lizards or frogs (18%), birds (11%) and other animals (insects or gastropods, 41%). In about half of the cases, the act had been committed in the presence of one or several other persons. When the researchers related animal abuse to delinquent and violent behaviour among participants, they found a significant link for every type of behaviour. For example, children who confessed to having abused animals had committed three times as many serious offences such as burglary or assault leading to injury.

The first French study on teenage animal abuse which I conducted in 2019 involved nearly 12,300 students aged 13 to 18. It found that 7.3% of them had abused animals – only once for 44% of them, twice for 15%, and more for the remaining 41%. Most acts of cruelty had been committed by the perpetrator alone (55%), and one quarter of those acts involved another person. The abused animals were mostly cats (22.5%), dogs (13.9%) or birds (11.6%), and sometimes rodents (8.2%) and fish (6.4%). As for the perpetrators, they were typically struggling students with a history of fighting or bullying.[36] Most of them were boys, which is consistent with the findings of the *Observatoire national de la délinquance et des réponses pénales* (The National Observatory of Crime and Criminal Justice) on individuals charged with animal abuse from 2016 to 2018: 80% were men.[37] In a more recent study carried out in a sample of more than 55,000 higher education students, 6.4% of the participants declared having perpetrated animal abuse in the past, with males having done so about three times more often than females.[38]

Psychological Deficiencies and Trauma

Beyond a simple description of acts of cruelty against animals, the studies allow us to examine a multitude of psychological or psychiatric traits associated with this violence. We have seen that the physical distance between the animal and the human perpetrator is relevant to understanding the logic of animal abuse. So is psychological distance. Thus, people with low empathy[39] or reduced emotional sensitivity[40] are more likely to abuse animals. That is also the case for people with sadistic,[41] psychopathic, narcissistic or Machiavellian tendencies.[42] In Michael Vaughn's study mentioned earlier, respondents who had committed violence against animals were afflicted with a myriad of psychiatric problems such as obsessive-compulsive disorder, histrionic personality disorder, or addictions (to alcohol, gambling, or others). In France, students who had abused animals we more likely to suffer from anxiety or depression, were less attached to their parents and had more problems at school. Furthermore, it was not uncommon for animal abusers to have witnessed domestic violence[43] or to have been physically or sexually abused during childhood.[44] In one study, Frank Ascione, at the University of Denver, found that children who had been victims of sexual abuse were six times more likely to commit acts of cruelty against animals. In the large study among higher education students mentioned above, animal abuse was linked with callousness, difficulties in impulse control and sensation seeking. Participants who reported a climate of violence in their family, or who had witnessed acts of violence by their father against their mother, were particularly prone to abuse animals.[45]

We can conclude that, in many cases, animal cruelty is only one facet of a psychiatric disorder. People with mental health problems are particularly prone to harming animals. The reverse is also true: according to a study on dog bites involving over 20,000 people, dogs are more likely to bite people with mental health issues.[46]

However, to believe that mental illness is the main cause of animal abuse would be as gross a mistake as thinking that most violence between humans can be explained by psychiatric disorders. In fact, mental disorders carry very little weight compared to other explanatory factors of violence, regardless of who the victims are.[47] Let us now turn to the most frequent and ordinary causes of violence.

Notes

1 Rupke N. (1987). *Vivisection in Historical Perspective*, London, Routledge, p. 37.
2 Wright J., Hensley C. (2003). "From animal cruelty to serial murder: Applying the graduation hypothesis," *International Journal of Offender Therapy and Comparative Criminology*, 47 (1), pp. 71–88.
3 https://www.vosgesmatin.fr/faits-divers-justice/2019/08/03/il-y-a-des-tueurs-en-serie-quiont-commence-par-des-animaux, accessed 13 April 2020.
4 See Arluke A., Madfis E. (2014). "Animal abuse as a warning sign of school massacres: A critique and refinement," *Homicide Studies*, 18 (1), pp. 7–22.
5 Sax B. (2007). "Culture, religion and belief system? Animals in Nazi Germany," in M. Bekoff (ed.). *Encyclopedia of Human–Animal Relationships*, Westport, Greenwood Press, pp. 442–443.
6 Herzog H. (2011). *Some We Love, Some We Hate, Some We Eat*, New York, Harper, p. 58.
7 Sax B. (2007). "Culture, religion and belief system? Animals in Nazi Germany."
8 Klee E. (1998). *La Médecine nazie et ses victimes*, Arles, Actes Sud; Lifton R. J. (2000). *The Nazi Doctors. Medical Killing and the Psychology of Genocide*, New York, Basic Books.
9 Arluke A., Sanders C. (1996). *Regarding Animals*, Philadelphia, Temple University Press. p. 133.
10 For psychiatry and psychology, see Bègue L. (2018). "Pour une criminologie animalière," *Revue semestrielle de droit animalier*, 2, pp. 211–218.; Gullone, E. (2012). *Animal Cruelty, Antisocial Behavior and Aggression*, London, Palgrave; Vaughn M. G., Fu Q., DeLisi M., Beaver K. M.,

Perron B. E., Terrell K., Howard M. O. (2009). "Correlates of cruelty to animals in the United States: Results from the National Epidemiologic Survey on alcohol and related conditions," *Journal of Psychiatric Research*, 43 (15), pp. 1213–1218; in the field of criminology, see Agnew R. (1998). "The causes of animal abuse: A social-psychological analysis," *Theoretical Criminology*, 2 (2), pp. 177–209; for social work and forensic medicine, see Ascione F. R., McDonald S. E., Tedeschi P., Williams J. H. (2018). "The relations among animal abuse, psychological disorders, and crime: Implications for forensic assessment," *Behavioral Sciences & the Law*, 36 (6), pp. 717–729); and in veterinary science, see Monsalve S., Ferreira F., Garcia R. (2017). "The connection between animal abuse and interpersonal violence: A review from the veterinary perspective," *Research in Veterinary Science*, 114, pp. 18–26; Gullone E. (2014). "An evaluative review of theories related to animal cruelty," *Journal of Animal Ethics*, 4 (1), pp. 37–57.

11 Monsalve S., Ferreira F., Garcia R. (2017). "The connection between animal abuse and interpersonal violence: A review from the veterinary perspective."

12 Ascione F. R., McDonald S. E., Tedeschi P., Williams J. H. (2018). "The relations among animal abuse, psychological disorders, and crime: Implications for forensic assessment," *Behavioral Sciences & the Law*, 36 (6), pp. 717–729.

13 Baron-Cohen S. (2011). *The Science of Evil*, New York, Basic Books.

14 Gleyzer R., Felthous A. R., Holzer C. E. (2002). "Animal cruelty and psychiatric disorders," *The Journal of the American Academy of Psychiatry and the Law*, 30 (2), pp. 257–265; Stupperich A., Strack M. (2016). "Among a German sample of forensic patients, previous animal abuse mediates between psychopathy and sadistic actions," *Journal of Forensic Sciences*, 61 (3), pp. 699–705.

15 Foucault M. (1973). *Moi, Pierre Rivière*, Paris, Gallimard, p. 158.

16 Mass murderers are defined as people who committed at least three homicides on the same day while serial killers are defined as perpetrators of planned homicides with at least three victims over a longer period and in different circumstances.

17 Leary M. R., Kowalski R. M., Smith L., Phillips S. (2003). "Teasing, rejection, and violence: Case studies of the school shootings," *Aggressive Behavior*, 29 (3), pp. 202–214.

18 See Arluke A., Madfis E. (2014). "Animal abuse as a warning sign of school massacres: A critique and refinement," art. cit.; Henry B. C., Sanders C. E. (2007). "Bullying and animal abuse: Is there a connection?" *Society and Animals*, 15 (2), pp. 107–126; Verlinden S., Hersen M., Thomas J., "2000. Risk factors in school shootings," *Clinical Psychology Review*, 20 (1), pp. 3–56.

19 See Gullone E. (2012). *Animal Cruelty, Antisocial Behavior and Aggression*, p. 5.

20 Macdonald J. (1963). "The threat to kill," *American Journal of Psychiatry*, 120 (2), pp. 125–130; Hellman D. S., Blackman N. (1966). "Enuresis, firesetting, and cruelty to animals: A triad predictive of adult crime," *American Journal of Psychiatry*, 122, pp. 1431–1435.

21 Parfitt C. H., Alleyne E. (2020). "Not the sum of its parts: A critical review of the Macdonald triad," Trauma, Violence & Abuse, 21 (2), pp. 300–310.

22 Parfitt C. H., Alleyne E. (2020).

23 Levitt L., Hoffer T. Loper A. B. (2016). "Criminal histories of a subsample of animal cruelty offenders," *Aggression and Violent Behavior*, 30, pp. 48–58.

24 Allen M. W., Hunstone M., Waerstad J., Foy E., Hobbins T., Wikner B., Wirrel J. (2002). "Human-to-animal similarity and participant mood influence punishment recommendations for animal abusers," *Society and Animals: Journal of Human–Animal Studies*, 10 (3), pp. 267–284; Rajecki D. W., Rasmussen J. L., Craft H. D. (1993). "Labels and the treatment of animals: Archival and experimental cases," *Society and Animals*, 1 (1), pp. 45–60.

25 Fischler C. (1998). "Le comestible et l'animalité," in B. Cyrulnik (ed.). *Si les lions pouvaient parler*, Paris, Gallimard, pp. 951–959.

26 Zaraska M. (2016). *Meathooked. The History and Science of Our 2.5 Million-Year Obsession with Meat*, New York, Basic Books, p. 158.

27 Tallichet S. E., Hensley C. (2005). "Rural and urban differences in the commission of animal cruelty," *International Journal of Offender Therapy and Comparative Criminology*, 49 (6), pp. 711–726

28 Miller K. S., Knutson J. F. (1997). "Reports of severe physical punishment and exposure to animal cruelty by inmates convicted of felonies and by university students," *Child Abuse & Neglect*, 21 (1), pp. 59–82.

29 Merz-Perez L., Heide K. M., Silverman I. J. (2001). "Childhood cruelty to animals and subsequent violence against humans," *International Journal of Offender Therapy and Comparative Criminology*, 45 (5), pp. 556–573.

30 Wright J., Hensley C. (2003). "From animal cruelty to serial murder: Applying the graduation hypothesis," *International Journal of Offender Therapy and Comparative Criminology*, 47 (1), pp. 71–88.

31 Ressler R. K., Burgess A. W., Douglas J. E. (1988). *Sexual Homicide: Patterns and Motives*, Lexington, Heath and Com.

32 Levin J., Arluke A. (2009). *The Link Between Animal Abuse and Human Violence: Reducing the Link's False Positive Problem*, Eastbourne, Sussex Academic Press.

33 Clark J. P., Tift L. L. (1966). "Polygraph and interview validation of self-reported deviant behavior," *American Sociological Review*, 31, pp. 513–523.

34 Lucia S., Killias M. (2011). "Is animal cruelty a marker of interpersonal violence and delinquency? Results of a Swiss national self-report study," *Psychology of Violence*, 1, pp. 93–105.

35 Studies on teenagers find rates of animal abuse varying between 11 and 50%, with an average of 25.3%. See Arluke A., Irvine L. (2017). "Physical cruelty and companion animal," in J. Maher, H. Perpoint, P. Beirne (eds.). *The Palgave International Handbook of Animal Abuse Studies*, Londres, Palgrave, pp. 39–57.

36 Bègue L. (2022). Explaining animal abuse among adolescents: The role of speciesism. *Journal of Interpersonal Violence*, 37 (7–8), pp. 5187–5207.

37 Frattini F. (2020). "Les personnes mises en cause pour maltraitance et abandon d'un animal domestique," *La Note*, 48, ONDRP.

38 Bègue, L., Garcet, S., Weinberger, D. (2025). Intentional harm to animals: A multidimensional approach. *Aggressive Behavior*, 51: e70028.

39 McPhedran S. (2009). "A review of the evidence for associations between empathy, violence, and animal cruelty " *Aggression and Violent Behavior*, 14 (1), pp. 1–4; Hartman C., Hageman T., Williams J. H., Mary J. S., Ascione F. R. (2019). "Exploring empathy and callous unemotional traits as predictors of animal abuse perpetrated by children exposed to intimate partner violence," *Journal of Interpersonal Violence*, 34 (12), pp. 2419–2437; Kotler J. S., McMahon R. J. (2005). "Child psychopathy: Theories, measurement, and relations with the development and persistence of conduct problems," *Clinical Child and Family Psychology Review*, 8 (4), pp. 291–325.

40 Walter G. (2017) "Animal cruelty and firesetting as behavioral markers of fearlessness and disinhibition: Putting two-thirds of Macdonald's triad to work," *The Journal of Forensic Psychiatry & Psychology*, 28 (1), pp. 10–23; Dadds M. R., Whiting C., Hawes D. J. (2006). "Associations among cruelty to animals, family conflict, and psychopathic traits in childhood," *Journal of Interpersonal Violence*, 21 (3), pp. 411–429; Hartman C., Hageman,T., Williams J. H., Mary J. S., Ascione F. R. (2019). "Exploring empathy and callous-unemotional traits as predictors of animal abuse perpetrated by children exposed to intimate partner violence"; Stupperich A., Strack M. (2016). "Among a German sample of forensic patients, previous animal abuse mediates between psychopathy and sadistic actions."

41 Stupperich A., Strack M. (2016). "Among a German sample of forensic patients, previous animal abuse mediates between psychopathy and sadistic actions."

42 Kavanagh P. S., Signal T. D., Taylor N. (2013). "The Dark Triad and animal cruelty: Dark personalities, dark attitudes, and dark behaviors," *Personality and Individual Differences*, 55 (6), pp. 666–670.

43 Baldry A. C. (2005). "Animal abuse among preadolescents directly and indirectly victimized at school and at home," *Criminal Behaviour and Mental Health*, 15 (2), pp. 97–110; Degue S., Dilillo D. (2009). "Is animal cruelty a 'red flag' for family violence? Investigating co-occurring violence toward children, partners, and pets," *Journal of Interpersonal Violence*, 24 (6), pp. 1036–1056.

44 Degue S., Dilillo D. (2009). "Is animal cruelty a 'red flag' for family violence? Investigating co-occurring violence toward children, partners, and pets"; McEwen F. S., Moffitt T. E., Arseneault L. (2014). "Is childhood cruelty to animals a marker for physical maltreatment in a prospective cohort study of children?" *Child Abuse & Neglect*, 38 (3), pp. 533–543.

45 Bègue, L., Garcet, S., Weinberger, D. (2025). Intentional harm to animals: A multidimensional approach. *Aggressive Behavior*, 51: e70028.

46 Yeh C. C. et al. (2012). "Mental disorder as a risk factor for dog bites and post-bite cellulitis," *Injury*, 43 (11), pp. 1903–1907.

47 Stuart H. (2003). "Violence and mental illness: An overview," *World Psychiatry*, 2 (2), pp. 121–124.

8   Why Are Human Societies Cruel to Animals?

Illustration: Magali Seghetto

"The cruelty we practise upon animals is but our training for the cruelty we inflict upon man."
Jacques-Henri Bernardin de Saint-Pierre, 1836.[1]

Long before the disclaimer "no animal was harmed in the making of this film" appeared during the credits, the seventh art had horses thrown off cliffs, monkeys beheaded, and rabbits sacrificed for no other purpose than popular entertainment. The Homeric chariot races in the eleven-Oscar-Winning film *Ben Hur* cost the lives of more than one hundred horses, the marine explosions of *Pirates of the Caribbean* (2003) killed countless marine animals, and two dozen sheep allegedly perished during the shooting of *The Hobbit* (2013).

In 2020, employees at the Puy du Fou historical theme park in France said that tigers, oxen, horses and cats were being abused there – but we can be certain that it could not

DOI: 10.4324/9781003561972-9

Figure 8.1 Filmed by Edison Studios, elephant Topsy was publicly executed with a 6,600-volt electric
shock at the Coney Island amusement park in 1903.
Source: Press photograph from January 4, 1903, https://en.wikipedia.org/wiki/Topsy_(elephant)

have been worse than the way they would have been treated during the historical periods
that inspired this attraction. For cognitive psychologist Steven Pinker, the decline of animal
cruelty in popular entertainment is part of a historical trend of decline in all forms of violence.[2] For example, in medieval France, cats were burned alive at the stake during summer
festivals, and in the Roman empire, the circus games were a terrifyingly bloody experience
for thousands of animals. To take just one example: the extravagant celebration of a military
victory by the emperor Trajan in the 1st century saw the slaughter of over 11,000 beasts.[3] In
ancient Greece, a festival in honour of the goddess Athena, the *Panathenaea*, involved the
ritual sacrifice of up to a hundred oxen. The word *hecatomb* (from the Greek *hekaton* – "hundred" – and *bous*, "ox") reflects this extravagant slaughter.

These few illustrations suggest that many of the abuses endured by animals are not the
consequence of individual weaknesses and deficiencies such as those described in the previous
chapter. However terrible they may seem, they are in no way the result of individual depravity,
but rather demonstrate that consideration for animals has evolved greatly throughout human
history. They force us to see that the way we treat animals is strongly influenced by collective
norms which define how we should behave towards them, and by the value that our societies
ascribe to them.

These norms and values are acquired through cultural influences to which individuals are
exposed from a very young age, which teach them that animals are not worthy of the same
consideration as humans. According to a study by Yale researcher Matti Wilks, our tendency
to disproportionately value human interests over animal interests increases from childhood to
adulthood.[4] Animal abuse also seems to be influenced by the observation of models, which it
often imitates. Thus, children who have witnessed animal abuse are three to eight times more
likely to abuse animals later in life.[5]

Reasons for Ordinary Violence

Animal abuse committed in the personal sphere or through institutionalised practices is
driven by several types of motivation, according to Yale researcher Stephen Kellert.

The first one is the desire to *control* animals so that their behaviour conforms with human expectations, for example when an owner hits their dog in an attempt to stop its barking. This coercive action is also observed in the training of bears, lions, tigers or elephants who are hit with metal rods or receive electric shocks if they refuse to stand on their hind legs for a circus act or to jump through a hoop placed in front of them.

Punishment is a second type of motive. It involves the use of painful measures to sanction the animal, for example when a dog relieves itself in the wrong place, bites a child or destroys a valued object.

Another form of motivation is *displaced aggression*.[6] In this case, the animal becomes a scapegoat, used as an outlet for an individual's unresolved fears and frustrations. For example, after an unfavourable meeting with a superior, the individual kicks his dog if he upsets him.[7]

Another form of violence consists in *using animals for aggression*. Animals are incited to attack other animals in staged fights which often lead to death or serious injury.[8] This tradition, which is usually illegal today (in France, animal fighting has been banned since 1833),[9] is still practised clandestinely and staggering sums of money are often wagered.[10] The animals most commonly used for fighting throughout the world are roosters and dogs, but may also involve horses, camels, buffaloes, rams or pigs.[11]

Amplification of violence consists in using the animal as an actual weapon to threaten or harm someone. A study comparing owners of so-called "high-risk" dogs such as rottweilers or pit bulls to owners of other breeds such as spaniels or Saint Bernards confirmed that the former had more often been convicted of assault, based on court records.[12] Another study showed that young adults who own "high-risk" dogs (but not large breeds) more often reported having committed crimes.[13]

In some cases, animals are abused for fun or to *shock* witnesses. This was the case in the notorious story of 25-year-old Frenchman Farid Ghilas, who was convicted after he posted a harrowing video of himself throwing a cat against a wall for "fun."

Another reason for animal cruelty is *revenge*, when an animal is harmed in order to retaliate against their owner. This includes, for example, the mutilation of farm animals.[14] It can also involve violence aimed at hurting a person who is emotionally attached to an animal. Several surveys on the circumstances of domestic abuse show that the fear of their partner harming the family pet often leads abused women to delay their departure[15] and sometimes to return home after leaving.[16]

One last reason pertains directly to *representations and prejudices* maintained towards a given species. Thus, people kill rats, snakes, insects or even cats and justify their actions by referring to the malignancy or insignificance of the species. Once an animal is labelled as a pest, it inspires only thoughts of eradication. Prejudices against animals result from the inconveniences they cause or from their perceived dangerousness, but, as we have seen earlier, they can also constitute the justifications used to rationalise their institutionalised exploitation.

In the French study on 12,300 teenagers mentioned in Chapter 7, the participants were asked to assess the value of animals in comparison to human beings. They were also asked whether they were in favour of sacrificing mice and rats for scientific research or whether it was acceptable to make animals suffer in experiments to find cures for human diseases. Their answers to all those questions were statistically associated with the number of times they had abused animals.[17] The correlation was robust and independent of gender, age and numerous other psychological variables measured in the study. Interestingly, the teenagers who were best integrated academically were slightly more likely to believe that it was acceptable to use animals and that they were less valuable than humans. This confirms that the devaluation of animal interests, although linked to universally condemned acts of cruelty, is not always socially deviant or inappropriate.

The Escalation Hypothesis

There are two ways of understanding the links between violence against animals and humans.

The first way is to see the violence as a manifestation of vulnerabilities or general deviant tendencies – either due to psychological disorders or behaviours inspired and modelled on one's entourage. In this case, a succession of increasingly violent acts (as illustrated by the story of Tom Nero described in the previous chapter) is only the result of pre-existing risk factors or deficits which may worsen with age. This is the *deviant syndrome model*: it alleges that animal abuse is part of a constellation of psychological and social issues.

According to another model, that of escalation, violence against animals could *prepare* its perpetrators for later violence against humans by desensitising them. This idea seems to have influenced the first French animal protection law, which was passed in 1850.[18] When he presented the bill, Jacques de Grammont recounted the harrowing story of a child who, after being fascinated by the bleeding of a pig, had slit his little sister's throat. The displacement of the abattoirs outside of Paris in the early 19th century was similarly motivated by moral imperatives in addition to health concerns: violence had to be removed from the city. Thanks to this measure, it was said that one's gaze would no longer "be painfully affected… by the streams of blood which used to run through the gutters of the great city."[19]

The escalation model implies that a gradual habituation to cruelty can occur and eventually influence behaviour. The desensitisation hypothesis had been made before, notably by Voltaire: "The children who cry at the death of the first chicken whose throat is slit before them laugh the second."[20] Today, we can illustrate it through the testimony of abattoir workers like Régis, a former slaughterhouse employee, who told an ethnologist:

> When I got here, I couldn't look at them – especially the cows, I couldn't look at them. Sometimes they kill the little kids, it's kind of sad because they're so small, they barely weigh 5 kilos. But, you know, you get used to it.[21]

It seems reasonable to acknowledge the phenomenon of habituation and desensitisation, but can we claim that these emotional adaptations to working conditions change the operators to the extent that they become more prone to violence? Can the concept of escalation really be applied to people who kill animals for a living?[22] There are persistent prejudices to in this regard. Throughout the centuries, butchers have often been looked upon with suspicion. The latin poet Ovid thus wrote in his *Metamorphoses*: "as he prepares to someday shed human blood, he who slits the throat of a lamb in cold blood and turns a deaf ear to its plaintive bleating."[23] In his *Tableaux de Paris au XVIIIe siècle*, philosopher Louis-Sébastien Mercier also wrote:

> It is neither good nor wise to slaughter the lamb in front of children's eyes or to shed the blood of animals on the street. Those bloody gutters affect man's moral and physical nature: he is doubly corrupted by the effluvia. Who knows whether a man did not become a murderer by walking through those streets and coming home with blood-red soles. He may have heard the whining of animals being slaughtered alive and become insensitive to the muffled cries of the one he struck.[24]

Novelists and philosophers have often described the butcher's trade as a cruel and hardened profession[25] upon which the police should keep a watchful eye.[26] Butchers have been disqualified from jury service.[27] The fear of bloody outbursts on the part of some "killers" (a term commonly used in French slaughterhouses) even led to recommendations for "moral training" of slaughterhouse workers.[28] In several Asian countries, the profession of butcher is considered impure and relegated to the lower classes.[29] Historian Eric Baratay observes that the opprobrium that affected butchers was "shared with executioners, animal castrators and knackers, all referred to by the same Latin word *carnifex* during the Middle Ages."[30]

As it was in the early 20th century at the start of industrialised slaughter described by Upton Sinclair, meat production workers were usually low-skilled, poorly paid workers[31] who felt that their job was "demeaning,"[32] as if there was a link between slaughter and social marginalisation.[33]

The concern that the gory use of animals could desensitise people has also been expressed in the field of animal experimentation. In a book about the debates around vivisection in 19th-century France, historian Jean-Yves Bory described the concerns of the medical establishment. According to the author of a French manual of professional ethics for doctors, "too frequent vivisection only led to the moral numbness of a butcher or a knacker."[34] Other authors have claimed that "vivisection hardened the heart and made one unable to sympathise with the suffering of the sick."[35] It was therefore necessary for the medical profession to be beyond reproach in the face of this risk. The author of an article on physiology claimed that, "But for the purity of our intentions, we, vivisectors, would be torturers."[36] When, in 1888, the criminal Jack the Ripper operated in the London district of Whitechapel, there was even a rumour that inflamed anti-vivisectionist circles: it was said that the serial killer was a vivisectionist who had grown tired of butchering animals and had turned to women instead.[37]

The escalation hypothesis also applies to violent conflict. In *Machete Season*, Jean Hatzfeld quoted this testimony obtained during his investigation of the Rwandan genocide:

> At the end of the day, a man is like an animal: if you cut his head or neck, he falls. In the early days, a man who had killed chickens, or better yet, goats, had an edge. It makes sense. But after a while, everybody got accustomed to this new activity and caught up...[38]

Some will go as far as to claim that the very existence of the animal category, conceived as the archetype of what is contemptible, could be a factor of violence. Writer Marguerite Yourcenar shared this view:

> Let us revolt against ignorance, indifference and cruelty – which, by the way, are only so frequent among humans from having been practiced on animals. Let us remind ourselves that, since we must always make everything about ourselves, fewer children would be abused if fewer animals were tortured, and fewer trains would take people to their deaths in dictatorships if we had not become accustomed to vans in which animals agonise without food and water on their way to the abattoir.[39]

The hypothesis that large-scale animal cruelty is an alarming sign and possibly an omen of genocidal violence is also voiced as a tragic enumeration by linguist Catherine Kerbrat-Orecchioni:

> The extermination of all American bison (tens or even hundreds of millions of them) by European colonists preceded and accompanied that of nearly all (95 percent) indigenous populations...; in 1910, the Armenian genocide was preceded by the elimination of large numbers of dogs living in the streets of Constantinople; in Czechoslovakia, the gradual implementation of a regime of terror under soviet occupation was prepared by large-scale campaigns to exterminate pigeons and dogs; and when they occupied Phnom Penh in 1975, the Khmer Rouge started by massacring domestic animals with unbelievable violence.[40]

We could continue listing historical events or fictional accounts that support the escalation hypothesis, but they alone are inadequate to provide sufficient demonstration. It is perhaps more useful to consider exactly what evidence would be required for this hypothesis to be scientifically grounded. Not only would it be necessary to prove that there is a chronological succession in which violence against animals precedes violence against humans. It would also be necessary to demonstrate that without the animal abuse, violence against humans would not have taken place. There is no such evidence. It is therefore more reasonable to consider that any animal cruelty is the expression of a general deviant syndrome and not necessarily the cause of later violence.

Of Mice and Norms

In a book on animal rights, philosopher Florence Burgat wondered about the psychology of the researchers behind the forced swimming test involving mice to evaluate antidepressants.[41] Peter Singer expressed the same perplexity with regard to the animal experimentation he criticized in *Animal Liberation*:

> How can people who are not sadists spend their working days driving monkeys into lifelong depression, heating dogs to death, or turning cats into drug addicts? How can they then remove their white coats, wash their hands, and go home to dinner with their families?[42]

To answer the question raised by the Australian philosopher, we need to remember the power of social norms. Although the human mind is inclined to find extraordinary causes for the facts that upset it, or to demonise those whose actions offend it, purely social factors are often enough to account for most facts, including those that seem unthinkable.

For example, the assumption that people who kill animals on hunting trips have less empathy towards humans or that they are more likely to be violent is not proven.[43] However, a taste for hunting is highly socially transmissible: according to one study, five out of six hunters indicated that during their childhood, someone in their family hunted.[44] The influence of norms is also evidenced by a comparative binational study. In this study conducted by an English researcher, violence against animals was eleven times higher in a cultural context that encouraged it (a Romanian village with many stray animals) compared to an urban context (a German metropolis).[45]

However, one study suggests that there is a link between the proximity of a slaughterhouse and the occurrence of violence, as the writer Upton Sinclair suggested in his 1906 novel on Chicago's slaughterhouses – a novel which contributed to social reforms in the meat industry. In *The Jungle*, he wrote: "There is but scant account kept of cracked heads in back of the yards, for men who have to crack the heads of animals all day seem to get into the habit, and to practice on their friends, and even on their families, between times."[46] Amy Fitzgerald, a researcher at the University of Windsor, Canada, looked at the changes in slaughterhouse employment in 581 US counties and at the evolution of violent crime rates from 1994 to 2002.[47] It appeared that, compared to other sectors of employment, the number of people employed in slaughterhouses was more strongly correlated with rates of arrest for violent offences, rape and sexual offences.[48] For the author of the study, these results show that the practice of industrial slaughter had a desensitising effect on employees. However, the Fitzgerald study, like another, more recent one,[49] does not find a direct link at the individual level but only a correlation in terms of geographical distribution. Yet one last study showed that, when comparing survey answers from butchers and farmers, butchers scored higher in verbal aggression, physical aggression and hostility.[50] However, the sample was particularly small (65 participants), making it difficult to draw a definite conclusion regarding the actual difference between the two groups.

Having presented the causes of violence against animals, we can conclude that not only is a purely psychological explanation insufficient, but that cultural and institutional factors also play a decisive role. We must now ask ourselves how individuals whose work involves harming animals manage to reconcile this activity with their personal moral values and with the empathy that is part of the standard human psychobiological equipment.

Notes

1 Original French quote in Ferry L., Germé, C. (1994). *Des animaux et des hommes*, Paris, Le Livre de Poche, p. 384.
2 Pinker S. (2011). *The Better Angels of Our Nature*, New York, Viking.
3 Shelton J. (2007). "Beastly spectacles in the ancient Mediterranean world," in L. Kalof (ed.). *A Cultural History of Animals in Antiquity*, London, Bloomsbury.
4 Wilks M., Caviola L., Kahane G., Bloom P. (2021). "Children prioritize humans over animals less than adults do," *Psychological Science*, 32 (1), pp. 27–38.
5 Kaufman K. L., Hilliker D. R., Daleiden E. L. (1996). "Subgroup differences in the modus operandi of adolescent sexual offenders," *Child Maltreatment*, 1, pp. 17–24.
6 Kellert S. R., Felthous A. R. (1985). "Childhood cruelty toward animals among criminals and noncriminals," *Human Relations*, 38 (12), pp. 1113–1129.
7 It has also been noted that violence against animals could be the expression of a form of general sadism leading people to take pleasure in making others suffer, or it could be the result of an obsession with pain and death.
8 A study on the psychological factors associated with approval of cockfights or dogfights shows that those are more often approved by men and people with lower empathy and who are more hostile to the idea of continuity between humans and animals. See Molina M., Arikawa H., Templer D. I. (2013). "Approval versus disapproval of dogfighting and cockfighting among college students," *Social Behavior and Personality*, 41 (2), pp. 345–352.
9 In Nord-Pas-de-Calais, France, and in overseas French departments, there is still an exception for cockfighting.
10 Up to $50,000 for some dog fights according to De Mello M. (2012). *Animals and Society*, New York, Columbia University Press, p. 118.
11 Nobrega Alves R. R., Albuquerque U. P. (eds.) (2018), *Ethnozoology*, New York, Academic Press. See also Digard J.-P. (1999). *Les Français et leurs animaux*, Paris, Fayard, p. 126.
12 Barnes J. E., Boat B. W., Putnam F. W., Dates H. F., Mahlman A. R. (2006). "Ownership of high-risk ('vicious') dogs as a marker for deviant behaviors: Implications for risk assessment," *Journal of Interpersonal Violence*, 21 (12), pp. 1616–1634.
13 Ragatz L., Fremouw W., Thomas T., McCoy K. (2009). "Vicious dogs: The antisocial behaviors and psychological characteristics of owners," *Journal of Forensic Sciences*, 54 (3), pp. 699–703.
14 See Beirne P. (2009). *Confronting Animal Abuse. Law, Criminology, and Human–Animal Relationships*, New York, Rowman & Litlefield, chapter 4.
15 18 to 45 percent of battered women postpone their decision to leave because they fear their pet will be abused by their partner.
16 That was the case for 35 percent of women according to a study by Carlisle-Frank P. L., Frank J. M., Nielsen L. (2004). "Selective battering of the family pet," *Anthrozoös*, 17 (1), pp. 26–42. See also Barrett B. J., Fitzgerald A., Stevenson R., Cheung C. H. (2020). "Animal maltreatment as a risk marker of more frequent and severe forms of intimate partner violence," *Journal of Interpersonal Violence*, 35 (23–24), pp. 5131–5156.
17 Bègue L. (2020). "Explaining animal abuse among adolescents: The role of speciesism," *Journal of Interpersonal Violence*, 37 (7–8) pp. 5187–5207.

18   The French law on the abuse of domestic animals from July 2, 1850, says: "Anyone who publicly and unfairly mistreats a domestic animal shall be sanctioned with a fine of five to fifteen francs and may be sentenced to five days in prison."

19   Quoted in Traïni C. (2011). *La Cause animale. 1820-1980. Essai de sociologie historique*, Paris, PUF, p. 21.

20   "Voltaire, traité sur la tolérance," chapter 22, 73, p. 170, quoted by Kerbrat-Orecchioni C. (2021). *Nous et les autres animaux*, Paris, Lambert-Lucas.

21   Rémy C. (2009). *La Fin de bêtes. Une ethnographie de la mise à mort des animaux*, Paris, Economica, p. 39.

22   This phenomenon is sometimes called the *Sinclair effect*, after the author of the novel *The Jungle* (1906), about the slaughterhouses of Chicago.

23   Lenoir F. (2017). *Lettre ouverte aux animaux (et à ceux qui les aiment)*, Paris, Fayard, p. 89.

24   Burgat F. (1995). *L'Animal dans les pratiques de consommation*, Paris, PUF, p. 51.

25   Serpell J. (1986). *In the Company of Animals*, Oxford, Blackwell, p. 165. In *The Lord of the Flies*, William Golding suggested that the practice of hunting by a group a children was a precursor to one of them being murdered. See also this testimony by a former poultry slaughterhouse: "You become violent more easily. When you get angry, you very easily tend to attack the person or thing that irritates you. You will use a knife more easily than you used to. Quite simply a knife, a sharp knife." Quoted by Rémy C. (2009). *La Fin de bêtes*, p. 66.

26   Pelosse V. (1882). "Imaginaire social et protection de l'animal," *L'Homme*, XXI, p. 16.

27   Pattenden R. (1999). "The exclusion of the clergy from criminal trials juries: An historical perspective," *Ecclesiastical Law Journal*, 5, pp. 151–163, quoted by Arluke A., Irvine L. (2017). "Physical cruelty and companion animal," in J. Maher, H. Perpoint, P. Beirne (eds.). *The Palgrave International Handbook of Animal Abuse Studies*, Londres, Palgrave, p. 47. As pointed out by Renan Larue, Rousseau noted in his *Émile* that "in England, even butchers are not allowed to testify" (*Émile*, Gallimard, 1969, vol. 4, p. 411), and Mme de Staël observed that a "fine law in England prohibits men who shed animal blood for a living from performing judicial functions" (*De la littérature*, Flammarion, 1991, p. 306). See Larue R. (2019). *Le Végétarisme des Lumières. L'abstinence de viande dans la France du xviiie siècle*, Paris, Garnier, p. 83.

28   Freminet J.-P. (1974). *De l'application des méthodes d'étourdissement préalables à l'abattage des animaux de boucherie*, veterinary PhD thesis, École nationale vétérinaire de Toulouse, p. 56, quoted by Rémy C. (2009). *La Fin de bêtes*, p. 32.

29   Joy M. (2010). *Why We Love Dogs, Eat Pigs, and Wear Cows*, San Francisco, Conari Press, pp. 84–85.

30   Baratay É. (2003). *Et l'homme créa l'animal*, Paris, Odile Jacob, p. 106.

31   Lamanthe A. (2013). "L'emploi peu qualifié et à bas salaire: problématiques nordeuropéennes," *Revue multidisciplinaire sur l'emploi, le syndicalisme et le travail*, 8 (2), pp. 9–34. Fitzgerald A. J., Kalof L., Dietz T. (2009). "Slaughterhouses and increased crime rates: An empirical analysis of the spillover from 'The Jungle' into the surrounding community," *Organization & Environment*, 22 (2), pp. 158–184; Schlosser E. (2004). *Fast Food Nation*, New York, Random House; Nicolino F. (2009). *Bidoche. L'industrie de la viande menace le monde*, Paris, Les Liens qui libèrent.

32   Rémy C. (2009). *La Fin de bêtes*, p. 38.

33   Rémy (2009), p. 45.

34   Bory J.-Y. (2013). *La Douleur des bêtes. La polémique sur la vivisection au xixe siècle en France*, Rennes, PUR, p. 65.

35   Bory J.-Y. (2013), p. 65

36   Bory J.-Y. (2013), p. 52.

37   See Traïni (2011). *La Cause animale*, p. 165. An analysis of the techniques he used to remove his victims' organs suggest that he was more likely a butcher. See Knight A., Watson K. D. (2017). "Was Jack the Ripper a slaughterman? Human–animal violence and the world's most infamous serial killer," *Animals*, 7 (4), p. 30.

38   Hatzfeld J. (2003). *Une saison de machettes*, Paris, Seuil. English translation: *Machete Season*. Londo: Picador, 2006.

39   Yourcenar M. (1983). *Le Temps, ce grand sculpteur*, Gallimard, p. 157, quoted by Lenoir F. (2017). *Lettre ouverte aux animaux (et à ceux qui les aiment)*, Paris, Fayard, pp. 137–138. In the same vein,

Leo Tolstoy reportedly said: "As long as there are slaughterouses, there will be battlefields." Quoted in Nicolino F. (2009). *Bidoche*, p. 17.

40 Kerbrat-Orecchioni C. (2021). *Nous et les autres animaux*, p. 424.

41 Burgat F. (2015). *La Cause des animaux. Pour un destin commun*, Paris, Buchet Chastel.

42 Singer P. (1975). *Animal Liberation*, New York, HarperCollins.

43 Flynn C. P. (2002). "Hunting and illegal violence against humans and other animals: Exploring the relationship?" *Society and Animals*, 10 (2), pp. 137–154.

44 Flynn (2002).

45 Plant M., Van Schaik P., Gullone E., Flynn C. (2019). "'It's a dog's life': Culture, empathy, gender, and domestic violence predict animal abuse in adolescents – implications for societal health," *Journal of Interpersonal Violence*, 34 (10), pp. 2110–2137.

46 Sinclair U. (1906), *The Jungle*, New York, Doubleday.

47 Fitzgerald A. J., Kalof L., Dietz T. (2009). "Slaughterhouses and increased crime rates: An empirical analysis of the spillover from 'The Jungle' into the surrounding community."

48 Another study analysed attitudes towards animals and agressive tendencies, and it confirmed that slaughterhouse employees seem more desensitised to violence. Richards E., Signal T., Taylor N. (2013). "A different cut? Comparing attitudes toward animals and propensity for aggression within two primary industry cohorts – Farmers and meatworkers," *Society and Animals*, 21 (4), pp. 395–413. However, this was not confirmed by other studies. See Flynn C. P. (2002). "Hunting and illegal violence against humans and other animals: Exploring the relationship".

49 Jacques J. R. (2015). "The slaughterhouse, social disorganization, and violent crime in rural communities," *Society and Animals*, 23 (6), pp. 594–612.

50 Richards E., Signal T., Taylor N. (2013). "A different cut? Comparing attitudes toward animals and propensity for aggression within two primary industry cohorts – Farmers and meatworkers."

9 How Empathy Gets Turned Off

Illustration: Magali Seghetto

"I work on ewes. I like my ewes. I say hello to them, and sometimes I explain the protocol to them... The problem is that at some point, I'll ask them to sacrifice themselves, because I need their brains. It's hard to manage your empathy with the animal."

A neurobiology researcher[1]

Double Sacrifice

The hard, smooth, white laboratory bench is the altar of a double sacrifice. The first applies to animal lives. Following protocols as inflexible as religious rituals, experimenters extract scientific omens from the entrails of their victims. Diagrams, charts and figures reduce the

DOI: 10.4324/9781003561972-10

Figure 9.1 Claude Bernard practising vivisection, surrounded by his students at the Collège de France.
Image: Léon Lhermitte (1889), https://fr.wikipedia.org/wiki/Claude_Bernard#Arriv%C3%A9e_%C3%A0_Paris

bodies that have been designated to feed the great march of science into two-dimensional representations. The experimenter's sensitivity, suppressed by professional guidelines, can sometimes seem like a second victim. This emotional self-denial, which conditions the execution of the scientific act, is the requirement to which the experimenter is bound to comply. Claude Bernard, the father of experimental medicine, stated it bluntly:

> A physiologist is not a man of the world; he is a scholar, a man who is seized and engrossed by the scientific idea he is pursuing: he does not hear the cries of animals, he no longer sees the blood that flows, he only sees his idea and perceives only organisms that hide the problems he wants to discover.[2]

Bernard goes on to say that to contribute to the advancement of science, the experimenter will have to go through a "long and horrible drudgery"[3] without letting "human passions moisten his eye."[4] Any sensitivity could only impede the sometimes-arduous process of research. François Magendie, for whom Claude Bernard was both assistant and student, and who founded the world's first laboratory at the Collège de France, "nailed dogs directly onto the vivisection table by their paws and ears. He recommended using blunted nails for this purpose because the animals' movements tore out nails that were too sharp and smooth."[5] Later, Claude Bernard would publicly electrocute rabbits after severing their spine to lower their temperature to 23°C, and then show his audience "the slowed movements of the heart with the help of a needle inserted into the organ and fitted with a small flag."[6]

This demand for emotional suppression still exists a century and a half after the foundational writings of Claude Bernard. Sociologist of scientific knowledge Isabelle Stengers noted that even today, "the non-consideration of animal suffering is still required of the researcher in some experimental fields."[7] At the French physiology master's school, entire generations of experimenters have endeavoured to achieve emotional numbing, following the example of French biologist Georges Chapoutier, head of research at CNRS:

> I experimented, mostly on rodents... In this post-Cartesian and Bernardian practice, my research method clearly treated animals like objects... I showed no "squeamishness" – that would have been frowned upon.[8]

Neuropsychiatrist Boris Cyrulnik was less compliant. He described his reluctance to incise animals on demand:

> When I was a student, I was asked to dissect live animals. They would scream when we cut their stomachs open. I would drop my scalpel. I couldn't do it. The professor showed surprise at my reaction and encouraged me to go on with the experiment. He asked me if I felt any emotions when I heard my bicycle squeak.[9]

The equating of animals to mere machines was introduced by Descartes and reinforced by Malebranche in the 17th century. The latter was adamant that one should not believe that animals were really capable of suffering: "What you take for cries of pain are only the creaking of pulleys inside the mechanism," he said.[10] The French philosopher and theologian also wrote that animals "eat without pleasure, cry without pain, grow without knowing it, they desire nothing, fear nothing, and know nothing."[11]

This objectifying view of animals had well-known consequences throughout history. Thus, one could read in one of the earliest treatises on livestock farming science and techniques, published in 1888:

> We know that, in the current state of science, animals must be regarded as machines, which must be built and fed to obtain useful transformations – whether into raw materials or motive force.[12]

The Harmful Principle

Whether in a lab or elsewhere, those who doubt that animals are just biological automatons and who are affected by the visible signs of animal suffering, may be suspected of attributing human emotions to animals – the notorious *anthropomorphic bias*. Isn't the practice of science, on the contrary, about resisting such naïve illusions, those projections which conceal rather than reveal the mental universe of the organisms being studied? Descartes himself stigmatised this anthropomorphic inclination as a childish prejudice: "The greatest prejudice of all we inherit from our childhood is the belief that animals think," he wrote.[13]

If, as philosopher Merleau-Ponty asserted, any scientific understanding of the animal world requires empathy on our part, then we must alter our approach to zoology.[14] But today, one is still expected to deny animals any significant mental life in order to have scientific credibility. In accordance with *Morgan's canon*, a scientific principle which says one should refrain from "interpreting any animal action as the exercise of higher faculties if they can be explained by lower-level faculties," any mental capacities will be granted to animals only with the utmost parsimony. This is why behaviourists would discard the accounts and observations of 19th-century naturalists, who were too inclined to report observations which credited animals with intentions, cognitive abilities or feelings, to pre-scientific oblivion. Since anthropomorphism is associated with empathy for animals,[15] would it not have posed a psychological obstacle to their complete objectivity? To avoid any potential for "mentalism," physiology Nobel laureate Ivan Pavlov is said to have fined laboratory personnel each time they used banned terms like "intention" or "mind" when referring to animals.[16] This constant suppression of anthropomorphism, bordering on actual "mentophobia" for some,[17] has resulted in the pitfall of another mistaken form of reductionism: "anthropodenial," which rejects any similarities between living beings and can impede the understanding of animal intelligence.[18] When it comes to building scientific knowledge, this new form of transcendence in a world freed from superstitions, are we not too quick to turn animals into cannon fodder in the name of Morgan's principle?[19]

A Risk of Emotional Anaesthesia?

The disciplined culture instilled throughout their training[20] enables researchers to control their emotions. They must commit, as Claude Bernard wrote, to turning a deaf ear to "allegations of cruelty from non-scientific individuals."[21] To those who have qualms about the 115 million animals raised and used for research every year),[22] the white paper on animal experimentation published by the CNRS and Inserm (French public research institutions) reminds us that "a biomedical researcher should feel no shame attached to the practice of animal experimentation."[23]

But doesn't this emotional anaesthesia dictated by *libido sciendi* erode scientists' ability to empathise with their fellow humans? Vivisection has been suspected of turning medical students into callous doctors by forcing them to detach from their emotions.[24] In the 19th century, the first campaigns against vivisection – which was already a controversial practice – sought to denounce the morally degrading effect it could have on experimenters[25] and they warned the public of the risk that "experimental rage" would not "stop at animals" and would eventually target humans.[26]

One century later, psychologist Richard Ryder, a former experimenter himself, asserted that animal experimentation had an emotionally crippling effect.[27] Even today, the psychological consequences of laboratory work are the subject of recurring ethical questions.[28] An employee of the French National Institute of agricultural Research (INRAE) lamented the fact that research institutions ignored their employees' suffering as well as the long-term effects of such experiments on their emotional well-being.[29]

This kind of habituation to pain is plausible, and one cannot rule out the possibility that experimenters may minimise the suffering that animals endure in their experiments. Is this not already the case with human medicine? A study conducted on health practitioners accustomed to treating pain showed that the areas of their brain involved in sharing pain were less activated when they were shown a video of a suffering patient compared to participants with no medical experience.[30] Moreover, the experienced doctors estimated that the painful sensory test undergone by the patients was easier to endure than the other participants did.[31]

This downplaying of pain was interpreted as a way of performing efficiently as a doctor while lowering the stress caused by negative emotions.[32] One survey of medical students confirmed that they showed more empathy during their first two years of training and became less empathetic when their interactions with patients increased.[33] This emotional erosion was further confirmed on a larger scale in a review of 18 studies focused on empathy trends among medical students and interns.[34]

Does the gradual desensitisation to human pain extend beyond professional practices? A scientist voiced the following question, which is reminiscent of Hannah Arendt's thesis on the banality of evil: "Why is it that a researcher can spend his or her weekend at home playing with a family pet and then, on Monday morning, return to their laboratory and test a potentially harmful chemical compound on stray or unwanted dogs?"[35] There is no evidence to suggest that those who experiment on animals have a specific profile or suffer any long-term effects. This is also because the institutional framework of animal experimentation is designed to minimise the emotional impact of the operations on their practitioners.[36] Not only are the animals highly standardised, but through their training as experimental technicians, humans manipulate them using procedures that are themselves standardised, transforming these operators into individuals who are, in a sense, also standardised.[37]

Laboratory Strategies and Semantic Tricks

"You mustn't think about the fact that you are now killing the animal. You just need to focus on following the procedure."

A researcher with training in animal experimentation[38]

There are in fact institutional tricks in place to prevent unnecessary emotions that an experimenter might feel when faced with animals subjected to unpleasant procedures. The overall organisation of the research process is based on the division of activities and dilution of responsibly – both are divided between all the actors involved. The lead researcher of a study may very well design an experiment, receive authorisation, have assistants conduct it, obtain the desired data, have it analysed and summarised without having any direct contact at any time with the animals that made the publication possible.[39]

Thus, for zootechnician Jocelyne Porcher, "pain..., if it affects the actors of the experimental procedure (both humans and animals), usually goes unnoticed by the researcher, who doesn't get his or her hands dirty and simply works with the data. Working on the results, getting value out of them and recognition from their peers – all this eclipses the suffering of the employees, who are often temps, as well as the suffering of the 'animal material.' "[40]

A functional distinction is also made between animal breeders, who have daily, prolonged contact with animals, and technicians, who are required to carry out experiments with researchers and to kill used or surplus animals. The first group knowingly interacts with live, sentient animals, while the second deals with animals that are treated like objects and meant to be turned into measurable results and data after a series of preestablished procedures.

The main purpose of a laboratory is to be a rationalised environment for the metamorphosis of a "naturalistic" animal – i.e., a whole, natural creature – into an "analytical" animal, literally an "object of science" whose original nature is forgotten and translated into statistics, diagrams and dissections.[41] For example, in the famous research on conditioning, for which thousands of dogs have been used since Pavlov's original findings, when we examine the 700 pages of the *Handbook of Classical and Operant Conditioning*, a reference text on the subject, we find only one mention of the fact that the Pavlovian studies were conducted on dogs.[42]

In her ethnographic study of a research laboratory, anthropologist Catherine Rémy noted that spatial segmentation physically separated those who cared for the animals from those who used them for experimentation or eliminated them when the research was over. The latter group were rarely in contact with the "naturalistic" animals. This "technico–moral" divide allowed for an efficient distribution of sensitivity among the participants. This was also illustrated by a study in which students were asked to practise vivisection on dogs under

Figure 9.2 "They're harmless when they're alone, but be very careful if there's a pack of them with a research grant."
Illustration: Magali Seghetto

general anaesthesia who were afterwards to be killed by an overdose of anaesthetic. For the students, the fact that the dog arrived completely inert on the laboratory bench allowed them to start dissecting without being troubled by the fact that it was their own intervention that ultimately doomed the animal: "Nobody really knew that we were the ones killing the dog," said one of them.[43]

But long before an experiment is even designed, it should be reiterated that animals are the objects of cultural representations that fully legitimise their use. *Human exceptionalism*, the belief that humans are fundamentally different from animals, provides the ideological framework that allows the instrumentalization of animals to be tolerated.[44] Depending on the species involved, additional justifications may come into play. During the industrial-scale development of animal experimentation in the 20th century, mice and rats (who now account for 98% of lab animals[45]) were still widely associated with uncleanliness and epidemic risks in the social imagination.[46] But symbols can change: today, these white rodents no longer evoke the Black Plague but an extremely sterilised and rationalised form for scientific research, fighting disease. Mice no longer scare us, but they are perceived somewhat more as objects.

As soon as they arrive in the laboratory, experimental mice are already partly objectified, as evidenced by the standardised model presentations in industry catalogues. Having once co-published a study on the chemical modulation of anxiety in rats,[47] I regularly receive mail trying to sell me cutting edge medical "equipment": rodents in which some genes have been altered or deactivated for targeted research. Their modest size, accelerated gestation (21 days) and physiological similarity to humans make mice the perfect scientific instruments. At least that is the message conveyed by multinational corporations of animal experimentation. These genetically modified, hyper-standardised mice with code names like "Gdf15KO mouse models," described and sold in imposing catalogues, are engineered to suffer from all sorts of medical pathologies that concern humans (e.g., myopathy, obesity, anorexia, or schizophrenia). There are over 2,500 varieties. To undertake research on muscular dystrophy, glaucoma or depression, simply select the correct "animal model." One of the most well-known models, the transgenic *Oncomouse*, was specially created and patented in 1988 for cancer research, and its tendency to develop tumours is accelerating research on carcinogenesis. From industry technical booklets, we also learn which genes have been deactivated or introduced, or simply the unit prices of the small quadrupeds, which range from a few euros to several thousand. The matching between particular species and pathologies is well established, as noted in a white paper on animal experimentation: "Rats for hypertension, pigs and rabbits for atherosclerosis, dogs for acute joint rheumatism, etc."[48]

It should be added that the type of species involved in the experiment is undoubtedly a modulating factor in the precautions that must be taken to preserve the experimenter's sensitivity. Indeed, the psychological discomfort or even the guilt that may be felt depends on the perceived closeness of the animal. As a lab technician stated in an interview:

> …it's different working with mice than goldfish. I'm sure goldfish don't evoke the same kind of response. I'm a lot more aware of [mice] and a lot more careful and compassionate, if you like, with a mouse, as an animal rather than just a thing that you do your experiment on.[49]

Experimenting on evolutionarily distant species makes the task less challenging, as Galen of Pergamon, one of the founders of Western medicine and animal experimentation already observed. He was emperor Marcus Aurelius's personal physician, and he influenced medicine for nearly fifteen centuries and is known to have carried out countless dissections on live animals (who, of course, had not been anesthetised, since the practice was not invented until the 19th century). Not inclined to feel needless empathy, the master advised his students to dissect animals "without pity or compassion."[50] In his experiments, when he severed the laryngeal nerves, he is said to have preferred to use sheep or pigs rather than apes as this allowed him to "avoid seeing the unpleasant expression of the ape when it is being vivisected."[51]

In the 19th century, during the heyday of animal experimentation, Claude Bernard also gave up experimenting on apes or monkeys because they were too physically similar to human beings. He reportedly only dissected one monkey in his entire career, claiming that "these animals will grab your hands and moan… they are too human-like."[52]

Picking species that are more phylogenetically or affectively distant from humans not only preserves the experimenter's sensitivity,[53] but also decreases the chance of public outrage. As a researcher explains in the white paper on animal experimentation published by the French research institutions CNRS and Inserm:

> Cardiology increasingly uses small rodents and has been using cats and dogs less and less often. This is primarily due to the cost of the animals, but also to the fact that experimenting on dogs has a strong impact on public opinion, whereas an operation on a rat leaves people indifferent.[54]

The same sort of caution was mentioned at a seminar for the American Association for Laboratory Animal Science. A lecturer recommended experimenting on "less popular animals like pigs and mice rather than cats and dogs."[55] This intuition is widely supported by surveys of the general public.[56] Even among animal rights activists, there is a clear hierarchy, both at the level of discourse[57] and in the actions carried out by activists against laboratories. Analysis of the webpages of the Animal Liberation Front indicates that three quarters of the actions undertaken target researchers experimenting on primates (although they account for fewer than 1% of animals used in research), whereas only 9% target researchers working with mice, who are by far the most often used species.[58] The preference for species closer to humans is also noticeable among philosophers specialising in animal issues: they are primarily concerned with vertebrates.[59]

Talking Points and Euphemisms

Making animals invisible or absent through linguistic sleight of hand is another way of preventing unwanted empathy. In 1920, in an edition of the *Journal of Experimental Medicine*, the editor laid out guidelines urging researchers to adopt sanitised language in their articles, for example by using the generic term "animal" instead of "dog." The abolition of personal pronouns was also recommended: "Never use 'he,' 'she,' 'his' or 'her' when referring to an animal."[60] He also suggested that illustrations never show a whole animal, only parts,[61] and advised against adjectives like "severe," "acute," and "intense" if they referred to animal suffering.[62] "Starving" was to be replaced with "limited food intake,"[63] "poison" with "toxic," and "bleeding" with "haemorrhaging."[64]

When large numbers of animals were used, the experimental subjects were numbered in a way that made it less apparent: thus, rabbit no. 102 was referred to as "rabbit 10-2."[65] In an article on the blood physiology of cats, an editor asked to substitute "the brain was cut in several places" with "the brain was removed."[66] According to this antiseptic logic, an electric shock becomes a "training stimulus," the cries of Guinea pigs injected with neurotoxins become "vocalisations," and convulsions become "symptoms of meningeal irritation."[67]

A review of current scientific publications shows that very little space is dedicated to the description of experimental procedures applied to animals or to their living conditions and well-being.[68] One study found that in 30% of the articles analysed, the number of animals used was not mentioned anywhere, and in 59% of the articles, there was no mention of the methods used to kill the animals, sometimes referred to as "preparations."[69]

The emotional neutralisation inherent in scientific publications is also sometimes found in the speech of technicians and experimenters. By observing the activity of twenty US laboratories, sociologist Arnold Arluke found that the employees tended to use the word "distress" instead of "suffering."[70] In France, journalist Audrey Jougla noted that laboratories used euphemistic language, preferring to speak of an "invasive" protocol rather than a "painful" one, or "making an animal work" rather than "using" it.[71]

"Nameless"

In the Bible, animals are initially mentioned as nameless beings.[72] Since man was given the privilege of naming them by his creator, should he not be able to revoke this individuation? "As soon as an animal bears a name, it becomes an individual," admitted novelist Isabelle Sorente, whose novel *180 Jours* recounts the short lives of pigs, from birth to slaughter.[73] As the animal is not meant to be seen as an individual in the laboratory, it seems natural to keep it nameless. This kind of deindividuation was tersely recommended in a scientific editorial written for researchers: "Never use names."[74]

This guideline was scrupulously observed in academia, and those who did not comply with it during their field observations, such as primatologist Jane Goodall or pachydermologist Cynthia Moss, were admonished by their colleagues.[75] In a study conducted over two years with several US laboratories, sociologist Mary Phillips found that the vast majority of the more than 5,000 animals used annually in the facilities she studied (many of them were cats or monkeys) were nameless. Only in two of 23 laboratories were names occasionally given to the animals. A primatologist remarked that "sometimes, as soon as a monkey has a name, it seems to be protected from invasive procedures; in a sense, its name protects it."[76]

This phenomenon is reflected in cultural content aimed at children. An analysis of Disney animated films produced between 1937 and 2016 shows that 90% of animals depicted as serving a utilitarian purpose (such as transport) remain nameless,[77] whereas this is only the case for 24% of pets.

According to Mary Philips, the systematic deindividuation that occurs in laboratories is partly due to the large number of animals used, but also to the limited time dedicated to them and to the brevity of their stay. This namelessness could also be explained by the difficulty of telling one from another. Naming animals requires the ability to distinguish them, and in a laboratory, genetic similarity is deliberately sought, since the lack of individual variation ensures more effective research. Thus, advertisements for lab animals sometimes show pictures of identical specimens, for example by presenting twelve photos of the same rat and reminding the reader that "for the same results... tomorrow... next year..." all rats "are created equal."[78]

Individual behavioural variations due to uncontrolled factors are disruptive for research. Therefore, laboratories prefer to use male individuals, as they are not subject to a menstrual cycle that is known to complicate observations. Thus, there are nearly four times more males than females in physiology studies, and five times more in pharmacology and neuroscience.[79] This is also the reason for the extreme standardisation of cage size, bedding, and of course, interaction with numerous animals. Another explanation for the tendency to keep animals nameless is the focus on a very specific part of their biology (for example the production of one enzyme), as one researcher explains in an experiment on a female rat:

> In the first step, your focus is on the pregnant animal. Is the female pregnant? That's the first question. Then your focus is on the foetus, and you start dissecting the foetus. Then your focus is on the brain, when you get it separated from the rest of the foetus. Then finally you're just thinking about cells. So you're reducing your focus at each step, until finally you get to the particular neurons you're interested in.[80]

The reason why it is so unusual to name lab animals is clearly because they will be killed in the end. Nearly a quarter of the experimenters interviewed by Mary Phillips said that abstaining from naming the animals allowed them to keep an emotional distance. Paradoxically, it is perhaps also to create that distance that some are named, but only in order to denigrate them. One dog, destined to be killed a few days later, was nicknamed "dead meat," and one cat who had been deliberately paralysed by severing its spine was called "Speedy Gonzales."[81] The proverbial humour of the medical world, which seems to serve the purpose of warding off the distress and human misfortune it faces on a daily basis, also manifests itself when animals are suffering.[82] Laughter then serves to exorcise the violence inflicted upon the bodies that must be mutilated and annihilated in the course of scientific practice.[83]

Notes

1 Despret V. (2009). *Penser comme un rat*, Versailles, Éditions Quæ, p. 77.

2 Bernard C. (1984). *Introduction à l'étude de la médecine expérimentale*, Paris, Flammarion, p. 189.

3 Bernard 1984, p. 54.

4 Bernard 1984, p. 9.

5 Bory J.-Y. (2013). *La Douleur des bêtes*, Rennes, PUR, p. 9.

6 Bory 2013, p. 13.

7 Stengers I. (1999). "Le développement durable: une nouvelle approche?," *Alliage*, pp. 40, 31–39; see also Porcher J. (2002). "L'occultation de l'affectivité dans l'expérimentation animale: le paradoxe des protocoles," *Nature*, Sciences, Société, 10, pp. 33–36.

8 Chapouthier G., Tristani-Potteaux F. (2013). *Le Chercheur et la Souris*, Paris, CNRS Éditions.

9 Lou Matignon K. (2012). *À l'écoute du monde sauvage*, Paris, Albin Michel, p. 42.

10 Malebranche N., "De la recherche de la vérité," VI, II, VII–394, quoted by Chauvet D. (2014). *Contre la mentaphobie*, Lausanne, L'Âge d'Homme, p. 35.

11 Chauvet 2014, p. 35.

12 Sanson A. (1888). *Traité de zootechnie*, tome II, Paris, Librairie agricole de la Maison rustique, p. 330, quoted by Porcher J. (2001). "Le travail dans l'élevage industriel des porcs. Souffrance des animaux, souffrance des hommes," in F. Burgat, R. Dantzer (eds.). *Les animaux d'élevage ont-ils droit au bien-être?* Paris, INRA Éditions, pp. 25–64.

13 Letter to Morus, Oph, t. III, p. 884, quoted by Fontenay É. de (1998). *Le Silence des bêtes*, Paris, Fayard, p. 286.

14 Merleau-Ponty M. (1968). *Résumés de cours au Collège de France*, Paris, Gallimard, p. 135, quoted in Fontenay, Elisabeth de. (2012). *Without Offending Humans: A Critique of Animal Rights*. University of Minnesota Press, p. 220.

15 On the links between anthropomorphism and empathy, see Preston S. D., de Waal F. B. (2002). "Empathy: Its ultimate and proximate bases," *Behavioral and Brain Sciences*, 25 (1), pp. 1–71. Amiot C. E., Bastian B. (2017). "Solidarity with animals: Assessing a relevant dimension of social identification with animals," *PLoS One*, 12 (1).

16 Dutton D. (2007). "Animal minds and human perspectives," in M. Bekoff (ed.). *Encyclopedia of Human–Animal Relationships*, vol. 3, Westport, Greenwood Press, pp. 930–934.

17 Chauvet D. (2014). *Contre la mentaphobie*.

18 "'Anthropodéni': le rejet a priori de traits proches des humains chez d'autres animaux ou proches des animaux chez nous," De Waal F. (2016). *Sommes-nous trop bêtes pour comprendre l'intelligence des animaux?* Paris, Les Liens qui libèrent, p. 40.

19 Sometimes this is literaly true, as it as in the 1980s when, according to a testimony collected by journalist Karine Lou Matignon: "Patrick was 22 when he was assigned to the army health service: 'I was one of the few people to participate in the first ballistic tests of the Famas (a French automatic rifle)... One day, I was asked to take delivery of this weapon at the base – which I did with a non-commissioned officer. Then, we walked into a building. The walls were covered with a thin layer of gelatin so that projectiles could not ricochet. There were several officers and doctors around me. They set up a Famas on its tripod in front of me, and then a pig weighing several hundred kilos, fitted with lots of sensors and catheters, was placed in front of me and I was asked to shoot it. I refused. An officer took my place, aimed and shot. The pig was startled, and it was enough to set off every measuring device it was hooked up to.'" Matignon K. L. (1998). *L'Animal, objet d'expérience. Entre l'éthique et la santé publique*, Paris, Anne Carrière, p. 360.

20 Birke L., Smith J. (1995). "Animals in experimental reports: The rhetoric of science," *Society and Animals*, 3 (1), pp. 23–42.

21 Bernard C. (1984). *Introduction à l'étude de la médecine expérimentale*, p. 189.

22 Linzey A., Linzey C. (2015). *Normalising the Unthinkable: The Ethics of Using Animals in Research*, Oxford, Oxford Centre for Animal Ethics.

23 Swynghedauw B. (1995). "Cœur," in *Livre Blanc sur l'expérimentation animale*, Paris, Inserm/CNRS Éditions, p. 29.

24   Turner J. (1980). *Reckoning with the Beast. Animals, Pain and Humanity in the Victorian Mind*, Baltimore, Johns Hopkins University Press, quoted by Traïni C. (2011). *La Cause animale*, Paris, PUF, p. 97.

25   Rupke N. (1987). *Vivisection in Historical Perspective*, London, Routledge.

26   Traïni C. (2011). *La Cause animale*, p. 100.

27   Ryder R. (1998). "Some basic objections to animal experiments. In The ethics of animal experimentation," *Proceedings of the European Congress*, 17–18 December 1998. Brussels, European Biomedical Research Associaton (EBRA), pp. 51–56, 1988, quoted by Rémy C. (2009). *La Fin des bêtes*, Economica, Paris. p. 134.

28   Herrman K., Jayne K. (eds.). *Animal Experimentation: Working Towards a Paradigm Change*, Boston, Brill.

29   Porcher J. (2002). "L'occultation de l'affectivité dans l'expérimentation animale: le paradoxe des protocoles."

30   The brain areas in question are the insula, the anterior cingulate cortex (ACC) and the periaqueductal gray (PAG).

31   Cheng Y. et al. (2007). "Expertise modulates the perception of pain in others," *Current Biology*, 19, pp. 1708–1713.

32   Haque O. S., Waytz A. (2012). "Dehumanization in medicine: Causes, solutions, and functions," *Perspectives on Psychological Science*, 7 (2), pp. 176–186.

33   Hojat M., Vergare M. J., Maxwell K., Brainard G., Herrine S. K., Isenberg G. A., Gonnella J. S. (2009). "The devil is in the third year: A longitudinal study of erosion of empathy in medical school," *Academic Medicine*, 84, pp. 1182–1191.

34   Neumann M., Edelhäuser F., Tauschel D., Fischer M. R., Wirtz M., Woopen C., Scheffer C. (2011). "Empathy decline and its reasons: A systematic review of studies with medical students and residents," *Academic Medicine*, 86, pp. 996–1009. See also Blackshaw J. K., Blackshaw A. W. (1993). "Student perceptions of attitudes to the human–animal bond," *Anthrozoös*, 6 (3), pp. 190–198.

35   Monamy V. (2017). *Animal Experimentation*, Cambridge, Cambridge University Press, p. 5.

36   Arluke A. (2006). *Just a Dog. Understanding Animal Cruelty and Ourselves*, Philadelphia, Temple University Press.

37   Holmberg T. (2008). "A feeling for the animals: On becoming an experimentalist," *Society and Animals*, 16, pp. 316–335.

38   Holmberg 2008, p. 328.

39   Gluck J. P. (1997). "Harry F. Harlow and animal research: Reflection on the ethical paradox," *Ethics and Behavior*, 7 (2), pp. 149–161.

40   Porcher J. (2002). "L'occultation de l'affectivité dans l'expérimentation animale: le paradoxe des protocoles."

41   Lynch M. E. (1988). "Sacrifice and the transformation of the animal body into a scientific object: Laboratory culture and ritual practice in the neurosciences," *Social Studies of Science* 18, pp. 265–289.

42   I borrowed this example from Adams M. (2020). *Anthropocene Psychology. Being Human in a More-Than-Human World*, London, Routledge, p. 17.

43   Arluke A., Hafferty F. (1996). "From apprehension to fascination with 'dog lab': The use of absolutions by medical students," *Journal of Contemporary Ethnography*, 25 (2), pp. 201–225. This dilution of responsibility has also been observed in a slaughterhouse by ethnologist Noëlle Vialles: "A first man stuns the animal and, alone or with a coworker, he hangs it; then the second man or a third one bleeds the animal... Since the anaesthesia is not lethal and the (supposedly) painless bleeding is not really a killing, there is no "real" killing any longer. As a result, no one is "really" killing anymore: the division of tasks leads to a total dilution of responsibility and possible feelings of guilt – even vague and repressed ones." Vialles N. (1987). *Le Sang et la Chair. Les abattoirs des pays de l'Adour*, Paris, Éditions de la Maison des Sciences de l'homme, pp. 48–49. The phenomenon of diluted responsibility and division of labour has been the object of many studies in social pshcyology. For an application to the domain of violence, see Baumeister R. (1997). *Evil. Inside Human Violence and Cruelty*, New York, Freeman; Kelman H., Hamilton V. (1989). *Crimes*

of Obedience, New Haven, Yale University Press; Bandura A. (1999). "Moral disengagement in the perpetration of inhumanities," *Personality and Social Psychology Review*, 3 (3), pp. 193–209.

44 Birke L. (2012). "Animal bodies in the production of scientific knowledge: Modeling medicine," *Body and Society*, 18, pp. 1–23.

45 Monamy V. (2017). *Animal Experimentation*, p. 65.

46 Holmberg T. (2011). "Mortal love: Care practices in animal experimentation," *Feminist Theory*, 12 (2), pp. 147–163.

47 Bell R., Duke A. A., Gilmore P. E., Page D., Bègue L. (2014). "Anxiolytic-like effects observed in rats exposed to the elevated zero-maze following treatment with 5-HT2/5-HT3/5-HT4 ligands," *Scientific Reports*, 4, p. 3881.

48 Swynghedauw B. (1995). "Cœur," in *Livre blanc sur l'expérimentation animale*, p. 22.

49 Birke L., Arluke A., Michael M. (2007). *The Sacrifice. How Scientific Experiments Transform Animals and People*, West Lafayette, Purdue University Press, p. 97.

50 Guerini A. (2003). *Experimenting with Humans and Animals. From Galen to Animal Rights*, Baltimore, Johns Hopkins University, p. 18.

51 Rupke N. (1987). *Vivisection in Historical Perspective*, p. 15.

52 Bory J.-Y. (2013). *La Douleur des bêtes*, p. 44.

53 Michael M. (2017). "Animals as scientific objects," in L. Kalof (ed.). *The Oxford Handbook of Animal Studies*, Oxford, Oxford University Press, pp. 380–396.

54 Swynghedauw 1995, p. 23.

55 Orlans F. (1993). *In the Name of Science. Issues in Responsible Animal Experimentation*, Oxford, Oxford University Press, p. 72.

56 Crettaz von Rotten C. (2012). "Public perceptions of animal experimentations across Europe," *Public Understanding of Science*, 22, pp. 691–703. Similar results are found in Driscoll J. W. (1992). "Attitudes toward animal use," *Anthrozoös*, 5 (1), pp. 32–39.

57 Paul E. (1995). "Us and them: Scientists' and animal rights campaigners' views of the animal experimentation debate," *Society and Animals*, 3, pp. 1–21.

58 Herzog H. (2011). *Some We Love, Some We Hate, Some We Eat*, New York, Harper, p. 250.

59 Chapouthier G. (2020). *Sauver l'homme par l'animal*, Paris, Odile Jacob, p. 72.

60 Dunayer J. (2000). "In the name of science: The language of vivisection," Organization & Environment, 13 (4) p. 443.

61 Guerini A. (2003). *Experimenting with Humans and Animals*, p. 113.

62 Dunayer J. (2000). "In the name of science: The language of vivisection," p. 434.

63 Dunayer 2000, p. 437.

64 McAllister Groves J. (1997). *Hearts and Minds. The Controversy over Laboratory Animals*, Philadelphia, Temple University Press, p. 47.

65 Plous S. (2003). "Is there such a thing as prejudice toward animals?," in S. Plous (ed.). *Understanding Prejudice and Discrimination*, New York, McGraw-Hill, p. 514.

66 McAllister Groves J. (1997). *Hearts and Minds*, p. 47.

67 Dunayer J. (2000). "In the name of science: The language of vivisection," p. 436.

68 Turner J. Z. (1998). "I don't want to see the pictures: Science writing and the visibility of animal experiments," *Public Understanding of Science*, 7 (1), pp. 27–40.

69 Smith J. A., Birke L., Sadler D. (1997). "Reporting animal use in scientific papers," *Laboratory Animals*, 31 (4), pp. 312–317.

70 Arluke A. (1992). "Trapped in a guilt cage," *New Scientist*, pp. 33–35.

71 Jougla A. (2015). *Profession: animal de laboratoire*, Paris, Autrement, p. 118.

72 Boyer F. (2010). "Un animal dans la tête," in J. Birnbaum (ed.), *Qui sont les animaux?* Paris, Gallimard, pp. 11—25.

73 Finkielkraut A. (2018). *Des animaux et des hommes*, Paris, Stock, p. 191; Sorente I. (2013). *180 Jours*, Paris, J.-C. Lattès.

74 Dunayer J. (2000). "In the name of science: The language of vivisection," pp. 441–442.

75 See De Waal F. (2001). *The Ape and the Sushi Master: Cultural Reflexions from a Primatologist*, New York, Basic Books; Moutou F. (2018). *Et si on pensait aux animaux?* Paris, Le Pommier, p. 181.

76 Vitale A. (2011). "Primatology between feelings and science: A personal experience perspective," *American Journal of Primatology*, 73, pp. 214–219.
77 Stranton R. R. (2021). *The Disneyfication of Animals*, Cham, Palgrave Macmillan.
78 Arluke A. (1994), " 'We build a better Beagle': Fantastic creatures in lab animals ads," *Qualitative Sociology*, 17, pp. 143–158, p. 148.
79 Haselton M. (2018). *Hormonal. The Hidden Intelligence of Hormones*, New York, Little, Brown and Cie.
80 Phillips M. T. (1994). "Proper names and the social construction of biography: The negative case of laboratory animals," *Qualitative Sociology*, 17.
81 Dunayer J. (2000). "In the name of science: The language of vivisection," p. 441. Speedy Gonzales is a cartoon mouse created in 1953 and known as "the fastest mouse in Mexico."
82 Birke L., Arluke A., Michael M. (2007). *The Sacrifice*.
83 See Rémy C. (2009). *La Fin des bêtes*, p. 176.

10 Arguing Over Animal Bodies

Illustration: Magali Seghetto

On January 18, 1982, an Animal Liberation Front activist entered the tall white stucco building that houses the Royal Society of London. Heading towards one of the rooms where a reproduction of a portrait of René Descartes was hanging, they stealthily pulled out a sharp blade and swiftly slashed the canvas of the father of modern philosophy before making their escape. The person was never found, but it was demonstrated that, three centuries after the death of the illustrious thinker, Descartes's image could still inspire most resolute forms of activism.

Descartes's Animal Machine: What Exactly Are We Talking About?

Descartes is still considered a nefarious figure among animal rights advocates. As the author of a theory of animals as machines, the philosopher and mathematician is often regarded as

DOI: 10.4324/9781003561972-11

one of the major deniers of animal sentience. In his *Treatise on Man* (1662), he explains that animals can be regarded as automata. Devoid of the spark of reason, they are only driven by inescapable physical determinism. In the bedside book of animal rights activists, *Animal Liberation*, in the best-selling essay published seven years before the London incident, philosopher Peter Singer reminded his readers that Descartes' theory of animal insentience[1] offered undeniable advantages, providing the perfect scientific endorsement of experimental cruelty at a time when "the practice of experimenting on live animals became widespread in Europe. Since there were no anaesthetics then, these experiments must have caused the animals to behave in a way that would indicate, to most of us, that they were suffering extreme pain. Descartes's theory allowed the experimenters to dismiss any qualms they might feel under these circumstances. Descartes himself dissected living animals in order to advance his knowledge of anatomy, and many of the leading physiologists of the period declared themselves Cartesians and mechanists."[2]

Richard Ryder, a close friend of Peter Singer known for coining the word "speciesism," explains Descartes' indifference to animal suffering through psychological speculation:

It is known that Descartes was a cold, neurotic and miserable man. Some have said that he was sadistic. But it is more probable that his fierce denial of the sufferings of others was an attempt to reinforce the denial of his own. Was he not one of those who, rejected by

Figure 10.1 Reproduction of the portrait of René Descartes vandalised by an activist in 1982 at the Royal Society in London.

Image: André Hatala [e.a.] (1997) Dde eeuw van Rembrandt, Bruxelles: Crédit communal de Belgique, ISBN 2-908388-32-4.

described, animals can polarise powerful collective emotional responses. Other, more recent examples are worth mentioning, as they highlight the social and political dimension of animals. This is the case with direct action movements.

Direct Action Movements

While the majority of activities carried out by these activist groups are limited to peaceful demonstrations or the removal and transportation of farm animals to shelters, at times more alarming acts are committed. According to American police authorities, the two principal direct-action organisations, namely, Animal Liberation Front and Earth Liberation Front have carried out over 600 illegal actions in the United States between 1996 and 2002, causing damage worth 43 million dollars.[17] Property damage, laboratory fires, intimidation of researchers performing animal experimentation and even use of homemade bombs – these incidents led the deputy director of the FBI to declare that ecoterrorism was one of the most serious threats on American soil. However, despite the extreme forms it may take in some countries, animal rights activism has never caused a single human death. In France, a study on animal rights organisations by economist Romain Espinosa showed that three quarters of them condemned any use of violence,[18] as does the organisation L214, famous for its viral videos exposing abuses in French farms and slaughterhouses.

In France, violent incidents motivated by environmental concerns or animal rights are very rare (a total of 77 have been claimed on the ALF website from 2002 to 2007 – mostly in the Paris or Toulouse areas) and they consist of property damage or destruction eight times out of ten.[19] Likely due to its apparently altruistic motives, this kind of activism maintains significant public sympathy.[20] Nevertheless, a special branch of the national police force, the *Cellule Demeter*, was created in 2019 to fight "intrusions, degradations and theft" targeting the farming and agribusiness sectors.

In the United Kingdom, a 2016 poll showed that 70% of respondents considered it acceptable for animal rights organisations to hand out leaflets on the streets or encourage passers-by to put stickers on their windows, 11% for them to demonstrate in front of the labs or even homes of people involved in animal experimentation, 9% for them to illegally release animals, 8% for them to occupy research labs, and 4% for them to destroy property.[21] The sector dedicated to animals manifests itself as highly dynamic, reflecting significant intensity and engagement, in ways not limited to quantitative measures.

Class Oppositions

The fate of animals lies at the heart of controversies fuelled by major sociological and political divides. Ever since the first laws prohibiting public cruelty to animals were passed, a class divide has been very much in evidence in France. The first animal protection law enacted in 1850 under the aegis of one of Napoleon III's ministers, General Jacques Philippe Delmas de Grammont, condemned the public abuse of animals[22] but it also reflected the government's concern about the brutality of an underclass whose mores were considered too violent.[23] This was labelled as an attempt at *demopedia* ("educating the people") by anthropologist Christophe Traïni: the idea was to eradicate the more visible forms of animal cruelty, like the horse abuse portrayed in the second picture of the story of Tom Nero discussed in Chapter 7.[24] Similarly, in England, the clergy and protestant groups suspected the working class of abusing their domestic animals.[25]

Class oppositions are also reflected in the stigmatisation of certain species of pets. It is common to equate a dog's alleged dangerousness with its owner's social class. In North

America, the media are prone to conflate scary pit bulls with poor Black or Hispanic populations.[26] In France, an anthropologist who studies domestication has suggested that the demonisation of that species of dog was evidence of the denigration of working-class neighbourhoods and inner cities. The alleged dangerousness of those "mean" dogs has been denounced and contrasted with the "friendly or fancy dogs of middle-class neighbourhoods."[27] In the aftermath of a series of riots in 2005 in France, a law on crime prevention even included a section on "dangerous dogs" in order to make it more difficult to own one. Although systematic studies of dog bites fail to demonstrate that one breed is more dangerous than another,[28] they do indicate individuals with close relationships to dogs are disproportionately represented among victims. Nevertheless, breeds reputed to be the most aggressive are still largely associated with the "dangerous classes" in the collective imagination.

The Political Denunciation of Vivisection

Another instance of the political use of animals is the denunciation of vivisection as a lack of civilisation. As early as the 19th century, English chauvinism was fuelled by pride in treating animals more humanely than other nations. Considered as the "moral birthplace of animal protection," England was home to the development of large numbers of humane societies from the very beginning of that century. No later than 1822, the country adopted the Martin's Act, which prohibited acts of cruelty against cows, horses and sheep, and a few years later, it prohibited animal fights. While England already numbered 15 antivivisectionist societies in 1885, France had only one.[29] In 1840, thanks to the official patronage of the Society for the Prevention of Cruelty to Animals by Queen Victoria herself, animal advocacy gained extra legitimacy.

The development of animal experimentation (called *vivisection* by its proponents until the early 20th century, when it was taken over by its detractors, who sometimes still use it today) fueled the accusation of "national cruelty" which the British associated with the executions carried out during the French Revolution,[30] and it was said that "Paris, far more than London, is the theatre of the cruel experiments of vivisection."[31]

The antivivisectionist cause thus became a facet of English nationalism, the true mirror of a superior civilisation. A milder version of this, the opposition between "decent" research and unacceptable practices, still shapes the discourse of those involved in research in the United Kingdom. A poll of British lab technicians and researchers showed that the practices of the French were commonly castigated, as evidenced in the words of this respondent: "I worked for some time in a French university, but I resigned due to the treatment seemingly reserved for animals."[32]

In a completely different context, animal rights were also exploited by German antisemites. Composer Richard Wagner allegedly called for the destruction of laboratories and the removal of vivisectors, whom he seemed to have associated with the Jews, who were then seen as the stereotypical scientists.[33] The enactment of some animal protection laws also reflected a clear hostility towards Jews, such as the law prohibiting ritual slaughter which was inspired by a veterinarian close to Hitler.[34] To this day, the topic is still instrumentalised by some xenophobic movements in Europe.[35]

The Overrepresentation of Women

Finally, the fight against animal experimentation is a cause in which women are notably overrepresented – to a degree that has changed little in 150 years. In the 19th century, 60% of antivivisectionist leaders were women – an impressive figure for a time when women were

Table 10.1 Differences between men and women in human–animal relationships.[44]

Domain	Direction of effect	Difference size
Favourable attitude towards animals	Women > Men	Moderate
Attachment to a pet	Women > or = Men	None to small
Field activism	Women > Men	Large
Hunting	Men > Women	Very large
Cruelty to animals (adults)	Men > Women	Large to very large
Compulsive animal adoption	Women > Men	Moderate

almost invisible in the public sphere. Moreover, three quarters of demonstrators for animal rights were women.[36] More recently, a review of nine studies conducted to determine the proportion of women participating in contemporary animal rights demonstrations in several countries showed that for every male participant, there were three women.[37] For other indicators of animal rights activism, the differences between men and women remain consistent, as shown in Table 10.1.[38]

This difference has often been presented as a case of divergence between masculine rationality, which is supposed to be scientifically informed and unswayed by emotions, and the "hysterical sentimentality" of women.[39] Animal rights advocates like the Irish suffragette Frances Power Cobbe, who founded the Society for the Protection of Animals Liable to Vivisection, or the Frenchwoman Marie Huot, who launched the *Ligue Populaire contre la vivisection*, were frequently depicted by their detractors as idle spinsters who transferred their unfulfilled maternal instincts onto animals.

In that spirit, one could read in the 1893 edition of the French *Guide pratique des maladies mentales* (a reference book on mental disorders) that "some people have an excessive affection for animals, to which they would sacrifice every human being. Antivivisectionists belong to that category of mental patients, and most of their members are women."[40] The denunciation of misplaced empathy and the pathologising of concern for animal welfare have long found fertile ground in anti-feminist prejudices.

Presidential Dogs

All these examples show that opposition to animal experimentation has frequently been linked to social and political goals that go far beyond the fate of animals. Closer to us, the political instrumentalization of animals seems obvious if we only consider the way political officials in many countries carefully stage their appearances with animals. Of course, there are exceptions: Mao Zedong condemned having pets as a sign of bourgeois degeneracy, and in the *Communist Manifesto*, Marx and Engels portrayed animal protection as a frivolous distraction for "armchair reformers."[41]

But many political leaders have understood that a well-staged appearance with an animal could be an effective way to convey a message – for instance, Vladimir Putin and Kim Jong Un showed themselves with powerful horses, whereas French far-right leader Marine Le Pen posed with a harmless feline companion. In the White House as in the French presidential palace, the Elysée, dogs have held a privileged place for at least 50 years. In France, every president since the beginning of the fifth Republic in 1958 has had one. Whether it's Georges Pompidou's dog Jupiter or Emmanuel Macron's four-legged companion Nemo, these pets have been used as tools of political communication to make their owners and the presidency appear friendlier. When Emmanuel Macron adopted a black Griffon-Labrador from an animal shelter, an implicit message seemed to emerge: a president who adopts a mixed-breed rescue dog cannot be bad to his fellow citizens. It was a judicious choice, as was that of President François Mitterrand with his dog Baltique. It's hard to imagine a German Shepherd, a Doberman or a Rottweiler in the Elysée Palace. The Labrador represents "quiet strength," explained paleoanthropologist Pascal Picq.[42]

It seems heads of state have concocted their own very political interpretation of Ghandhi's famous statement that the greatness of a nation can be judged by the way it treats its animals.[43] They have invited their fellow citizens to measure the greatness of their President by the way he welcomes their favourite animal in the gilded halls of the Republic.

Notes

1 Singer wrote that, according to Descartes' philosophy, animals "experience neither pleasure nor pain, nor anything else". *Animal Libération*, New York, HarperCollins, p. 292.

2 Singer P. (1975) *Animal Libération*, p. 172.

3 Ryder R. (1975). *Victims of Science. The Use of Animals in Research*, London, Davis-Poynter, p. 169. On May 5, 2021, Ryder wrote to me about this psychological analysis of Descartes: "I haven't done any research on Descartes for many years. I remember thinking he must have been concerned about the pain he had caused animals and tried to find excuses."

4 Tom Regan, another major animal rights theorist, is just as critical of Descartes. See Regan T. (1983). *The Case for Animal Rights*, Berkeley, University of California Press, pp. 3–31.

5 Bory J.-Y. (2013). *La Douleur des bêtes*, Rennes, PUR, p. 31.

6 Traïni C. (2011). *La Cause animale*, Paris, PUF, p. 171.

7 Letter to the Marquess of Newcastl, November 23, 1646, quoted in Ferry L., Germé C. (1994), *Des animaux et des hommes*, Paris, Le Livre de Poche, p. 183.

8 Fontenay É. de (1998). *Le Silence des bêtes*, Paris, Fayard, p. 277.

9 Auberger J., Keating P. (2009). *Histoire humaine des animaux*, Paris, Ellipses, p. 74.

10 Cottingham J. (1978). " 'A brute to the brutes?': Descartes' treatment of animals," *Philosophy*, 53, pp. 551–559.

11 Descartes R., *A Discourse on Method*, part 5.

12 Oph, t. II, p. 887, quoted in Fontenay É. de (1998). *Le Silence des bêtes*, p. 281.

13 Cottingham J. (1978). " 'A brute to the brutes?': Descartes' treatment of animals,", p. 557. See also Harrison P. (1992). "Descartes on animals," *Philosophical Quarterly*, 42, pp. 219–227.

14 Fontenay É. de (1998). *Le Silence des bêtes*, p. 293.

15 The monument bears the following inscription: "In memory of the Brown Terrier dog done to death in the laboratories of University College in February 1903 after having endured vivisection – extending over more than two months and having been handed over from one vivisector to another till death came to his release. Also in memory of the 232 dogs vivisected at the same place during the year 1902."

16 The story was told by Joseph Andras (2021). *Ainsi nous leur faisons la guerre*, Arles, Actes Sud.

17 Gagnon B. (2010) "L'écoterrorisme: vers une cinquième vague terroriste nord-américaine?," *Sécurité et Stratégie*, 3, p. 15–25.

18 Espinosa R. (2021). *Comment sauver les animaux? Une économie de la condition animale*, Paris, PUF, p. 166.

19 Sommier I. (2021). *Violences politiques en France*, Paris, Les Presses de Science Po.

20 Gagnon B. (2010). "L'écoterrorisme: vers une cinquième vague terroriste nordaméricaine?" See also Segal J. (2020). *Animal radical. Histoire et sociologie de l'antispécisme*, Montréal, Lux.

21 Clemence M., Leaman J. (2016). *Public Attitudes to Animal Research in 2016*, London, Ipsos Mori.

22 As indicated by Jean-Pierr Marguénaud, this law did not apply to animal experimentation. See Marguénaud J.-P. (2011). *Expérimentation animale. Entre droit et liberté*, Versailles, Éditions Quæ.

23 The oldest known legal text devoted to the protection of animals was promulgated during the Babylonian Empire. It was the Code of Hammurabi (who was emperor from 1792 BCE to 1750 BCE).

24 See Agulhon M. (1998). "Le sang des bêtes. Le problème de la protection des animaux en France au xixe siècle," in B. Cyrulnik (ed.). *Si les lions pouvaient parler*, Paris, Gallimard, pp. 1192–1198.

25 Carrié F. (2019). "La cause animale en France et dans les pays anglo-saxons: contrastes et influences," in Carrié F., Traïni C. (eds.). S'engager pour les animaux, Paris, PUF, pp. 27–39; see also Carrié, F., Doré, A., Michalon, J. (2023). *Sociologie de la cause animale*. Paris: La Découverte.

26 Arluke A., Sanders C. (1996). *Regarding animals*, Philadelphia, Temple University Press. p. 185.

27 Digard J.-P. (1999). *Les Français et leurs animaux*, Paris, Fayard, p. 173.

28 Reisner I. R., Shoffer F. S., Nance M. L. (2007). "Behavioral assesssment of child-directed canine aggression," Injury Prevention, 13, pp. 348–351; Casey R. A., Loftus B., Bolster C., Richards G. J., Blackwell E. J. (2014). "Human directed aggression in domestic dogs (Canis familiaris): Occurrence in different contexts and risk factors," *Applied Animal Behaviour Science*, 152, pp. 52–63.; ANSES (2020). *Risque de morsure du chien. Avis de l'ANSES. Rapport d'expertise collective*, Maisons-Alfort, ANSES.(https://www.anses.fr/fr/system/files/SABA2015SA0158Ra. pdf)

29 Traïni C. (2011). *La Cause animale*, p. 5.

30 Traïni 2011, p. 66.

31 Traïni 2011, p. 70.

32 Michael M., Birke L. (1994). "Accounting for animal experiments: Identity and disreputable others," *Science, Technology and Human Values*, 19, pp. 189–204.

33 Arluke A., Sanders C. (1996). *Regarding Animals*, Philadelphia, Temple University Press, p. 143.

34 Ibid., p. 153.

35 Sägesser C. (2018). "Les débats autour de l'interdiction de l'abattage rituel," *CRISP*, 2385, pp. 5–48.

36 French R. D. (1975). *Antivivisection and Medical Science in Victorian Society*, Princeton, Princeton University Press, pp. 239–240.

37 Herzog H. A. (2007). "Gender differences in human–animal interaction: A review," art. cit.; see also Vezirian, K., & Bègue, L. (2023). The gender gap in animal experimentation support: The mediating roles of empathy and speciesism. *Anthrozoös*, 36(6), pp. 1115–1127.

38 One might add that the overwhelming majority of people involved in research on human–animal relations are women. See https://www.psychologytoday.com/gb/blog/animals-and-us/202105/women-dominate-research-the-human-animal-bond.

39 Traïni C. (2011). *La Cause animale*, p. 17.

40 Sollier, P. (1893). *Guide pratique des maladies mentales*, Paris, G. Masson, p. 363, cité par Traïni C. (2011). *La Cause animale*, p. 178.

41 Agulhon M. (1998). "Le sang des bêtes. Le problème de la protection des animaux en France au xixe siècle," in B. Cyrulnik (ed.). *Si les lions pouvaient parler*, p. 1186.

42 Schneider V. (2018). "Les chiens du pouvoir," *Le Monde 2*, 356, pp. 27–32.

43 Serpell J. (1986). *In the Company of Animals*, Oxford, Blackwell, p. 29.

44 Adapted from Herzog H. A. (2007). "Gender differences in human–animal interaction: A review," *Anthrozoös*, 20 (1).

11 How Many Dogs for Every Human?

Illustration: Magali Seghetto

"Is one person equivalent to a thousand mice?"
Frans de Waal[1]

The Trolley Problem

A trolley is rushing towards a worker who is working on a track, and if you don't activate a switch lever in front of you, he will be crushed. However, if you divert the tram to spare the worker, the vehicle will hit ten dogs on the other track. So, what do you do?

The trolley problem is a thought experiment invented by philosopher Filippa Foot in the 1960s, which is now part of the collection of dilemmas used by researchers to analyse moral decision-making. Millions of people have answered it on the MIT website. It has become a staple of popular culture, and it is sometimes replaced by stories about lifeboats too small to

DOI: 10.4324/9781003561972-12

Figure 11.1 A variation on the "railroad track" version of the trolley problem. Close to 31% of respondents choose to save the ten dogs.

Illustration: Magali Seghetto

save everybody, or burning houses in which one must decide whom to save. In the above dilemma, which is a variation on the trolley problem, nearly 31% of participants usually decide to save the ten dogs.[2] Replace the dogs with pigeons and there is little doubt that the percentage will drop close to zero. Substitute the dogs with humans (as in Filippa Foot's original version), and it will rise to nearly 100%.[3]

As George Orwell would have us know, "all dogs are equal, but some dogs are more equal than others." A researcher at the University of Augusta, USA, presented participants with a slightly different imaginary dilemma, in which they had to decide whether to save their dog or someone else's dog from a fatal accident. The animal's life also had to be weighed against the lives of people who were either socially very close to or very distant from the respondent and who were in danger of being run over by a bus. When the life of a foreign tourist was at stake, 40% of participants preferred to save their dog. But the percentage dropped to about 10% when the dog was not their own.[4]

The bias which makes us prefer people or animals with whom we have a closer relationship is reflected in our beliefs regarding the ability to suffer. For example, just as the entire medical profession in the 19th century assumed that Black people were less sensitive to pain than Whites, experimenters attributed more sensitivity to pain to domestic animals than to wild animals.[5] Our preference for people closer to us follows a purely emotional logic. If you encourage people to "think emotionally" when solving a dilemma, they tend to increase their preference for pets such as dogs over species like pigs.[6]

Now imagine that we replace the switch lever in the trolley problem with a far more radical procedure: if you push a fat man who happens to be standing on a bridge over the track, his massive body will stop the trolley's deadly course and you will have saved several people who were about to perish on the tracks.[7]

In this case, reactions differ widely: nearly 90% of people are reluctant to push the man onto the track. Even though it is a purely imaginary situation, being physically responsible for a homicide seems unconscionable. According to neuroimaging studies, the emotions caused by

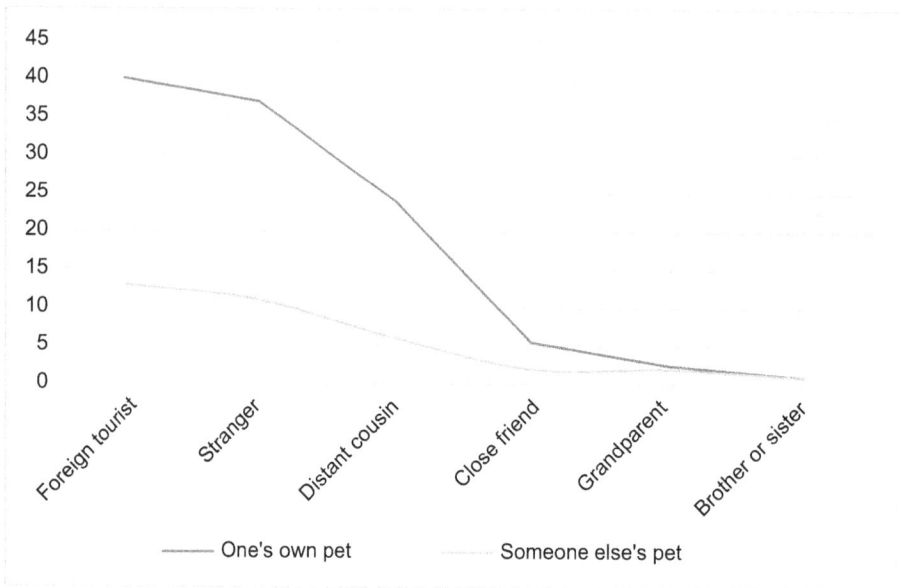

Figure 11.2 Willingness to save an animal instead of a human depending on social distance.

this simulation are more intense than those felt in the "railroad switch" situation.[8] What seems to be obviously the right choice in terms of the number of lives saved still seems unacceptable to nearly everyone. The absolute rule "Thou shalt not kill" takes up the entire mental space. Some participants may even remember fragments of their high school philosophy classes, like Immanuel Kant's famous principle that we should never treat people as "mere means to an end." In other words, whatever one's goal, one should never *use* someone to reach it.

But now imagine that we replace one species with another, and we are now asked whether we would push an ape, not a fat man, off the bridge to save 10 apes. Lo and behold, most people are now willing to treat one animal as a means to save its peers![9]

With animals, who are regarded as interchangeable, a strict application of the utility principle does not seem so shocking. It certainly did not bother Kant, who stated that "animals are not self-conscious and are there only as a means to an end." The philosopher even added, lest anyone should wonder what he really meant: "That end is man."[10] Studies conducted by a team of Oxford researchers have shown that whether we can sacrifice a member of a species to save others depends on how much we value that species. For example, we prefer to sacrifice a pig to save ten other pigs rather than sacrifice a dog to save ten other dogs.[11]

The same research team studied the way favouritism develops with age. In a series of studies, they showed that the strong pro-human bias observed in adults did not appear among 5- to 9-year-old children. Whether it's pigs or dogs, children care more about the sheer number of living beings at stake. While nearly 60% of adults would rather save a human than 100 dogs, nearly 70% of children favour the 100 dogs. When a dog's life and a human life are at stake, 35% of children prioritise the human life, 28% prioritise the dog, and the rest cannot make up their minds. In the same situation, 85% of adults sacrifice the dog and 8% do the opposite. When the dog is replaced with a pig, 57% of children prioritise the human, 18% the pig, and the rest are undecided. In the same case, 93% of adults choose the human and only 3% save the pig's life.[12]

Studies devoted to the trolley problem have thrived. An academic book entitled *Would You Kill the Fat Man?* was even published by an Oxford philosopher.[13] Studies have analysed

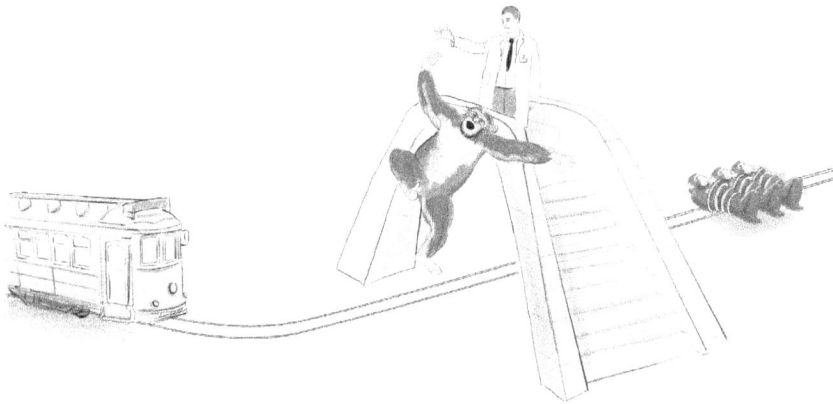

Figure 11.3 A variant of the "bridge" version of the trolley problem in which the victims are apes.
Illustration: Magali Seghetto

the influence of our moods and temporary mental states on our decision-making, and even the effect of the language in which the dilemma is presented (we are more utilitarian when responding in a language other than our mother tongue, since we are less emotionally involved).[14] Others have highlighted the way in which the identity of the protagonists influences us (participants are more likely to take the utilitarian decision when the lives of members of minorities are at stake). A third type of study focuses on the individual variables that influence choices. For example, there is one category of people who are far less reluctant to push someone off a bridge: men.[15] This is also the case with participants of any gender whose previous answers had shown that they had low levels of empathy[16] or high levels of psychopathy.[17]

Opinion Polls on Animal Experimentation

Studies show that support for animal experimentation varies widely, depending on which aspects of the issue are emphasised. As with most opinion polls on sensitive subjects, the way the questions are introduced or phrased can lead to different or even opposite results. A review of no less than 56 different polls has shown that, depending on the phrasing and on the population samples polled, 27 to 100% of respondents said they were in favour of animal experimentation, and 0 to 68% were against it.[18] For example, if the word *painful* or *death* was mentioned in the question, support for animal experimentation dropped.[19]

A brief awareness-raising introduction to a poll is enough to sway results. In one study, researchers asked participants to what extent they would accept researchers being allowed to experiment on animals. Half of the sample was presented with a "priming" introduction: "Researchers are developing and testing new drugs to cure deadly diseases like leukaemia or AIDS. By performing experiments on live animals, they think we can make more rapid progress than would otherwise be possible." While 61% of respondents were against animal experimentation when asked directly about it, only 41% those who had previously read the priming introduction opposed it.[20] Emphasising the fight against life-threatening diseases in humans overshadows animal interests.

Support for animal experimentation also depends on the species under consideration. Acceptance of the use of animals from various species rests on a combination of factors: familiarity with the species, evolutionary distance from it, and the mental abilities attributed to the animals. A study conducted in 28 European countries indicated that everywhere, experimentation on mice was more widely accepted than experimentation on dogs or monkeys.[21] In a study of students and researchers, the hierarchy of species that emerged put small fish at the bottom, then rats and mice, pigs or sheep, monkeys, and finally cats and dogs at the top.[22]

Other parameters come into play, such as the purpose of the research, the perception of a lack of viable alternatives, or the degree of severity of the procedure. For example, most respondents (65%) considered that experimentation on animals was acceptable when it was carried out for medical purposes and presented as having no alternative.[23] But this acceptance is modulated by the severity of the disease being studied: sacrificing animals to cure leukaemia is considered more legitimate than doing so to put an end to allergies.[24]

The nature of the research which uses animals also matters. Only 9% of people think that cosmetic testing on animals should be allowed,[25] whereas 50% accept experimentation for therapeutic purposes.[26] In a study of students and researchers, acceptance of research decreased depending on the type of study in the following order: experiments on animals to find cures for animal diseases, then human diseases, basic research, human medicine, animal production, chemical testing, and cosmetics.[27]

Animal suffering is a crucial issue for the public, carrying even more weight than species, according to a major opinion poll.[28] Finally, the number of animals involved is also important: when people are asked to assess a research protocol, the larger the number of animals required for the research, the greater the opposition to animal experimentation.[29]

Among the individual variables influencing responses, those in support of animal experimentation are disproportionately male.[30] A review of 56 studies conducted in 23 countries showed that men were more supportive in 84% of studies. On average, participants who answer in support of animal experimentation are older,[31] more likely to live in rural areas, less likely to have a pet,[32] have an omnivorous diet,[33] and live in less industrialised countries[34] where physical labour is more common[35] and GDP is lower.[36] It can also be observed that medical students and researchers (notably in biology)[37] are more in favour of animal experimentation.[38] A three-year follow-up study of a cohort of veterinary students found that they became increasingly supportive of animal experimentation throughout their training.[39]

Mental Attributions and their Uses for Research

The way in which the Cartesian "machine animal" thesis was interpreted certainly legitimised the rise of vivisection in the 18th and 19th centuries. To this day, the denial of mental abilities in animals is a major factor in legitimising their use in scientific research. In one study, researchers measured participants' naïve beliefs about these abilities (see Box 11.1) and related them to questions measuring support for animal experimentation.

Box 11.1 Attributing mental states to animals: Questionnaire[40]*

1. Most animals have no awareness of what happens to them.
2. Most animals can experience a wide range of feelings and emotions.
3. Most animals can somehow think, solve problems and decide what they should do.
4. Most animals are like computer programs: they mechanically respond to instinctive impulses without being aware of what they're doing.

*Participants respond by picking the extent to which they agree with each statement on a scale of 1 ("not at all") to 7 ("completely agree"). Questions 1 and 4 are reversed prior to aggregating all responses.

Figure 11.4 A rabbit presented as an experimental subject was perceived as having lower mental abilities than a rabbit presented in a natural context.

Photo: Shutterstock

The results showed that the more participants attributed cognitive or emotional abilities to animals, the less they supported using them for research.[41] Since the attribution of mental abilities to animals determines what one will allow to be done to them, we can expect that, conversely, when they are subjected to harmful treatments, they will be deemed to have lower mental abilities.

We tested this hypothesis through a series of studies with Kevin Vezirian, from the University of Grenoble, France, and Brock Bastian, from Melbourne University. The following rabbit photo was presented to participants who had just been made aware of the fact that, in their daily lives, they used products that had been tested on animals, so as to put them in a state of slight cognitive dissonance. Half of them were told that the animal lived in a forest, while the others were told that the animal would be used for research, then euthanized. Then, they were asked whether the rabbit was able to experience various mental states such as fear, pleasure, pride, and joy. The results largely confirmed that a rabbit destined to be sacrificed for research was perceived as having lower cognitive abilities.[42]

Mental Frameworks and Animal Instrumentalisation

When a human considers that another living being belongs in the "animal" category, this has profound implications. If it's another human, this usually implies serious denigration: calling someone a rat, a dog or a cockroach, as we saw in Chapter 3, can pave the way for violence. If the targets are non-human animals, there is usually no barrier to prevent their objectification. This triggers a specific perceptual process, which includes seeing animals as more similar to one another than humans are. Moral boundaries are established and hierarchical divides emerge – one between humans and animals, another between some animals and others (e.g., dogs vs pigs, or sheep vs horses), depending on their affective proximity or utilitarian purpose for humans.[43]

Research on intergroup relations indicates that competition for scarce resources or the experience of threats – real or perceived – shapes our representations of other groups, both human and non-human. However, this perception is also influenced by our values and ideologies.[44] One of the most important dimensions is called *social dominance orientation*[45] and it appears to be closely linked to discrimination against both human and non-human groups. First theorized by Harvard researcher Jim Sidanius, this psychological dimension refers to an individual's opposition to egalitarianism and adherence to social hierarchies. It is more strongly correlated with support for the sacrifice of animals for research or food production than most other known sociopolitical variables.[46] This result suggests that people who believe in the necessity of hierarchical relationships between humans also tend to view human–animal relationships in the same way.

In order to test the relation between this anti-egalitarian ideological trait and support for animal experimentation in France, a study surveyed 1,048 men and women aged 20 to 40 from various social backgrounds. The participants answered a questionnaire that measured their support for social dominance and animal experimentation.

Example of questions measuring social dominance orientation*

No group should be dominant in society. We should all strive to give every group the same chance to succeed.

Example of questions measuring support for animal experimentation*

It is normal to sacrifice animals like mice or rats for scientific research.

　　When it comes to finding the best treatments for diseases, experimenting on animals is justified even if it may harm them.

*Participants respond by picking the extent to which they agree with each statement on a scale of 1 ("not at all") to 7 ("completely agree").

The results showed that the more a participant (both men and women) subscribed to social dominance, the greater their level of support for animal experimentation.[47]

Although it is clear that the value people attribute to animals is related to broader sociopolitical representations, this does not tell us very much about the actual behaviour of the people who answer those polls. There is no shortage of examples showing that behaviour does not derive in a simple, straightforward manner from individual attitudes.

In social psychology, observable behaviour is often the litmus test which confirms or disconfirms hypotheses. Even though this adds an additional challenge, it is an irreplaceable step in any demonstration.[48] But is it possible to measure behavior that directly harms animals, and if so, how?

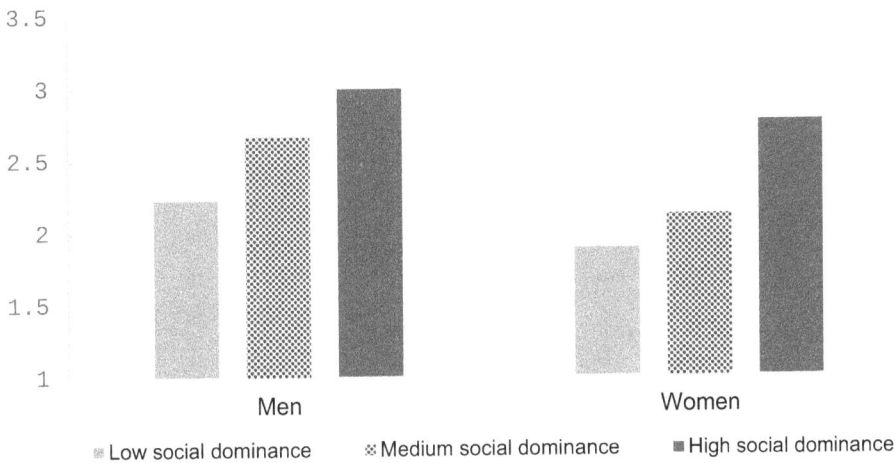

Figure 11.5 Support for animal experimentation depending on social dominance level in men and women.

Notes

1 De Waal F. (2013). *The Bonobo and the Atheist*, New York, Norton.
2 Amiot C. E., Bastian B. (2017). "Solidarity with animals: Assessing a relevant dimension of social identification with animals," *PLoS One*, 12 (1), study no. 7. It also appears that people who strongly identify with animals are significantly less likely to save the human on the track.
3 Awad E., Dsouza S., Kim R., Schulz J., Henrich J., Shariff A., Rahwan I. (2018). "The moral machine experiment," *Nature*, 563, pp. 59–64.
4 Topolski R., Weaver J. N., Martin Z., McCoy J. (2013). "Choosing between the emotional dog and the rational pal: A moral dilemma with a tail," *Anthrozoös*, 26, pp. 253–263.
5 Guerini A. (2003). *Experimenting with Humans and Animals*, op. cit. Baltimore, Johns Hopkins University, p. 81.
6 Caviola L., Capraro V. (2020). "Liking but devaluing animals: Emotional and deliberative paths to speciesism," *Social Psychological and Personality Science*, 11 (8), pp. 1080–1088.
7 The dilemmas were originally developed by Filippa Foot. See Foot F. (1967). "The problem of abortion and the doctrine of double effect," *Oxford Review*, 5, pp. 5–15.
8 Greene J., Somerville R. B., Nystrom L. E., Darley J. M., Cohen J. D. (2001). "An fMRI investigation of emotional engagement in moral judgment," *Science*, 293, pp. 2105–2108.
9 Edmonds D. (2014). *Would You Kill the Fat Man?* Princeton, Princeton University Press, p. 132.
10 Kant E. (1997). *Leçons d'éthique*, Paris, Le Livre de Poche, p. 391, quoted by Ricard M. (2014). *Plaidoyer pour les animaux*, Paris, Allary, p. 32.
11 Wilks M., Caviola L., Kahane G., Bloom P. (2021). "Children prioritize humans over animals less than adults do," *Psychological Science*, 32 (1), pp. 27–38.
12 Wilks et al. 2021, pp. 27–38.
13 See also Greene J. (2015). *Moral Tribes: Emotion Reason, and the Gap Between Us and Them*, London, Atlantic Books.
14 Costa A., Foucart A., Hayakawa S., Aparici M., Apesteguia J., Heafner J., Keysar B. (2014). "Your morals depend on language," *PLoS One*, 9 (4), p. e94842.
15 Friesdorf R., Conway P., Gawronski B. (2015). "Gender differences in responses to moral dilemmas: A process dissociation analysis," *Personality and Social Psychology Bulletin*, 41, pp. 696–713; Armstrong J., Friesdorf R., Conway P. (2019). "Clarifying gender differences in moral dilemma judgments: The complementary roles of harm aversion and action aversion," *Social Psychological and Personality Science*, 10 (3), pp. 353–363.

16 Bostyn D. H., Sevenhant S., Roets A. (2018). "Of mice, men, and trolleys: Hypothetical judgment versus real-life behavior in trolley-style moral dilemmas," *Psychological Science*, 29 (7), pp. 1084–1093.

17 Bartels D. M., Pizarro D. A. (2011). "The mismeasure of morals: Antisocial personality traits predict utilitarian responses to moral dilemmas," *Cognition*, 121, pp. 154–161.

18 Hagelin J., Carlsson H.-E., Hau J. (2003). "An overview of surveys on how people view animal experimentation: Some factors that may influence the outcome," *Public Understanding of Science*, 12 (1), pp. 67–81.

19 Hagelin, Carlsson, Hau 2003, pp. 67–81.

20 Herzog H., Rowan A., Kossow, D. (2001). "Social attitudes and animals," in D. J. Salem, A. N. Rowan (eds.). *The State of Animals*, Washington, Humane Society Press, pp. 55–69.

21 Crettaz von Roten F. C. (2013). "Public perceptions of animal experimentation across Europe," *Public Understanding of Science*, 22Comparable results have been found by Driscoll J. W. (1992). "Attitudes toward animal use," *Anthrozoös*, 5 (1).

22 Sandgren E. P., Streiffer R., Dykema J., Assad N., Moberg J. (2020). "Attitudes toward animals, and how species and purpose affect animal research justifiability, among undergraduate students and faculty," *PLoS One*, 15 (5), p. e0233204.

23 Clemence M., Leaman J. (2016). *Public Attitudes to Animal Research in 2016*, London, Ipsos Mori; Ormandy E. H., Schuppli C. A. (2014). "Public attitudes toward animal research: A review," *Animals*, 4 (3), pp. 391–408.

24 Herzog H., Rowan A., Kossow D. (2001). "Social attitudes and animals."

25 Such tests have been officially prohibited in Europe since 2013.

26 Psychological studies involving animals fall somewhere in-between. See Herzog H., Rowan A., Kossow D. (2001). "Social attitudes and animals."

27 Sandgren E. P., Streiffer R., Dykema J., Assad N., Moberg J. (2020). "Attitudes toward animals, and how species and purpose affect animal research justifiability, among undergraduate students and faculty."

28 Lund T. B., Mørkbak M. R., Lassen J., Sandøe P. (2014). "Painful dilemmas: A study of the way the public's assessment of animal research balances costs to animals against human benefits," *Public Understanding of Science*, 23 (4), pp. 428–444.

29 Schuppli C. A., Molento C. F., Weary D. M. (2015). "Understanding attitudes towards the use of animals in research using an online public engagement tool," *Public Understanding of Science*, 24 (3), pp. 358–374.

30 Sandgren E. P., Streiffer R., Dykema J., Assad N., Moberg J. (2020). "Attitudes toward animals, and how species and purpose affect animal research justifiability, among undergraduate students and faculty"; Schuppli C. A., Molento C. F., Weary D. M. (2015). "Understanding attitudes towards the use of animals in research using an online public engagement tool."

31 Schuppli et al. 2015; Ormandy E. H., Schuppli C. A. (2014). "Public attitudes toward animal research: A review.".

32 Paul E. S., Serpell J. A. (1993). "Childhood per keeping and humane attitudes in young adulthood," *Animal Welfare*, 2, pp. 321–337; Hagelin J. et al. (2002). "Influence of pet-ownership on opinions towards the use of animals in biomedical research," *Anthrozoös* 15, pp. 251–257; Driscoll J. W. (1992). "Attitudes toward animal use."

33 Hagelin J., Hau J., Carlsson H. (1999). "Undergraduate students views on the use of animals in biomedical research," *Academic Medicine*, 74, pp. 1135–1137; Broida J. et al., (1993). "Personality differences between pro- and anti-vivisectionists," *Society and Animals*, 1, pp. 129–144; Furnham A., Heyes C. (1993). "Psychology students' beliefs about animals and animal experimentation," *Personality and Individual Differences*, 15, pp. 1–10; Furnham A., Pinder A. (1990). "Young people's attitudes to experimentation on animals," *The Psychologist*, 10, pp. 444–448; Plous S. (1996). "Attitudes toward the use of animals in psychological research and education: Results from a national survey of psychology majors," *Psychological Science*, 7, pp. 352–358; Sandgren E. P., Streiffer R., Dykema J., Assad N., Moberg J. (2020). "Attitudes toward animals, and how species and purpose affect animal research justifiability, among undergraduate students and faculty."

34 Pifer L., Shimizu K., Pifer R. (1994). "Public attitudes toward animal research: Some international comparisons," *Society and Animals*, 2 (2), pp. 95–113.

35 Crettaz von Roten F. C. (2013). "Public perceptions of animal experimentation across Europe."

36 Crettaz von Roten F. (2019). *Experimentation animale. Analyse de la controverse de 1950 à nos jours en Suisse*, Neuchâtel, Éditions Livreo-Alphil, p. 147.

37 Sandgren E. P., Streiffer R., Dykema J., Assad N., Moberg J. (2020). "Attitudes toward animals, and how species and purpose affect animal research justifiability, among undergraduate students and faculty"; Schuppli C. A., Molento C. F., Weary D. M. (2015). "Understanding attitudes towards the use of animals in research using an online public engagement tool."

38 Joffe A. R., Bara M., Anton, N., Nobis N. (2016). "The ethics of animal research: A survey of the public and scientists in North America," *BMC Medical Ethics*, 17, p. 17; Masterton M., Renberg T., Kälvemark Sporrong S. (2014). "Patients' attitudes towards animal testing: 'To conduct research on animals is, I suppose, a necessary evil,'" *Biosocieties*, 9 (1), pp. 24--41.

39 Machado G. F., Melo G. D., Perri S. H., Fernandes F. V., Moraes O. C., Souza M. S. et al. (2017). "Perceptions of animal experimentation: A longitudinal survey with veterinary students in Araçatuba, São Paulo, Brazil," *Journal of Biological Education*, 51 (4), pp. 391–398.

40 Knight S., Vrij A., Cherryman J., Nunkoosing K. (2004). "Attitudes towards animal use and belief in animal mind," *Anthrozoös*, 17 (1), pp. 43–62.

41 Knight et al. 2004, pp. 43–62.

42 Vezirian, K., Bègue, L., & Bastian, B. (2024). Mindless furry test-tubes: Categorizing animals as lab-subjects leads to their mind denial. *Journal of Experimental Social Psychology*, 114, 1–11.

43 One speaks of *vertical speciesism* in the first case and *horizontal speciesism* in the second.

44 The dimensions that have been studied the most are political conservatism, authoritarianism and antiegalitarianism, which also predict support for animal experimentation.

45 Sidanius J., Pratto F. (1999). *Social Dominance: An Intergroup Theory of Social Hierarchy and Oppression*, Cambridge, Cambridge University Press.

46 Dhont K., Hodson G., Loughnan S., Amiot C. E. (2019). "Rethinking human–animal relations: The critical role of social psychology", *Group Processes and Intergroup Relations*, 22 (6), pp. 769–784; Dhont K., Hodson G., Costello K., MacInnis C. C. (2014). "Social dominance orientation connects prejudicial human–human and human–animal relations," *Personality and Individual Differences*, 61/62, 105–108; Dhont K., Hodson G., Leite A. C. (2016). "Common ideological roots of speciesism and generalized ethnic prejudice: The social dominance human–animal relations model (SD-HARM)," *European Journal of Personality*, 30, pp. 507–522.

47 The differences between the tree categories are statistically significant. The index of association between the two scales was r=.34, p.<.001. Analysis also showed that women were more critical of animal experimentation. They also had lower social dominance levels than men, which was consistent with most studies on this issue. Wilson M. S., Liu J. H. (2003). "Social dominance orientation and gender: The moderating role of gender identity," *British Journal of Social Psychology*, 42 (Pt 2), pp. 187–198; Dambrun M., Duarte S., Guimond S. (2004). "Why are men more likely to support group-based dominance than women? The mediating role of gender identification," *British Journal of Social Psychology*, 43 (Pt 2), pp. 287–297.

48 Baumeister R. F., Vohs K. D., Funder D. C. (2007). "Psychology as the science of self-reports and finger movements: Whatever happened to actual behavior?" *Perspectives on Psychological Science*, 2 (4), pp. 396–403; Doliński D. (2018). "Is psychology still a science of behaviour?" *Social Psychological Bulletin*, 13 (2), pp. 1–14.

12 Human Obedience in the Lab
The Milgram Experiment

Illustration: Magali Seghetto

"As the water approached the 180-degree mark, it dawned on me that I simply could not "do" the mouse. I turned off the flame and, with trepidation and relief... I am now struck by the similarity between my task that afternoon and the plight of the subjects in Stanley Milgram's infamous obedience experiments."[1]

Hal Herzog, professor at Western Carolina University[2]

In this short account, one of the leading researchers in the field of human–animal relations recalls a situation that many biology students have faced at some point. Most of them obediently perform the experiments requested by their professors. Some, like Hal Herzog, later remember this event. When I discussed the mouse and Bunsen burner incident with him, he

DOI: 10.4324/9781003561972-13

told me he had kept this story under wraps for 15 years before coming back to it, bringing up the theme of moral guilt.

Hal Herzog was not the first to notice a similarity between animal experimentation and Milgram's research on submission. Peter Singer had already suggested it in 1975, and others followed.[3] Philosopher of science Isabelle Stengers goes as far as to write that any experimental program including animals may evince "a disturbing similarity between researchers and torturers."[4] That is one of the deepest paradoxes of animal experimentation, despite its complete overhaul under the Nuremberg Code after WWII. To protect future generations from the kinds of atrocities that had been committed on a massive scale, including cruel experiments conducted on humans, this piece of legislation from 1947 consisting of ten articles, stipulates that any potentially harmful test on human subjects must first include a phase of systematic animal experimentation.[5] Today, no drug, no surgical procedure or medical device can be authorised without fulfilling this requirement.

Psychologist Stanley Milgram was also motivated by the atrocities perpetrated by the Nazis. When he started his research at Yale in the 1960s, he was trying to prove that "ordinary people, simply doing their jobs, and without any particular hostility on their part" could become "agents in a terrible destructive process."[6]

Looking Back at Milgram's Experiment

For his first study, the psychologist recruited 40 volunteers aged 20 to 50 from the general population. They were given the equivalent of 27 present-day dollars to contribute to a study on memory and learning. Upon arrival at the lab, the participants met two people who were in fact actors. The first was a 30-year-old experimenter who wore a white lab coat and personified scientific authority (E in Figure 12.1). The other was a 47-year-old man who played

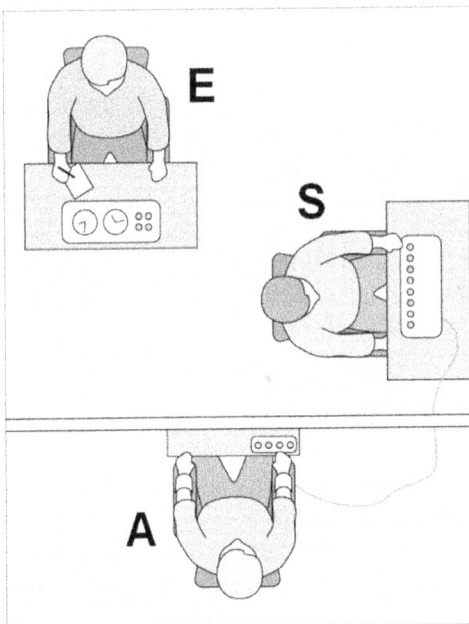

Figure 12.1 Spatial distribution of the participants in the Milgram experiment.

Source: Expérience de Milgram.png. (2020, October 17). *Wikimedia Commons.* Retrieved June 26, 2025, from https://commons.wikimedia.org/w/index.php?title=File:Exp%C3%A9rience_de_Milgram.png&oldid=491943030.

the part of the learner (A in the figure). The role of the "teacher" was given to the participant (subject S in the figure). With every mistake, the unknowing subject (the "teacher") was to administer an electric shock to the learner through a generator that went up to 450 volts in increments of 15 volts. On the generator panel, information about the increasing intensity of the electric shocks could be read: "mild shock," "medium shock," "very strong shock," "intense shock," "extremely intense shock," "danger," "danger, severe shock," and finally several buttons labelled "XXX."

Participants were told how the shock generator worked, and they were then subjected to a 45-volt shock to personally experience the unpleasant effect of a shock of that intensity. The learner was then tied to a chair, an electrode was attached to his right wrist where an ointment was applied, allegedly to prevent burns. During the experiment, when the subjects turned to the experimenter for guidance or to express their reluctance to continue, they would receive a preestablished response from the scientific authority encouraging them to continue until the end of the experiment.[7] As the experiment progressed, the reactions of the pseudo-victim became increasingly intense as he received the fictitious shocks. They began with light moans at 75 volts, then rose to an insistent request to stop from 150 volts onward (repeated at other thresholds), up to agonised screams at 270 volts, and painful roars followed by a frightening lack of response after 330 volts. The results were very striking: most participants inflicted 450-volt shocks despite the learner's screams and heart-wrenching supplications.[8]

Variations in the protocol allowed Milgram to demonstrate to what extent human behaviour can be shaped by a situation. For example, when the scientific authority was physically close to the participants, 90% of them inflicted the maximum shock to the learner, whereas this was the case for only 22% of subjects when the orders were given by telephone and 12.5% when the orders were played on a magnetic tape. When the distress signals of the victim were intensified, the subjects became less obedient. Thus, up to 66% of participants obeyed in a *no-feedback condition* in which there was no communication between the experimenter and the victim, who were in two different rooms. Conversely, in a *contact condition*, the subjects had to reattach a strap to the learner's arm, who had managed to free it while attempting to leave the chair and quit the experiment. In that situation of physical contact with the learner, only 30% of participants obeyed until the completion of the experiment.

It was not long before the idea of adapting Milgram's experiment to nonhuman victims emerged. In 1975, one year only after the book *Obedience to Authority* came out, philosopher Peter Singer wrote: "If this can happen when the participants believe they are inflicting pain on a human being, how much easier is it for students to push aside their initial qualms when their professors instruct them to perform experiments on animals?"[9] As if in response to this question, a researcher from the University of California, Berkeley, and his colleague conducted a study at the same time, which aimed to answer one of the most common critiques of Milgram's experiment. Indeed, it had been suggested[10] that during the experiments, participants might have simply played a role and administered the electric shocks without really believing that the victim felt them. To test this, the researchers devised a horrendous protocol in which a "silky-haired puppy" whose paws touched a metal grid received real electric shocks, which increased with every mistake it made in a perceptual discrimination task. The intensity of the shocks was such that during the last stage of the experiment, the puppy would bark and howl continually.[11] The results of this study confirmed those found by Milgram: three quarters of the participants went through with the experiment. They were similar to those of Milgram's *vocal and visual feedback* condition, in which participants could see and hear the victim suffering. But above all, they show that, in the pursuit of science, psychologists can act like the worst experimenters.

Milgram, 60 Years After the First Shocks

Sixty years after the initial studies conducted at Yale in 1961–1962,[12] to what extent has Milgram's view of obedience to authority been borne out by further research? How can we explain obedience, and can this help us understand animal experimentation?

Regarding the robustness of research on obedience to authority, beyond the 20 experimental variations published by Milgram which involved a thousand participants from the general population,[13] two dozen replications have been performed in ten different countries with adults and sometimes even children. In the vast majority of studies, over two thirds of participants administered strong electric shocks, and when the pressure applied in the situation changed, the rate of obedience varied in a consistent way. It has also been demonstrated that the rate of obedience did not vary significantly depending on the year when the experiment was carried out.[14] Although individual variables were not part of Milgram's main focus, it was found that they had very consistent effects on observed behaviour.[15] For example, participants with authoritarian or highly conservative beliefs were more obedient.[16]

As for the possibility that participants might have played the expected role without truly believing in the reality of the experiment, there is further evidence suggesting that this criticism is unfounded.[17] An analysis of Milgram's archives at Yale shows that many participants expressed great relief when they learned that the experiment was completely fake and that they had been genuinely worried about the health of the victim. One of them even said he had checked the obituaries for several weeks in the city where the experiment took place to make sure he was not responsible for someone's death.[18]

Milgram had indicated that, with a few exceptions, his participants were convinced that the experimental situation was real.[19] His evidence was based on the participants' answers to a questionnaire given after the experiment: 62% believed the victim was really receiving the shocks and 22% believed the victim was probably receiving them.

Obedience to Authority is Not What Milgram Thought it Was

Although the scientific community now considers that the phenomenon highlighted by Milgram is well-established, most researchers disagree with the explanation he put forward.[20] In *Obedience to Authority*, he developed the concept of an *agentic state*, which is the cornerstone of his analysis of obedience. For Milgram, "individuals are in an agentic state when, in a given situation, they define themselves in such a way that they accept to be fully under the control of an individual possessing a higher status. In that case, participants no longer feel responsible for their actions. They only see themselves as instruments meant to follow someone else's commands."[21] Milgram thinks participants "blame someone else for their actions"[22] and, through this "ideological surrender,"[23] betray their usual moral criteria.

However, a first fact challenges Milgram's interpretation: when participants were questioned after the experiment, they took responsibility for their actions.[24] A more recent study which replicated Milgram's experiment confirmed that those who quit the experiment before the end were not more likely to blame someone else than those who completed it.[25]

In addition, the concept of an agentic state does not account for the small acts of defiance which were often seen in Milgram's experiments. Analysis of the recordings of participants' verbal behaviour during the experiments shows that they were not abjectly submissive: they negotiated their participation,[26] sometimes even attempting to subtly help the victim in order to avoid having to administer the shocks. In a study conducted in France in which Milgram's protocol was adapted for a TV show, I observed that, as soon as it was no longer possible to doubt the painful nature of the shocks, one quarter of the participants discretely attempted to help the victim suffering in front of them.[27]

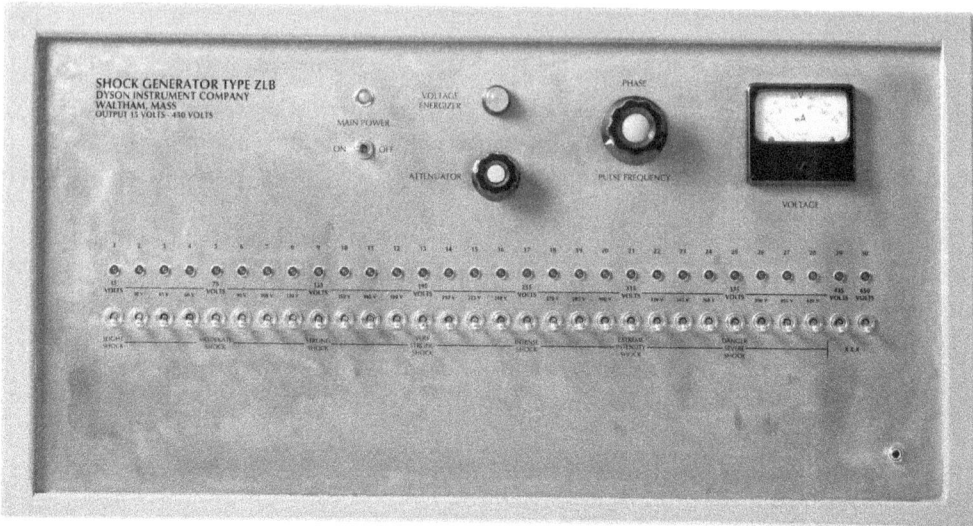

Figure 12.2 Electroshock machine used in a recent series of studies in Poland.
Photo: Courtesy of Dariusz Dolinski

Moreover, if the participants had truly submitted to authority, their obedience would have increased as the commands became more forceful. Yet analysis of Milgram's archives[28] as well as a more recent study[29] have shown that, when the authority gave them overly directive orders, participants were *more* reluctant to obey. And finally, if participants were blindly obedient to authority, would there have been so much variation in the rates of submission depending on experimental conditions?

A Ratchet Effect?

For Milgram, "binding factors" of the action contribute to increasing obedience. The gradual increase in the intensity of the shocks is one example. Based on the theory of cognitive dissonance, Milgram suggested that the gradual increase in the shocks made it difficult for participants to quit the experiment because doing so would have meant disavowing their previous conduct.[30]

A similar idea was suggested by a researcher who wondered whether the effects observed by Milgram would have been the same if the participants had been immediately asked to press the 450-volt button without having gone through the preliminary steps.[31] Two recent experiments conducted in Poland by Dariusz Doliński and his team tested this hypothesis by comparing the gradual process with a protocol in which the subjects had to administer 150 volts (study 1) or 225 volts (study 2) as soon as the learner made his first mistake.

Much to the surprise of the researchers, the results completely refuted the ratchet effect hypothesis. Since there is a lack of evidence for the agentic state hypothesis and for an explanation based on the incremental nature of the protocol, we must consider other possible explanations.

Science as a Higher Goal

Authority is a social function and sometimes the way we dress can amplify its effects. When, in one of his experiments, Milgram asked a man who did not wear a lab coat to give commands to the participants, only 20% administered the strongest shocks.[32] When the experiment took place in a low-prestige facility like an old commercial building in a small town, the rate of obedience was only 47.7%,[33] which is nearly 20% lower than it was at Yale. Of course, the external forms that authority takes are only effective when the institutions they represent are recognised by the individuals to whom they give orders. A captain's hat or bishop's mitre would not be enough to elicit unanimous obedience in a research laboratory.

These examples introduce the issue of the legitimacy attributed to authority and science in a given context. In Milgram's experiment as in most studies in psychology, the participants are far from being solely driven by the material reward. It is often curiosity and the desire to learn something during the experiment that leads volunteers to walk through the laboratory door. Once Milgram's experiment was over, the majority said they were happy to have helped with the research. Qualitative analysis of the interviews with the participants showed that adherence to scientific aims was a major component of the experiment. Milgram himself noted that the experiment was shrouded with the "mystique of science."[34]

Some clues confirm the hypothesis that the personal commitment of the participants to scientific goals is what best explains Milgram's results. Thus, when presenting the various versions of Milgram's experiment and asking outside observers to indicate the extent to which they identify with the learner or experimenter based on each different protocol, it appears that stronger observer identification with the experimenter corresponds to higher levels of obedience among participants.[35] Finally, a study in which participants followed a virtual simulation of Milgram's experiment found that when they identified more with the experimenter than with the learner, the average intensity of the shocks administered was higher.

Perhaps we should grant individuals the coherence that seems to have been denied them and recognise that they are not only cognitive recipients but also agents.[36] Far from being, as Milgram wrote, "mindless" performers of an action,[37] individuals appear more like agents with attitudes and goals (such as an appreciation of science) to which they subscribed before entering the lab, and who not only consent to but actively commit to a sequence of behaviours, no matter how harmful, which are expected of them.[38] Without denying the importance of the context and influences on the individual, reinterpreting Milgram's work means granting some rationality to the cultural animals that we are.[39]

A Model of Rational Obedience

Considering the critiques of Milgram's theory of obedience to authority, we can draw the following conclusions. First, an individual who deliberately harms another may be influenced by a specific experimental context, but they are also pursuing pre-existing goals. Second, the prevailing situationist interpretation of the experiment which suggests that contextual factors had an overwhelming influence neglects some important facets of obedience, even though they were suggested by Milgram himself. Those neglected aspects involve the cultural prestige of science and its influence on individual behaviour.[40] In experiments on obedience to authority, contributing to a scientific project was a decisive motivating factor for participants. Milgram recognised that they administered shocks to "serve the cause of science."[41] The degree to which an individual values the aim of an experiment is an essential motivator for behaviour.

People usually support animal experimentation because they support scientific research in general. Despite perceptible signs of scepticism from the public, science now ranks as the number one cultural authority in the Anglo-European sphere.[42] In his conclusion to the latest national survey on the French population and science conducted in 2020, CNRS researcher Michel Dubois observed that "the French still overwhelmingly trust researchers and their institutions."[43]

Support for animal experimentation can also vary within the same culture depending on one's familiarity with the practice of science. Researchers have a more favourable attitude towards it than the general population[44] and, while 44% of the public approves of animal experimentation even though it causes harm to animals, that number soars to 80% among medical students.[45]

Another aspect to consider is the psychological cost to the individual who is required to harm the animal, in accordance with the fundamental moral rule presented as follows by Milgram: "The absolute obligation not to harm a defenseless, innocent being who poses no danger to anyone."[46] This cost naturally results from the severity of the procedure undergone by the animal. It also depends on the animal's evolutionary proximity with humans:[47] as we have seen, we have less empathy for more evolutionarily distant species.

Finally, the psychological cost of sacrificing an animal depends on the extent to which one believes in a hierarchy of species. Since we have created mental barriers between ourselves and the animals we use, it becomes much easier to regard them as living test tubes. Let us now address the experimental setting which allows us to test these ideas.

Notes

1 Herzog H. (2011). *Some We Love, Some We Hate, Some We Eat*, New York, Harper, p. 207.
2 Herzog 2011, p. 207.
3 For example Joy M. (2010). *Why We Love Dogs, Eat Pigs and Wear Cows*, San Francisco, Conari Press; Arluke A. (2006). *Just a Dog*, Philadelphia, Temple University Press, pp. 79–80.
4 Stengers I. (2002). *Sciences et pouvoirs. La démocratie face à la technoscience*, Paris, La Découverte, p. 80.
5 Katz J. (1996). "The Nuremberg code and the Nuremberg trial. A reappraisal," JAMA, 276 (20), pp. 1662–1666. A crtitical analysis of the implications of the code can be found in Greek R., Pippus A., Hansen L. A. (2012). "The Nuremberg code subverts human health and safety by requiring animal modeling," *BMC Medical Ethics*, 13, p. 16.
6 Milgram S. (1974/2009). *Obedience to Authority: An Experimental View*, New York, Harper Perennial Modern Classics, Reprint edition.
7 "Prompt 1: Please continue; prompt 2: The experiment required that you continue; prompt 3: It is absolutely essential that you continue; prompt 4: You have no other choice, you must go on." Milgram S. (2009). *Obedience to Authority: An Experimental View*, New York, Harper Perennial Modern Classics, Reprint edition.
8 Every participant went as far as administering shocks of 285 volts, 12.5% went up to 300 volts, 20% between 315 and 360 volts, one participant stopped between 375 and 420 volts, and the remaining 65% went all the way to the maximum, 450 volts.
9 Singer P. (1975). *Animal Libération*, New York, HarperCollins, p.69.
10 Orne M. T., Holland C. C. (1968). "Some conditions of obedience and disobedience to authority. On the ecological validity of laboratory deceptions," *International Journal of Psychiatry*, 6 (4), pp. 282–293.
11 Sheridan C. L., King R. G. (1972). "Obedience to authority with an authentic victim," *Proceedings of the Annual Convention of the American Psychological Association*, 7 (Pt. 1), pp. 165–166.
12 The first study was published in 1963. For an overview of Stanley Milgram's contributions, see Blass T. (2004). *The Man Who Shocked the World. The Life and Legacy of Stanley Milgram*, New York, Basic Books. On recent neuroscientific studies on Milgram's obedience, see Caspar, E. (2024). *Just following order. Atrocities and the brain science of obedience*. Cambridge: Cambridge University Press.
13 These publications include Milgram's book as well as complementary articles.
14 Blass T. (ed.). (2000). *Obedience to Authority: Current Perspectives on the Milgram Paradigm*, Mahwah, Lawrence Erlbaum Associates Publishers.

15 Blass T. (1991). "Understanding behavior in the Milgram obedience experiment: The role of personality, situations, and their interactions," *Journal of Personality and Social Psychology*, 60, pp. 398–413.

16 Bègue L., Beauvois J.-L., Courbet D., Oberlé D., Lepage J., Duke A. A. (2015). "Personality predicts obedience in a Milgram paradigm," *Journal of Personality*, 83 (3), pp. 299–306.

17 Orne M. T., Holland C. C. (1968). "Some conditions of obedience and disobedience to authority. On the ecological validity of laboratory deceptions."

18 Perry G. (2013). *Behind the Shock Machine. The Untold Story of the Notorious Milgram Psychology Experiment*, New York, New Press, pp. 79–80.

19 Milgram S. (1963). "Behavioral study of obedience," *Journal of Abnormal and Social Psychology*, 67, pp. 371–378 (p. 375).

20 Miller A. (2016). "Why are the Milgram obedience experiments still so extraordinarily famous– and controversial?," in A. Miller (ed.). *The Social Psychology of Good and Evil*, New York, Guilford Press, pp. 185–223; Russell N. (2018). *Understanding Willing Participants. Milgram's Obedience Experiments and the Holocaust*, vol. 1., Cham, Palgrave.

21 Milgram S. (1974/2009). *Obedience to Authority: An Experimental View*, New York, Harper Perennial Modern Classics, Reprint edition.

22 Milgram S. (1974/2009). *Obedience to Authority: An Experimental View*, New York, Harper Perennial Modern Classics, Reprint edition.

23 Milgram S. (1974/2009). *Obedience to Authority: An Experimental View*, New York, Harper Perennial Modern Classics, Reprint edition.

24 Ibid.; Mantell D. M., Panzarella R. (1976). "Obedience and responsibility," *British Journal of Social and Clinical Psychology*, 15 (3), pp. 239–245. On this topic, see also Caspar, E.A. (2024). *Just following orders. Atrocities and the brain science of obedience.* Cambridge: Cambridge University Press.

25 Burger J. M., Girgis Z. M., Manning C. C. (2011). "In their own words: Explaining obedience to authority through an examination of participants' comments," *Social Psychological and Personality Science*, 2 (5), pp. 460–466.

26 Gibson S. (2014). "Discourse, defiance, and rationality: 'Knowledge work' in the 'obedience' experiments," *Journal of Social Issues*, 70, pp. 424–438.

27 Bègue L., Duke A., Courbet D., Oberlé D. (2017). "Values and indirect noncompliance in a Milgram-like paradigm," *Social Influence*, 12 (1), pp. 29–40. Similar strategies were observed by Milgram in his early experiments. He had noted that "some would signal the right answer to the victim by verbally accentuating it when they read the word associations." However, he doesn't seem to have made much of this.

28 Haslam S. A., Reicher S. D., Birney M. E. (2014). "Nothing by mere authority: Evidence that in an experimental analogue of the Milgram paradigm participants are motivated not by orders but by appeals to science," *Journal of Social Issues,* 70, pp. 473–488. See also Reicher S., Haslam S. A. (2011). "After shock? Towards a social identity explanation of the Milgram 'obedience' studies," *British Journal of Social Psychology*, 50, pp. 163–169.

29 Burger J. M., Girgis Z. M., Manning C. C. (2011). "In their own words: Explaining obedience to authority through an examination of participants' comments."

30 Milgram S. (1974/2009). *Obedience to Authority: An Experimental View*, *op. cit.*

31 Gilbert S. J. (1981). "Another look at the Milgram obedience studies: The role of the gradated series of shocks," *Personality and Social Psychology Bulletin*, 7 (4), pp. 690–695.

32 Milgram S. (1974/2009). *Obedience to Authority: An Experimental View*, New York, Harper Perennial Modern Classics, Reprint edition.., experiment 13.

33 Milgram S. (1974/2009). *Obedience to Authority: An Experimental View*, New York, Harper Perennial Modern Classics, Reprint edition.experiment 10.

34 Milgram S. (1974/2009). *Obedience to Authority: An Experimental View*, New York, Harper Perennial Modern Classics, Reprint edition.

35 Reicher S. D., Haslam S. A., Smith J. R. (2012). "Working toward the experimenter: Reconceptualizing obedience within the Milgram paradigm as identification-based followership," *Perspectives on Psychological Science*, 7 (4), pp. 315–320. See also Birney, M. E., Reicher, S. D., Haslam, S. A.,

Steffens, N. K., Neville, F. G. (2023). Engaged followership and toxic science: Exploring the effect of prototypicality on willingness to follow harmful experimental instructions. *British Journal of Social Psychology*, 62 (2), pp. 866–882.

36   Billig M. (1991). *Ideology and Opinions*, London, Sage.

37   Milgram S. (1974/2009). *Obedience to Authority: An Experimental View*, New York, Harper Perennial Modern Classics, Reprint edition.

38   Sunstein C.R. (2019). *Conformity*, New York, New York University Press.

39   Baumeister R. (2005). *The Cultural Animal. Human Nature, Meaning and Social Life*, Oxford, Oxford University Press.

40   For example, Milgram, using the principles governing everyday interactions revealed by sociologist Erving Goffman, observed that his participants had "a certain compassionate impulse towards the experimenter, an instinctive reluctance to hurt his feelings" (1974). This compliance sheds light on a result that was recently found in France: people who tend to be the most agreeable in ordinary social situations have the highest obedience rates. See Bègue L., Beauvois J.-L., Courbet D., Oberlé D., Lepage J., Duke A. A. (2015). "Personality predicts obedience in a Milgram paradigm."

41   Milgram S. (1974/2009). *Obedience to Authority: An Experimental View*, New York, Harper Perennial Modern Classics, Reprint edition.

42   Bauer M. W., Pansegrau P., Shulka R. (2019). "Image, perception and cultural identity of science," in M. W. Bauer, P. Pansegrau, R. Shukla (eds.), *The Cultural Authority of Science. Comparing Across Europe, Asia, Africa, and the Americas*, London, Routledge, pp. 3–21. Milgram did not express anything else when he wrote, probably in reference to the work of the anthropologist Bronislaw Malinowski: "if the experiment were carried out in a culture very different from our own – say, among Trobrianders – it would be necessary to find the functional equivalent of science in order to obtain psychologically comparable results," Milgram S. (1974). Obedience to Authority, p. 142.

43   *Le Monde. Science et médecine*, 17 November 2021, p. 8.

44   Plous S. (1996). "Attitudes toward the use of animals in psychological research and education: Results from a national survey of psychology majors," *Psychological Science*, 7, pp. 352–358; Sandgren E. P., Streiffer R., Dykema J., Assad N., Moberg J. (2020). "Attitudes toward animals, and how species and purpose affect animal research justifiability, among undergraduate students and faculty,." *PLoS One*, 15 (5).

45   Joffe A. R., Bara M., Anton N., Nobis N. (2016). "The ethics of animal research: A survey of the public and scientists in North America," *BMC Medical Ethics*, 17.

46   Milgram S. (1974/2009). *Obedience to Authority: An Experimental View*, New York, Harper Perennial Modern Classics, Reprint edition.

47   Miralles A., Raymond M., Lecointre G. (2019). "Empathy and compassion toward other species decrease with evolutionary divergence time," *Scientific Reports*, 9.

13 An Experimental Study Using a Robotic Fish

A Variation of the Milgram Experiment

Illustration: Magali Seghetto

"Setting up an experiment is much like producing a play."
Stanley Milgram[1]

In the opening chapter of *Obedience to Authority*, Milgram evokes the tragedy of Antigone, and as in a Greek drama, the victim occupies a privileged position in his experiment.[2] Part of that victim's role is easy to play: he or she must simply alternate between right and wrong answers in a memory test, following a planned sequence. But another aspect is harder to perform: the victim must also simulate increasingly distressed verbal and postural responses when he or she receives the electric shocks sent by the participant. In Milgram's experiments, the victim's role was played by a 47-year-old accountant, Jim McDonough, a friendly and likeable Irish American man. In the study I am about to present, the victim's role was played by a highly sophisticated, 20-inch-long Korean biomimetic fish robot. It was made to look so realistic with the help of a plastic artist that the vast majority of participants did not realise it was fake.

The aim of this study was not simply to replace a flesh-and-bone human being with a fake animal with fins and electronic components. This variation on the Milgram study was mainly

DOI: 10.4324/9781003561972-14

about exploring a different explanation for obedience to authority. Whereas Milgram saw the individual as having "robotic impassivity" (in his own words), I thought, conversely, that participants would act in a mostly conscious, explainable and rational manner. This is very far from the hypothesis of an "agentic" state alleged to make individuals lose their sense of responsibility, in Milgram's terms. In other words, the robot fish was intended to prove that human participants were not robots as Milgram suggested, even under the influence of a scientific authority.

In the experimental situation, participants had to resolve a sort of dilemma in which the scientific benefits of the experiment came into direct conflict with the psychological cost of their actions. As with the Milgram experiment, I expected most of the participants to comply with the task, but not for the same reasons. Furthermore, I thought that the conflict between the two interests at stake (that of science and that of the victim) would be shaped by several individual factors as well as the context. But first, let me give you an overview of the experimental setting so you can better picture it before I delve into the hypotheses in detail.

In Silico: The Scientist and the Artist

The office consisting of two adjoining rooms occupied by one of my colleagues, a biologist at the University of Grenoble, is a chaotic jumble of boxes of small electronic devices, precision tools, obsolete computers, stacks of books and articles, and most importantly, there are several aquariums in which mormyrids swim, whose microelectric discharges he meticulously measures. The presence of those fish, also known as elephantfish because of their trunk-shaped barbel, combined with the liquid sounds of the room and the continual humming of the water pumps, creates an indescribable atmosphere that hits you as soon as you walk into the room. It is the only place in this building where animals live, but a few dozen meters away, in another building, a vast research animal facility is home to colonies of rodents and batrachians.

During a recent visit, my colleague briefly explained to me how the gas chamber is used to euthanise rodents. The fully transparent acrylic box has a valve for the injection of CO_2, which causes the painless death of animals placed into it after experiments, as well as those who will not be used. My colleague told me that other methods were also used with rats and mice, including intoxication, cervical dislocation, and decapitation.

In a booklet of about a hundred pages entitled "An Ethical Approach to Project Design," which he gave me after our conversations in the middle of the old white-tiled lab benches, the famous "3Rs" of animal experimentation were explained. These are overarching principles introduced in 1959 by zoologist William Russell and microbiologist Rex Burch. They stipulate that scientific research should:

- *Reduce* the number of animals used;
- *Refine* their methods to make procedures less invasive and painful; and
- *Replace in vivo* methods with other methods.

Alternatives include the *in vitro* method, where research is carried out on a cellular level rather than on a whole organism, and the *in silico* method, using biomathematical modelling. *Silico* refers to silicium (Si), an indispensable ingredient in computer chips. Coincidentally, silicium was also part of the silicone rubber that allowed us to avoid using a real animal for our experiment. In fact, silicone gel was a key ingredient that allowed us to shape the scaly skin of the robot fish, combining elasticity and strength. This material also allowed us to apply colours to achieve the appearance of a perfectly natural, live fish.

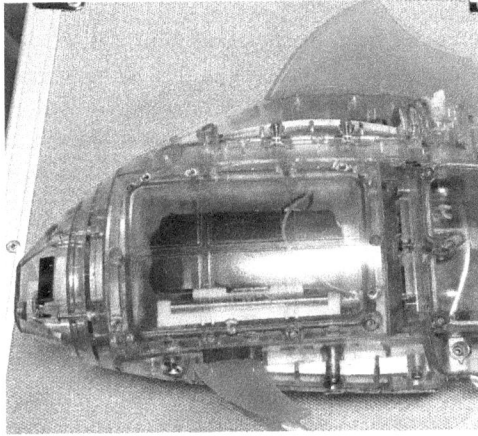

Figure 13.1a Robot fish (Airo 9).

Figure 13.1b Making the mould.

Figure 13.1c Covered fish.
Photos: Laurent Begue Shankland

A Biomimetic Fish

At least that is what I remember from plastic artist Alain Quercia's explanations. This master of the art of creating artificial skin and creator of unsettling sculpted chimeras, used his art to achieve a daring transformation: transforming a robot fish with strangely fluid movements into a fish that appeared completely real to the human eye (see Figures 13.1a–c). Over lunch, he explained the different phases of moulding the fish's skin as he enjoyed a plate of herbed tilapia. He described the steps through which he would bring the animal to life, knowing that my participants would be instructed to sacrifice it.

The trial phase included several unsuccessful attempts before we achieved a promising result. In fact, the movements of the fish robot used for the study (model Airo 9) were slowed down by the weight of its artificial scales. Water would accumulate between the robot and its silicone skin, and the sensors that allowed the robot to move in an autonomous manner were partly blocked by the new layer. The glass eyes, which Alain Quercia had obtained from a taxidermist, and which moved many participants (sometimes even making their own eyes tear up), also needed major adjustments.[3]

Despite the highly realistic movements of the fish and its very convincing appearance, the pretests showed that a small number of observers still had doubts. When the fish changed direction, it formed creases on its side that sometimes gave away the artificial nature of the skin. That problem was solved by dampening the vertical lighting of the room and adding a 1,200-lumen light panel under the aquarium, facing the participants. The glare from the light effectively concealed the last hints of artificiality.[4] After these adjustments were made, only a negligible minority of participants still perceived something fishy about our fish.[5] Most believed they were seeing a real, live fish. This came out in the spontaneous verbal responses we recorded during the interviews after the experiment. They will be presented later.

Describing the Injection Protocol

Milgram considered that, in his experiments, the specific action performed by the individual regarding the victim was not very significant.[6] Yet can we really believe that he would have observed such impressive levels of submission without the electric shock generator? It is hard to believe that the massive, 16-inch wide, 16-inch-deep box with its rows of thirty switches, its humming sound, its two lights – one red, one blue – and its voltmeter only played a minor role in Milgram's theatrical setup. Authenticated by a manufacturing plaque bearing the inscription "Shock Generator, Type ZLB, Instrument Dyson Company, Waltham, MA, output 15-450 volts," its mere presence lent a unique scientific touch to the protocol – a gravity that sociologist of science Bruno Latour calls the *phenomenotechnical effect*.[7]

The generator was an important part of the setup because of the essential psychological distance it created between the protagonists.[8] The participants may have pushed the buttons, but it was the electric shock from the generator that physically "hurt" the victim. This technical mediation lessened the psychological cost of the action for the individual. Introducing a mediator diminishes the individual's sense of responsibility and guilt. When hunting monkeys with blowguns and curare-tipped darts, the Huaorani people of the Amazon rainforest consider the vine that produces the neurotoxin to have killed the monkeys, not their own actions.[9] In our study, the method chosen to "injure" the "animal" was neither electricity nor a natural toxin, but a synthetic chemical presented as being harmful: *piracetam*.

Figure 13.2 A 3D representation of the experimental setup.
Image: Louise Bègue Teissier

The participants were told that, to assess the toxicity of this drug intended for elderly patients suffering from memory disorders, it was necessary to run a preliminary test on fish. Since the motions of the animal had to be monitored, participants were also told that there was a subjective dimension to the observation and that this was why we asked both experts with training in animal experimentation as well as novices like themselves to perform the same test.

The participants were informed that the fish had previously been conditioned to respond to certain signals. In the presence of light signals and bubbles in specific parts of the aquarium, the fish generally moved to a given area in the aquarium, and we were trying to measure the effect of injecting a memory-boosting substance in the aquarium on their performances while identifying the threshold at which the chemical became harmful. An overdose of the drug would be fatal to the fish.

The setup included a computer connected to a motor-activated syringe that made it possible to inject twelve doses of yellow liquid into the water of a vast aquarium that was almost a metre deep and contained 3,000 litres of water. A red and white, 21-inch-long fish that looked like a goldfish swam in the aquarium.

Participants had to successively click on the 12 buttons on the screen, using a mouse. Each button triggered an injection of 10 milliliters of piracetam along with an intermittent sound signal. Then bubbles would rise from the bottom of the aquarium for 12 seconds, a spotlight illuminating a specific area of the aquarium would turn on, and green LEDs would start blinking.

Finally, a 25-second countdown would start. During this time window, participants had to click a button to count the number of times the fish swam through the perimeter delineated by orange tape on the side of the aquarium. The risk that the fish would die was indicated under each button, in the following order: 0% (button 1), 33% (button 3), 50% (button 6), 75% (button 9), and 100% (button 12).

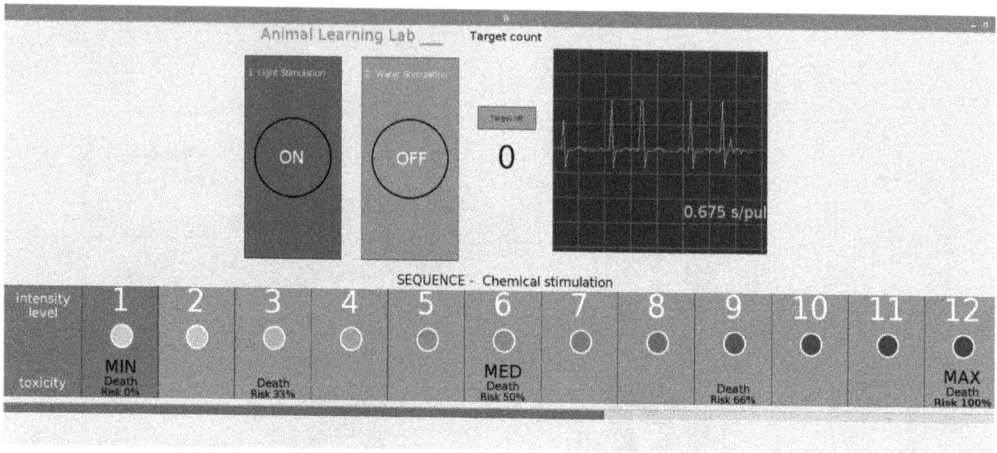

Figure 13.3 Control screen.
Image: Laurent Begue Shankland

In the original design of his experiment, Milgram had imagined that the indications expressing how dangerous each type of shock was (e.g., "danger, extremely strong shock") would suffice to create a moral pressure that would limit the obedience of the participants. However, his preliminary tests showed that nearly every subject would complete the experiment without any qualms, which did not allow him to measure different degrees of obedience. To overcome this "ceiling effect," Milgram had to introduce the protests and screams of the victim.[10] In our protocol, since we obviously could not use the same trick (as one of our participants said, "fish don't scream"), I chose to show participants a simulation of the fish's heart rate. Participants were told that this was measured directly through a sensor that had been implanted inside the fish. The heart rate was visualised as sine waves on the screen, accompanied by increasingly erratic beeping sounds as the experiment went on, which unambiguously reflected the cardiac distress of the fish. One 49-year-old participant, a special needs teacher, said, "I was more impressed by the heart rate of the fish than by its behaviour. You could really hear it and it showed you what was going on inside."

For the duration of the experiment, an experimenter would sit to the right of the participant. His role was limited to explaining the technical aspects of the interface and to three occasions when the syringes would have to be changed.[11] If a participant indicated wanting to quit the experiment, the assistant was to give the initial following reply, "For our research, it is important that you go all the way to button 12 but, as you were told before, you may stop at any moment." If the participant confirmed his or her wish to stop, the experimenter would reply: "Do you want to stop? Are you sure?" The experiment would stop if the participant insisted or once the 12 doses had been injected. A short clip of the setup can be viewed at the following address: https://www. youtube.com/watch?v=exNHKprKNwI or by using the QR code below.

The Recruitment Process and the Different Steps of the Experiment

Nearly 750 men and women of various ages and social backgrounds participated in this research programme. To recruit them, we advertised several times in the local newspapers, on social networks and through posters and leaflets placed in various shops. The recruitment pool consisted of roughly 400,000 people living in the city of Grenoble and its surrounding area. Each of the five studies required the participation of 150 participants who received 15 euros for the pre-test and for the first four studies, and 30 euros for the fifth study.[12] Participants completed an online questionnaire beforehand to check that they met the inclusion criteria[13] and completed various individual measurements. They were then given an appointment for an hour-long interview at the site of the experiment, at the *Maison des Sciences de l'Homme Alpes*, which is part of the Grenoble campus.

On arrival, participants were greeted by an assistant who showed them a 6-minute video on a large screen, in which a 55-year-old professor wearing a white lab coat (actually an actor) explained the aims and method of the study:

We are trying to determine how the behaviour of a fish is encoded by experts in biology as opposed to people who have no training in the field. The study is about the effect of administering a chemical compound, piracetam, on the behaviour of fish after a learning task. This substance is said to be *nootropic*, which means it boosts the functioning of neurotransmitters. It is currently prescribed in the treatment of cognitive and neurosensory deficit as well as dizziness in elderly humans. Piracetam is known for its effects on memory. However, a debated question is the maximum safe dosage. This protocol will allow us to test a highly concentrated form of piracetam. Your task will be to inject successive doses of piracetam into the water of a large aquarium and then code the behaviour of a fish in the tank. The animals being observed are goldfish. In their natural habitat, goldfish can reach a length of 40 centimetres in adulthood and their life expectancy is about 30 years. Contrary to popular belief, goldfish have long-term memory. They are capable of sophisticated learning and they can feel pain. They can build complex spatial mental representations of their environment and navigate various types of mazes to find food. For this experiment, several dozen fish have been conditioned over the previous weeks to respond to certain stimuli. We now want to determine if piracetam will significantly increase the target behaviour, which consists in heading towards the front, right-hand part of the aquarium. Your task is to administer standard doses of piracetam at various times to the fish in the aquarium. All you will have to do is to click on the round buttons, from the first to the last, which will automatically cause two sensory and hydraulic stimuli in the aquarium: light and bubbles. You must count as precisely as possible how many times the fish swims through the orange frame by clicking on the counter every time the fish swims through. When the syringe is empty, an assistant will replace it. In this protocol, the piracetam causes the death by overdose of over half the animals tested on level 5 (medium), and nearly 100% on level 12 (maximum), either immediately or over the next two hours. During the experiment, the fish may experience paralysis or abnormal movements induced by the treatment. An implanted cardiac sensor provides immediate feedback on the physiological impact of piracetam on the fish. The heartbeats are visualised as a curve on the screen and are accompanied by audible beeps. If you notice that the fish does not move for more than five minutes, warn the assistant so that he removes it from the aquarium. Another fish will be immersed, and the experiment will start again from the beginning. You may stop at any moment, and you will still receive the same payment.

The participants were then led to a 34-square-meter room in which the experiment was to take place and they sat in front of a screen on which they could see the commands. If they refused to begin or to continue, or when the experiment was over, they were taken to another room where a second experimenter gave them a final assessment questionnaire and had a short, filmed interview with them.[14] Every participant was then told that the experiment was fake, and we made sure that no one left thinking that they had actually hurt or killed an animal.[15] The experiment was approved by our university's ethics committee.[16]

The Impact of the Protocol

We paid special attention to two significant aspects of the protocol. The first one was the impact of the experiment on the participants. Social psychology sometimes designs social simulations that are only explained to their participants after the experiment. By definition, this use of deception[17] temporarily suspends the principle of informed consent and thus requires special ethical precautions. It also necessitates that the "technical illusions"[18] we use have the desired effects on participants, thanks to a sufficient degree of experimental realism.[19]

Our observation of the participants' behaviour during the experiment as well as our filmed interviews with them have confirmed that, for the overwhelming majority, the experimental situation was highly realistic. Some participants felt conflicted and they sometimes experienced high levels of anxiety. The following extracts from interviews offer a glimpse into the way the participants interpreted the situation as well as its psychological impact.

> *I was afraid that it would make it suffer, that it would be so unbearable that it would die.*
>
> A 36-year-old male technician

> *I almost cried in the middle of it, I couldn't press the button, the fish didn't look okay.*
>
> A 21-year-old female law student

> *On my way out, I wasn't feeling well. I was asking myself: why did I do this?*
>
> An unemployed 46-year-old man

> *I prayed that it wouldn't die in front of me.*
>
> A 33-year-old secretary

> *It was quite stressful. I was surprised. I didn't think I could feel those kinds of emotions. It felt like every time I pressed a button, I killed the fish a little more, so it made me quite uncomfortable, I felt a little guilty. I tried to detach myself emotionally.*
>
> A 19-year-old female mathematics student

The questionnaire that was given to the participants after the experiment[20] showed that, even though the task was considered stressful and disturbing by the majority, nearly 84% expressed a neutral opinion or said they were glad to have participated. As in the Milgram experiment, analyses showed that women were significantly more stressed than men.[21] This is consistent with the results of a study on people who used a helpline for staff practicing animal experimentation: there were more women using the service than men.[22]

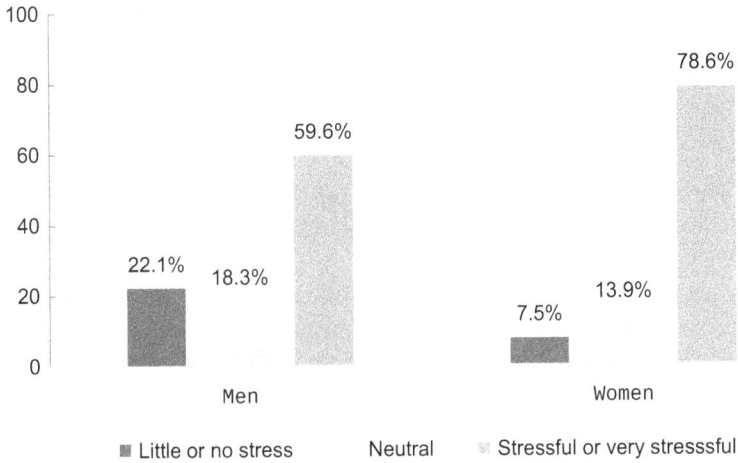

Figure 13.4 A study examining stress levels in men and women.

Spotting Suspicious Participants

To draw reliable conclusions from the experimental protocol, we had to pay attention to a second aspect: some participants might become suspicious about the true aims of the study. In Milgram's experiments, the few participants who had serious doubts about the reality of the shocks were the ones who administered the strongest shocks. Unfortunately, the clues that can reveal suspicious participants are sometimes hard to interpret. A participant may look like he or she did not suspect the true aims of the study, but still claim that they were onto something once the true aims of the study are revealed during the final interview. This *ex post* suspicious attitude can be adopted in a disingenuous way to save face with the interviewer, but it can also appear when an individual who was vaguely, unconsciously sceptical learns about the true nature of the experiment, which gives meaning to the obscure feelings he or she had felt before.

One might think that all we had to do was ask the participants directly once the experiment was over if they had had any doubts during the experiment, but again, such a straightforward question might artificially increase the number of participants claiming to have had suspicions. To overcome this obstacle, we had to encourage participants to freely tell us about their experience and ask them if some things seemed particularly interesting, surprising or even intriguing to them. Their answers were filmed and viewed by people who were not directly involved in the experiment, who then shared their opinions.

After watching the films, the evaluators were asked to sort the participants into three categories:

- those who had expressed explicit doubts about key aspects of the protocol (e.g., the reality of the fish, the toxicity of the injected substance, or the intentions underlying the experiment), who made up 14.1% of the sample;
- those who had not expressed significant doubts and whose naïve belief in the protocol was very likely (they made up 70.5% of the sample);

• and finally, those for whom it was hard to decide. They seemed to believe in most of the experimental scenario, but during the post-experiment interview, they said things that implied limited or occasional doubts, which did not compromise the protocol (15% of the sample).[23]

When analysing the results that are presented in the following pages, participants who had clear doubts were systematically excluded. The other two categories (about 85% of the sample) were clustered together and they are the focus of our study.

The way the participants described the experiment or responded when we told them about its true purpose showed how engaged and surprised they were.

I never thought I would care so much about a fish. It was big, it was beautiful.

An unemployed 55-year-old woman

I'm relieved. I thought I had committed a murder today.

A 19-year-old woman (no known occupation)

Wow, I'm so relieved. I have chills.

A 53-year-old woman, self-employed in administrative services

This stuff is amazing! I can't believe it. Wow, I feel much better now.

A 50-year-old female choreographer

Now that you know about the experimental framework and the methodological precautions that were taken, we can address the heart of the matter: the behaviour of human beings when confronted with an animal whose life they are being asked to take for the sake of their own species.

Notes

1 Perry G. (2013). *Behind the Shock Machine*, New York, New Press, p. 50.
2 In *Obedience to Authority*, Milgram mentions Antigone as an embodiment of the conflict between individual conscience and authority that he wants to analyse.
3 During one of the earliest pre-tests of the setup, the fish lost one of its eyes as it swam by. Much to my surprise, the participant in the experiment, an engineering school student, did not doubt the authenticity of the fish and she exclaimed that the product she had injected must be highly toxic indeed.
4 A few additional props were introduced into the room: a rubbish bin with the "biohazard" symbol, a large net intended to collect dead fish from the pond, and pharmaceutical vials.
5 The exact detection rates are given later in the chapter.
6 Milgram S. (1974/2009). *Obedience to Authority: An Experimental View*, New York, Harper Row.
7 Latour B., Woolgar S. (1979). *La Vie de laboratoire. La production des faits scientifiques*, Paris, La Découverte.
8 Russell N. (2018). *Understanding Willing Participants*, vol. 1., Cham, Palgrave.
9 Bradshaw J. (2017). *The Animal Among Us. How Pets Make Us Human*, New York, Basic Books, p. 33.
10 Milgram S. (1965). "Some conditions of obedience and disobedience to authority," *Human Relations*, 18 (1), pp. 57–76.
11 In the first experiment, the participants themselves had to replace the empty syringes. However, this operation would cause additional complications. For one thing, sometimes participants were not able to properly change the syringe, and in addition, even though they had been issued with gloves,

the alleged toxicity of the product made them worry about contamination. This led us to discard this part of the experiment in the following four experiments.

12 To make up for the difficulties we faced during the recruitment phase, a compensation of 30 euros was offered to participants in the fifth study. The difficulty of recruiting large numbers of participants for a lab study was also experienced by Milgram, who had published his ads in a newspaper with 106,000 readers but only got 296 replies. Professor Dariusz Doliński, the author of the recent Milgram-like studies in Poland, describes similar difficulties.

13 The participants we were looking for had to be 18 or over and were not to have any training in medicine, biology, psychology, sociology, sports science, or cognitive neuroscience.

14 Participants were invited to explain what they remembered about the aims of the experiment, to mention the aspects that had seemed especially interesting or surprising to them and to share their feelings and impressions during the experiment.

15 Disclosing the aims of this type of study is an ethical requirement. However, if participants disclose the details of the study they have participated in, it can compromise the validity of later experiments. One of the main criticisms that can be made against Milgram is that he did not consistently inform his participants that the victim did not receive real shocks. See Perry G. (2013). *Behind the Shock Machine*. The participants in our studies were told that the chemical was fake right after the experiment. During a collective meeting that was proposed a few months later, the entire protocol was explained in detail, and it is only then that they were told that the fish was fake as well.

16 Namely, the research ethics committee for Grenobles-Alpes (*Comité d'éthique pour les recherches Grenobles-Alpes*, IRB IRB0001029020200050162.)

17 This is less common nowadays. Between 1965 and 1985, nearly half of all social psychology experiments used some form of deception.

18 This is Milgram's term.

19 One usually distinguishes between two types of realism in social psychology. The first kind is *experimental realism*, which implies that participants are involved in the experimental situation enough for it to have an impact on them. The second kind is *ordinary* realism, which makes the situation in which participants are placed similar to a situation they might encounter outside the laboratory. Aronson E., Carlsmith J. M. (1968). "Experimentation in social psychology," in G. Lindzey, E. Aronson (eds.), *The Handbook of Social Psychology, Reading*, Addison-Wesley, 2nd ed., vol. 2, pp. 1–79.

20 The answers were collected before the debriefing. Out of a sample of 128 participants from the first sample (study 1), 93.8% thought the directions were clear. They had found out about the study in the press (7.8%), on the radio (1.6%), through posters of flyers (26.4%), by word of mouth (30.2%), on social networks or on the internet (34.1%).

21 To make the results easier to read on the graph, the answers that were initially given out of 5 degrees were mapped onto 3 degrees. Statistical analyses on the initial version of the stress scale showed that stress was significantly higher in women. $M = 4.08$ (SD = 0.99) vs $M = 3.60$ (SD = 1.19), $t(183.38) = 3.50$, $p.<.001$).

22 Capaldo T. (2004). "The psychological effects on students of using animals in ways that they see as ethically, morally or religiously wrong," *Alternatives to Laboratory Animals*, 32 (suppl. 1B), pp. 525–531.

23 Another category was created later to include participants who did not seem to have understood the protocol and whose behaviour was impossible to interpret. There were two such participants.

14 What the Study Reveals About Us

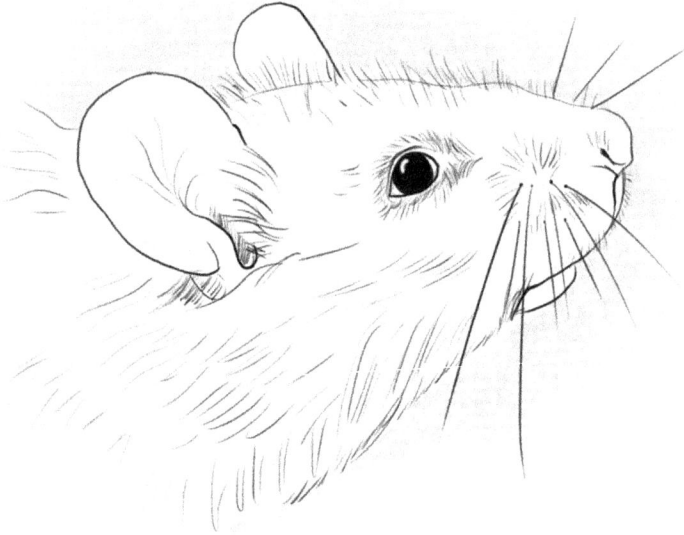

Illustration: Magali Seghetto

"At some points in my moral development, I could have participated in a commando to liberate animals from a laboratory."

Élisabeth de Fontenay, emeritus associate professor at
Panthéon-Sorbonne University, 84 years old.

In a radio interview, the philosopher Élisabeth de Fontenay, who wrote a book that has become a modern classic, *Le Silence des bêtes*, confessed that, when she was younger, she could have "participated in a commando to liberate animals from a laboratory."[1] But this rebellious thought remained in the realm of pure abstraction and, if we look at the demographics of opposition to animal experimentation, the probability of Élisabeth de Fontenay taking part in such illegal activity decreases every year. When examining the profiles of

DOI: 10.4324/9781003561972-15

individuals who claim to be ready to engage in activism for this minority cause, we see a higher proportion of women and people who score highly on a scale of nonconformity (reproduced in Box 14.1).[2]

Box 14.1 Statements measuring non-conformity orientation

I do things others are afraid to do because of other people's opinions.
I am something of a rebel.
I like to do things that people find offensive.
I like to get to know people who are weird or different.

However, this is still only in the realm of ideas. Psychologists know that intentions are limited predictors of actions.[3] The sizeable gap between the way we plan to behave and what we actually do was illustrated in a compelling way by Milgram himself. When he asked psychiatrists, sociology professors, middle-class adults and students to predict what they would do if they participated in his experiment, their answers were unanimous: no one would go beyond the first harmless shocks. "I can't bear to see someone suffer. If the learner wanted to stop, I would free them immediately," one of the respondents assured us. Since all those predictions were false, the observation of actual behaviour sheds a unique and irreplaceable light.

Behavioural Predictions: A Better-Than-Average Effect

Before we turn to observed behaviour, let us focus for a moment on hypothetical behaviour – behaviour that people think they *might* engage in. This is an interesting question because we might expect to observe a phenomenon known as the *better-than-average effect* (or *BTA effect*).[4] This is a very common bias that makes us think we are more impartial than other people,[5] less prejudiced and less easily influenced.[6] It is what invariably happens when people are first introduced to Milgram's experiment: they are surprised that so many people are obedient, and they swear that they would have been among the rebels.

To test the BTA effect in the context of my experiment, I showed 1,623 individuals[7] the entire video tutorial that had been viewed by participants before the experiment as well as videos of the setup. Thus, they had a good understanding of the important aspects of the study, such as the computer interface controlling the injection of the drug, the motorised syringe, the aquarium and of course the fish itself. Participants were then asked what level of injection they would personally have gone up to if they had taken part in the experiment and their opinion on the typical threshold for people of their age and gender in the same situation.

The results showed a striking BTA effect: nearly 29.5% of respondents thought they would not have injected a single dose of the toxic chemical and only 12% thought they would have completed the experiment and injected all 12 doses. In contrast, nearly 93% of participants believed that other people would administer at least one dose. To summarize it in two numbers: on average, participants estimated that they would have administered 4 doses and predicted that others would have administered 6.5 doses.[8] Women expressed significantly lower estimates than men, both for themselves and others.

Did it make a difference when participants had heard about Milgram's work on obedience to authority? Yes, it did, but in very different ways, depending on whether they were asked about themselves or about others. Those who were aware of the experiment (about half the sample) predicted that *others* would go further in the experiment while they themselves

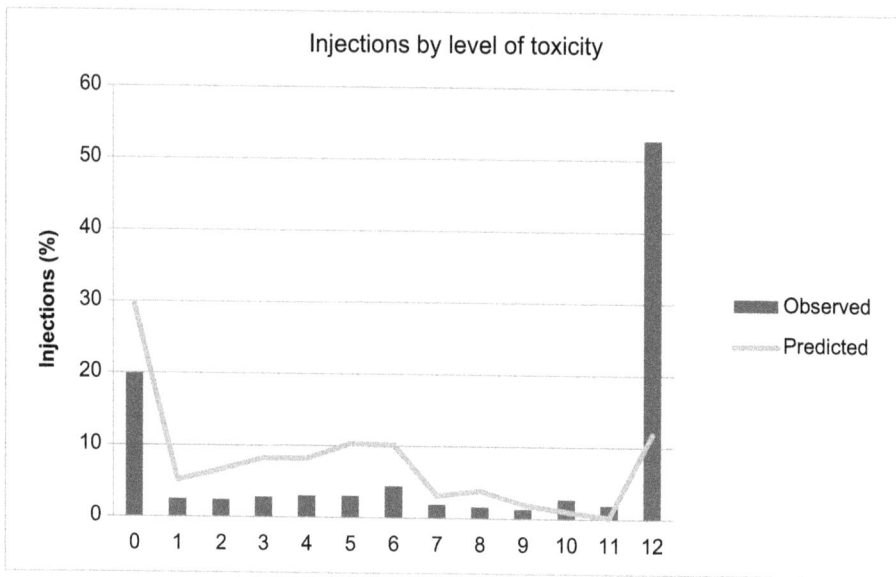

Figure 14.1 Injections by level of toxicity.

would go less far. Thus, knowing more about the way authority can influence people leads us to predict that others are more easily influenced, but that we would more easily escape the social influences that work on others!

Concerning the behavioural results we obtained on the whole experimental sample,[9] you can see in the graph in Figure 14.1.

- Nearly 20% of participants refused to begin the task;
- Nearly 53% completed the task and injected all 12 doses of the toxic chemical;
- 1 to 4.5% of participants stopped the experiment at one of the intermediate levels;
- On average, women administered lower doses than men (7 doses for women vs 9 for men).[10]

By comparing the curve of predictions with the results that were actually observed (illustrated as bars in the graph),[11] we can see that the number of doses injected is much higher than the number predicted by people who were not involved in the situation – once again in accordance with Milgram's observations.

Consented Authority

In essence, the scientific approach has no regard for authority: only observable facts can refute beliefs and overthrow belief systems, including scientific ones. Claude Bernard, a historical figure in animal experimentation, expressed no difference in his view: to him, the experimental sciences were about *non-obedience to authority*,[12] scientific ideas being merely "intellectual instruments which… serve to look into phenomena; they must be changed when they have fulfilled their purpose, as one changes a blunted scalpel when it has been used long enough."[13] This ability of scientists to give up their own hypotheses made them "heroic" in the eyes of philosopher of science Karl Popper, who pointed out that researchers constantly expose their ideas to the risk of refutation.[14]

However, it is important to distinguish the logic of science from established scientific practices which, as sociologist of science Thomas Kuhn has shown, are embodied in majority paradigms and, as such, are partly guided by conformity.[15] Although it has historically replaced systems of knowledge that involved blind deference to religious or philosophical authorities,[16] modern science still retains a role as a cultural authority. We are therefore faced with a paradox: trust in scientific authority can undermine the nonconformist logic that defines science, if science is granted the kind of deference and blind adherence that unscientific belief systems tend to command.[17] For example, a recent series of studies demonstrated that people with high levels of trust in science were more likely to believe fake news than other respondents when the news was accompanied by scientific references.[18]

The experiment I am about to describe aims to demonstrate that the appeal to science facilitates the exploitation of animals. There is nothing irrational about this scientific legitimisation: animal experimentation is based precisely on the promise of scientific benefit. Has medicine not won many Nobel prizes in this way?[19] This justification is therefore based on a rational trust in scientific authority. Although they naturally do not have any evidence that the death of the animal will benefit science or medicine, we expect participants to consent to carry out the protocol. This is a different approach to that described by Milgram, who attempted to explain the behaviour of his participants as a temporary suspension of their autonomy and by their having entered a state of blind obedience which he called the *agentic state*.[20]

How Does a Pro-science Attitude Influence Behaviour?

We tested the following hypothesis: if participants were prompted to adopt a more pro-science mindset, would they inject the fish with a higher number of toxic doses? The participants were randomly given either a handout encouraging a pro-science mindset (half the sample received it), or one that encouraged a science-critical mindset (the other half received it)[21] to compare the effects of this positioning on harmful behaviour towards the fish. In the pro-science version of the handout, participants had to briefly mention three important aspects of science in their opinion, then three things they liked about science, and finally three traits they believed they shared with scientists. Conversely, in the science-critical condition, they were asked to write down three things they saw as problems with science, three things they did not like about science, and three things that personally distinguished them from scientists.[22]

One participant, Isabelle K., a 51-year-old secretary at a major NGO, was randomly assigned to the pro-science group. She had learned about the study through an ad on a second-hand marketplace website. Temperatures were still cool that April in Grenoble, and she was wearing a white cable-knit wool jumper and a blue polka dot scarf. She wore large, violet-tinted glasses which highlighted her round, dark-complexioned face framed by very curly hair. After showing her the video tutorial for the experiment, she was asked to write down three things she thought were important about science on a form. She replied: "research," "results," and "means." Then, she said that what she liked about science was "uncertainty," "unexpected discoveries," and what she thought she had in common with scientists was "patience" and "perseverance." She was then taken to the room with the aquarium. She exclaimed: "That's a really big fish!" She clicked on the first few buttons without any apparent difficulty. After administering the eighth dose, she asked out loud: "Is that the fish's heart rate we're hearing? It seems really stressed out!" When she reached the ninth button, she questioned the experimenter again, asking him whether she should consider that the fish had swum through the orange frame if it did so towards the back of the aquarium. Her comments during the post-experiment interview suggested that she had been concerned about the fish.

The idea was simple, wasn't it? You just had to inject the drug. But watching the behaviour of the fish wasn't easy…

In the beginning, the fish always turned in the same direction, clockwise, around the aquarium, up to the glass, and then it limited its movements, and near the end I think it wanted to get it over with too, so it went to the area where it knew it was expected, and it looked around… It was a bit like suicide, I saw it a bit like a suicide…

I thought to myself "I'm killing it," but I told myself "it's just a fish, we fish them." The first thing that surprised me was that I didn't expect such a big fish…

I was killing that animal. I know it's for research… it makes progress possible, it's normal. Actually, I don't even know if it's normal or not.

I heard the animal's heartbeats, so it stressed me out, hearing those beeps. In the numbers from 1 to 12, you can see "risk of death 50%." That makes you think, too, you know.

Her answers to the final questionnaire indicated that she was rather satisfied with having participated in the study. She thought it was quite interesting and useful, but stressful and technically difficult to carry out.

When she later learned about the true nature of the experiment, relief was clearly visible on her face, which brightened up: "This is reassuring. I was going to lose sleep over this." Indeed, she had injected all twelve doses of the chemical, so the probability of the fish dying was 100%.

Laetitia D., a 33-year-old product manager, was in the "science-critical" branch of the study. She had signed up for the experiment after reading an advert in a free newspaper. She gave the impression of being an attentive and curious person with her bright, lively eyes. She had a tanned face, wore a necklace alternating between large red and pearly white buttons, and her grey jumper was draped over her shoulders. On her form, she had notably mentioned her concern that research could be influenced by industry and lobbying, she wondered whether most scientific discoveries were really useful for the average person, and she mentioned the pressure on researchers to "publish or perish."

During the interview, she repeated several times that the chemical affected the fish:

The fish seemed to lose a great deal of mobility as the doses increased. Then again, I'm not particularly sensitive to animals' emotions, but just seeing how it changed from 1 to 6 was something. From 1 to 2 and 3, it swam a bit around the aquarium. Then with 4, 5, and 6, you could tell it was getting sort of limited… I feel like there's a real connection between the dose that's administered and its behaviour in the aquarium, so I don't want to go further so I don't see it die in the aquarium and tell myself I did it because I pushed the button.

She also commented on the fast pace of the experiment: "I think that within 15 minutes you can get acquainted with the fish and its environment and then see it lying dead in the aquarium and even in the bin as biological waste," and she concluded that "you can turn into a fish killer within 10 minutes." Laetitia decided to stop at the sixth injection. Her answers to the questionnaire showed that, like the previous participant, she found the task stressful and difficult to carry out. However, she had a less favourable opinion of the interest of the study, and was less satisfied with having participated in it, which is consistent with the results of most participants: the less they progressed in the experiment, the less useful they found the task, and the less satisfied they were with their participation.

The behaviour of Isabelle K. (12 injections) and Laetitia D. (6 injections) perfectly represent the experimental group to which they belonged. Our comparison of the behaviour of individuals in the "pro-science group" and the "science-critical group" confirmed that those in the first group administered significantly more doses of the toxic chemical into the aquarium than those in the second group. Emphasizing the importance of science clearly made it easier for them to see the animal purely as an instrument for research. In fact, the significance of science was spontaneously mentioned by many participants after the experiment.

It's still interesting for science and for the aim of curing human diseases especially.

A 46-year-old male R&D project manager

To be honest, I felt pretty bad afterwards, but I told myself "Well, it was a good thing because it helped the advancement of science."

A 19-year-old female literature student

I want to say that it kind of sucked to have to inject that, but what's reassuring is that it was all for science.

An unemployed 43-year-old woman

I guess you have to accept doing that kind of thing if you want research to make progress.

A 45-year-old female health insurance technician

It's hard, but to do research, at some point you have to... .

A 60-year-old male caretaker

As we have just seen, the emphasis on science contributed to a significant increase in the number of doses administered to the fish.[23] But what goes on in the minds of the participants when they sacrifice the animal?

Notes

1 Finkielkraut A. (2018). *Des animaux et des hommes*, Paris, Stock, p. 43.
2 Goldsmith R. E., Clark R. A., Lafferty B. (2006). "Intention to oppose animal research: The role of individual differences in nonconformity," *Social Behavior and Personality*, 34 (8), pp. 955–964.
3 Hagger M. S., Chatzisarantis N. L. D., Biddle S. J. H. (2002). "A meta-analytic review of the theories of reasoned action and planned behavior in physical activity: Predictive validity and the contribution of additional variables," *Journal of Sport and Exercise Psychology*, 24 (1), pp. 3–32. The relationship between the two might even be artificially inflated by the fact that subjects answer a question that prompts them to project themselves into the future, as observed in voting behaviour. See Greenwald A. G., Carnot C. G., Beach R., Young B. (1987). "Increasing voting behavior by asking people if they expect to vote," *Journal of Applied Psychology*, 72 (2), pp. 315–318.
4 Zell E., Strickhouser J. E., Sedikides C., Alicke M. D. (2020). "The better-than-average effect in comparative self-evaluation: A comprehensive review and meta-analysis," *Psychological Bulletin*, 146 (2), pp. 118–149.
5 Messick D. M., Bloom S., Boldizar J. P., Samuelson C. D. (1985). "Why we are fairer than others," *Journal of Experimental Social Psychology*, 21 (5), pp. 480–500.

6   Dunning D., Johnson K., Ehrlinger J., Kruger J. (2003). "Why people fail to recognize their own incompetence," *Current Directions in Psychological Science*, 12 (3), pp. 83–87. This general bias even extends to our pets: it has been observed that on average, people think their dog is smarter than other people's dogs. See El-Alayli A., Lystad A. L., Webb S. R., Hollingsworth S. L., Ciolli J. L. (2006). "Reigning cats and dogs: A pet-enhancement bias and its link to pet attachment, pet-self similarity, self-enhancement, and well-being," *Basic and Applied Social Psychology*, 28 (2), pp. 131–143.

7   1,623 participants aged 18 to 86, made up of 36.6% of men and 63.4% of women. See Bègue, L. Vezirian, K. (2024). The blind obedience of others: A better than average effect in a Milgram-like experiment. *Ethics & Behavior, 34* (4), pp. 235–245.

8   The differences between the two averages were statistically significant. The order effect was controlled for: half the participants answered the first question first and the other half answered it second and vice versa. In a recent study about a Milgram protocol conducted in Poland, the authors also observed a BTA. See Grzyb T., Dolinski D. (2017). "Beliefs about obedience levels in studies conducted within the Milgram paradigm: Better than average effect and comparisons of typical behaviors by residents of various nations," *Frontiers in Psychology*, 8, pp. 1632.

9   The sample included 746 participants; 106 of them (14.2%) had expressed doubts about the experiment and were removed from the sample, and three others were removed for other reasons (not understanding the instructions or making mistakes in following the protocol).

10 The difference was statistically significant at the threshold p.<.001.

11 As in the Milgram studies, the distribution of data was bimodal. See Packer D. J. (2008). "Identifying systematic disobedience in Milgram's obedience experiments: A meta-analytic review," *Perspectives on Psychological Science*, 3 (4), pp. 301–304.

12 Bernard C. (1984). *Introduction à l'étude de la médecine expérimentale*, Paris, Flammarion, p. 93.

13 Bernard 1984, p. 93.

14 See Stengers I. (2002). *Sciences et pouvoirs*, Paris, La Découverte, p. 19.

15 Kuhn T. (1962). *The Structure of Scientific Revolutions*, Chicago and London, The University of Chicago Press.

16 I am using the categories of Auguste Comte's theory of the three states (1925).

17 This is why Claude Bernard asserted that "one must not have absolute faith in the formulas of science, but instead absolutely believe in its principles" (*Introduction à l'étude de la médecine expérimentale*, p. 300).

18 O'Brien T.C., Palmer R., Albarracin D. (2021). "Misplaced trust: When trust in science fosters belief in pseudoscience and the benefits of critical evaluation," *Journal of Experimental Social Psychology*, 96, p. 104184.

19 Crettaz von Roten F. (2019). *Experimentation animale*, Neuchâtel, Éditions Livreo-Alphil, p. 20.

20 Before testing this hypothesis with an experiment based on observing behaviour, we had to check to what extent support for science and animal experimentation were associated. To that purpose, I compared two groups that could be expected to differ in that respect. A questionnaire was presented to medical and pharmacy students. These are fields that are known to be based on experimental practices that are largely legitimised by the theoretical and practical training in these subjects. A group of physiotherapy and midwifery students were also tested. (Animal experimentation is less important in those fields.) Participants had to respond to a series of statements such as "I believe science can contribute to making the world a better place" in order to measure their pro-science beliefs, and to other statements such as "Sacrificing animals like rats and mice for research is justified" to assess their support for animal experimentation. The results confirmed that, in a sample of 321 students, those two attitudes were indeed associated, in men as in women. It was confirmed that men were more supportive of animal experimentation than women and that medical and pharmacy students were more supportive than the rest. More importantly, the relationship between the field of the students and their support for animal experimentation partly reflected different pro-science attitudes, with medical students being more pro-science than others. This effect was independent of age and gender. Thus, different levels of support for science differentiate between those groups and are involved in the contrast between them in terms of support for animal experimentation. To consolidate those observations, another study used date from the Eurobatometer study, which

included over 31,000 participants from 28 EU countries (as well as a few additional countries like Switzerland or Turkey). The data were collected from a sample of randomly selected participants who were interviewed face-to-face in their own homes. To estimate the association between pro-science attitudes and support for animal experimentation while making sure this association was not an indirect consequence of other variables, several other measures were introduced in the statistical analyses as control variables. In accordance with many previous studies, support for animal experimentation was more widespread among men, older, more religious people, and people who were on the right side of the political spectrum or who were extremely conservative. More importantly for our demonstration, it came out that pro-science attitudes were significantly related with support for animal experimentation, independent of any other variables. Those two surveys therefore allowed us to confirm that support for animal experimentation is associated with pro-science attitudes. For more detail about them, see Bègue L., Vezirian K. (2021). "Sacrificing animals in the name of scientific authority: The relationship between pro-scientific mindset and the lethal use of animals in biomedical experimentation," *Personality and Social Psychology Bulletin*, 2022.

21 This protocol had been used before. See Bègue, Vezirian 2021.

22 The experimenter did not know what experimental condition the participants were in. To check if the experimental suggestion had worked, participants had to immediately respond to five statements testing their opinions regarding science, such as "I completely share the aims of science". Analyses confirmed that the two groups expressed the difference that was expected.

23 The link between valuing science and supporting animal experimentation is also explained by the fact that one of the modes of thinking associated with science might be a form of ethical neutrality, as if engagement in the realm of facts and logic tended to make the realm of values less salient. That is what a later survey showed: the more pro-science participants were, the more they subscribed to a utilitarian ethics (expressing more agreement with statements like "sometimes, it is morally necessary for innocents to die as collateral damage if it means more people get saved"), and the more this utilitarian attitude was related to support for animal experimentation. See Bègue L., Vezirian K. (2021). "Sacrificing animals in the name of scientific authority: The relationship between pro-scientific mindset and the lethal use of animals in biomedical experimentation.". It would be a mistake to conclude that the practice of science and support for animal experimentation are inextricably linked. As we have seen, we are dealing here with a favourable attitude towards science as an abstraction rather than a concrete practice. When we focus not simply on attitudes towards science but on scientific reasoning, the association does not appear as inextricable. Sometimes the effect is even reversed: when one measures students' level of scientific knowledge, those who oppose animal experimentation the most are the ones with the highest scientific skills. See Pifer L., Shimizu K., Pifer R. (1994). "Public attitudes toward animal research: Some international comparisons," *Society and Animals*, 2 (2).

15 Neutralising the Gaze of Animals

Illustration: Magali Seghetto

"When the fish looked [at me], I looked at the screen… I felt like it was looking at me more and more desperately. I didn't look, I turned away."

Nathalie, 20 years old

On several occasions during the experiment, Nathalie expressed how uncomfortable she felt about gradually poisoning the fish to death. As I listened to the testimony of this computer science student who was upset that the fish was staring at her, I could not help thinking about

DOI: 10.4324/9781003561972-16

the German philosopher Theodor Adorno, who thought that the root of all violence could be found in our reluctance to "look back into the eyes of a mortally wounded animal."[1]

The eyes of an abused animal, even when they are as flat and inexpressive as those of a goldfish, can trouble our conscience by reminding us of their sentience. This may explain why laboratory assistants sometimes say that they prefer animals to be put in opaque rather than transparent cages: seeing mice looking at them makes them uncomfortable.[2] The writer Franz-Olivier Giesbert also felt that, in "meat factories," in the face of "calves with children's eyes," one has to look away.[3] This was confirmed by a former slaughterhouse worker, Mauricio, who, after working for six years in one of the largest slaughtering facilities in Limoges, France, explained why he could no longer continue: "I couldn't stand to see the live animals, because you can see the distress in their eyes."[4] Finally, when a reformed experimentalist, Michael Slusher, had to choose a title for the book in which he described the job he had quit, he named it *They All Had Eyes: Confession of a Vivisectionist*.[5]

Is it because of the power of the gaze, or what we project onto it, that in some cultures hunters gouge out the eyes of their prey?[6] Among humans, avoiding eye contact during a social interaction can be a symptom of a psychological disorder,[7] though more commonly a sign of embarrassment and sometimes disrespect. An old American study found that the duration of eye contact that White men made with a Black person during an interview could be predicted from a questionnaire measuring how much they valued equality.[8]

Touched by a Gaze

"Why do some animals spontaneously look into our eyes?

If they thought we were only bodies moved by physical forces, like falling stones or trees, or if they did not think at all, they would look indifferently at any part of our bodies without latching onto our gazes."

Baptiste Morizot, *Sur la piste animale*[9]

The eyes of animals move us for at least two reasons. First, like most vertebrates, we have eyeballs with three pairs of muscles that make them mobile and clearly distinguish them from the rest of our bodies.[10] This anatomical similarity raises questions. How can we not value the lives of animals that show such obvious morphological similarities with our own species? Humans have a particularly strong interest in animals with large, expressive eyes with starkly contrasted colours, as when a coloured iris stands out from the sclera. But eyes that look less like ours do not leave us indifferent either. For his book *Les Yeux de la Mer* ("the eyes of the sea"), photographer David Doubilet photographed hundreds of fish, and very often it is their eyes rather than their fins, the shape of their mouths or their amazing colours that have a magnetic and disturbing effect upon us. The eyes of animals evoke wonder and sometimes overwhelm us, or inspire philosophical reflection, as they did for Jacques Derrida who, in his vast poetic self-analysis, declared, "The animal gazes at us, and we are naked before it. Thinking perhaps begins there."[11]

The eyes, those doors to the inner self in which "the soul is concentrated,"[12] are magnified by cinema, which, through the gazes it presents, can make our own eyes tear up. When filmmakers explore our relationships with animals, the exchange of gazes is essential, both in documentary and in fiction, such as John Huston's *Moby Dick* (1956), in which the gazes of the whale and captain Ahab constantly challenge each other, or Robert Redford's *The Horse Whisperer*, in which the gazes of Pilgrim and Grace express the communion of their wounds.[13]

We have all experienced the importance of eye contact in the forming of bonds with fellow humans and in connecting with other species. In a study by Micho Nagazawa at Azabu University in Japan, participants came to the lab individually with their dogs and interacted

Figure 15.1 Pilgrim and Grace in the film *The Horse Whisperer* by Robert Redford (1998).
Illustration: Magali Seghetto

with them for 30 minutes. The behaviour of the dog–human pair was carefully observed and both the dog's and the owner's oxytocin (the "bonding hormone") levels were measured before and after the experiment. It appeared that the interaction with the dog increased the owner's oxytocin level, especially when the dog looked into its owner's eyes.[14] Dogs who maintain eye contact with their owner for an extended period also experience an increase in oxytocin of about 30%.[15]

Without eye contact, empathy seems impossible, suspended, or apathetic. In Milgram's classic experiments, simply removing the ability to see the victim being shocked (while still being able to hear his screams), caused the proportion of people administering 450 volts to increase from 40% to 62.5%. Many signals can trigger empathy, especially when they show a victim's vulnerability,[16] but eyes have a unique way of doing this. This was confirmed by the responses of a 32-year-old hospital cleaner in our experiment (he stopped after 9 injections).

Interviewer: What made you stop at that specific moment?
Participant: The eyes of the fish. I don't know. They affected me. I felt something in its eyes.

A 32-year-old male hospital cleaner

A 25-year-old man summed up the power of eye contact in establishing a bond filled with empathy:

When you meet his gaze, you really feel like you have a conscience in front of you and you see, I don't know, there's a kind of connection that's created, you almost put yourself in his place and you don't want to be there. Why impose that on him?

A 25-year-old male law student

But empathy is not the most common response to a fish. Few people can say, as Kafka did: "I feel things the way a fish does."[17] Its aquatic appearance does not elicit the kind of protective response we experience with animals like mammals, who are closer to us. Empathy is a biased emotional response, as we have seen, and not all victims seem entitled to it.

Selective Empathy

Empathy is defined as the "ability to share and understand other people's emotional and mental states."[18] This echoing of other people's experiences is strongly modulated by the appearance of said others. For example, we are more likely to empathise with living beings that remind us of helpless children. In one study, researchers measured participants' empathetic responses and their willingness to help Kayla, an accident victim. Participants were told that her leg was broken. The victim was either a student, a dog, a child, or a puppy. The researchers found that the child and the puppy elicited more empathetic responses[19] than the other victims.

Empathy evolved primarily to benefit living beings that look like us, and it plummets when there is less physical resemblance between us and the species involved.[20] Scott Plous, a researcher at Wesleyan University, showed participants scenes of animal abuse while measuring their stress levels through sensors that detected sweat. This electrophysiological phenomenon, known as skin conductance, results from the activity of the sympathetic nervous system, which, during stressful experiences, stimulates sweat glands and thus increases the electric conductivity of the skin. When participants viewed scenes of animal abuse, their physiological stress response (manifesting as weak electric currents measured in *micromhos*) was higher when confronted with a monkey compared to a frog or a pheasant.[21]

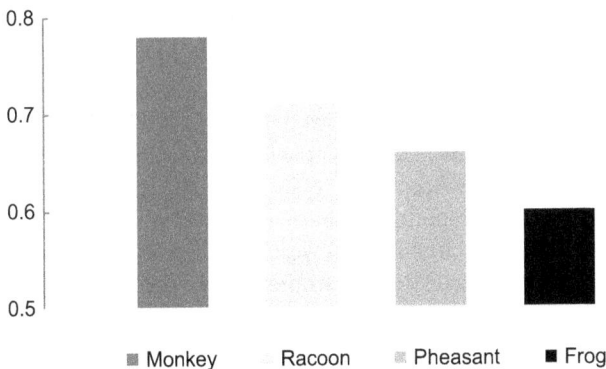

Figure 15.2 Skin conductivity (in Mmhos) of participants shown films of mistreated animals, depending on the species. High conductivity manifests a more intense emotional response.

Many other studies have confirmed that basic information about the identity of a victim (such as their being a fellow citizen or a foreigner) was enough to dramatically alter the level of empathy they elicited.[22]

Zero Degrees of Empathy

We care more about primates than toads, but not everyone has the same emotional response to the mistreatment of monkeys. Harry Harlow, who dedicated his career to ground-breaking but cruel studies, separated baby rhesus monkeys from their mothers to study their stress responses. He provided the monkeys with nursing dummies – surrogate mothers that dispensed milk but were physically repellent (their bodies were made of steel wires) or comforting dummies made of fabric but without any nursing function. The monkeys preferred the cloth dummies. However, Harlow found that, when all that was available was a repellent "mother" (which sometimes blew cold air on them or poked them with spikes), the baby monkeys would still cling to it.

In other studies, Harlow confined monkeys to a cramped room in order to induce and study depression, and what he said about his experimental subjects could make you wonder if he felt any empathy for them at all: "We have spent the last four years deep in depression – fortunately, the depression of others and not ourselves – and we regard this period of animal research as one of the most successful and promising we have experienced."[23] During an interview about his research, he did not hesitate to admit the following: "The only thing I care about is whether the monkeys will turn out a property I can publish. I don't have any love for them."[24]

The callousness of this researcher, who was awarded the US National Medal of Science, triggered outrage among animal rights advocates like Peter Singer and Donna Haraway. Haraway was of the opinion that a psychiatric examination would have revealed a sadistic trait in his personality.[25] But here, as in many other instances of institutionalised animal abuse, there is no need to appeal to psychopathology to understand how normal people can mistreat animals.

Indeed, in those horrific studies on primate attachment, the division of labour in Harlow's laboratory made it possible to "view an experiment, be authorised to use animals, make sure they were exposed to the relevant variables, gather and analyse data, and check the results without being directly exposed to the consequences of the whole process on the animals."[26] One of Harlow's former students suggested that "the reality of the fate of the experimental animals may have been obscured by the abstract goals of the experiment." These were abstract but also somehow very tangible, since the publish-or-perish principle is part of the career-driven logic that motivates many studies on "animal models" whose scientific value is not always certain.[27] For example, a review published in *Nature* indicated that half of all animal studies on cancer could not be replicated.[28] According to another article from the same prestigious journal, over 80% of potential therapeutic applications failed when transferred from animals to humans.[29] The most commonly cited reasons were the physiological and metabolic non-equivalence of species,[30] the limited quality of the studies and of their analyses,[31] and the presence of systematic disturbances in the lab environment that could affect the physiology and behaviour of the animals.[32]

It is often inaccurate to suggest that individuals who harm animals in an institutional setting are characterised by a sadistic trait. Before one of our experiments with the fish-robot in Grenoble, I asked nearly 150 participants to answer questions measuring their sadistic tendencies, based on the degree to which they agreed with statements like "I have hurt people for fun before," "I like to see people suffer," or "I have fantasies about hurting people".[33]

The results showed that there was absolutely no correlation between an individual's level of sadism and the number of doses with which they injected the fish.

However, concluding that sadism and cruelty towards animals are completely unrelated would also be a mistake. The fish experiment was not just about cruelty. Most participants consented to do what was expected of them because they deemed that serving science was a higher purpose that justified not only sacrificing the fish but also, for many of them, overcoming their heartfelt reluctance to do so. Nevertheless, we cannot conclude that the participants' individual psychological traits were unrelated to their behaviour, as we will see in the case of empathy.

The Empathy Quotient and Behaviour

I did what I was told. I didn't feel anything in particular.

Marc V., an unemployed 23-year-old man

Not everyone reacts the same way to animal or human suffering. Some people feel concern or distress. Others find justifications to make the fate of the victims seem acceptable ("They're only animals"; "He's responsible for what happened to him"),[34] focus on something else or, on the contrary, sometimes find the means to express their disapproval. Personality differences are one of the factors that explain why people have different attitudes towards victims. Marc V., the participant quoted above, was among the 2% with the lowest empathy scores in the sample.[35]

Milgram did not want to focus on the role of personality or individual variables in his work: only three pages are dedicated to this in *Obedience to Authority*. His aim was rather to shed light on the role of context in determining behaviour. However, Milgram's experiments provided compelling evidence for the relevance of individual variables.[36] We can think of personality as a set of partly learned patterns that determine our reactions, shape our interpretations and influence our decisions. Empathy, which we will especially focus on, is a response that is activated at different thresholds in different individuals. The most direct way to measure it is to ask people about their own habitual reactions to others. In the *Empathy quotient* questionnaire developed by psychologist Simon Baron-Cohen, one finds statements such as "I can easily tell if someone wants to join a conversation" or "Seeing people cry doesn't affect me much" (reversed question). Believing, somewhat like the poet Lamartine, that "we do not have two hearts, one for humans and the other for animals," Baron-Cohen considers that our relationships with other species mobilise emotional resources that are not fundamentally different from those we use with our own. When it comes to relationships with other species, several surveys show that people with high levels of empathy are less likely to support the use of animals as food or research subjects.[37] However, we do not know about the actual behaviour of the people behind these profiles. To measure the precise influence of empathy, participants were asked to answer the empathy questionnaire developed by Mark Davis,[38] which includes a series of statements such as "When I see someone being taken advantage of, I feel kind of protective towards them" or "I often have tender, concerned feelings for people less fortunate than me."

The results showed that the higher the empathy of the men and women in the sample were, the fewer doses of toxic chemical they administered to the fish.[39] The statistical association was significant but modest. For example, the empathy score of the participants who had refused to even begin the experiment was only almost 7% higher than that of those who had gone all the way to the twelfth injection. This result is consistent with that obtained in a recent replication of the Milgram study by Jerry Burger at Santa Clara University: empathetic individuals expressed reluctance to continue the experiment earlier than the others.[40]

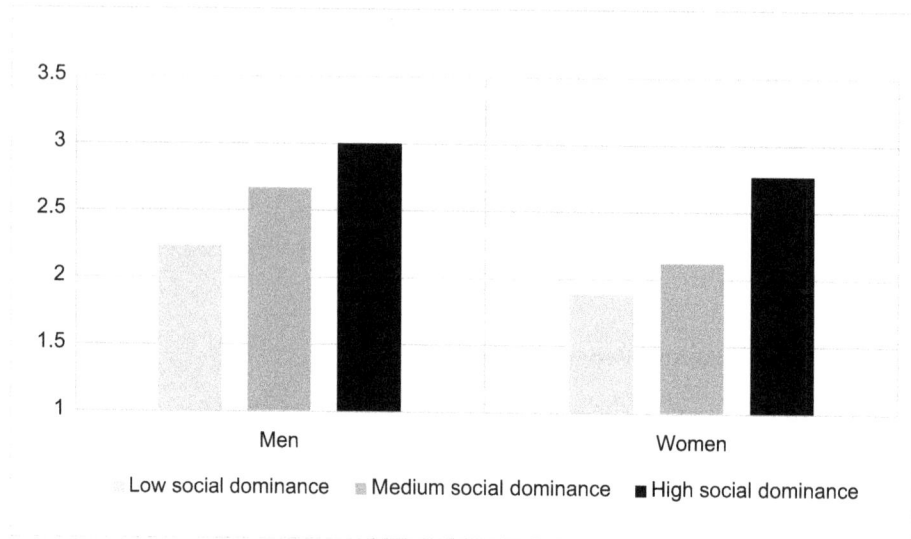

Figure 15.3 Number of injections depending on social dominance orientation, by gender.

Hierarchising Living Beings

People who have an inegalitarian view of human groups approach human–animal relationships in the same way. In Chapter 11, I showed that adherence to social hierarchies and anti-egalitarianism were associated with support for animal experimentation. To determine whether this trait, called *social dominance orientation*, was statistically associated with the administration of toxic injections, I related the number of injections administered by each individual with their social dominance score as measured before the experiment, through responses to statements such as "No group should dominate society" (reversed question) or "Some groups are just inferior to others."

The results have largely confirmed that the higher the participants' preference for social dominance, the more injections they administered.[41] For example, the social dominance score of the participants who had refused to begin the experiment was 18% lower than that of the participants who had gone all the way to the twelfth injection. Table 15.3 provides a simplified view of the results, distinguishing three levels of social dominance.

A third variable was found to be especially correlated with the number of injections administered to the fish: speciesism. This ideological dimension, a form of moral discrimination based on species membership, implies ascribing lower value to animals. It can be measured with a set of six questions developed by a team of Oxford researchers.[42] Here are two examples: "Morally, animals always count for less than humans" and "Humans have the right to use animals however they want to." The experiment revealed that the speciesism score of the participants who had completed the experiment (all 12 doses) was 22% higher than that of those who had refused to inject the first dose. A series of deeper analyses allowed us to test whether the associations between all the variables (empathy, social dominance and speciesism) remained significant regardless of the gender, age and food preferences of the participants.[43]

Converging Influences

The way participants viewed their aquatic victim certainly resulted from the low regard currently accorded to fish, who are regarded as "lower vertebrates." Participants' behaviour was also influenced by the cultural authority of science and its therapeutic promises. Finally, individual factors such as empathetic tendencies, adherence to hierarchy between groups (i.e., social dominance) and the moral divide between humans and animals (i.e., speciesism) are significant influences on behaviour.

Since, as we have seen earlier, Milgram's theory of obedience does not accurately predict the behaviour of our participants, it is interesting to listen carefully to their discourse to understand how they account for their own behaviour. If we consider that, in situations with serious implications, people also base their actions on explicit motives, then considering the reasons offered by the protagonists allows us to better understand the mental context in which they made their decision to sacrifice the animal or let it live by confronting the researcher.[44]

Notes

1 Adorno T. (2003). *Minima moralia. Réflexions sur la vie mutilée*, Paris, Payot, p. 142. A writer that was dear to Adorno, Franz Kafka, is on the other hand alleged to have talked to the fish in the Berlin aquarium, telling them: "Now at last I can look at you in peace, I don't eat you anymore."

2 Birke L. (2003). "Who-or what-are the rats (and mice) in the laboratory," *Society and Animals*, 11 (3), pp. 207–224.

3 Giesbert F.-O. (2014). *L'animal est une personne. Pour nos sœurs et frères les bêtes*, Paris, Fayard, p. 63.

4 Clément H. (2019). *Comment j'ai arrêté de manger des animaux*, Paris, Seuil, p. 102.

5 Slusher M. (2016). *They All Had Eyes: Confession of a Vivisectionist*, Boston, Vegan Press.

6 Digard J.-P. (1999). *Les Français et leurs animaux*, Paris, Fayard, p. 149.

7 Tanaka J. W., Sung A. (2016). "The 'eye avoidance' hypothesis of autism face processing," *Journal of Autism and Developmental Disorders*, 46 (5), pp. 1538–1552.

8 Penner L. A. (1971). "Interpersonal attraction toward a black person as a function of value importance," *Personality: An International Journal*, 2 (2), pp. 175–187.

9 Morizot B. (2017). *Sur la piste animale*, Arles, Actes Sud, p. 34.

10 Balcombe J. (2018). *À quoi pensent les poissons?* Paris, La Plage, p. 38.

11 Derrida J. (2006/2008). *The Animal that Therefore I Am* Fordham U P, p 29.

12 Hegel (1995). *Cours d'esthétique*, t. III, Paris, Aubier, p. 207.

13 See Burt J. (2002). *Animals in films*, Londres, Reakton Books.

14 Nagasawa M., Kikusui T., Onaka T., Ohta M. (2009). "Dog's gaze at its owner increases owner's urinary oxytocin during social interaction," *Hormones and Behavior*, 55 (3), pp. 434–441. Another study complemented this result by showing that when people hug their dog, the dog's heart rate slows down. Lynch J. J., McCarthy J. F. (1969). "Social responding in dogs: Heart rate changes to a person," *Psychophysiology*, 5 (4), pp. 389–393.

15 Nagasawa M., Mitsui S., En S., Ohtani N., Ohta M., Sakuma Y., Onaka T., Mogi K., Kikusui T. (2015). "Social evolution. Oxytocin-gaze positive loop and the coevolution of human–dog bonds," *Science*, 348 (6232), pp. 333–336.

16 Staub E. (1989). *The Roots of Evil. The Origins of Genocide and Other Group Violence*, Cambridge, Cambridge University Press.

17 *Journal de F. Kafka*, quoted by Cervellon C., (2020). *L'Animal*, Paris, Belin Éducation, p. 57.

18 Singer T., Decety J. (2011). "Social neuroscience of empathy," In Decety J., Caccioppo J. T. (eds.). *The Oxford Handbook of Social Neuroscience* (pp. 551-–564), Oxford, Oxford University Press.

19 Batson C. D., Lishner D. A., Cook J., Sawyer S. (2005). "Similarity and nurturance: Two possible sources of empathy for strangers," *Basic and Applied Social Psychology*, 27 (1), pp. 15–25. 20. Miralles A., Raymond M., Lecointre G. (2019). "Empathy and compassion toward other species decrease with evolutionary divergence time," art. cit.

20 Miralles A., Raymond M., Lecointre G. (2019). "Empathy and compassion toward other species decrease with evolutionary divergence time," *Scientific Reports*, 9.

21 Plous S. (1993). "Psychological mechanisms in the human use of animals," *Journal of Social Issues*, 49 (1), pp. 11–52. See also Westbury H., Neumann D. L. (2008). "Empathy-related responses to moving film stimuli depicting human and non-human animal targets in negative circumstances," *Biological Psychology*, 78 (1), pp. 66–74.

22 Avenanti A., Sirigu A., Aglioti S. M. (2010). "Racial bias reduces empathic sensorimotor resonance with other-race pain," *Current Biology*, 20, pp. 1018–1022; Xu X., Zuo X., Wang X., Han S. (2009). "Do you feel my pain? Racial group membership modulates empathic neural responses," *Journal of Neuroscience*, 29 (26), pp. 8525–8529.

23 Harlow H., Suomi S. (1974). "Induced depression in monkeys," *Behavioral Biology*, 12, pp. 273–296, quoted by Despret V. (2020). *Quand le loup habitera avec l'agneau*, Paris, Les Empêcheurs de penser en rond, p. 105.

24 Gluck J. P. (1997). "Harry F. Harlow and animal research: Reflection on the ethical paradox," *Ethics and Behavior*, 7 (2), pp. 149—161.

25 Harraway D. (1989). *Primate Visions: Gender, Race and Nature in the World of Modern Science*, New York, Routledge.

26 Gluck J. P. (1997). "Harry F. Harlow and animal research: Reflection on the ethical paradox."

27 Knight A (2011). *The Costs and Benefits of Animal Experiments*, New York, Palgrave Macmillan; Herrman K., Jayne K. (2019). *Animal Experimentation*, Boston, Brill; Akhtar A. (2015). "The flaws and human harms of animal experimentation," *Cambridge Quarterly of Healthcare Ethics*, 24 (4), pp. 407–419; Van Norman G. A. (2020). "Limitations of animal studies for predicting toxicity in clinical trials: Part 2: Potential alternatives to the use of animals in preclinical trials," *JACC. Basic to Translational Science*, 5 (4), pp. 387–397.

28 Mullard A. (2021). "Half of top cancer studies fail high-profile reproducibility effort," *Nature*, 600 (7889), pp. 368–369.

29 Perrin S. (2014). "Preclinical research: Make mouse studies work," *Nature*, 507, pp. 423–425; Pound P., Ebrahim S., Sandercock P., Bracken M.B., Roberts I. (2004). "Reviewing animal trials systematically (RATS) Group. Where is the evidence that animal research benefits humans?," *BMJ*, 28, 328 (7438), pp. 514–517.

30 LaFollette H., Shank N. (1996). *Brute Science*, London, Routledge.

31 Perel P., Roberts I., Sena E., Wheble P., Briscoe C., Sandercock P., Macleod M., Mignini L. E., Jayaram P., Khan K. S. (2007). "Comparison of treatment effects between animal experiments and clinical trial: Systematic review," *BMJ*, 334 (7586), p. 197.

32 Herrman K., Jayne K. (2019). *Animal Experimentation*; Ram R. (2019). "Extrapolation of animal research data to humans: An analysis of the evidence," in K. Herrman, K. Jayne (2019). *Animal Experimentation*, pp. 341-375.

33 146 participants filled out the sadism questionnaire.

34 Hafer C. L., Bègue L. (2005). "Experimental research on just-world theory: Problems, developments, and future challenges," *Psychological Bulletin*, 131, pp. 128–167.

35 His score was 2.7 on the Interpersonal Reactivity Index.

36 Bègue L., Beauvois J.-L., Courbet D., Oberlé D., Lepage J., Duke A. A. (2015). "Personality predicts obedience in a Milgram paradigm," *Journal of Personality*, 83 (3).

37 Furnham A., McManus C., Scott D. (2003). "Personality, empathy and attitudes toward animal welfare," *Anthrozoös*, 16 (2), pp. 135–146; Taylor N., Signal T. D. (2005). "Empathy and attitudes to animals," *Anthrozoös*, 18 (1), pp. 18–27.

38 Davis M. H. (1983). "Measuring individual differences in empathy: Evidence for a multidimensional approach," *Journal of Personality and Social Psychology*, 44 (1), pp. 113–126.

39 For a sample of 609 participants, the association index was as follows: rho = −.09, p.<.001.

40 Burger J. M. (2009). "Replicating Milgram: Would people still obey today?" *American Psychologist*, 64, p. 1–11.

41 For a sample of 604 participants, the association index was: rho = .219, p.<.000.

42 Caviola L., Everett J., Faber N. S. (2019). "The moral standing of animals: Towards a psychology of speciesism," *Journal of Personality and Social Psychology*, 116 (6), pp. 1011–1029.

43 See Bègue, L. Vezirian, K. (2023). Instrumental harm toward animals in a Milgram-like experiment in France. The role of nonpathological personality traits. In *Animal Abuse and Interpersonal Violence* (eds. H. C. Chan and R. W. Y. Wong). https://doi.org/10.1002/9781119894131.ch9

44 For a rhetorical approach to phenomena of obedience to authority, see Gibson S. (2019). *Arguing, Obeying and Defying. A Rhetorical Perspective on Stanley Milgram's Obedience Experiments*, Cambridge, Cambridge University Press.

16 Moral Dilemmas

Illustration: Magali Seghetto

"I had a feeling that it was suffering. I told myself: I have to put it out of its misery."

Clémence F., a 31-year-old financial manager

"I prayed that it wouldn't die in front of me."

Sandra A., a 28-year-old medical secretary

As she is administering a ninth toxic dose to the fish swimming in front of her, Clémence F. holds her head and seems very concerned. Her post-experiment account confirms the

DOI: 10.4324/9781003561972-17

tension she visibly exuded during those long minutes sitting in front of the aquarium. Like Clémence, every volunteer was debriefed after the experiment. We conducted nearly 750 interviews to allow each participant to express themselves individually, to find out if they had any doubts about the study, and finally to inform them of its true aims.[1]

In this chapter, I will delve into the experiment as it was described by the participants themselves, which will allow you to feel and understand how they tried to reconcile their values, their representations of animals, the promises of science, as well as various elements of their individual backgrounds.

Stress and Tension

Watching a fish swim is often experienced as a relaxing activity, of a deeply soothing nature that can even lower one's blood pressure[2] and relieve anxiety in young children.[3] But in this experiment, things are very different. According to their responses to the questionnaire completed immediately after the experiment, nearly 60% of men and 80% of women found the experience very stressful. This was largely confirmed by their oral accounts:

My heart was racing. My hands were sweaty. I was afraid to see it die. I felt sorry for it.

A 23-year-old literature and language student

I felt stressed. I could feel my heart beating faster and faster.

A 42-year-old saleswoman

I could feel the pressure rising because I could see that the fish was suffering, and I could see how it was going to end.

A 64-year-old unemployed woman

My heart was pumping. I was actually afraid to kill it.

A 23-year-old economics student

In theory, the behaviour of the fish robot was supposed to be the same for the entire duration of the experiment. It would swim freely in its 3,000-litre aquarium thanks to four sensors that allowed it to detect obstacles and automatically adjust its trajectory in the water. However, it would sometimes hit the glass panels of the aquarium instead of smoothly avoiding them or staying in a given area. This was completely random behaviour, but it did not stop participants who kept giving one injection after another from thinking that the animal was gradually getting worse and to associate any abnormal behaviour with the effects of the chemical they were injecting. After all, they had been told that the fish might experience paralysis or abnormal movements during the experiment.

Thus, in some sense, the imperfections of the biomimetic robot contributed to increasing its emotional impact on participants, who could not help associating any abnormal behaviour with their own actions.

With the last couple of injections, you could see it was violent. It seemed violent for the fish.

A 27-year-old woman working in the tourism industry

I could clearly see I was injecting it with something that had some kind of neurological effect.

A 50-year-old female choreographer

Its eyes would open wider and wider. It was getting worse and worse. You could hear the heartbeat.

A 21-year-old male law student

I could feel that the fish was in pain. It was suffering.

A 30-year-old paramedical student

When the fish started hitting its head against the glass, that's what made me stop.

A 22-year-old female literature student

Near the end, I think the fish also wanted to get it over with.

A 51-year-old female NGO secretary

The tension felt by the participants also came from their immersion in an unfamiliar and probably stressful experimental set up, with its control screen, buttons and dials, the high-pitched and increasingly rapid sounds of the heartbeat, the motorised syringe filled with toxic, fluorescent yellow liquid, and the particular luminous atmosphere that filled the room.

It's kind of like in those dystopian films where things are pushed to an extreme, with this white light glaring at you and this huge fish swimming round and round.

A 20-year-old female physics student

It was like being in a torture chamber.

A 20-year-old literature and language student

Several participants seemed so worried about the fate of the fish that they felt a parallel and a kind of emotional or even physiological closeness between themselves and the aquatic animal:

My heart would beat faster and faster as the fish's heart beat faster and faster.

A 24-year-old unemployed man

I felt like I was the fish. For half a second, I saw myself in the aquarium.

A 21-year-old female business student

I could feel the suffering of the fish.

A 20-year-old male physics student

My own stress increased as the heart rate of the fish went up.

A 32-year-old female restaurant employee

Hearing that sound, that heartbeat. It's... When you're a woman and you've heard your baby in your womb, there's a connection.

A 62-year-old female employee

This concern for the fish was at its strongest in several participants who said they felt particularly bad for what the animal was undergoing:

I almost cried in the middle of it. I couldn't push the button.

A 21-year-old female management student

It made you sad when you imagined what it would be like to be that fish.

A 24-year-old secretary

I didn't think I would be so overwhelmed. I was on the verge of having a panic attack.

A 49-year-old female social service assistant

The evolutionary and emotional distance that separates us from fish does not make it easy to empathise with them, and indifference constantly threatens our relationships with them. Speaking of the bonds we form with fish – even those we keep as pets – an Oxford veterinarian went so far as to claim that "no child really loves their goldfish."[4] We must admit that when they die, they do not always get a decent funeral. As a young HR assistant put it bluntly (perhaps forgetting that our fish was nearly 50-centimetres long): "I told myself: am I not sending that fish right down the toilet?" Still, some people, and not only children, cry when their fish die. This also happens to prominent adults such as great orator Hortensius, a close friend of Cicero, who had a strong attachment to his turbot and was inconsolable when it died.[5]

Few people cried during the experiment. Four female participants cried during the interview afterwards, and they mainly spoke of the regrets or guilt they felt. Consistent with the stereotype (but also with cross-cultural research),[6] no men cried, but guilt and regret were frequently mentioned by both genders. Many participants had imagined how badly they would have felt if they had gone as far as killing the animal. This anticipation of guilt is an important mental phenomenon in moral behaviour.[7]

I think I would have felt guilty if I had gone all the way to 12.

A 21-year-old female humanitarian project management student

If the fish dies because of me, how am I going to feel?

A 20-year-old unemployed man

Its life is in my hands. If I kill it, I'm going to feel terrible.

A 19-year-old female childcare student

Conversely, some participants who had sacrificed the fish or who thought they had injected it with too many doses blamed themselves or expressed a form of psychological discomfort involving regret and sometimes intense guilt.

I kind of wish I hadn't pressed the button. Yeah, I'm not going to feel good about this later.

A 46-year-old unemployed man

The more it went on, the more I felt I was being cruel to that fish and the more I empathised with it.

A 49-year-old female educator

I feel really guilty.

A 40-year-old woman (profession unknown)

I felt I had done something that was against my own principles. When I was carrying out the experiment, I felt ashamed thinking about her (my girl-friend) – she loves animals.

A 26-year-old video producer

For other participants, the feeling of guilt was attenuated by that of having performed an important duty and they mentioned the benefits that would result from their participation in the experiment.

You feel guilty but it's for a good cause.

A 63-year-old woman (profession unknown)

It's never very pleasant to hurt a fish, but in this case, it was for a good cause.

A 26-year-old woman working in the tourism industry

I would always remind myself that the resulting benefits were more important.

A 49-year-old female employee in the public education sector

It's heartbreaking but we've got to keep making progress in medicine.

A 37-year-old female childcare assistant

Such benefits were mentioned as obvious reasons because the decision-making rule under-lying the use of the animal was crystal clear: fish obviously counted for less than humans.

Some animals must die so we can improve the human condition.

A 21-year-old male history student

It's always better to do it with fish rather than humans.

A 21-year-old male student

Moral Pain Relief

In some cases, participants seemed to feel less guilty if they contrasted their actions with other behaviours that they considered to be much more problematic. Thus, sacrificing fish for research was presented as more justifiable than sacrificing other species (e.g. humans, pets, animals considered to have more emotional capacity or more individuality, or animals we do not usually eat). In the same spirit, using fish for medical research seemed more legitimate than using them for more frivolous purposes such as cosmetics.

When you think we can carry out experiments on humans, a fish, well...

A 54-year-old male temporary worker

If it had been a dog, a cat, or a monkey, I would have left.

A 50-year-old female choreographer

There are thousands of fish.

A 39-year-old woman (profession unknown)

Dogs, cats, those kinds of animals – I'm pretty sure they're sentient. They can feel pain, sadness, and so on. But a fish, I can't really imagine.

A 47-year-old unemployed woman

It's the aim of the experiment that justified my doing it. If I had been told it was about testing lipstick, I wouldn't have done it.

A 44-year-old training consultant

Sometimes, participants mentioned the culinary use of fish – both very common and presented as less legitimate than science.

I told myself "We kill thousands of fish for food, so why not for science?"

A 20-year-old male industrial science student

This justification could already be found in the writings of Claude Bernard. In his *Introduction to the Study of Experimental Medicine*, we can read: "It would be strange indeed if we recognised man's right to make use of animals in every walk of life, for domestic services, for food, and then forbade him to make use of them for his own instruction in one of the sciences most useful to humanity."[8] The same argument could be heard again from a 27-year-old animal keeper working with dogs in a laboratory. In the same testimony, he invoked a powerful figure of justification: the sick child:[9] "You've got to find things to cure kids. And I tell myself: we eat meat anyway, don't we? Well, this is the same, except it's useful."

By evoking various thresholds of acceptability for research, participants actively explored the frontiers of licit and illicit practices, sometimes in unexpected ways, evoking quantitative criteria of value such as the size or age of the animal, or alternative human or animal categories.

It would be better to test it on an old fish, because it's okay to die when you're old.

A 63-year-old woman (profession unknown)

If it's a little one, I won't touch it, but if it's a big one, it's already had a full life.

A 31-year-old female accounting and finance civil servant

It would have been less stressful with a small fish.

A 21-year-old female physics student

Personally, I feel less sorry for insects.

A 22-year-old management student

Why not experiment on paedophiles, criminals? It's okay to experiment on them, but not on animals.

A 42-year-old female personal carer

The idea that some humans can be experimented on because they have lost any right to moral consideration has a long history. The French philosopher Maupertuis wrote in 1752: "I would gladly see criminals used for those operations,"[10] echoing the Roman physician Celsus, who stated more than 20 centuries earlier: "There is no cruelty in seeking ways of curing countless honest citizens by tormenting a small number of criminals."[11] Experimentation was still being carried out on murderers in 16th-century Pisa, where authorities had provided a professor of anatomy with a criminal "with permission to kill him or dissect him at pleasure"[12] and it was practiced in the same century by Ambroise Paré in France.[13]

Self-exoneration

On a different note, several forms of moral disengagement we have until now largely observed in the discourse of experimenters appeared in the justifications offered by participants. They exonerated themselves by mentioning the inevitability of the death of animals destined for research.

I told myself that if I didn't do it, someone else would.

A 23-year-old female geoscience student

The fish was already 50% dead, so I might as well go all the way.

A 29-year-old lab technician

I told myself someone would do it anyway, so the fish was doomed in any case.

A 50-year-old female choreographer

It was unlikely to make it out alive, so I might as well finish the experiment.

A 20-year-old male environmental science student

In my opinion, when an animal is locked up, it's already dead. It needs either to be freed or to be killed.

A 19-year-old biochemistry student

Consistent with the strategies described in Chapter 5, some participants justified the animal's plight by debasing it or downplaying its capabilities.

I think fish are pretty but I think they're stupid, to be honest.

A 21-year-old web and multimedia student

I thought that fish just swam around, that they couldn't think or feel pain.

A 49-year-old personal care assistant

Altruism or Rebellion?

Listening to participants discussing their conflicting feelings and the challenges they faced during the experiment showed us that many of them had to overcome their visceral reluctance to do what was being asked of them, and they did so to be helpful and contribute to a good cause. We were looking at people who believed in what they were doing and wanted to do it right, agreeing to overcome their inhibitions and seeking to control their emotions.

I tried not to get emotional about it.

A 29-year-old male physics student

I tried not to be sensitive about it.

A 21-year-old male mathematics student

I wanted to help you guys.

A 26-year-old real estate executive assistant

At one point, I told myself "I'm going to stop, I don't want to hurt that fish," but at the same time, I thought "But they need those results."

A 24-year-old female art student

If it can help science… And honestly, I didn't have too many qualms about it.

A 49-year-old female educator

You think you're doing something good. At least that's what I hoped. I'm glad I participated.

A 59-year-old female musician

To justify their participation, several participants also mentioned close relatives who could benefit from scientific advances resulting from animal experimentation. Additionally, some mentioned their own medical conditions:

I'm glad to participate. I lost my mother to that disease.

A 63-year-old unemployed man

A lot of people in my family suffer from dizziness.

A 20-year-old female engineering student

I had a stroke four months ago, so I feel concerned.

A 45-year-old female administrative and financial assistant

In my family, we have a history of Alzheimer's.

A 49-year-old female communications officer

Participants who refused to participate or who quickly quit the experiment were not a homogeneous category. Some would appeal to general principles and oppose the moral hierarchy of species, or they would refer to the cognitive or emotional capabilities of animals to justify their position.

Administering a chemical to an animal and watching it wither and die is against my principles. I'm a vegetarian.

A 50-year-old administrative manager

Humans don't own animals. I consider fish as my equals.

A female 19-year-old art student

It has been proven beyond any doubt that animals have a form of sentience, a form of intelligence, that you can't use them as if they were rubbish.

A 29-year-old woman (self-described as "multi-job")

Many participants explained that even though they were in favour of animal experimentation, they did not want to actively participate in it. In a more direct and surprising way, the participant I have just quoted appealed to the conscience of the interviewer:

I could ask you if you would be able to put chemicals in aquariums and watch fish die, but then again, it's your career, it's your choice.

A 29-year-old woman (self-described as "multi-job")

The "Pet as Ambassador" Hypothesis

Several participants highlighted their proximity with, consideration for, or long-time commitment to animals, explaining that this bond kept them from acting in a way that would harm them.

I save spiders. I save bees in swimming pools.

A 22-year-old female digital communication student

I don't even use bug spray against ants, so I'm not going to kill a fish.

A 56-year-old female sales coordinator

I spend a lot of time taking care of animals. I even came here thinking "Cool, I'm going to give the money to the RSPCA," so I'm not going to participate in a study that kills animals.

A 49-year-old female educator

I have a cat. I have a special bond with animals.

A 51-year-old female teacher

The phenomenon evoked by the last quotation above has been the subject of several studies. In psychology, the theory of *moral licensing* predicts that caring for pets might decrease behaviour that benefits other animals in different contexts.[14] For example, a person who contributes to the well-being of her cat, being convinced that she takes good care of animals, might be less receptive to the needs of other animals.

Contrary to this hypothesis, several studies show that pet owners have more favourable attitudes towards animals in general, and they are more opposed to their being used for food or science. Thus, a pet could be regarded as an ambassador of its category for humans, or even as an ambassador for animals in general.[15] A survey showed that pet owners were more likely to oppose the use of animals for research.[16] However, there remains some uncertainty about this result. For example, having a pet is positively associated with attributing mental and emotional abilities to animals in some studies[17] but not others.[18] If attachment to a pet was associated with greater concern for other animals, one would expect this to result in avoiding meat consumption, but this does not seem to be the case.[19]

In our research, participants were asked if they had had a pet when they were children and if they currently had one. The results showed that nearly a third had had a pet as a teenager and half had one at the time of the experiment. However, no correlation was found between those two variables and the number of doses administered to the fish during the experiment. Several participants who, like this 23-year-old caretaker, had said "I love fish, I have some at home" or who were fishkeeping enthusiasts, still injected all 12 doses. This gap between attachment to a pet and indifference towards other animals is reminiscent of the example of François Magendie, one of the most eminent vivisectors of the 19th century, who was said to be "the slave of the little dog he had at home and who slept on or in his bed."[20]

Poignant Personal Experiences

Participants' personal backgrounds are usually influences that laboratory experiments try to minimise and control. In an experiment, any individual variation can compromise the measurement of the statistical effect of the specific factors being studied by the researcher. Like laboratory animals, humans who participate in most psychology experiments are usually not studied as individuals with singular stories, but for the quantitative data that can be obtained from them collectively, depending on the conditions of the study.

But in some cases, poignant biographical information emerges from interviews. A 70-year-old woman described the strong impression she had been left with after a bird she had picked up had died in her hands. A 54-year-old caretaker who, after bluntly stating "I don't give a shit about fish," recalled that, since his father was a hunter and hated the sight of blood, he had been responsible for dressing the pheasants or rabbits he brought back dead. A 60-year-old computer scientist explained that her daughter, a student, had suffered during her years at veterinary school when she had to experiment on animals. It is impossible to have any certainty about the link between those memories and the behaviour of the participants in the laboratory, but their testimonies include significant experiences:

When my sister's goldfish died, it affected me. That's why I didn't go all the way to the 12th step.

A 21-year-old performing arts student

I've had aquariums before, and my biggest fear was dead fish.

A 32-year-old restaurant employee

I've slaughtered animals before: sheep, chickens…

A 23-year-old art student

In my biology classes, when we had to dissect animals, I wouldn't do it.
A 23-year-old communications student

Once the Experiment is Over

After the experiment, and once they were able to give their spontaneous account of it, participants were informed that the product they had injected was non-toxic and that they had actually been the subjects of the experiment. Many of them expressed relief when they understood that they had not killed the fish. One thing they frequently mentioned during this phase was that they had found peace again. Participants thought they would sleep better now that they were relieved of that moral burden.

Oh! (Silence) Ok. That's reassuring. I was going to lose sleep over this.
A 51-year-old woman working as a secretary for an NGO

At one point I told myself: "That fish is going to keep squirming in the aquarium and I'm not going to be able to sleep all night."
A 58-year-old female social worker

This idea can be linked to the sleep disorders sometimes experienced by professionals involved in killing animals or experimenting on animals.[21] Such was the case for Stephen Suomi, an eminent student and collaborator of Harry Harlow, who was world renowned for his work on attachment). As part of his doctoral research in the 1970s, Suomi had conducted experiments on depression by keeping juvenile monkeys in boxes for several months. He claimed that this research caused him to have recurrent nightmares. Slaughterhouse workers can experience similar sleep disorders. One of them told an anthropologist: "I've been here for seventeen years and it's true that in the beginning – wow, it's hard. I had dreams about it, I kept thinking about it and everything."[22]

In conclusion, the many interviews conducted with the participants show that, on the one hand, they had been deeply engaged with the experiment and, on the other hand, they could not simply be considered to have abandoned their principles to passively obey a scientific authority. Most of them finished the experiment, but their decision to sacrifice the animal for science was part of a system of representations that largely pre-existed their arrival at the lab. The moral dilemma posed by the experiment often elicited sophisticated thinking on their part as they searched for an equilibrium between their personal ethics and the scientific and therapeutic goals they believed they were serving.

Notes

1 However, 14% of the participants were removed from the sample for that reason, following a systematic assessment of the interview videos by outside observers.
2 Katcher A., Segal H., Beck A. (1984). "Comparison of contemplation and hypnosis for the reduction of anxiety and discomfort during dental surgery," *The American Journal of Clinical Hypnosis*, 27 (1), pp. 14–21.
3 Montagner H. (2002). *L'Enfant et l'Animal*, Paris, Odile Jacob, p. 201.
4 Foster C. (2016). *Being a Beast: Adventures Across the Species Divide*, London, Metropolitan Books, p. 173.
5 Serpell J. (1986). *In the Company of Animals*, Oxford, Blackwell, p. 37.
6 Van Hemert D. A., Van de Vijver F. J. R., Vingerhoets A. J. (2011). "Culture and crying: Prevalences and gender differences," *Cross-Cultural Research*, 45 (4), pp. 399–431.

7   Baumeister R. F., Stillwell A. M., Heatherton T. F. (1994). "Guilt: An interpersonal approach," *Psychological Bulletin*, 115, p. 243-267; Hoffman M. (2008). *Empathie et développement moral: les émotions morales et la justice*, op. cit Grenoble, PUG.

8   Bernard C. (1865/1957). *Introduction to the Study of Experimental Medicine*. Chelmsford, Massachusetts: Courier Corporation, p.102.

9   This 27-year-old animal keeper working with dogs was interviewed by Audrey Jougla. See Jougla A. (2015). *Profession: animal de laboratoire*, Paris, Autrement, p. 98.

10 Maupertuis J.-B. (1759). *Lettre sur le progrès des sciences*, p. 375, quoted by Poliakov L. (1998). "Le fantasme des êtres hybrides et la hiérarchie des races aux xviiie et xixe siècles," in B. Cyrulnik (ed.). *Si les lions pouvaient parler*, Paris, Gallimard, p. 1167.

11 Quoted by Sarasca H. (2006). *Animaux, cobayes et victimes humaines*, Esqualens, Dangles, p. 14.

12 Bernard C. (1865/1957). *Introduction to the Study of Experimental Medicine*. Chelmsford, Massachusetts: Courier Corporation, p. 100.

13 Chapouthier G., Tristani-Potteaux F. (2013). *Le Chercheur et la Souris*, Paris, CNRS Éditions, p. 87.

14 Merritt A. C., Effron D. A., Monin B. (2010). "Moral self-licensing: When being good frees us to be bad," *Social and Personality Psychology Compass*, 4 (5), pp. 344–357.

15 See Possidónio C., Piazza J., Graça J., Prada M. (2021). "From pets to pests: Testing the scope of the 'Pets as ambassadors' hypothesis," *Anthrozoös*, 34, pp. 707–722.

16 Bradley A., Mennie N., Bibby P. A., Cassaday H. J. (2020). "Some animals are more equal than others: Validation of a new scale to measure how attitudes to animals depend on species and human purpose of use," *PloS One*, 15 (1), p. e0227948.

17 Morris P., Knight S., Lesley S. (2012). "Belief in animal mind: Does familiarity with animals influence beliefs about animal emotions?" *Society and Animals*, 20 (3), pp. 211—224.

18 Knight S., Vrij A., Cherryman J., Nunkoosing K. (2004). "Attitudes towards animal use and belief in animal mind," *Anthrozoös*, 17 (1).

19 Rothgerber H., Mican F. (2014). "Childhood pet ownership, attachment to pets, and subsequent meat avoidance. The mediating role of empathy toward animals," *Appetite*, 79, pp. 11--17.

20 Bory J.-Y. (2013). *La Douleur des bêtes*, Rennes, PUR, p. 39.

21 https://www.cbc.ca/radio/outintheopen/done-and-done-1.4712114/i-began-having-nightmares-former-animal-tester-reveals-the-reality-of-working-in-animal-research-1.4712368

22 Rémy C. (2009). La Fin des bêtes, op. cit., p. 67. A recent review of 14 studies on mental health in slaughterhouse workers carried out in seven different countries has shown that they could experience post-traumatic stress disorder and had higher levels of anxiety and depression that the control groups. See Slade, J., Alleyne, E. (2023). The psychological impact of slaughterhouse employment: A systematic literature review. *Trauma, Violence, & Abuse*, 24 (2), pp. 429–440.

17 Afterword

A Canary in the Coalmine

"Behold! I've brought you a man," triumphed Diogenes, brandishing a plucked chicken at the Academy. He was responding to the philosopher Plato, who had defined man as a "featherless, hornless biped."[1] But in seizing the bird to refute Plato, Diogenes was unaware that his irony was also somehow prescient.

Today, the chicken, or rather its skeleton, has become a symbol of the Anthropocene (or "human epoch"), the period of history marked by the footprint of human activity across the planet. That bird, whose industrial farming has reached unprecedented proportions, has become the most widespread vertebrate species on Earth. Scientists say that the current accumulation of billions of chicken bones will remain as a geological marker of our era for thousands of years to come.[2] We are the species that have produced and consumed astronomical quantities of fast-growing chickens. This will be remembered as one of the most striking things we did with animals, in addition to the creation of hypoallergenic cats,[3] fluorescent rabbits,[4] and cannulated cows.[5]

However, we are also the generation that has surpassed all others in its scientific understanding of the animal world, and the one that has enacted laws by which humanity has imposed obligations upon itself towards these *sentient beings*, as they are now referred to in laws after years of evolution. And finally, we are the generation that has sometimes prioritized

DOI: 10.4324/9781003561972-18

other species over its own kind: in France, for example, individuals spend twice as much money on their pets (nearly 5 billion euros a year) as they give away to charity.

Our Compromises with Animals

As I described our paradoxical behaviour with animals, I tried to show that, instinctively or deliberately, we engage in strange intellectual contortions in search of a balance between the emotional bonds we have with these ancestral companions of our evolution and the possessive impulses that prompt us to use them without any limits. Since cunning is in our nature, we have come up with narratives about our own superior value and about the fate of animals in order to soothe our moral anxiety.

The way human cognition works allows us to dehumanise the "others" we encounter on the basis of their appearance (human vs animal, similar vs foreign) and then treat them accordingly. This also applies to invisible characteristics such as cognitive or emotional activity. The rule is a basic one: the mental worlds we attribute to others determine the moral consideration they deserve. This works both ways: when, in a study, we lead people to believe that a lobster[6] has significant emotional activity, this increases the moral consideration it receives.[7] The same phenomenon occurs if you replace the crustacean with a primate.[8] Conversely, if you let the participants know that the animal will soon be served on their plate[9] or laid out on the experimenter's lab bench,[10] they think less of its mental abilities.

Processes of dehumanisation can lead us to deshumanise other people but also to "de-animalise" animals. For example, when a human belongs to a deshumanised social minority, he or she ranks very low on two crucial dimensions of social perception: ability to elicit affection, and perceived competence. As can be seen in the specific activity of a brain area involved in social cognition– the medial prefrontal cortex – our brain treats that person as subhuman.[11] Except perhaps for the ones we choose as pets, most animals are perpetually at risk of being treated the same way. The human mind spontaneously assimilates them to a negligible outgroup: as in Orwell's *Animal Farm*, we make a moral distinction between four-legged and two-legged creatures. Too many or too few legs can make a crucial difference to the way one is dehumanised and treated.

When researchers deactivate oxytocin-producing genes in mice, some of their social abilities are permanently damaged.[12] Our species has more behavioural flexibility: it can deactivate its empathy towards animals through ideological filters shaped by our history. These create powerful moral hierarchies between the species we love, those we do not, and, above all, our own. The effects of these boundaries have been demonstrated in the psychological studies on animal experimentation presented in this book. For instance, cultural beliefs that downplay the moral worth of animals and the more general ones which support strong hierarchies between human groups were directly related to more harmful behavior towards animals. These lab results confirm the anthropological intuition expressed by Claude Lévi-Strauss 40 years ago: there is a close correspondence between the hierarchical boundary separating humans from animals and an inegalitarian view of human groups.

After Milgram: Revisiting Our Conceptions of Submission to Authority

The approach defended by Milgram more or less treated individuals as predictable cogs in a hierarchical system. As they turned into mindless operators in a merciless chain of command, according to the Yale researcher, they gave up their personal beliefs out of pure deference to the white coat. But the studies presented in this book tell a different story: Authority can only be effective with some degree of acceptance from those who submit to it. It appears that a participant's level of identification with the scientific cause may affect how willing they are to continue with a destructive task.[13]

Milgram and Hannah Arendt reached similar conclusions when, at the same moment in history, they introduced a highly paradoxical notion of violence, the "banality of evil," which may have led to a misunderstanding of what is most often at play in situations of destructive violence. To believe that people blindly follow orders is to ignore that the obedience that is sometimes manifested in such contexts has been prepared by their history, their former commitments, and their underlying interests.

Through the study of the case of Adolf Eichmann, the high-ranking Nazi official who organized the deportation of Jews, Hannah Arendt suggested that the most unbearable crimes were not necessarily committed by monsters or hateful ideologues. This was a seductive and thought-provoking idea, which showed how demonising those responsible for violence could blind us to some realities. However, the theory of the banality of evil to which Milgram subscribed[14] was undermined when several of Eichmann's biographers revealed that he was less an obedient civil servant than an ideologue fueled by racial hatred.[15] With the contemporary questioning of Milgram's radical situationism, the notion of the "banality of evil" seems more like a literary trope today than a useful scientific concept.

By rejecting the notion that submission to authority is merely a "moral abdication," we can acknowledge the influence of social factors that Milgram overlooked: their historical and cultural roots. According to historian of medicine Nicolaas Rupke, animal experimentation emerged precisely when, in the intellectual history of the West, science was being invested with a higher power. This "scientocratic"[16] view of society is still the basis for the prevailing consensus on animal experimentation.

With a Canary in the Coalmine

In the 19th and 20th centuries, underground, far from the light of day, coal mining brought together countless lives. Draught animals like Trompette, the mining horse in Emile Zola's classic novel *Germinal*, but also donkeys and dogs sacrificed their lungs to the same toxic underground dust as the black-faced miners. A colorful, melodious animal, the canary, was probably the most tragically unexpected occupant of the lignite tunnels. Much more sensitive than we are to carbon monoxide (a noxious but odourless gas), the bird was used as a biological alarm system until the 1980s in some mines. When its singing abated or when it showed signs of distress and eventually died, the miners understood that they too were in danger.[17]

In a sense, animal experimentation reflects the same logic: to preserve our lives, we put theirs on the line. They are our biosentinels. When our conscience reproaches us for treating them in this way, we can come up with solutions to ease the dissonance and perhaps even to appease our gods. In South Korean medical labs, religious ceremonies are performed to honor the animals that are sacrificed for science.[18] Rabbits and mice are honored with incense, Guinea pigs with prayers, and food offerings are laid out. Other biomedical institutions in Japan, Thailand, the United States, and Canada encourage similar initiatives.[19] In Moscow, a plaque commemorates the dog Laïka, who died of stress and overheating seven hours after Sputnik 2 was launched into orbit in 1957.[20]

But the use of candles and incense does not guarantee that the sacrifice of animals is justified. Researchers acknowledge that many animals whose lives were offered to science have done little to contribute to the "welfare of mankind."[21] According to the chief veterinary officer at NASA, most of the mice that are locked up in small plastic and metal cages in labs are considered surplus and are simply disposed of like expired consumables once the research protocols are complete.[22] Other sources confirm this systematic waste of animal lives. We also

Figure 17.1 Photo of a bronze plaque on the wall of the University of Rochester School of Medicine.

know that the clinical applications of "animal models" are far from miraculous: only two out of 20 extensive reviews of the biomedical literature concluded that animal experimentation was useful,[23] and more advanced scientific techniques could often replace it.[24]

No one can predict how our relationships with animals will evolve in the future. All we know is that some species will be missing. Between 1970 and 2016, populations of mammals, birds, amphibians, reptiles and fish have decreased by 68%,[25] and we are the ones to blame.[26] We also know that our future is filled with uncertainty, as evidenced from books and articles with striking titles such as *Farmageddon*[27] or *Aquacalypse Now*,[28] which document the environmental havoc we continue to cause. In the face of these alarming signs, will we acknowledge that we are now deep in the coalmine with the canary, breathing the same air?

Notes

1 Paquet L. (1975). *Les Cyniques grecs. Fragments et témoignages*, Ottawa, Presses de l'Université d'Ottawa.

2 Bennett C. et al. (2018). "The broiler chicken as a signal of a human reconfigured biosphere," *Royal Society Open Science*, 5 (12), 180325.

3 Dance A. (2020). "The race to deliver the hypoallergenic cat," *Nature*, 588 (7836), pp. S7–S9.

4 https://www.lemonde.fr/archives/article/2000/10/04/les-animaux-fluorescents-fascinent-che rcheurs-artistes-et-militaires_102022_1819218.html.

5 See Nicolino F. (2009). *Bidoche*, Paris, Les Liens qui libèrent, pp. 43–46.

6 Robbins J. P. (2012). "The phenomenal stance revisited," *Review of Philosophy and Psychology*, 3 (3), pp. 383–403. See also Kasperbauer T. J. (2017). "Mentalizing animals: Implications for moral psychology and animal ethics," *Philosophical Studies: An International Journal for Philosophy in the Analytic Tradition*, 174 (2), pp. 465–484.

7 Gray K., Young L., Waytz A. (2012). "Mind perception is the essence of morality," *Psychological Inquiry*, 23, pp. 101–124.

8 Sytsma J., Machery E. (2012). "The two sources of moral standing," *Review of Philosophy and Psychology*, 3, pp. 303–324. See also Piazza J., Landy J. F., Goodwin G. P. (2014). "Cruel nature: Harmfulness as an important, overlooked dimension in judgments of moral standing," *Cognition*, 131, pp. 108–124.

9 Loughnan S., Haslam N., Bastian B. (2010). "The role of meat consumption in the denial of moral status and mind to meat animals," *Appetite*, 55 (1); Loughnan S, Bastian B, Haslam N. (2014). "The psychology of eating animals," *Current Directions in Psychological Science*, 23 (2), pp. 104–108.

10 Vezirian, K., Bègue, L., Bastian, B. (2024). "Mindless furry test-tubes: Categorizing animals as lab-subjects leads to their mind denial," *Journal of Experimental Social Psychology*, 114, 1–11.

11 Harris L. T., Fiske S. T. (2006). "Dehumanizing the lowest of the low: Neuroimaging responses to extreme out-groups," *Psychological Science*, 17 (10), pp. 847–853; see also Harris L. (2017). *Invisible Mind. Flexible Social Cognition and Dehumanization*, Cambridge, MIT Press.

12 Bielsky I. F., Young L. J. (2004). "Oxytocin, vasopressin, and social recognition in mammals," *Peptides*, 25 (9), pp. 1565–1574.

13 Birney, M. E., Reicher, S. D., Haslam, S. A., Steffens, N. K., Neville, F. G. (2023). "Engaged followership and toxic science: Exploring the effect of prototypicality on willingness to follow harmful experimental instructions," *British Journal of Social Psychology*, 62 (2), pp. 866–882.

14 "After witnessing hundreds of ordinary people submit to the authority in our own experiments, I must conclude that Arendt's conception of the *banality of evil* comes closer to the truth than one might dare imagine." Milgram S. (1974), *Submission to Authority*, p. 6.

15 Cesarani D. (2004). *Becoming Eichmann: Rethinking the Life, Crimes, and Trial of a "Desk Murderer,"* Cambridge, Da Capo Press; Stangneth B. (2014). *Eichmann before Jerusalem: The Unexamined Life of a Mass Murderer*, New York, Knopf; Lipstadt D. (2011). *The Eichmann Trial*, New York, Shocken.

16 Rupke N. (1987). *Vivisection in Historical Perspective*, London, Routledge.

17 Other animals were used as alarm systems. In Japan, bowls of fish were used to detect earthquakes: when they got frantic, people would hurry out of their houses to avoid being buried alive under the rubble. In Korea, but also in Germany, fish were used to monitor the quality of drinking water.

18 Choi H. W. (1998). "Koreans honor dead lab animals (who knows – they may return)," *Wall Street Journal*, 10 November 10, p. B1.

19 Iliff S. A. (2002). "An additional "R": Remembering the animals," *ILAR Journal*, 43, pp. 38–47.

20 Burgess C., Dubbs C. (2007). *Animals in Space. From Research Rockets to the Space Shuttle*, Berlin, Springer.

21 Herzog H. (2011). *Some We Love, Some We Hate, Some We Eat*, New York, Harper, p. 223.

22 Herzog 2011, p. 223.

23 Harris R. (2017). *Rigor Mortis. How Sloppy Science Creates Worthless Cures, Crushes Hope, and Wastes Billions*, New York, Basic Books; Herrman K., Jayne K. (2019). *Animal Experimentation*, Boston, Brill; Knight A. (2011). *The Costs and Benefits of Animal Experiments*, New York, Palgrave Macmillan.

24 Herrman K., Jayne K. (2019). *Animal Experimentation*.

25 https://www.wwf.fr/sites/default/files/doc-2020-09/20200910_Rapport_Living-PlanetReport-2020_ENGLISH_WWF-min.pdf.

26 Maxwell S. L. et al. (2016). "The ravages of gun, nets, and bulldozers," *Nature*, 536, pp. 143–145.

27 Lymbery P., Oakshott I. (2014). *Farmageddon. The True Cost of Cheap Meat*, London, Blomsberry.

28 https://newrepublic.com/article/69712/aquacalypse-now.

Acknowledgements

I would like to thank Odile Jacob for the interest she has shown in this book project and for her unfailing support so that it could be published in the best possible conditions. This book benefited from the reading, thoughts and influence of several people I would like to thank: Hélène Brissaud, Mireille Brochot, Émilie Dardenne, Hélène De Roche, Renan Larue, Maitane Sebastian and Nicolas Treich. Naturally, they are not are not responsible for the book's limitations. In addition to her attentive reading, Rebecca Bègue-Shankland has encouraged the writing of these pages, month after month, with her bright enthusiasm, and as a specialist in gratitude, she can be sure that mine is complete. Thanks to the reading and comments of Caroline Rolland, not only have inaccuracies been avoided, but valuable additions have been made in several chapters.

This book was translated by François Tharaud. I would like to thank him for the elegance of his work and his meticulous attention to detail in the manuscript. The translation also benefited from the invaluable help of Sylvia MacGregor, who, as a wordsmith, had the inspiration for the right words, for which I am most grateful.

The research program presented throughout the last chapters of the book was facilitated by funding from the French Institute of Higher Education (Institut Universitaire de France). Lee Khan, from the Korean company Airo, provided me with several biomimetic robots under very advantageous conditions, and I thank him for that. My work could not have progressed without the help and support of many individuals, especially Kevin Vezirian, but also Jérôme Maisonnasse, Véronique Aubergé, Christian Graff, Alain Quercia, Teo Pesci, Mae Pincin, Mathieu Tarpin, Violette Hassani-Champlong, Marion Swider, Melissa Lahuerta, Camille Jaquet, and Juliette Faure.

The presentation of preliminary results from my research at LIP/PC2S (Grenoble-Alpes University), CREC (University of Lausanne), and LAPPS (University of Paris-Nanterre and Paris-VIII) gave me the opportunity to delve deeper into some of the ideas presented in this book. Finally, I greatly benefited from the suggestions of Lucian Conway from the University of Montana, as well as five anonymous experts during the publication of a portion of this work in the *Personality and Social Psychology Bulletin*. I also thank Magali Seghetto for her beautiful illustrations, Louise Bègue-Teissier for the 3D rendering of the experimental setup, and Benjamin Girard from BProd for the video preview. Dariusz Doliński from the University of Wroclaw in Poland and Aurélien Miralles from the National Museum of Natural History in Paris granted me permission to use certain visual content of which they are the authors. I sincerely thank them for this.

For Product Safety Concerns and Information please contact our EU
representative GPSR@taylorandfrancis.com
Taylor & Francis Verlag GmbH, Kaufingerstraße 24, 80331 München, Germany